AN ABRIDGMENT OF MAURICE'S KINGDOM OF CHRIST

The Original Two Volumes Abridged into One Based on the 1842 Edition Emended with an Introduction

William J. Wolf

UNIVERSITY PRESS OF AMERICA

LANHAM • NEW YORK • LONDON

University Press of America,™ Inc.

4720 Boston Way
Lanham, MD 20706

3 Henrietta Street
London WC2E 8LU England

ISBN (Perfect): 0-8191-3151-2
ISBN   (Cloth): 0-8191-3150-4

Co-published by arrangement with
the Episcopal Divinity School

In Loving Memory

Of Our Son

STEPHEN HALE WOLF
1951-1981

ACKNOWLEDGEMENTS

Some abridged and revised material from my chapter on Maurice in The Spirit of Anglicanism by Wolf, Booty and Thomas (1979) has been included in the Introduction with the permission of the publisher, Morehouse-Barlow Co., Inc., Wilton, Connecticut.

PREFACE

Frederick Denison Maurice's two-volume classic, The Kingdom of Christ, has been out of print and only rarely available from lists of used books. Over a period of more than thirty years I have developed a series of readings from The Kingdom of Christ for a course on theological issues. Continued use and class criticism of these selections has led at last to an abridgment in one volume. It is possible today to omit much of the original work that remains of interest mainly to the Victorian specialist in church-state relations and in the cultural confrontations of that era. This abridgment has been achieved by severe cutting from chapter IV (Part I) on religious, philosophical and political movements and from chapter V (Part II) on church and state. The omission of almost half of the original material, painful to the Maurice aficionado, somewhat undercuts Maurice's broad purpose to show Christ, in H. Richard Niebuhr's terminology, as "the transformer of culture," but it makes up for its losses by concentration on Maurice's theological principles and their ecumenical significance. Enough has been included about the reduced areas to suggest Maurice's approach to a critique of culture in general.

The Introduction is designed to help readers understand the setting of The Kingdom of Christ in Maurice's life. There is discussion of his method and of some of his obscurities of style and substance. The purpose of the abridgment is to stimulate reflection on the significance of his theology for today. With the permission of the publisher Morehouse-Barlow, material from sections of my chapter on Maurice in The Spirit of Anglicanism (Wolf ed., Booty and Thomas) has been included in an abridged and revised form. There is new matter and notes with updated bibiliographical helps. Those who are approaching The Kingdom of Christ for the first time may want to read the chapter entitled "Recapitulation" (Part II) in which Maurice gives a birdseye view of the terrain covered in the previous part.

The basis for this edition is Maurice's second edition of 1842 in two volumes by publisher J.G.F. Rivington and J. Rivington and entitled The Kingdom of Christ, or, Hints to a Quaker respecting the Principles, Constitution, and Ordinances of the Catholic Church. That text has been compared with subsequent editions and altered in a few places to correct probable slips of his pen or typographical errors. His few quotations in Latin or Greek have usually been translated with quotation marks within parentheses. Maurice's own table of contents has been restored as more appropriate for the abridgment than the lengthy substitute by an unknown hand first inserted into the Macmillan edition of 1883 and reprinted in all subsequent editions of 1891 (Macmillan), 1906 (Everyman's Library) and 1958 by Alec Vidler (Student Christian Movement Press).

I am indebted to my friend and colleague John Skinner for the invitation to publish this abridgment under the imprint of the Episcopal

Divinity School-University Press of America publications. This is an opportunity also to thank the donors of the Fund for Theological Writing who have made it possible for me to invest the fall semester in research and writing.

William J. Wolf,
Howard Chandler Robbins Professor
The Episcopal Divinity School

TABLE OF CONTENTS

Page

Introductory Dialogue with a Quaker   (not included)

Part I: On the Principles of the Quakers, and of the   1
          Different Religious Bodies which have Arisen
          Since the Reformation and of the Systems to
          Which They have Given Birth

    Chapter I   Quakerism   2

        Section I   - On the Positive Doctrines of the   2
                       Quakers - The Indwelling Word - The
                       Spiritual Kingdom - Spiritual
                       Influences

        Section II   - Objections to the Quaker Theology   6
                       Considered

        Section III - The Quaker System   9

        Section IV   - On the Practical Working of the   12
                       Quaker System

    Chapter II   Pure Protestantism   19

        Section I   - The Leading Principles of the   19
                       Reformation - Justification by
                       Faith - Election - The Written
                       Word - Authority of National
                       Sovereigns

        Section II   - Objections to the Principles of the   25
                       Reformation Considered

        Section III - Protestant Systems   40

        Section IV   - The Practical Working of the   44
                       Protestant Systems

    Chapter III Unitarianism   47

                 Connection of Unitarianism with Pure
                 Protestantism, with Natural Philosophy and
                 with the System of Locke - Its Positive
                 Side - Its Negative Side - Final Results

Chapter IV   On the Tendency of the Religious,   55
             Philosophical and Political Movements
             Which Have Taken Place in Protestant
             Bodies, Since the Middle of
             the Last Century

   Section I   - Religious Movements   55

               Methodism - Religious Societies -
               Search for a Theology

   Section II - Philosophical Movements   (not included)

               Feelings Respecting Man - Poetry and
               Criticism - Pure Metaphysics -
               Eclecticism

   Section III - Political Movements   59

               American Revolution - French
               Revolution - Individual Rights -
               Individual Will - Schemes of Universal
               Society - Education - Power of the
               State

Part II: Of The Catholic Church and the Romish System

   Chapter I   Recapitulation   64

   Chapter II   Indications of a Spiritual Constitution   75

   Chapter III The Scriptural View of This Constitution   81

   Chapter IV   Signs of a Spiritual Society   97

      Section I   - Baptism   97

      Section II - The Creeds   114

      Section III - Forms of Worship   124

      Section IV - The Eucharist   138

      Section V   - The Ministry   159

      Section VI - The Scriptures   178

Chapter V   On the Relations of the Church with   195
             National Bodies

    Section I   - The Old Testament - Ancient Pagan   195
                    History - History of Modern Europe -
                    General Inferences

    Section II   - The Quaker - Sermon on the Mount -   (not included)
                    Different Passages in It Considered -
                    Provision for Ministers

    Section III - The Pure Theocratist   (not included)

    Section IV   - The Separatist   (not included)

    Section V   - The Patrician   (not included)

                    Idea of a Golden Age - Allegorical
                    Interpretations of the Old Testament -
                    Church Discipline - Extrusion of
                    Heretics - Catholic Unity Amidst
                    National Peculiarities

    Section VI   - The Modern Statesman   (not included)

    Section VII - The Modern Interpreters of Prophecy (not included)

Part III: The English Church and the Systems which Divide It

    Chapter I   How Far This Subject Is Connected with   198
                 Those Previously Discussed

    Section I   - To the Signs of a Universal and   199
                    Spiritual Constitution Exist in
                    England?

    Section II   - Does the Universal Society in England   207
                    Exist Apart from its Civil Institutions,
                    or in Union with Them?

    Section III - What is the Form of Character which   212
                    Belongs Especially to Englishmen? To
                    What Kind of Depravation Is It Liable?

    Chapter II   Modern English Systems   217

Section I   - The Liberal System: The Evangelical   217
System: The High Church or Catholic
System

Section II - Reflections on These Systems, and on   218
Our Own Position Generally

INTRODUCTION

MAURICE'S EARLY LIFE

John Frederick Denison Maurice, as he was christened, was born at Normanstone on the coast of Suffolk, England, on August 29, 1805.[1] His father, Michael Maurice, was a Unitarian minister who did not object to the doctrines of the creeds so much as to their use as a test for church membership. He had been a younger colleague of Joseph Priestly during the time a fanatical mob had burned Priestly's house. Frederick, the only boy to survive infancy, had three older sisters and four younger ones.

The family was tightly knit and affectionate until serious dissentions began to rend its unity. His sister Elizabeth became a member of the Church of England. Two other sisters and finally the mother joined Baptist fellowships with strict Calvinistic theologies. Young Frederick was bewildered at the quarrels these religious changes occasioned. Forbidden by their father to engage in religious discussions at home, members of the family wrote long letters to each other to explain their stands. Maurice's later drive to realize unity and to bring reconciliation to warring factions may have been rooted psychologically in these family confrontations or enforced silences that were so painful to the growing boy. Later he was to write: "I not only believe in the Trinity in Unity, but I find in it the center of all my beliefs: the rest of my spirit, when I contemplate myself or mankind. But, strange as it may seem, I owe the depth of this belief in great measure to my training in my home. The very name that was used to describe the denial of this doctri⁻ is the one which expresses to me the end that I have been compelled, even in spite of myself, to seek."[2]

In 1823 Maurice entered Cambridge University, where he became a member of the Apostles' Club and developed skills in literary criticism. His tutor, Julius Hare, introduced him to Plato and to German thought. Hare later became his close friend and married his sister Esther. His most intimate friend was John Sterling. Sterling shared Maurice's enthusiasm for Coleridge and helped him to overcome the great shyness that prevented him from participating in university life. Maurice took a First in civil law, but could not receive his degree because he would not at tᵗ is time subscribe to the Thirty-nine Articles.

The dissatisfaction with Unitarianism that Maurice had been feeling since boyhood was resolved for him when he became a member of the Church of England by baptism on March 29, 1831 and returned to university study, this time to Exeter College, Oxford, to prepare for ordination.

In 1837 Maurice married Anna Barton, sister-in-law of John Sterling. Two sons, Frederick and Edmund were born. Frederick, who would become a major general in the British Army and a military writer, deserves the gratitude of all students for the wonderfully understanding and balanced two-volume biography of his father and collection of his letters which he published in 1883 and 1884. Unfortunately, most of the actual letters used and abridged at times by his son have been lost, impov rishing Maurician scholarship.

The Kingdom of Christ

Maurice's masterpiece, The Kingdom of Christ, was written in his mid-thirties. He may well have derived the concept of the Kingdom of Christ from his curacy in 1833 under the Millenarian rector of Lympsham, Joseph Adam Stephenson, who also helped to bring him to ordination in the Church of England. In his memoir of Stephenson, Maurice wrote that his rector believed the events surrounding the destruction of Jerusalem actually brought the real establishment of Christ's Kingdom, the creation of a new heaven and a new earth. The evidence for a Millenarian origin for the phrase "the Kingdom of Christ" is that it does not occur in his writings before his association with Stephenson and that it is after this period his central organizing theological concept. Maurice expressed his gratitude in a letter to Stephenson on July 24, 1834.

"I have often desired to express to you how much more lively my impressions of your kindness and of the truths which I heard from you are now than when I was in the neighborhood of Lympsham.... But since I have been engaged in preaching myself, I have found the advantage of your instructions in a degree that I could scarcely have believed possible; especially as they have led me, almost unawares, into a method of considering many subjects, and of setting them forth, which I should not have naturally fallen into...but I have found myself in all my private meditations, as well as in preaching, drawn to speak of Christ as a King, and His Church as a Kingdom; and whenever I depart from this method, I feel much less clearness and satisfaction, much less harmony between my own feelings and the work of God."3

Shortly after this letter, Maurice became aware through his sister Elizabeth of a controversy that was threatening to divide the Society of Friends. As a result of the deism and rationalism of the eighteenth century, the older body of Quaker divinity had been largely reduced to a universalist emphasis upon the spirit in everyone with a loss of the evangelical understanding of incarnation and atonement. In direct opposition to this development and inspired by the rising evangelical movement in England, a group of Quakers began to interpret Quaker doctrine in terms of personal salvation from sin. They organized separate worship with readings from the Bible, evangelical witness and even sacramental ordinances. Maurice became fascinated with the controversy as illustrating for him a hunger in the sect for the reality of church and yet as also showing the preservation by the sect of a truth needed in the church. He connected these thoughts with his continued reflection upon Pusey's views on baptism and saw a way of addressing both controversies in a larger context. At the urgent request of Samuel Clark, a Quaker publisher who was in later years to become ordained in the Church of England as a result of Maurice's influence, Maurice began in January 1837 a series of twelve "Letters to a Member of the Society of Friends" published in monthly installments by Darton and Son. The second letter was really Maurice's answer to Pusey. Other topics treated were Quaker, sect and church principles, eucharist, Scriptures, unity, liturgy, church and state, education and family relationships. We have Maurice's own testimony as to the genesis and development of The Kingdom of Christ.

"Reflecting much on this controversy and connecting it with what was passing in the English Church, it seemed to me that the old Quakers were affirming a most grand and fundamental truth; but that it had become narrow and contradictory, because they had no ordinance which embodied it and made it universal; that we on the other hand, forgetting their Quaker principles, or rather the words of St. John, necessarily made baptism a mere ceremony or a charm. The two being united expressed to me the reconciliation of the High Church Baptismal regeneration with the Evangelical demands for personal faith. Starting from this text, I wrote a series of tracts addressed to Quakers, but really concerning ourselves more than them. They formed the book called the "Kingdom of Christ," of which a second edition, much altered appeared in 1841. In the second of these tracts I commented on Dr. Pusey's theory of baptism. Nothing I have written had so important an effect on my life. It set me in direct antagonism with his school, to which I had many attractions, and by some members of which my "Subscription No Bondage" had been partially approved."[4]

The letters were collected and published toward the end of 1838 in three volumes by Darton and Clark as The Kingdom of Christ: or Hints on the Principles, Ordinances, and Constitution of the Catholic Church in Letters to a Member of the Society of Friends.[5] Maurice was urged by many to turn the book into a treatise on the church by reducing its discussion of the Quaker controversy and by enlarging its scope to survey all the churches and sects of the Christian West, together with a critique of philosophical and social movements. He accepted the latter advice, but rejected the former, feeling that to keep its context with the Quaker controversy better illustrated his conception of doing theology by digging down to foundations than by constructing systematic theologies. It also justified his comprehensive apologetic as he explained in an advertisement prefixed to the second edition in 1842 as "the circumstances which induced me to attempt a comparison between our own position and that of those who seemed to be at the greatest distance from us." The second edition, moreover, contained a dedication to the Reverend Derwent Coleridge with an acknowledgement of the influence of his father Samuel Taylor Coleridge upon him.[6] Maurice, writing confidentially to is friend Strachey on September 10, 1841, revealed his own evaluation of the second edition: "I like my own alterations in it, but I question if that portion of mankind which read the first edition will. As it expresses more of what I really think and believe, it is better quoad me, and if the universe don't approve it, the universe must write a book for itself."[7]

The first part of the book consists of an analysis of Quakerism, Pure Protestantism (Lutheranism, Calvinism, Zwinglianism and Arminianism), Unitarianism and, later in the book, Roman Catholicism. There are many historical flashbacks in this survey, particularly one on the early Luther which communicates Maurice's deep sympathy with him. Maurice describes Luther's need to speak out on issues in language identical with statements elsewhere of his own need to speak out. If it can be said that the Tractarians rediscovered the catholic heritage, Maurice rediscovered the Reformation and reclaimed it from the contemporary evangelical deformation of it and the Tractarian contempt for and ignorance of it. Seeking to counter a widely held view that religious views and churches were dying out and that what was really valuable in them was preserved in philosophical theories (Carlyle), Maurice added a rambling section, refuting the view by showing that these philosophical ideas became contradictory and untenable once severed from their religious rootage. The material on religious, philosophical, historical and social movements is probably more confusing to a modern reader because of a lack of clear identification of the persons or movements discussed than it would have been for Maurice's contemporaries who shared the consciousness of the age with its conventional short-cut allusions and coded references. There is discussion, seldom clearly interrelated or convincingly organized to promote his purposes, about Locke, Hume, the Romantic school, American sectarianism, Kant, Rouseau, Hegel, Bentham, Saint-Simon and Owenite socialism. A far more responsible wrestling with the history of philosophy can be found much later in his two-volume Moral and Metaphysical Philosophy (1873). Maurice's basic conclusion is that nearly every one of these movemnts is right in its positive assertions, but wrong in its negations. These negations are compounded into systems that further divide people and shatter the unity of Christ's Church. When Maurice is at his best in describing alternative Christian positions, he shows an imagination and appreciation of the beliefs of others, living and thinking himself into other ways of experiencing reality. He becomes a Christian Socrates almost without a rival trying to meet other Christians on their own ground.

The second half of The Kingdom of Christ describes the "hidden hunger" of the previous sects and systems and interprets the Bible as the progressive manifestation of covenantal relations between God and ι *Benhoff* humanity in the given institutions of family, of the nation and, finally, of the church as the Kingdom of Christ. The Catholic Church is for Maurice not just a theological idea or a Platonic universal, but a *pw*·concrete, historical reality, unfortunately obscured by systems that have been forced upon it. The six "signs of a spiritual society" are then analyzed in the usual order in which people are drawn into living communion with Christ: baptism, the creeds, the forms of worship, the eucharist, the ordained ministry and, undergirding and interpreting them all, the Bible. Maurice's usual method is to describe the sign and its true meaning in the Bible or in tradition. Then he discusses and disposes of the various sectarian and philosophical objections to the sign. Lastly, he acknowledges the presence of the sign in the Roman Catholic Church, but argues that it has been corrupted there.

Maurice is convinced that the Roman Catholic Church has become the "sworn enemy of nations and national churches" and that the Reformation rightly restored the principle of national churches. The long and rambling section on church and nation is of more interest to the Victorian specialist than to the general reader today. Maurice believes that if the New Testament discloses the principles of the universal society which is the church, then the Old Testament reveals chiefly through the Ten Commandments the basic institutions of national life. He could not really conceive the separation of church and state in a Christian nation. The church was required as a conscience to keep political institutions from becoming instruments of internal oppression or of external imperialism. The state was needed to keep the church from becoming a worldly despotism. In a letter to Ludlow, who developed the principle of democracy from the sovereignty of the people and found a way of adjusting monarchy to this analysis, Maurice wrote in protest:

> "Twist the word as you will it must imply a right on the part of the people to choose, cashier, and depose their rulers. It must imply that power proceeds from them that it does not find them....Do they make Christ their King? Might they choose another if they liked?...I must have Monarchy, Aristocracy and Socialism, or rather Humanity, recognized as necessary elements and conditions of an organic Christian Society."[8]

Depending on whether one finds Maurice emphasizing monarchy and aristocracy or socialism, he can be described as a conservative or a revolutionary. His interpreters have often followed either one of these options.[9] The significant reality, however, is that he is both at the same time because he holds paradoxically the two poles together as "necessary *e* elements and conditions of an organic Christian society."

Behind Maurice's analysis there is a basic presupposition: the contrast and correlation of church and world. The church must remain a distinct society, but this is held alongside the conviction that "the State is as much God's creation as the Church." In the same passage Maurice adds: "I have been most anxious to rescue the idea of a national society from those who would make it out to be something cruel and devilish...."[10]

His clearest statement of the correlation of church and world occurs in the Theological Essays.

"The world contains the elements of which the Church is composed. In the Church, these elements are penetrated by a uniting, reconciling power. The Church is, therefore, human society in its normal state; the World, that same society irregular and abnormal. The world is the Church without God; the Church is the world restored to its relation with God, taken back by him into the state for which He created it. Deprive the Church of its Center and you make it into a world."[11]

The last section of Maurice's The Kingdom of Christ discusses the Church of England, particularly its party structure, with respect to the previous problems and concerns. The Prayer Book becomes the key for understanding the views of the Church of England on the six signs of the Catholic Church. Maurice understands the political forces which shaped the Anglican reformation, but beyond that he finds the English character itself to be politically oriented. English literature exhibits this tendency as seen in Shakespeare's historical dramas, Spenser's Faerie Queene and Milton's writings on government and much of his poetry. This political orientation, with its political metaphors to describe religion, meant that the English would naturally look upon Christ's Church as a kingdom rather than a system. Elsewhere differences in theology would lead to varying schools of thought responsive to great theologians, but in England differences would be expressed politically as parties in church life. The great Anglican classic, Richard Hooker's The Laws of Ecclesiastical Polity, reveals in its very title this political concern and orientation. Maurice's own classic incorporates the political image into its title as The Kingdom of Christ.

Maurice's book has commonly been misunderstood, although there is some evidence for the charge, as an apology for the Church of England, whereas his theological principles, despite his failure at times to apply them fully, are the basis for a Christian ecumenism that has yet to be recognized and accepted in the churches. Maurice clarifies his intention in these words:

"I am not ignorant, also, that the hints which I have offered in opposition to systems, may, themselves, be turned by myself or by others into a system...On the other hand, if there be anything here which may help to raise men above their own narrow conceptions and mine, may lead them to believe that there is a way to that truth which is living and universal, and above us all, and that He who is Truth will guide them in that way -- this which is from Him and not from me, I pray that He will bless."[12]

Later Life

Maurice is often described as the founder of Christian Socialism.[13] This description may actually be the source of more confusion than light because Maurice's socialism bears no resemblance to the modern, post-Marxian varieties. He was not interested in government ownership of the means of production, but in producers' cooperatives, a radical innovation in his day. More important to him than a specific set of social goals for which legislation should be sought, was the theological anal ·sis of political and economic reform. He wanted to challenge his theological students to a concern for the social implications of the Gospel. He was as committed to provide educational opportunities for working men and women by founding colleges for them as he was to improve social conditions. In fact, he saw the first helping to bring about the second. If Christ had redeemed them all, then all human life must express this redemption.

Further, the real founder of the Christian Socialist movement was J.M. Ludlow, an English social critic who had been born in India and educated in France. He interested Maurice in the cooperative movement and originally proposed the formation of an association dedicated to the reform of English society along Christian lines. After the revolutionary events of 1848, a group of outstanding young men gathered around Maurice and Ludlow, meeting weekly for Bible study. They promoted producers' cooperatives, conducted classes in a slum section of London and published Tracts on Christian Socialism.

The name "Christian Socialism" had been seized upon by Maurice because, as he put it, "It will commit us at once to the conflict we must engage in sooner or later with unsocial Christians and unChristian socialists."[14] "Competition is put forth as the law of the universe. That is a lie. The time is coming for us to declare it is a lie by word and deed. I see no way but by associating for work instead of for strikes...This is my notion of a Tailors' Association."[15]

Within one year of the Communist Manifesto, Maurice opened his first Tract on Christian Socialism as follows:

"Somebody (a person of respectability): Christian Socialism! I never saw that adjective united to that substantive before.

Do you seriously believe that a Socialist can be a Christian, or a Christian a Socialist?
Nobody (the writer): I seriously believe that Christianity is the only foundation of Socialism and that a true Socialism is the necessary result of a sound Christianity."16

Though it made a great impact on English society, the movement did not achieve all that Ludlow envisaged for it, partly because of dissension among the members. Maurice quickly became the real head of the movement and dominated it according to his own understanding that society was already constituted in Christ. His interest was not in social revolution, but in the regeneration of English society by reasserting its foundation in Christ. This regeneration involved, in Maurice's eyes, raising the laboring classes up to take their rightful place in the social order, but it did not involve the formation of a new society by revolutionary force. Consequently, he ultimately turned the energies of the Christian Socialists from producers' cooperatives to Workingmen's College, founded in 1855. Maurice is one of the sources of that concern for social redemption that has characterized Anglican theology in the modern period and which, through men like Headlam and Temple[17] has been a tributary stream to the Life and Work movement of modern ecumenism.

Maurice's discussions with the radical Chartists and revolutionaries of his day may be seen as a daring anticipation of the Marxist-Christian dialogue of our day which can be as dangerous to contemporary participants on both sides in terms of the security of their jobs and standing as it proved for Maurice. Attacked on all sides by the politically conservative papers of both low and high churchmanship, Maurice gave his enemies the opportunity they were seeking to impugn his orthodoxy when in 1853 he published his Theological Essays. In his book he criticized the popular equation of eternity with endlessness in reference to future punishment. His own understanding of the word eternal was drawn from such Johannine texts as "This is life eternal that they might know thee the only true God and Jesus Christ whom thou hast sent." He denied that he was a universalist, but to the self-consciously orthodox of his generation any weakening of the traditional picture of hell seemed to subvert the sanctions for morality and social control. After much controversy he was dismissed by the Council of King's College for undefined opinions on eternal punishment "of dangerous tendency, and calculated to unsettle the minds of the theological students."

His earlier writing on education and his conviction that the church had a primary responsibility to educate the nation led to the founding of Queen's College, London, in 1848. Started at first as a school for governesses, it quickly became a pioneering agency for the higher education of women.[18] From 1848 to 1854 Maurice served as its principal. After his expulsion from King's he founded the Workingmen's College, giving a set of six subscription lectures to raise funds for it.

In 1866 he became Knightbridge Professor of Moral Theology and Moral Philosophy at Cambridge. His books, The Conscience and Social Morality, are the fruits of his Cambridge lectures. The remainder of his life was spent in these university surroundings, where he also accepted the unpaid cure of souls at St. Edward's Church. Maurice died on Easter Monday, 1872, as he prepared in his sickbed to receive the Holy Communion. His last words were the Trinitarian blessing.

Most of Maurice's books were developed from sermons he delivered on the Scriptures. Some of his outstanding books on biblical theology are: The Prophets and Kings of the Old Testament, The Patriarchs and Law Givers of the Old Testament, The Doctrine of Sacrifice, The Unity of the New Testament, The Gospel of the Kingdom of Heaven, The Gospel of St. John, The Episles of St. John, the Acts of the Apostles and The Apocalypse. Liturgical theology today would be enriched by his biblically oriented sermons on The Prayer Book, The Lord's Prayer and The Church a Family, twelve discourses on the occasional services of the Book of Common Prayer.[19] The extent of his writing throughout an active life is amazing. One estimate runs to more than 16,300 octavo pages.[20]

Two things about Maurice seem to have attracted people to him wherever he went and to have given him a certain fame. One was his encyclopedic mind and the other his Christlike character. Even his enemies, once they met him face to face, admitted that they had never known so good a man. He knew how to reach out to others in deepest sympathy and he constantly chose to work with the ignorant, the suffering and the poor of English society. Friends liked to parody his frequent references to a bedridden old woman as the criterion of truth. Yet he was a shy person at the beginning of his life and was always filled with self-doubt and self-reproach. The sense of unworthiness and of sin displayed in his correspondence may strike the modern reader as morbid. Apparently it did not so strike those who knew him best. R.H. Hutton attributes it to his intense sympathy with others, claiming that Maurice literally felt the sins and the shame in others as his own, yet constantly accused himself of not having entered more generously into their doubts and feelings. He felt himself implicated in the sins of the age.

In theological discussion his aim was not to defeat, but to find the point of reconciliation between various truths. In this he lived out personally his understanding of the vocation of Anglicanism, which was "to hold together things which were never meant to be separated."

All this, however, grew out of his understanding of the Christian life. It was a life of repentance, if repentance is understood as constant dependence upon God-in-Christ. He was a living embodiment of the righteousness which he felt the Scriptures revealed. He trusted in a deliverer. Though it is fashionable to call him a Johannine thinker, the principle of his life was Pauline. He trusted in a justifier. His understanding of John opened his eyes to the meaning of Paul's phrase, "Christ in you."

> "That truth, of Christ being in us the hope of glory...I have found most necessary to sustain my own spirit when it has been sinking with the sense of its own unworthiness; for it shows that we can have no goodness apart from Him, that all our goodness must be by union with Him who is perfectly good."[21]

His Method and Christological Principle

There is an inner consistency in Maurice's thoughts from the time he sought ordination in the Church of England until his death. Very few changes are to be recorded. He remained loyal to the basic principle of Christ as King, which he had accepted very early. He found, however, ever more fascinating ways of illuminating the cultural task in its light.

Many times Maurice made clear his opposition to system-building. While he modestly described his vocation as "metaphysical and theological grubbing," this phrase really expressed his deliberate choice of the method of laying bare the theological presuppositions of culture and of dogma. In The Kingdom of Christ he observed:

> "Now to me those words (system and method) seem not only not synonymous, but the greatest contraries imaginable: the one indicating that which is most opposed to life, freedom, variety; and the other that without which they cannot exist."[22]

His chief opposition to systems of doctrine, however, was founded on his respect for the facts of historical existence. In this Maurice expressed both English empiricism against the conceptualism of continental thinkers and the Anglican's respect for historical institutions as points of departure for theological analysis.

> "When once a man begins to build a system the very gifts and qualities which might serve in the investigation of truth, become the greatest hindrances to it. He must make the different parts of the scheme fit into each other; his dexterity is shown, not in detecting facts, but in cutting them square."[23]

One of his letters provides this insight into his understanding of the theologian's task:

"Theology is not (as the schoolmen have represented it) the climax of studies, the Corinthian capital of a magnificent edifice, composed of physics, politics, economics, and connecting them as parts of a great system with each other - - but is the foundation upon which they all stand. And even that language would have left my meaning open to a very great, almost an entire, misunderstanding, unless I could exchange the name theology for the name God, and say that He Himself is the root from which all human life, and human society, and ultimately, through man, nature itself are derived."[24]

Maurice's style presents a hurdle for the reader. It is often opaque, and confusing. This is partly the result of Maurice's extensive use of the Socratic method of inquiry in which it is not always clear whether Maurice is stating his own argument or that of his imaginary interlocutor. In spite of all this he frequently exhibits a gift of epigrammatic utterance that more than compensates for the difficult task of reading him.

Though it may be said of almost any theologian that Christology is central to thought, with Maurice Christology furnishes in a unique way the underlying principle of all that he said and did. It is the element that gives unity and coherence to his thought, yet saves him from constructing a system. He saw the unifying power of Christology more ✓ clearly, perhaps, than any other Christian thinker.

In a letter to his son he wrote: "I was sent into the world that I might persuade men to recognize Christ as the center of their fellowship with each other, that so they might be united in their families, their countries, and as men..."[25]

The basic principle of Maurice's theology is that God has created and redeemed the whole race in Christ. The heart of the Gospel, as he understood it, is that Christ, the Eternal Son of God, is "the Head and the King of our entire race." He believed this to be the witness of the creeds and behind them of the biblical revelation. He interpreted every Christian doctrine, and the human situation as well, in the light of the doctrines of the Incarnation and Atonement, placed in a Trinitarian setting. The cosmic Christ of Ephesians, Colossians and Hebrews and the Logos Christ of the Fourth Gospel became for Maurice the key to understanding both the scriptural revelation and the human situation.

"My desire is to ground all theology upon the name of God the Father, the Son, and the Holy Ghost, not to begin from ourselves and our sins; not to measure the straight line by the crooked one. This is the method I have learned from the Bible. There everything proceeds from God; He is revealing himself; He is acting, speaking, ruling."[26]

Maurice felt that the theology of his day, whether Roman Catholic or Protestant, whether Anglo-Catholic or Anglican Evangelical, had wrongly oriented itself around human sinfulness as the actual (even if not the explicit) starting point. He proposed instead the early divinity of the creeds which do not mention the fall. Although he took a literalistic view of Genesis and thus believed the fall as historical fact, he maintained that we know Adam and humanity through Christ, and not vice versa.

> "Protestants and Romanists, even while they denounce and excommunicate each other, yet appear to recognize the fact of depravity, of Evil, as the fundamental fact of divinity. The fall of Adam -- not the union of the Father and the Son, not the creation of the world in Christ -- is set before men in both divisions of Christendom as practically the ground of their creed."[27]

Such a passage reveals to us what Maurice meant when he called himself a theological digger. Using the revelation of God in Christ, the union of all in the Head of the race, he probed into every problem and every area of human life, tracing every abuse or evil in Christendom to an inadequate faith in Christ. This is why, in his book Christ and Culture, H. Richard Niebuhr cites Maurice as expressing more clearly than "any other modern Christian thinker and leader" the position that Christ is the transformer and converter of culture.[28]

Maurice, however, never leaves in isolation the principle that Christ is the Head of all. It is always correlated with the nature of the church and its function in the world. To Miss Williams Wynn he wrote in 1858:

> "I do anticipate a very deep and searching reformation, one which cannot be attended with less trials, one which I trust is to issue in greater blessings than the Reformation of the sixteenth century....I feel very strongly that the ascension of our Lord into the heavens, and the glorification of our nature in Him with the corresponding truth that the Church exists to witness of Him, not only as her Head, but as the Head of every man, will be the battle-cry that will rally Protestants and Romanists, hungry seekers after wisdom, lonely tatterdemailions without bread, about the one standard...."[29]

It remains to underline the significance of this fundamental christological principle for such other doctrines as revelation, sin and atonement, the church and sacraments, and for the principle of ecumenism.

Revelation and Scripture

In spite of his largely precritical attitude toward biblical study, Maurice anticipated many of the theological commonplaces today about revelation and its modes. For Maurice revelation is not a set of dictated propositions, but is given in events particularly in relationship to the person of Christ. "The revelation which the reason demands cannot be one of merely moral principles or axioms -- it must be the revelation of a living Being. It cannot therefore be one in which events are merely accidents that can be separated from some idea which has tried to embody itself in them."[30]

He distrusted the scholastic distinction between natural and revealed theology on at least two grounds. He could not accept the notion that there were two distinct pathways to the knowledge of God, especially that there could be one initiated from the human side by something called "unaided reason." In today's terminology we should say that he believed in general revelation: "I hold that all our knowledge may be traced ultimately to Revelation from God."[31] In the second place, he refused to class the Gospel as one among the religions of the world. The Bible is not about religion, but about the acts of the living God: "We have been dosing our people with religion when what they want is not this but the living God."[32]

Maurice's use of the Bible has sometimes been criticized as "Platonizing eisegesis." There is no question about the impact of Plato on his thought. Yet the influence is often more in terms of a method of inquiry than in substantive propositions. Maurice's method in The Kingdom of Christ will remind the reader at once of Socrates' method when seeking the definition of justice by questioning conflicting schools of opinion. Maurice, of course, is leading his respondents on to the admission that there actually is a Catholic Church in their midst and that to it each bears a partial witness. The problem of Platonism is rooted in the recognition that, for Maurice, the Johannine writings are very much the clue to his understanding of the Bible as a whole. It might even be permissible to limit the field further by saying that, within the Fourth Gospel, it is the prologue which is the key. Careful study, however, reveals that Maurice integrated Pauline and Johannine Christianity. What may partially explain the persistent charge of Platonism is more the form than the substance of his exposition. Maurice asserts that what God had intended things to be and has made them through redemption is the real though unseen world. What the world has become through rebellion is the false though seen world.

The Bible is the witness to the Kingdom of Christ, and that Kingdom is the real theme of the Old Testament and the source of truth in other religions and philosophies. In interpreting any passage, Maurice tried to understand its simplest and historical context. Then he sought to show how the historical facts therein narrated also were pointers to

God's universal kingdom and, in particular, to the constitution of all in Christ. He believed that the Holy Spirit would reveal the relevance between these insights and the situation of the preacher or reader of the Bible. He believed deeply in the self-authenticating character of revelation.

> "I use them (the Scriptures) because I conceive they set forth Christ as the Son of God and the Lord of every man. I do not use them because I think they set forth some standard which is good for a set of men called Christians, who are different from other men, and who have not the same God with other men. I use the Scriptures to show us what I believe is the law and the life for all of us, that law and life of which men in the old world had only a partial glimpse. I should not use them if I thought them less universal and more partial than the books of heathens or of later moralists."[33]

For Maurice the Bible is not a solitary fact. He seeks to lay bare the organic connection that actually exists between church, creeds and Bible. His Anglican heritage, with its respect for Bible, tradition and reason interpreted in a pastoral way, received a creative evaluation in depth. The following passage of his about these relationships is genuinely illuminating and relevant in view of the discussion at the Second Vatican Council.

> "He who dwells with us and governs us, the Ever-blessed Word, has formed us to be one in Him; He seeks to make us one by bringing us to a knowledge of Himself; for this end He has revealed Himself to us, and has preserved the revelation in a book; this revelation He has entrusted to His Church, that she may impart it to men, and train men to apprehend its contents; the Church, in the exercise of her functions, has from Scripture formed a creed which is the first step in her scheme of education; when men were awakened by this creed, it became her duty to use the Bible, that they might know the certainty of those things wherein they have been catechized; with this Bible, she is able to cultivate the reason, which is the organ wherewith we apprehend spiritual matters; the Church tried what she could do without the Bible, and she became weak; the Bible has been set up against the Church, and has been dishonored; the Reason has been set up against both Church and Bible, and has become partial, inconsistent, self-contradictory. Finally, bitter experience must lead us at last to a conviction, that God's ways are higher than our ways; that a universal Church, constituted in His Son, and endowed with His Spirit, is the proper instrument for educating the universal reason."[34]

Sin and Atonement

Maurice's method of evaluating the human situation flows quite logically from his basic christological principle. Christ precedes Adam in the order of being. When it is written in Genesis that man has been created in the image of God, Maurice at once understands that the human being has been created by the Eternal Son and that this image can therefore not be destroyed by sin. We are "not to think that the world was created in Adam, or stood in his obedience for the Scriptures of the New Testament, illustrating those of the Old, teach us that it stood and stands in the obedience of God's well-beloved Son; the real image of the Father, the real bond of human society and of the whole universe, who was to be manifested in the fullness of time, as that which he had always been."[35] This means that Christ comes not as an alien intruder into the world, but as the redeemer of his own creation. While Christ brings us the utterly new gift of redemption, he does not extricate us from the race, but restores us to our true life as persons created in his image.

It is clear that such a premise will entail a different understanding of sin from the traditional one which speaks either of a total loss of the image of God or only of certain aspects of the image. Maurice does not understand sin prospectively as the prelude to redemption. He sees it retrospectively, in the sense that we are now members of a race that has been redeemed by the incarnation of the Word, by Christ's bearing the sins of the whole world, and by his resurrection from the dead on the plane of our history.

There is no minimizing of the Atonement in Maurice. Indeed, the opposite is the case, for his firm convictions about the work of Christ in overcoming sin led him to demote the doctrine of sin from its too dominant place in popular theologies. Maurice's view of the Atonement, as set forth in his Theological Essays, has been characterized as one close to the moral-influence theory. This is only a partial description, although perhaps justified because of the obscurity of expression in that work. His own view of the Atonement is best set forth in The Doctrine of Sacrifice, one of the clearest of his writings. Tracing the sacrifices of the Old Testament in a way that would need correction today from newer historical perspectives, Maurice holds that the New Testament asserts sacrifice as the great principle of the divine obedience of the Son before the world existed. What is new here is the careful linking of the Trinity and the idea of creation with the concept of Atonement.

> " We see beneath all evil, beneath the universe itself, that eternal and original union of the Father and the Son...which was never fully manifested till the Only Begotten by the eternal Spirit offered Himself to God. The revelation of that primal unity is the revelation of the ground on which all things stand, both things in heaven and things in earth. It is the revelation of an order which sustains all the intercourse

and society of men. It is the revelation of that which sin has ever been seeking to destroy, and which at last has overcome sin. It is the revelation of that perfect harmony to which we look forward when all things are gathered up in Christ...when the law of sacrifice shall be acknowledged law of all creation."[36]

Maurice criticized Calvinism for misinterpreting God's election and predestination in a narrowly individualistic and exclusivistic way. It made a travesty of the biblical witness that Christ was himself the elect One and that the whole race, not just a favored few, was included in him. This perspective is quite close to Barth's criticism of Calvin. Maurice claimed that the constitution of the race in Christ was the proper background for appreciating the power of Luther's concern for justification by faith and of keeping that cardinal insight uncorrupted. But protestantism found it almost impossible to submit its doctrine of justification by faith to the experience of justification by faith, with the result that, as Maurice shrewdly observed, "when assent to the doctrine of justification was substituted for belief in the Justifier, Protestantism went into the lean, sickly and yet contentious stage of its existence only to emerge from that into indifference -- a mere denial of Romanism."[37]

The Church and Its Six Signs

For Maurice the church was organic to the Gospel. The church is the body of Christ, given life by its Head. It exists to show the world its true center and to support, by articulating the law of mutual sacrifice, the unity of both nations and families. Maurice held that the church was really the world when the christological principle was rightly understood.

It was not customary in Maurice's time to develop the idea of the church as the Israel of God. With a thoroughly scriptural analysis he traced a series of covenants between God and Abraham and the Israelite nation to show that family and nation are preliminary manifestations of church structure. The Church a Family continued consideration of this theme. The ultimate pattern of unity is God who as the Trinity expresses the ground of the family principle. He described his fundamental position in The Kingdom of Christ as follows:

"There rose up before me the idea of a Church Universal, not built upon human inventions or human faith, but upon the very nature of God Himself, and upon the union which He has formed with His creatures; a Church revealed to man as a fixed and eternal reality by means which infinite wisdom had itself devised."[38]

The fundamental sign of church life is baptism, wherein we are forgiven our sins, are incorporated into Christ and realize our status as children of God in the power of the radial atonement effected by Christ.

• Maurice liked to call baptism "the sacrament of constant union." He stressed the importance of sacraments as demonstrations of the free grace of God in Christ and as salutary checks to any excessive preoccupaiton with our own feelings or faith:

"Outward signs and tokens have a great worth. They attest the reality and universality of God's gifts, as in the case of the water in Baptism and the bread and wine in the Lord's Supper. They prevent men from fancying that their thoughts, and impressions, and beliefs, create the blessings which are bestowed upon us by God's free grace."[39]

Baptism interprets the human situation. Maurice has a way of bringing all his previous insights together when he seeks the depth of his next point. Notice the themes, hitherto separately developed, now focused on baptism.

"I have maintained that Christ, by whom, and for whom all things were created, and in whom all things consist, has made reconciliation for mankind; that on the ground of this atonement for mankind, God has built His church, declaring men one family in Christ...And (we believing) that the mark of that universal body or fellowship, appointed by God Himself is Baptism, do, without fear or scruple, asseverate of ourselves, and of all others who will come to this holy Baptism, of all who bear the marks and impress of that nature which Christ took, in His birth, of the blessed Virgin; that they are admitted into these high and glorious privileges; that they are brought into a state of salvation; that they are made sons of God and heirs of everlasting life...And in saying this, we contend that we give faith...a ground upon which to stand, and which otherwise it cannot have."[40]

The second sign, which he elaborated in The Kingdom of Christ, is the two creeds which confess the triform name into which we are baptized. The creeds are not digests of doctrines; they are our protection against theological systems. To say the creed is to confess the Name, to make an act of allegiance to a person. Baptism is the sign that we are saved by grace, the creed that we are saved by faith.

The third sign of the church is the existence of set forms of worship, such as are collected in the Book of Common Prayer. Maurice is a profound interpreter of liturgics. He rejoiced that ordinary English people expressed their worship in forms derived from the Hebrews, the Greeks and the Latins. It was evidence to him that the church transcended space and time. Like many engaged today in the liturgical movement, he held the prayers written in the first ages of Christianity to be "in general more free, more reverent, more universal, than those which have been poured forth since."[41]

The eucharist is the fourth sign. It testifies that, because of Christ's sacrifice once and for all perfected on Calvary, a "living and perpetual communion" has been established between God and humanity. It expresses Christ's "continual presence with His universal family." More significant than the debates over the manner of Christ's presence, Maurice maintained, was the reality of that presence as sheer fact. There was, moreover, social meaning to the eucharist and an eschatological anticipation of the new age. Maurice felt personally that the eucharist expressed a depth and a practicality that one could not find elsewhere. "Ask yourself then solemnly and seriously -- 'Can I find Christianity for men of all countries and periods, all tastes and endowments, all temperaments and necessities so exhibited as I find it in this Sacrament?'"[42]

The ordained ministry is the fifth sign of the Catholic Church. It testifies that there is a permanent structure in the life of the church, a representative office of sacrificial service. Unless it serves faithfully it may congeal into a hierarchy of power and become only another expression of the world. Maurice wrote that the four gospels might be described as "the Institution of a Christian Ministry." The historic episcopate, he believed, expressed the reality of universal communion in the church and was the order that stood in succession to the apostolate. He expresses the idea in these words:

> "I believe that He meant His Church to stand in certain permanent and universal institutions...in a permanent ministry through which He should declare his will, and dispense His blessings to the whole body, and the main office in which should be that apostolic office, which belongs characteristically to the new dispensation, seeing that it expresses the general oversight of Him, who no longer confines himself to any particular nation, but has ascended upon high that He might fill all things."[43]

Although he considered the episcopate necessary, he did not, as the Tractarians did, unchurch those who lost it. This bond of communion might be broken and yet many ties with the universal church might still stand. He refused to define the limits of the church. "I cannot answer the question; I believe only One can answer it. I am content to leave it with Him."[44] The sixth sign, the Bible, has already been discussed. For Maurice, it is the reality behind all the previous signs.

Maurice and Ecumenism

Maurice's The Kingdom of Christ, and many other writings and letters of his, set forth a theology of Christian ecumenism that has yet to come into its own.[45] As the Protestant Churches see beyond pan-Protestantism to an ecumenism that is genuinely catholic and as the Roman Chatholic Church comes out of its isolationism and loses what

one of its own theologians has called its "anti-Protestant face,"
Maurice's modestly offered "hints" will become increasingly central to
ecumenical discussion and action. A surprising number of studies on the
nature of the church by Roman Catholic ecumenists follow a
methodology similar to Maurice's. One of these theologians, Louis
Bouyer, explicitly mentions Maurice's work well before Vatican II.[46]
    With this awareness of the universal applicability of Maurice's
ecumenical principles, it may be well to illustrate just how he saw the
vocation of his own communion as a reconciler. Anglicanism, he
maintained, had never defined itself in sectarian terms. The word sect
represents one of Maurice's basic distinctions in ecclesiological analysis.
The real opposit of catholicism, in his mind, was not protestantism, but
sectarianism. The sect principle was opposed to the principle of
catholicism in that a sect built itself upon some human formula of truth.
To paraphrase his own words, the Church Catholic is a community united
in the acknowledgment of a living person, Christ. Every sect is a body
united in the acknowledgment of some notion or system of divinity. The
sect invariably considered Christianity as an ecclesiastical organization
to which one must adhere.

    True catholicism, however, looked upon Christianity as the
bestowal of a relationship with God. The relationship was given by God
to all. The church existed to bear witness to it in the world. It was, one
might say, the necessary means by which God proclaimed people his
children and heirs and invited them to receive their heritage. Thus the
church could never be conceived as simply a human organization pitted
against the organizations of the world. It was part of the "constitution
of the race." The sect, on the other hand, always saw itself pitted
against the world. It could make no peace with those outside its
confines. Its only approach to unity was to demand agreement with or
submission to itself.

    All of this analysis is common enough today. For a variety of
reasons modern Christians are much aware of the sect type of
Christianity. Maurice's concern, however was the manner in which the
sect principle had infected all of Christendom, whether originally
sectarian or not. The tendency of church bodies to identify themselves
with "the true church" meant that the sect principle triumphed almost
everywhere in Western Christianity. The ecumenical movement is a sign
that responsible Christians have now become aware of these evils and
are seeking a way out of the impasse. Though he came long before the
movement had established itself, Maurice too felt the impasse and
thought Anglicanism had something to contribute toward its solution.

    Many Anglicans today fail to let the depth of Maurice's distinction
between church and sect judge their understanding of the Anglican
Communion. They seem never to question whether they are members of
a church. From this uncritical assumption they look down their noses in
scorn or pity at the historic Protestant churches as "sects" because, for

example, they may not exhibit all the points of the Lambeth Quadrilateral. It has been ironic that the points of the Quadrilateral which were really "principles" or "signs of the Catholic Church" for Maurice have been converted by many latter-day Anglicans into a sectarian system. (Maurice speaks today to this element of self-righteousness and legalism in the Anglican system. Often we have prided ourselves since the formation of the Anglican Communion on being delivered from being a national or regional sect when all that we have really become is a world sect.)

> "I can well conceive how galling it is to a Dissenter to be told that he is the member of a Sect, and that we are not members of one. Moreover, the words seem to me unjust. I think he claims to be a member of Christ's Church as I do. I think I am as liable to sink into a Sectarian, and to be only that, as he is."[47]

Maurice made his point clearly in his criticism of the Episcopal Church of Scotland: "They have stood too much upon their ecclesiastical dignity, that they have seemed too much mere anti-presbyterians."[48]

Anglicanism, he contended, was an important expression of Christianity precisely because it did not have a "system of divinity" or a confessional formulation. It was not a church that insisted upon an official point of view, but embraced warring factions within itself dedicated to catholic, protestant, or liberal principles. This holy pandemonium might be the despair of the strict Roman Catholic or of the pure Protestant, but it did emphasize the fact that the church was founded not upon a humanly contrived system, but directly upon God.

> "Our Church has no right to call herself better than other churches in any respect, in many she must acknowledge herself to be worse. But our position, we may fairly affirm, for it is not a boast but a confession, is one of singular advantage. If what I have said be true, our faith is not formed by a union of the Protestant systems with the Romish system, nor of certain elements taken from the one and of certain elements taken from the others. So far as it is represented in our liturgy and our articles, it is the faith of a Church and has nothing to do with any system at all. That peculiar character which God has given us, enables us, if we do not slight the mercy, to understand the difference between a church and a system better perhaps than any of our neighbors can, and, therefore, our position, rightly used, gives us a power of assisting them in realizing the blessings of their own."[49]

Maurice did not attribute the advantages of the Anglican position to human wisdom and foresight. Rather he contended that the events of the English Reformation had prevented the Church of England from formulating its understanding of itself in sectarian terms. The result was a church body in which the catholic constitution of the church was united to a Protestant protest against the papacy. In her insistence upon national freedom, in her emphasis upon justification by faith, in her refusal of a human, visible head for the church, the Church of England was thoroughly a church of the Reformation. Yet none of the classic marks or "signs" of the church, he believed, were abrogated. The apostolic ministry, the catholic creeds, Scripture as the Word of God, the two dominical sacraments and liturgical worship all remain. It is interesting to note that these very items, which Maurice treats at great length in The Kingdom of Christ, were later also affirmed in the Chicago-Lambeth Quadrilateral as essentials of church life.

It is not usually recognized that Maurice's writings were the real source of the Chicago-Lambeth Quadrilateral since most commentary on its development stops on this side of the Atlantic with William Reed Huntington's The Church Idea, published in 1870. Huntington telescoped Maurice's six signs of the Catholic Church into four by bracketing baptism and holy communion into one point and by omitting Maurice's forms of worship. Huntington compared his four points to the foursquare City of God in the Apocalypse and unfortunately borrowed the name "quadrilateral" from the four Lombard fortresses. The liturgical setting within Anglicanism is so dominant that a "pentelateral" might have been more realistic and possibly more productive than the Lambeth Quadrilateral. Gone also from the Quadrilateral was much of the spirit of Maurice, the replacement of Maurice's view of principles and process by a somewhat legalistic and static ultimatum about "this sacred deposit."[50] The Lambeth Conferences of 1920 and 1968 in their commentary on the Quadrilateral have come closest perhaps to Maurice's spirit, whereas, in general, Anglicanism has been fairly stodgy, defensive and myopic in its use. The Decree on Ecumenism of the Second Vatican Council comes much closer to the spirit of Maurice.

Maurice was not an especially accurate prophet of what would happen to the religious systems of his day. He saw them headed for a speedy dissolution but in a way that history simply has not confirmed. Also, he was not without a certain anti-Roman bias that may largely be accounted for in the dismal condition of the Italian church in his day. On most points he has been vindicated since the renewalist theologies of Vatican II have often taken positions surprisingly similar to his.[51]

The Kingdom of Christ gives us an indication of Maurice's views on the unity of the church. As indicated above, he tries to show that in the positive witness of each sect some basic living Christian principle is recognized, but not the whole of Christian truth. In constructing a system to embody and defend its partial truth, each sect denied other truths and excluded other Christian bodies from its fellowship. In the process, it betrayed the truth it set out to enshrine. The trouble lay in the sectarian conviction that it must construct the church anew to purify it from error. There was no remedy for this trouble, Maurice contended, unless the church already existed, built upon the foundation of the living Christ, reconciling all the fragments of truth which the various sects had championed, liberating them from the distorted shapes into which their defenders had forced them. Maurice joined the Church of England because in it he saw the partial fulfillment of this vision.

Far from claiming anything for itself, Anglicanism simply witnessed to the living foundation underlying all sects. Far from excluding all those who disagreed with it, Anglicanism claimed for itself and others membership in Christ's one, holy, catholic and apostolic church. Its role was to affirm and defend major catholic truths denied by Rome or by protestant churches. Thus, Maurice saw the ideal of Anglicanism to be just as concerned to defend justification as the Lutheran, just as occupied in proclaiming election as the Presbyterian, just as zealous for the inner light as the Quaker, just as insistent upon the preservation of catholicism as the Roman Catholic. Precisely because it had no system of its own except, of course, this very formula itself, it was in a better position, he believed, to champion the truths others had perceived.

> "Let us make the members of sects to understand that we are setting up no opinions of ours against theirs, no leaders of ours against their leaders; that we desire to justify all that they and their fathers have clung to in their darkest and bravest hours, all that their leaders have taught them when they were inspired with most indignation against our indifferences to Christ and His Gospel; that what we preach is Christ the One Head of a body which time and space cannot bound, Christ the source and object of their faith and ours. Christ is the destroyer of all sects, inasmuch as He joins man to God. Let us make Spaniards, Frenchmen, Italians understand that we do not ask them to leave their churches for ours, to accept any single English tradition which is not also theirs, or to travel through the path by which God led the Teutonic nations in the sixteenth century."[52]

From the perspective of its ecumenical vocation, the parties of Anglicanism could be of considerable value. The Tractarians preserved the catholic witness to a constitution and order for the whole race and to the reality of the Church Catholic in the world. Evangelicals witnessed to the fact that there was a real bond for all in Christ's sacrifice. The liberals or broad churchmen insisted that the church must be comprehensive and throw off all partial truths. Each party, unfortunately, became as narrow and as divisive as any sect in the defense of its principles. But between them they outlined the things to which any branch of the church must witness. The fact that they stayed together in one communion testified to the divine union which the church was meant to proclaim to the world. It has often been remarked that Anglicanism itself is a microcosm of the ecumenical movement. This is precisely Maurice's point.

Maurice's opposition to parties within the Church of England is well known. Although he had been influenced by each of the three parties of his day, he never joined one. He also saw the dangers of a "no-party" and even of a Maurician party. His insight into the tendency within the Church of England to form parties is quite profound. This tendency has characterized Anglicanism far beyond its first homeland. "Elsewhere the defenders of a system may merely form a school. In England because by constitution we are politicians and not systematizers, they must form a party."[53]

Maurice's "ecumenical" ecumenism is still needed by us and we need to listen to his warnings about party divisions within. The fine quality of Maurice's spirit breathes through this well-known passage as he concludes The Kingdom of Christ.

"But if shame and humiliation are needful for English clergymen generally, they must be especially needful in those who have presumed to speak of our sins, and to offer any suggestions for our amendment....I have in this book attacked no wrong tendency to which I do not know myself to be liable....I am not ignorant, also, that the limits which I have offered in opposition to systems may, themselves, be turned by myself or by others into a system; and that neither its weakness and inconsistency, nor the insignificance of its originator, may prevent it from connecting itself with some new party....But since a school, which should be formed to oppose all schools, must be of necessity more mischievous than any of them, and since a school, which pretended to amalgamate the doctrines of all other schools, would be, as I think, more mischievous than that, I do pray earnestly that, if any schools should arise, they may come to nought."[54]

How was the ecumenical vocation of Anglicanism to be carried out? This would not be done by calling other groups to unite with it as one possessing all the essentials of church life. That would be a return to sectarianism. Yet neither would it do to propose indiscriminate mergers with other groups. Few of the religious bodies in Maurice's day understood the truth he was driving at. His approach was to invite those of sectarian views to see that they were not really members of a sect at all, but of the church. On this ground he justified refusal of the Church of England to permit itself to be called a sect. Though this seemed pretentious to non-conformist churchmen, its purpose was to preserve a witness against their own view of themselves. "We will not submit to be called an episcopalian sect, because we do not want you to consider yourselves as sects. We want you to feel that you are members of a Church, members of Christ, children of God."⁵⁵

Thus Maurice stumbled across the very principle which has made the ecumenical movement possible -- the recognition that somehow all Christians are already united in Christ and members of his Church. He was perfectly willing to associate with other Christians on the grounds of "common membership in Christ." But he sharply rejected any sort of union based on the lowest common denominator of belief. Such a union would only be the dead residue of all sectarian systems.

The ecumenical vocation of Anglicanism, on the other hand, was to be carried out by claiming for others the privileges and the position Anglicanism claimed for itself. Rather than unchurch those who disagree with it -- which is, in effect, the approach of sectarianism -- it is to "church" them. It is to insist that what is true of itself is also the truth about them. Maurice even approached the thorny question of apostolic orders in this way. (The doctrine of apostolic ministry, he insisted, was not held in order to cast doubt on the validity of other ordained ministries, but to testify to the fact that every minister is more than a denominational official.) God himself had brought the pastoral office into being. The nonconformist minister, it was granted, could stand in a deeper, more organic relation to his congregation than he himself recognized or admitted. The intention of Anglican insistence upon apostolic orders was in part to enable such a minister to see the real validity of the ordained ministry and the catholicity of the given communion.

Maurice did not feel that the vocation he envisaged for Anglicanism could be undertaken with any sense of self-righteousness. Essentially he was contending that the Church of England was to call others to repent the sectarian temper which led them away from Christ and divided them from each other. Such a call could only come out of a like repentance from the Anglican. Maurice was extraordinarily aware of the sins of his own church, of the way it had treated its catholic structure as a pretext for a sectarian temper, of its treatment of both the Bible and Prayer Book as a "series of inspired sentences" and of its neglect of the poor in England. There was no sin in any church that was not also a sin of the Church of England. Only out of repentance could a call for unity come. But come it must, for God was "a destroyer of sects." On the horizon of the nineteenth century Maurice saw a "fearful crushing of sects"; this made him hopeful for the unity of the church, but not optimistic about the future. "Permitted destroyers of faith" would force the church back to its oneness in Christ.

Maurice's understanding of the ecumenical vocation of Anglicanism and of the much larger focus, the reconciliation in depth between catholicism and protestantism, is the message of the Spirit to the churches in our day. Maurice many times described his whole ministry and authorship as a search for unity. He knew, however, that its deepest ground was there all the time, in the given unity of the Triune God:

"The idea of the unity of the Father and the Son in the Holy Spirit, as the basis of all unity amongst men, as the groundwork of all human society and of all thought, as belonging to little children, and as the highest fruition of the saints in glory, has been haunting me for longer time than I can easily look back to."[56]

NOTES: Introduction

1. Frederick Maurice, The Life of Frederick Denison Maurice (New York: Charles Scribner's Sons, 1884), referred to hereafter as Life. This remains the indispensable biographical source. There is also a very short biography, Frederick Denison Maurice, by Florence Higham (London: SCM Press, 1947). See also John F. Porter and William J. Wolf Toward the Recovery of Unity: The Thought of Frederick Denison Maurice (edited from his letters with an introduction) (New York: Seabury Press, 1964). Some additional unpublished letters of Maurice are quoted by Frank McClain in his useful Maurice: Man and Moralist (London: S.P.C.K., 1972). McClain includes an exhaustive list of the published works of Maurice and of manuscript sources.

2. Life, I, 41.

3. Ibid., I, 167.

4. Ibid., I, 237. Subscription No Bondage, Maurice's first theological book, is a defense of the Articles of Religion as requirements in the universities. Near the end of his life he wrote: "No book which I have written expresses more strongly what then were, and still are, my deepest convictions." (Life I, 174).

5. It is to be hoped that some day the first edition of The Kingdom of Christ will be republished because his views are often expressed more clearly there than in the ecumenically richer second and revised edition. Meanwhile it is possible to acquire some feeling for the first edition from the extensive quotations from it made by W. Merlin Davies in An Introduction to F.D. Maurice's Theology: Based on the First Edition of The Kingdom of Christ (1838) and The Faith of the Liturgy and the Doctrine of the Thirty-Nine Articles (1860) (London: S.P.C.K., 1964).

6.   The Kingdom of Christ, or Hints to a Quaker respecting the Principles, Constitution, and Ordinances of the Catholic Church. Second edition revised and altered. Two volumes, J.G.F. Rivington and J. Rivington, 1842.

7.   Life, I, 309.   Alec Vidler in Witness to the Light (New York: Charles Scribner's Sons, 1948) quotes from almost the full range of Maurice's books.   Vidler's commentary provides a useful introduction to Maurice's thought.

8.   MS.letter; September 8, 1852 quoted by McClain, op.cit., p. 128.

9.   Olive J. Brose in her helpful Frederick Denison Maurice: Rebellious Conformist 1805-72 (Athens: Ohio University Press, 1971) calls Maurice "the Burke of the Church of England." (p. 279). See also Robert Tom Hall's doctoral thesis (Drew University, 1967) entitled The Unity of Philosophy, Theology and Ethics in the Thought of F.D. Maurice.

10.   Kingdom of Christ (1838), III, p. 76.

11.   F.D. Maurice, Theological Essays (New York: Harper, 1957), pp. 276-277.

12.   The Kingdom of Christ, II, pp.346-47 (SCM Press).

13.   Torben Christensen, The Origin and History of Christian Socialism 1848-1854 (Universitetforlaget Aarhus, 1962) is an excellent critical analysis of the movement.   Christensen has revised his Danish doctoral thesis Logos og Inkarnation, and translated the revision into English as The Divine Order: A Study in F.D. Maurice's Theology, (London: Brill, 1973). It is the most comprehensive study of Maurice's theology that we have.

14.   Life, II, 35.

15.   Ibid., II, 32.

16.   F.D. Maurice, Tracts on Christian Socialism (London: Christian Social Union, Oxford University Branch, 1849), p.2.

17.   Maurice B. Reckitt, Maurice to Temple: A Century of the Social Movement in the Church of England (London: Faber and Faber, 1947).

18.   See the chapter "Maurice on Women" by Frank McClain in F.D. Maurice: A Study (Cambridge, Massachusetts: Cowley Publications, 1982).

19. See The Prayer Book by F.D. Maurice (London: James Clarke and Co., 1966) with a forward by Archbishop Michael Ramsey and Worship and Theology in England from Watts and Wesley to Maurice 1690-1850 by Horton Davies (Princeton: Princeton University Press, 1961).

20. Claude Jenkins, F.D. Maurice and the New Reformation (London: S.P.C.K., 1938), p. 23.

21. Life, I, 230.

22. The Kingdom of Christ, I, p. 236.

23. Ecclesiastical History, p. 222.

24. Life, II, 136.

25. Ibid., I, 239-40. See John F. Porter The Place of Christ in the Thought of F.D. Maurice (Doctoral thesis, Columbia University, 1959).

26. Doctrine of Sacrifice, p. xli.

27. Conflict of Good and Evil, p. 170.

28. H. Richard Niebuhr, Christ and Culture (New York: Harper and Row, 1956) p. 229.

29. Life, II, 317.

30. The Kingdom of Christ, I, p. 177.

31. Sequel to What is Revelation, p. 97.

32. Life, I, 369.

33. Epistles of St. John, p. 14.

34. The Kingdom of Christ (1838), II, p. 87 ff.

35. Patriarchs and Lawgivers, p. 66.

36. Doctrine of Sacrifice, p. 194.

37. Life, II, 615.

38. The Kingdom of Christ, II, p. 363.

39. Acts of the Apostles, p. 188 ff.

40. The Kingdom of Christ (1838), I, 88 ff.

41. The Kingdom of Christ, II, p. 45.

42. The Kingdom of Christ (1838), I, 287.

43. Three Letters to the Rev. William Palmer (London: Rivington, 1842), p. 8.

44. Epistle to the Hebrews, p. cxxxiv.

45. For a more detailed discussion see William Wolf, "Maurice and Our Understanding of 'Ecumenical'" in The Anglican Theological Review (No. 4, October 1972, Vol. liv), pp. 273-90. This issue is given over to articles delivered at the American Maurice Centenary held at Seabury-Western Theological Seminary.

46. See L. Bouyer, The Spirit and Forms of Protestantism (Westminster, Md.: Newman Press, 1956). See also more recent doctoral theses by Roman Catholics: John Haughey, The Ecclesiology of F.D. Maurice (Catholic University of America, 1967) and David Murphy, The Ecumenical Theology of F.D. Maurice (Ottawa University, 1971).

47. F.D. Maurice, A Few Words on Secular and Denominational Education, p. 12. Quoted from Vidler, op. cit., p. 80.

48. The Kingdom of Christ, II, p. 340.

49. Ibid., p. 343.

50. "Do not let the Church stand, Narcissus-like contemplating the comeliness of her proportions and the greatness of her powers. That comeliness will appear most when she moves, these powers will be felt when she is acting." The Kingdom of Christ (1838), III, pp. 131-32.

51. See David Murphy, "Maurice and Contemporary Theology," chap 6 op.cit.

52. Lincoln's Inn Sermons, II, p. 86.

53. Kingdom of Christ, II, p. 331.

54. Ibid., p. 347.

55. Life, I, 258-59.

56. Ibid., I, 414.

PART I

ON THE PRINCIPLES OF THE QUAKERS AND OF THE
DIFFERENT RELIGIOUS BODIES WHICH HAVE ARISEN
SINCE THE REFORMATION, AND ON THE SYSTEMS TO
WHICH THEY HAVE GIVEN BIRTH

1

CHAPTER I

QUAKERISM

SECTION I -- ON THE POSITIVE DOCTRINES OF THE QUAKERS

The Indwelling Word -- The Spiritual Kingdom -- Spiritual Influences

In Mr. Gurney's work on the religious peculiarities of the Society of Friends, we are told that the doctrine "which lies at the root of all their particular views and practices, is that of the perceptible influence and guidance of the Spirit of Truth." This author maintains in a previous passage that "a measure of the influence of the Spirit is bestowed upon all men whereby they are enlightened, and may be saved." But it is obvious that he does not look upon this principle as in any degree so important or so characteristic of the Quakers, as the other. I do not see how a mere theory respecting the condition of the world generally can ever seem so important to any man, as a principle which concerns his own conduct and responsibility. But I question whether the old Quakers would have stated the latter doctrine precisely in the terms which Mr. Gurney has used; I think they would have given it a much more practical form and signification, and that by doing so they would have exhibited the relative position and value of these two portions of their creed very differently.

Anyone who reads Fox's Journal will find that he adhered most literally and practically to a belief in perceptible impressions and influences. His whole conduct was regulated by the conviction, that he was commanded to do certain acts and utter certain words; wherever he went, whomsoever he denounced, whatever tone or manner he gave to his discourses, he believed undoubtedly that he was obeying a divine instigation. But, however strange this conviction may seem in our days (and some of the results of it would seem strange to the Quakers themselves), no one who is at all acquainted with the history of the period between 1645 and 1660 will fancy that Fox or his disciples were in this particular distinguished from a number of other religious men. There were hundreds, perhaps I might say thousands, in Cromwell's army who lived and acted as much under this belief, and who followed it out as consistently, as any Quaker could possibly do. Fox himself was frequently brought into collision with such men. He speaks, again and again, of a body of Ranters who gave him much trouble, on this very ground that they all believed themselves under perceptible spiritual influences. And in one very remarkable passage of his Diary, he says that a convert of his, Justice Hotham, told him, that he (Fox) had been raised up to utter a principle which discomfited these Ranters, and that but for this principle they would have overrun the whole land and destroyed it.

I. This principle, and not the doctrine respecting perceptible influences, must then, one would think, have been the central one of Primitive Quakerism. Nay, a really earnest Quaker would have been willing that the truth and value of his spiritual impressions should be tried by their conformity to it or disagreement with it. What then was this principle? William Penn, in his preface to Fox's Journal, expresses it in the following words: "They were directed to the light of Jesus Christ within them as the seed and leaven of the kingdom of God; near all, because in all, and God's talent to all. A faithful and true witness and just monitor in every bosom, the gift and grace of God to life and salvation, that appears to all, though few regard it." This, he says, was "their fundamental principle, the corner-stone of their fabric, and, to speak eminently and properly, their characteristic or main distinguishing point or principle;" this principle of "the light of Christ within, as God's gift for man's salvation, is the root of the goodly tree of doctrines, that grew and branched out of it."

That this doctrine was the ground of Fox's teaching every page of his Diary proves. It might be a conviction, that he was sensibly led by the Spirit, which induced him to break forth in this or that steeplehouse, or to attack this or that Independent, Baptist, Presbyterian, or "Common-Prayer man." But, when he did speak, the words he uttered were, "Brother, there is a light within thee: resist it and thou art miserable; follow it and thou art happy." And he again and again expressed his assurance that these were the words which produced a real moral effect upon his hearers; that whatever else he said was valuable only as it arose out of them, or tended to illustrate and enforce them. He believes that he spoke to something which was in those to whom he spoke, and that, being there, it answered his appeal.

It was not from the teachers or popular books of the day that Fox learnt this doctrine. The language in which he describes his early life is remarkably unlike that which we meet with in Puritan biographies. "At eleven years of age," he says, "he knew pureness and righteousness;" while he was a child he was taught how to walk to be kept pure; when he grew up and "was put to a man that was a shoemaker by trade, and that dealt in wool, and used grazing, and sold cattle, and a great deal passed through his hands, he never wronged man or woman, for the Lord's power was over him to preserve him...people had generally a love to him for his honesty and innocency." The conflicts of mind, which he describes afterwards, had no relation to any of the controversies, religious or political, by which England was then torn asunder. Of Prelacy or Covenant, King or Parliament, he knew nothing. The awful question, What am I? -- what have I to do in this strange confused world? occupied his soul. It is one which must be new to each man, though thousands may have been vexed with it before him. Those whom Fox consulted about it afforded him little help; he withdrew from the society of his fellow-creatures, and studied his Bible. Even that seemed not to tell him the secret which he wanted to know: one thing however he learnt; there was

3

in him that which shrank from this inquiry, and would fain forget it altogether, and there was that in him which would have no rest till he found the answer to it. Now, was not this in itself a great discovery? Did it not shew him (in part at least), what kind of being he was? He had desires which drew him down to things which he saw, and tasted, and handled; he had desires which aspired after something with which his senses and appetites had nothing to do. And was there not another discovery contained in this? They were actual earthly objects which attracted him towards themselves; his nature inclined him to them, yet, when he obeyed that nature, he seemed to lose what was most real in him. Must there not be a counter-attraction, a power as real as any of those things which he beheld, raising him out of them, urging him to seek something above himself, a real substantial good? Must not that power be in truth greater, though the contrary might seem to be the case, than all which were resisting it? Could he not obey that higher influence, and, by obeying it, obtain life and peace? He felt that he could; that he was meant to do so. The light was stronger than the darkness. He was privileged to dwell in it.

But was this light, then, afforded only to George Fox the shoemaker? How could this be? Did it not witness to him, that whenever he was setting up himself he was resisting it, not following it; when he was obeying the selfish inclinations, he knew that he was flying from this great teacher; when he desired to be led by it he knew that he was a man? Surely, then, this must be a light vouchsafed to him, because he was a man; it must be "a light which lighteneth every man who cometh into the world." A terrible majority might be striving against it, but their very strivings proclaimed the truth; the kind of misery which men experienced shewed the happiness which was intended for them.

When he arrived at this conviction, the Bible seemed to him a new book altogether. From first to last it witnessed to him of that invisible good which men are to seek after, and against the visible idolatries which are drawing them away from it. The lives of the patriarchs, of Moses, of the prophets, were the lives of men who were following the light, the teacher of their hearts, the Lord of righteousness, and were resisting the evil inclinations and appetites which would make them the slaves and worshippers of outward things. On the other hand, all the records of the sins of the Jewish nation, or of heathen nations, were records of revolts from this mysterious guide and teacher, by men who chose darkness rather than light, the outward and apparent good rather than the real and inward. As might be expected, the darkness became continually more gross in each individual who gave himself up to it, and the light brighter and clearer in each one who steadily pursued it. And so it had been in each new period -- greater blindness and sensuality, greater and more immediate illumination: Jews and Gentiles becoming more estranged from Him who was yet revealing Himself to them both; holy prophets holding more wonderful converse than their fathers had

4

done with the WORD OF GOD -- rising more above outward emblems and institutions, obeying more implicitly his inward suggestions. Such, or nearly such, was the form in which the Old Testament history seems to have presented itself to Fox; and therefore the words at the beginning of the Gospel of St. John appeared to him to stand in the most natural connection with all the records to which they refer. And St. Paul's declarations, in the first and second of Romans, that the Gentiles knew God, but glorified Him not as God, and liked not to retain Him in their knowledge; and that the Gentiles as well as the Jews, if they sought for glory and honour and immortality, would obtain eternal life; while the Jews as well as the Gentiles, if they were contentious and obeyed not the truth but obeyed unrighteousness, would have tribulation and wrath -- far from containing a puzzle, which it required critical ingenuity to surmount, appeared to him the simple announcement of a truth with which all the rest of Scripture was in agreement.

II. But how was the condition of men affected by the appearance of our Lord in human flesh? This was a question which probably did not at first present itself to Fox; but by degrees he and the other Quakers found an answer to it. Men having foregone their spiritual privileges and given themselves up to the flesh, were not indeed forsaken by their heavenly Teacher, but they could not be treated as spiritual. By outward emblems and images, the elements of the world, they were trained: to the Jews was given a direct intimation of the nature and purpose of their discipline; the Gentiles, through a thicker film of sense, and with fewer helps to penetrate it, might yet, if they would, discover their invisible guide. But these were preparations for a clearer day. Christ, the Living Word, the Universal Light, appeared to men, and shewed in His own person what processes He was carrying on in the hearts of all; subduing the flesh, keeping Himself separate from the world, submitting to death. This manifestation was the signal for the commencement of a new dispensation; sensible emblems were no longer to intercept man's view of his Lord; national distinctions were to be abolished; men might be treated as belonging to a higher state than that which they lost in Adam; they might attain a perfection which did not exist in Adam.

The Scriptural testimonies to this doctrine seemed to them most numerous. Stripped of the fantastical covering in which they were sometimes enveloped, few readers will think that they received a forced or unnatural construction. The announcement by the Prophets of a dispensation which should have these two characteristics above all others -- spirituality and universality; the evident annulling, in the Sermon on the Mount, of rules and maxims which had been previously current and the substitution of a spiritual principle for them; our Lord's constant declaration that He came to establish a kingdom, and that that kingdom was to be within us; the announcement of the Evangelists that His parables were the discovery of mysteries which had been hidden from the foundation of the world; His own words that He would yet shew His disciples more plainly of the Father; the language of the Epistle to the

5

Galatians, affirming that a spiritual covenant had succeeded to the fomal Jewish covenant; the language of the Epistle to the Ephesians, affirming that an economy hidden from ages and generations was then made known to His Holy Apostles by the Spirit; the exhortations in the Philippians and the Hebrews to press onwards to perfection -- exhortations evidently grounded upon the new position into which those who were addressed had been brought: these are only specimens of the evidence which every page of the New Testament seemed to the Quakers to contain of the doctrine that our Lord came to bring in a universal Light, to establish a perfectly spiritual Kingdom, and to encourage men to seek a perfectly spiritual Life.

III. It is implied in the very idea of this constitution, that men are brought under a directly divine government or influence. Those who yield themselves to the light, and become members of the spiritual kingdom, recognise this influence in all their acts. They will not move without it; they will be ready to move anywhere at its bidding. The sacrifice of all personal inclinations, energies, will, in short self-annihilation in its highest form, is their duty and their privilege; so they become fit to utter the divine voice, and prompt to perform the divine will.

In support of this doctrine the Quakers would plead the words of John the Baptist, announcing the baptism of the Holy Spirit and fire as the great promise of the new covenant; the ignorance of the Apostles till they received the gift from on high; the silence and waiting that were enjoined upon them till it arrived; the whole tenor of the Apostolic history, shewing that the first ministers of Christ believed themselves to be acting under an immediate inspiration, and to be incapable of acting without it; the principle so often asserted, and everywhere implied, that the kingdom was to be everlasting, and that those who first witnessed its establishment were to be patterns and precedents of all who succeeded them.

SECTION II -- OBJECTIONS TO THE QUAKER THEOLOGY
            CONSIDERED

I am far from saying that the early Quakers acknowledged no theological principles except these three. In a sense they admitted most of the doctrines which other men embody in creeds or articles. But these three principles determined that sense; these had been realised in their minds; the rest hung loosely about them, and at one time might be heartily recognized, at one time almost rejected, as they seemed to square with the primary truths or to contradict them. These three doctrines, then, may be said to constitute the positive theology of the Quakers; from these their system has been deduced. Before I inquire what that system is, and how far it is legitimately connected with the principles of which I have spoken, I may state in a few words why I cannot join some conspicuous opponents of Quakerism in denouncing

6

these principles -- why I believe them to be either truths or hints of truths which are most vital and important.

I. There are three objections usually taken against Fox's doctrine of the Inward Light or the Indwelling Word. First, it is said to be mystical; secondly, it is said to be unscriptural; thirdly, it is said to be unsupported by fact, or by any authority, save that of an ignorant mechanic and his credulous disciples.

1. I shall not evade the first charge, by saying that the word mystical may mean anything, everything, or nothing; that it may be applied -- has been applied -- against the most recognized principles in physics as well as in morals; that if mystical and mysterious mean the same thing, all science is mystical. I will at once give the word a sense which may be a legitimate sense, which at all events is a common one. The tendency to invest certain feelings, consciousnesses, temperaments of individual men with the sacredness which belongs only to such truths as are of universal character, and may be brought to a universal test, is often designated by the name Mysticism; it is unquestionably one to which religious men in all ages have been prone; and I do not know any records which contain more frequent instances of it than those of the early Quakers. But the question is, whether, if this be the definition of mysticism -- and I know no definition which distinctly condemns it except this -- the doctrine we are considering be not essentially unmystical, nay, whether we might not almost venture to call it emphatically the antagonist principle to mysticism. For surely it disclaims, more vehemently than almost any, exclusive appropriation; it submits itself more directly than most to a universal test. Fox did not say, "This light is mine;" he said, "It is yours as much as mine: it is with you; and in the healthiest, truest, soberest states of your mind, you know that it is with you." This principle stood out, then, in marked contrast to those peculiar experiences and interpretations upon which he often laid so much stress; attesting its difference from them by the effects which it produced, and obtaining at least some sanction in its being forced upon the conviction of men whose characteristic infirmities would have led them to an entirely different conclusion.

2. The notion that the doctrine is unscriptural has derived support, partly from the opinion that Fox and his followers habitually disparaged the Scriptures, partly from his own confession that he knew the doctrine before he saw it in the Bible, though afterwards he learnt how to support it from the Bible. How far the general charge against them is true I may consider presently; that it does not affect this particular case is evident from the appeal which they make not to a few isolated texts merely, but to the whole tenor and context of the inspired volume, in defence of their position. Neither can I see in Fox's account of the mode by which he arrived at an apprehension of this principle anything different from the statements which are common in writers who are the most opposed to him; that, after they were spiritually awakened, the Bible, which had

7

been a dead letter to them, seemed to be full of meaning to them, the only wonder being that they had not perceived it before -- language which I believe is very simple, reasonable, and accordant with the experience of most earnest men, no wise derogatory to the Bible, and not at all incompatible with the belief that the study of it may have been one of the principal instruments whereby that capacity which makes its words comprehensible was called forth. And surely no considerations about the course of thought which another man has followed, need hinder us from inquiring whether the view which he takes of a book do throw a light upon it, and render the contents of it more coherent and intelligible.

I have stated a few of the reasons which have led others, and, I acknowledge, compel me, to believe that the denial of Fox's doctrine makes the scheme, the spirit, and the letter of Scripture alike perplexing. If it were necessary to add further proofs, I should find them in the violent and tortuous expedients to which critics have resorted for the sake, as they profess, of escaping from the extravagances and absurdities of mystical interpretation.   When, for instance, I hear a grave, learned, and (so far as hostility to Socinianism is a title to that name) orthodox interpreter, suggesting that 'o logos in the first verse of the Gospel of St. John means only 'o legomenos (the person talked of -- promised), supporting the gloss by the question of John's disciples, Su ei'o erchomenos; and treating the two phrases as equivalent; when I find such an opinion as this adopted by respectable scholars, as a convenient refuge from mysticism -- I am constrained to think that I am not likely to preserve my respect for the letter of the inspired volume more uncorrupted, or my apprehension of what is reasonable in human language more clear, by determining not to believe that the Word of God before He came in the flesh was the light which lightened all men -- a principle as much confirmed to me by the evidence of profane as of sacred history.

* * *

One thing at least is evident, that Fox, the shoemaker of the 17th century, was not the first person who understood the verses at the beginning of St. John's Gospel in a literal, not a metaphorical sense. Before I quit this part of my subject, I must take leave to remark, that the kind of charge which is brought against the Fathers who adopted this doctrine shews very clearly whence the main objection to it has been derived. We are told, and sometimes in a very solemn manner, to beware how we corrupt the simplicity of the Gospel by philosophy and vain deceit.   Perhaps the caution may be less applicable to Fox and the Quakers, than to some others; for he hated Greek and Philosophy most cordially, and his followers have in general retained this part of his opinions with great fidelity; still, it is an important caution, which those to whom it is offered should receive gratefully, and for which they cannot shew their value in any way so effectually as by returning it. I believe that anyone, who is at the pains to investigate the origin of his own opinions, will discover that neither reverence for Scripture, nor a great love for simplicity, but precisely the addiction -- I must call it, the slavish addiction -- to a certain system of philosophy which established itself in this country about the time of the Revolution, is consciously or unconsciously the cause of his dislike to a principle which has been recognized by the humblest and most ignorant men, as well as by the most profound. Ever since the position was adopted as a new and surprising truth (which previous thinkers had looked upon as one of the most plausible, most natural, and most degrading forms of error), that there is no knowledge but that which comes to us through the senses, the idea of a communion between the Divine Word and the heart and conscience and reason of men has been of course rejected. The subject will often recur it the course of our inquiries.

II. I need say very little about the two other main articles of the Quaker faith; first, because the principle of them is contained in that which we have been examining, and secondly, because they are admitted to a certain extent, and under some conditions, by nearly all Christians. The proposition, for instance, that Christ came to establish a spiritual kingdom, a kingdom not of this world, different from the Jewish, in being less carnal and more spiritual, is constantly proclaimed by those English dissenters who are most inclined to denounce Fox's primary tenet as unscriptural and false. Only they think that he pushed this truth to an extreme. They think the kingdom is spiritual but not quite so spiritual as he fancied. So also with reference to the gift of the Spirit and the subordination of man's powers and utterances to His government -- they believe that what Fox said was true up to a certain point, but that there is great danger of going beyond that point. I shall have opportunities of examining the plea for these restrictions hereafter. At present, I will only say that, far from thinking that the Quakers have carried their principles to an excess, I believe all their errors have arisen from the narrow imperfect and earthly notions which they entertain respecting the nature of a spiritual kingdom, and from the low estimate which they have formed of that transcendent gift which God bestowed upon His creatures when His Holy Spirit came down to dwell among them. My meaning will appear more clearly when I have spoken of the negative articles of Quaker Theology.

SECTION III -- THE QUAKER SYSTEM

1. It is not difficult to imagine in what way the principle of an inward light must have affected the mind of a man educated as Fox was, provided he were perfectly earnest and sincere. I have spoken of his doctrine -- unquestionably it was his doctrine, for it was that which he taught wherever he went; if I had called it a dogma I should perhaps have described very exactly that which it has become to modern Quakers; but assuredly neither word would have seemed to him the correct one. He had actually discovered a law to which he himself was subject -- to

9

which every other man was subject; would anyone tell him that this was a mere notion like those about justification, sanctification, final perseverance, and so forth, which he had heard proclaimed from the pulpits of the day? The language of the preachers and of the books might be about something which concerned him and all men; but he had discovered the very thing itself; he had a fact to proclaim, not a theory or a system. From the very first therefore he began to denounce dogmas and formulas as corrupting and misleading. The young mechanic told the preachers, who had been trained in all the distinctions and divisions, which the Westminster Assembly with such infinite labour and discussion had wrought out, that they knew nothing about the matter they were talking of. Those who had silenced their brethren for their want of spiritual knowledge were rebuked, and sometimes silenced (by the voice of a man, not the vote of a trying Committee), for the self-same sin. But if formulas were evil things, could forms be better? Here were men professing outward acts and ceremonies, and between these and the Christian life they said or signified that there was an intimate connexion. Strange, almost incredible blindness! Did not the Christian life consist in following an inward Guide, an invisible Teacher, in eschewing that which was visible and sensible? What could these outward things have to do with that? The argument was irresistible. It was a main part of Fox's vocation to bear witness against such idolatries.

2. Possibly the thought may sometimes have occurred to one who studied the Old Testament diligently, that forms had been in the olden time the very testimonies for this light, the very means by which the Jews were warned against sensual worship; that they were converted by those Jews into excuses for the indulgence of a natural idolatry; but yet that being God's appointed protests against it, and the means which He had devised for delivering men from it, they were actually appealed to, from age to age, by the prophets who were raised up to tell the people of their sins; these prophets being in fact far more diligent observers of the forms than the sensualists and the hypocrites whom they denounced for neglecting their meaning. I say, such a thought as this may have glanced into the mind of Fox, and with it the reflection, that possibly a method which was good once might be good still. But he was able to silence such suggestions, or to dismiss them as proceeding from an evil source, by the second doctrine of which I spoke. Till the appearance of Christ this might be true; but he came to establish a Spiritual and Universal Dispensation. A spiritual dispensation; therefore outward institutions, like that of circumcision, like that of a passover, like that of a priesthood, like that of an outward sacrificial worship, like that of particularly sacred seasons, are abolished. But are not Baptism, the Eucharist, a Ministry appointed by impositions of hands, and divided into three permanent orders, Liturgies, the observance of Fasts and Festivals, equally visible and outward? On what plea then have you substituted one set of ceremonies for another, when you profess to be members of a spiritual kingdom?

Moreover, the dispensation is to be universal as well as spiritual. National distinctions, therefore, are no more; they belong to the economy of the world. War has been the fruit of these; under a spiritual and universal dispensation, war is a sin. Nations have always, the Jewish nation as much as the rest, invoked God as the witness of their ordinary transactions; Oaths are forbidden under the new dispensation. Nations have generally made a provision for the ministers of religion, and regarded them as parts of the commonwealth. Such arrangements are altogether inconsistent with a spiritual and universal dispensation.

3. As the Quakers turned away with disgust from all confessions whatsoever, it was not likely they would distinguish between the dogmatic articles which were drawn up in later ages of the Church, and the creeds which had been adopted in its infancy. At all events, even the simplest of these creeds was objectionable to them, because it directs our thoughts to the outward acts and events or our Lord's life upon earth, rather than to His presence in the heart. It was a more difficult question how they should regard the Scriptures. These recorded actual events, and appeared to have an outward character. Yet the Bible was the only book of which Fox and several of his brethren knew anything. In it he had found the strongest confirmation of all that he believed. The language, therefore, of the Quakers became more tinctured with the phraseology of Scripture than that of any sect; while, nevertheless, they described it in language which the members of no other sect would have ventured to use. The reading of it was said to be rather a luxury than necessity to the believer, and nothing was more important than that he should derive his knowledge from the inward teacher, not from the outward book. No doubt warnings about the danger of trusting in the letter, and still more about the impossibility of finding a meaning in it without help of another kind, had been common in the writings of learned doctors before, and even since, the Reformation. But it was evident that they acquired a new and much stronger meaning among the Quakers. That meaning was deduced from the doctrine concerning Spiritual Influences. He only was a true teacher who had been called by the inward voice; he was only teaching rightly at any moment when he was obeying that voice. How then, they argued, can he be at the same time subject to the dominion of a book? He may read it, and passages in it might be brought to his mind; but he will only apply them properly when he feels in the position of those who wrote the book; speaking by the same inspiration which actuated them. The book may be the best of all books, but it must be valuable as an instrument, not strictly as an authority. Such seems to have been their practical conclusion, though the words in which it was expressed might often vary.

It seemed to follow still more obviously, from this belief of an immediate spiritual influence, that preparatory studies for the work of the ministry were unlawful and faithless. Studies as such might not be positively forbidden, but as the teachers were in some sense the standards of thinking and feeling, it was impossible that a sense of the

11

inexpediency, if not the sinfulness, of any high mental cultivation should not have diffused itself among the disciples generally.

A body asserting the positive doctrines, and having the negative characteristics I have described, gradually formed itself, and assumed to itself the name of The Society of Friends. This Society, its members believed, was called into existence to exhibit the features of that kingdom which Christ came into the world to establish. Without wishing to be uncharitable, or denying that there might be good men who did not belong to it, yet they practically looked upon it as the Church of God on earth -- the witness against the world. They were, therefore, to keep themselves entirely from the habits of this world, from its varying fashions, from its amusements, and, as far as might be, from its phraseology. With these, the so-called Christian body had become defiled; nay, the very devices by which it had seemed to assert its existence were themselves earthly and sensual, bearing no testimony whatever to the distinction between the light and darkness, to the spirituality and universality of the kingdom, and to the presence of the Spirit.

SECTION IV -- ON THE PRACTICAL WORKING OF THE QUAKER
                SYSTEM

We are now to inquire whether this body has fulfilled the office to which its founders believed that it was divinely appointed. Let us see what evidence is admissible in this case, and how much it will prove. Quakers are agreed with us in believing that one of the characteristics of a divine Church is permanency. It was never intended to last only for a generation; on the contrary, it exists to testify against a changing, capricious world. Neither we then, nor they, are entitled to plead the ordinary law of decay in human bodies, as an excuse for the Church failing to perform the functions to which it has been appointed. Both of us must suppose that this tendency has been foreseen by Him whose handiwork the Church is, and that in some way or other its effects have been counteracted. The peculiarity of the Quakers is, that they suppse permanent institutions, permanent symbols, which man may misinterpret from time to time, but which continue to testify, in spite of his misinterpretations and against them, are not the remedy or even one of the remedies which has been provided against this danger. The condition of a spiritual body, according to them, is that it rests in the faith, the purity, the vitality of its individual members. This being the case, it must, I conceive, be admitted, that all confessions by them of degeneracy from an older standard are very startling. They can intimate little less than this, that the constitution or kingdom which God has set up in the world, has been overcome and crushed by the world's kingdom which is opposed to it. Yet such confessions are most numerous in the writings, not of one but of all the different divisions of Quakers in the present day. They take different forms according to the views of the persons who make them; but in one form or other they may be traced

12

everywhere. Still I am far from thinking that such evidence as this, however much it may excite the anxious inquiries of Quakers, could be sufficient of itself to prove, either to them or to us, that the experiment had failed. The indications of that fact should be very palpable; they should not rest upon the feelings or observations of any particular persons, however impartial or even however prejudiced in favour of the system, and they should be clearly and obviously connected with the form and order of the Society; otherwise I think they ought not to be produced, at least for the purpose of disturbing the confidence of anyone who still cleaves to it.

1. One such indication must, I think, suggest itself to every thoughtful person. All, said the Quakers, who are not walking in the divine light, who do not recognize the presence and. the guidance of an invisible teacher, are of the world. The pure and holy company, the Church, the Society of Friends, must consist of all who are led by the Spirit to perceive their connection with the invisible Guide, and to follow Him whithersoever He may lead them. Seeing that there was no body of men answering to this description, such a body must be formed; and all who did not attach themselves to it must in practice be treated as belonging to the world. Thus far all seems easy. One might fancy there was a little exclusiveness; that a few persons were treated as aliens, who might possibly be citizens of the household of God; but this could not be helped. There was need of a palpable distinction between the true men and the false. If the distinction were not perfect, it was at least good so far as it went; and faithful men must expect that the Spirit of God would, in due time, bring all to see that this was the Society to which they should belong. But soon a difficulty arose, for which the founders of the Society seem to have made no provision. Children are born to the members of it. What are these? Friends or world-citizens? The consistent answer would have been, "They are of the world; they are not consciously following the light; till they do so, it is mere dream and contradiction to reckon them in the Society." But feeling, and, as I believe, conscience, gave a different answer. They said, these must by all means belong to the Society; if not, it is a sin to have been agents in giving them existence. The only resource was to use all possible means for separating these children, outwardly at least, from the surrounding world. The parents would then feel that they had done their best, and they would think as little as possible of the falsehood which lay at the root of the whole proceeding. But it is only for a certain time that any falsehood can be hidden. This one is now making itself palpable. The younger Quakers look about, and ask themselves what it means that they are kept from the world? If the world means those who do not walk in the light, there is a world within the Society as well as without it. Would not their fathers have been right to exclude the idea of consanguinity from the Society altogether? For it is evident that between the law by which human society is propagated, and the law which governs this body, there is no connecting link. The heavenly kingdom has nothing to do with earthly relationships. Unless the body could be continually recruited by

13

conversions from the ranks of the world, it seems as if it could never escape from the penalty of constantly violating the very distinction for which its presence was meant to be the abiding testimony.

2. But the Quaker Society was to be the witness for the existence of a Universal Kingdom. In this faith Penn went forth and preached to the Indians. He was satisfied that they had in them a sense of right and wrong, that the Word was speaking to them as well as to other men. I believe the results of his very interesting mission shew how true the conviction was which encouraged him to undertake it. But what else do they prove? Did the settlement of Pennsylvania become the nucleus of a great missionary society? Did it attract to itself the aboriginal Indians and the English settlers? It grew up into a colony of prosperous traders, maintaining a very creditable position in the States distinguished by certain badges of dress and manners from the neighbouring people, increasing according to the ordinary rate of increase in the population, indifferent beyond the rest of the sects to missionary enterprises. I speak of America, because it cannot be said that the system has not been fairly tried there. But whether you look at Quakerism in that country in which it flourished by persecution, or in that where it had the greatest opportunities for expansion, I ask what witness has it borne for universality, what signs does it make to prove that it is the universal kingdom which was to be set up on earth?

Perhaps it may be said that the philanthropy of the Quakers is a testimony to that feeling of fellowship with the whole human race, which their principles of a universal light and a universal kingdom were likely to foster. I am very far indeed from wishing to deny the existence of this philanthropy, or to detract from its merits. I can have no motive to do so, for I inwardly and heartily subscribe the doctrine which is supposed, and I think rightly, to be the only ground of sympathy with man as man. I have no doubt that it is that principle, or the tradition of it, which has brought forth whatever has been sound and good in the feelings of the Quakers for their white and black brethren. But the question which we are now considering is, How far is the Quaker system a witness on behalf of that principle? and to this question, I fancy, the mode in which the benevolence of Quakers, in late years especially, has displayed itself, is a most striking and conclusive answer. For the moment that they began to do anything besides bearing individual testimonies, the moment they attempted to perform some general, social, organic acts on behalf of their fellow-creatures, that moment they found it necessary to fraternise with the members of other societies. They became members of societies for distributing the Bible, societies for emancipating the negroes, societies for promoting universal peace. Assuredly Fox and Penn would have done no such thing. They would have said: "Our Society being raised up and constituted by God Himself to be the witness for what is spiritual and universal against that which is earthly and national, is the Bible society, the emancipation society, the peace society; we know of no other -- there can be no other." The notion of uniting with the world for the sake of promoting spiritual objects would have seemed to them most monstrous; and yet their followers have adopted this method as the only one they know of for carrying out the Quaker principles.

3. Among the benevolent projects of this day, there is none which has interested the Quakers more than the progress of education; they have been almost the founders of the British and Foreign School Society, and its greatest supporters. The present is not the opportunity for discussing any point connected with this subject in which I may differ from them. I refer to their exemplary zeal in reference to it for the purpose of noticing how much it clashes with the Quaker system, so far as that system puts forward an assertion of the doctrine of spiritual influences. The Quaker minister speaks only when an immediate perceptible impression determines him that he ought to speak. To prepare for his work, to receive any regular appointment to it, to be paid for it, is incompatible with the spiritual nature of the function. But the Quaker teacher, or the teacher whom the Quaker supports in a school, must have a formal appointment, must prepare regular lessons, must receive a regular salary. It follows either that the spiritual minister is not appointed to educate, or that education is not spiritual. If education be as important as the Society of Friends and as I think that it is, what testimony is borne here to the spiritual economy, or to the spiritual influences which go forth that men may be able to administer that economy? Education, which is to have so mighty an influence upon society, is to be conducted upon principles precisely the reverse of those which are proclaimed to be the only spiritual principles.

"But the Qakers," it is said, "have borne a more consistent testimony than others against the habits and maxims of the world.": I do not mean, at present, to inquire what precise meaning we ought to attach to this word world -- I take the signification which it bears among religious people generally, and the Society of Friends especially. Now the world, in their sense, though it may be built upon one common evil principle, assumes many shapes and appearances; and it must be admitted, I think, that the body which is raised up to protest against it at any particular period, or in any particular locality, ought to bear witness mainly against the form or appearance which is most characteristic of that time or locality. A society which should testify against gladiatorial exhibitions in the nineteenth century, or against cannibalism in Europe, might be entitled to the praise of great prudence, but could scarcely allege any strong evidence of a divine vocation. The position of the Quakers has been exclusively or almost exclusively in Great Britain and the United States of America during the period between the Civil Wars and the reign of Queen Victoria. I ask any plain person to tell me what he thinks has been the characterisic sin of these two countries during this time especially. That there have been persons, a large body of persons in each, who have been devoting themselves to amusements of one kind or other, and have made them the end of life, I do not doubt;

but assuredly no one, comparing England and America with France or Italy, would affirm that the pursuit of pleasure has been the especial sin of us and our Transatlantic children; least of all, that it has been the especial sin of that part of our respective populations with which the Quakers are brought into contact, and whose evils therefore, they ought most to have denounced. Again, it is indisputable that a certain number of persons have pursued literature and mental cultivation as the end of life, and have, for the sake of it, overlooked higher and more universal ends. But certainly this has not been our chief infirmity; other European nations have been far more tempted by it. One deep radical disease has been infecting our two countries, and during the last two centuries has been entering deeper and deeper into our constitution, till it has now nearly reached the vitals of both. Will not everyone say that it has been money-getting? How, then, has the Society of Friends borne witness by its habits and constitution against this sin? It says, indeed, that no portion of the wealth of the body is to be set apart for the support of its ministers; that their subsistence is to be entirely precarious. This may be construed into a proof that money has nothing to do with that which is spiritual. But I confess I do not see how this testimony is to act upon the world, when they find that Friends -- believing all amusements, and many branches of mental cultivation, to be necessarily evil, to be actually incapable of being sanctified to a good purpose -- believe that the acquisition of wealth is not only a safe and lawful thing, but is to be emphatically, and by the very nature of the community, the business of everyone who enters it. A Society, the members of which are, to all outward appearance -- its ministers as well as others -- principally occupied in trade, nay, which till lately had a fear of being occupied in anything else, is to be the witness against a world, which has for its most characteristic, most irreligious distinction, the worship of mammon.

But has the existence of such a body as the Society of Friends had no influence at all in inducing men to believe that the heart and spirit of men are intended to converse with holy and invisible things? I hope that it has had this effect. I cannot believe that any system is permitted to exist which is not working some good; possibly there are minds (out of the Society I mean; of course, there must have been many in it) to whom Quakerism has suggested thoughts which nothing else would have suggested. But yet it seems to me that the positive witness which it has borne in favour of spirituality is of the most equivocal kind. I am afraid if the majority of Quakers were asked wherein the peculiar spirituality of their body consisted, they would answer: "In our not baptizing, not keeping an outward feast, not offering up prepared prayers, not having an outwardly ordained ministry." And unquestionably this answer would express very much the feeling which the sight of such a Society communicates to indifferent persons who behold it from a distance. A man of the world, who thinks the ordinances of the Church troublesome or unmeaning, observes, perhaps, to himself now and then, that the Quakers contrive to dispense with these ordinances, and yet are a very religious and thriving people. But at another time he will be equally

16

struck with the observation, that though they have none of these indications, they have others which seem to him not less outward and visible. They have no fixed forms of prayer, but they have a fixed form of dress; they have rejected sacraments, but they retain a peculiar kind of language. Surely a man who is inquiring with some confusion what spiritual Christianity means, must be somewhat puzzled when he is told: Those are the marks of a formal earthly body; these of one essentially spiritual and divine.

It may be supposed that these are mere accidents of the Quaker profession, which shew what a tendency to formalism there is in the human mind, but which may be laid aside by those who understand the true objects of the Society. There cannot be a greater mistake. The younger Quakers are probably very impatient of these restrictions; but it is not because they have an insight into any essential principles; on the contrary, indifference to the outward badges is very generally accompanied by indifference to the ideas on which Quakerism rests, or by an attachment to them only as far as they are opposed to something else. All the older and more earnest members of the Society maintain, and I believe on the most just and philosophical grounds, that these peculiarities, unimportant as they may seem, cannot be safely abandoned; that the very existence of Quakerism is involved in their preservation. They assert, it seems to me with equal truth, that every relaxation of the rules which the first Quakers laid down respecting amusements, or literary pursuits, tends to make the existence of the body less intelligible; nay, tends to a directly immoral result, by exhibiting all restraints upon self-indulgence as hard and unnecessary burdens, which are to be avoided as far as prudence and the opinions of others will permit.

I do not venture to predict how rapid may be the process of decay in a body which exhibits these symptoms. At present Quakerism is threatened from without on two sides -- on the Evangelical side, and on the Unitarian. Here in England the younger Quakers desire, in general, to be more like those who profess what are called the doctrines of the Reformation; in America they have been powerfully attracted in the opposite direction. It is quite possible that these feelings may not lead to any great secessions from the Society, besides those which they have caused already. But one or other of these influences will be henceforth predominant; Quakerism will have less and less a basis of its own. All its grand pretensions are at an end; its greatest defenders speak of it now not as the Church or Kingdom of God, but as the best of the sects which compose the religious world. Such language can never satisfy those who retain any of the old Quaker spirit. They must believe that there is a spiritual kingdom somewhere; if they cannot find it in the Society of Friends, they will look for it in those opposing systems of which I have spoken. Let us inquire what prospect they have of being rewarded for their search.

17

CHAPTER II

PURE PROTESTANTISM

SECTION I -- THE LEADING PRINCIPLES OF THE REFORMATION

Justification by Faith -- Election -- The Written Word -- Authority of
National Sovereigns

1. The inward struggles of Martin Luther were at least as terrible
as those of George Fox, and they have left far more remarkable
testimonies of themselves in the history of Europe. For as the character
of Quakerism was determined by the conflicts in the mind of the Drayton
shoemaker, so the character of the Reformation is interpreted by those
which tormented the Monk of Wittenberg.

In some respects there was a resemblance between them. Anyone
who reads attentively the first document which Luther put forth against
the sale of indulgences, must perceive how deeply and inwardly he had
realised the conviction, that he was a two-fold being; that there was in
him that which required to be crushed and destroyed; that there was that
in him which was meant to enjoy life and peace and freedom. A man
could hardly have arrived at such a conviction, or at least have been able
to express it in such language, who had not experienced much of what
Fox describes. But yet the history of their minds was altogether
different; nay, the contrast is as remarkable as we can expect to find in
the lives of two men, both equally sincere and brave.

Of a light speaking to his conscience, and warning him of the evil
he had done, and of the temptations within and without which were
tempting him to forsake it, Luther knew as much as any Quaker could
have told him. But the thought of such a light, instead of giving him
peace, was the cause of all his tumult and confusion. It spoke to him of
a Being of absolute power and wisdom and righteousness, between whom
and himself there was no sympathy. It bade him seek, by all means, to
be reconciled to that Being, and account all trials and sufferings light, if
so be they might but give a promise, now or hereafter, of such a blessing.
But it told him also of a strict, irreversible law, from which there could
be no departure, no dispensation; and the recollection of which made
every effort to heal the breach between him and his Maker a new witness
to him that it was perpetual. Then came the dream of a possible
deliverance from the curse of this law, brought to him in words which he
had heard from his infancy, but to which till then he had been unable to
attach any meaning. He had been told of a Mediator between the
Creator and His creatures; of His having offered a sacrifice for men; of
their being united with or grafted into Him; of their possessing a
righteousness in Him which they had not in themselves. These words, or
words like these, had been uttered again and again by doctors and
schoolmen whom he had studied. But they had been mixed with the

19

strangest perplexities about cases of conscience; the effects, kinds, and degrees of repentance; the distinction of mortal and venial sins; the nature and the mode of justification. And if there were such scholastic obstructions to a man's escape from that which he felt and knew to be a state of evil, there were still more monstrous practical obstructions which seemed to destroy all intercourse between the soul of man and his Deliverer. The sops which were given to the conscience by indulgences, the unfulfilled promises held out to it by penances which really tormented the spirit more than the flesh, all the notions of intervening mediators, beseeching for the removal of the curse which had been already borne by Him who alone could bear it, and who alone could fully sympathise with the miseries of those for whom He suffered, were so many bandages and fetters upon the human soul; making it content with the sin that it loved, or hopeless of real deliverance from the sin which it loathed.   It was the Bible which set Luther's mind free from the perplexities of the scholastic logic. It was by help of the creeds and sacraments of the Church that he was able to disengage himself from the intricate web of papal inventions. The written word of God seemed to him, from beginning to end, to be witnessing that a man is justified by faith; no school phrases being used to express the idea, but every act of affiance in a Divine Person who had revealed Himself to man as the object of his trust and confidence being an exemplification of it.   He could thus see the meaning of St. Paul's assertion, that Abraham was justfied by faith. *He trusted in God's promise and word, and that made him a godly and righteous man. All the Psalms, in like manner, were nothing but acts of faith and affiance, whereby a man, crushed down with all kinds of evils, inward and outward, rose up and claimed that relation to God which His covenant had given him, and shook off the sins into which he had fallen through forgetting it.   Still these, properly speaking, were acts of trust in a Mediator; they were recognitions of one to whom the suppliant himself was related, who was a bond between him and the absolute God, in whom alone he could dare to call upon Him. Therefore all these justifications were foretastes and anticipations of that justification which the Son of God made for all who would trust in Him, when, having offered up His body as a sacrifice, He rose again from the dead. To announce this work as accomplished; to tell men that they became righteous by believing it, and so entering into union with their Lord and Master -- this was, Luther believed, the great end of St. Paul's life. *He believed also that it was his own appointed office. It was the business of the preacher in every age to tell men this truth simply, using the direct personal language of the Bible, instead of the formal and dogmatic language of the schools. But not the man only was bearing witness of this principle. The Creed was preaching it, the Sacraments were preaching it, and the truly instructed doctor would find in these the deepest wisdom, and would labour that they might carry that home practically and in effect to men, which he could only utter in words. This, it seems to me, is Lutheranism according to Luther; and in this Lutheranism lies the germ of all the doctrines which peculiarly belong to the Reformation, though it might be the work of other minds than his distinctly to evolve them.

2. The principal of these is that which Luther proclaimed with so much vehemence in his controversy with Erasmus, but which yet, it is quite evident, could not have been as habitually present to his mind as it was to that of the Genevan Reformer, John Calvin. The idea of an object to which a man might look, and in which he might rest, took precedence of all others in the heart and reason of Luther. Unless when he were driven to it by some dogma like that of Erasmus, which seemed to him to threaten the revival of all Papal contrivances for the reconciliation of man, he troubled himself little about the origin of those feelings and acts, whereby a man apprehends Him who offers himself to his faith and hope. It is clear, however, not only from this treatise of Luther, but from the very character of his doctrine, that this question must suggest itself, and that it must receive some such solution as he and Calvin found for it. The idea of an absolute will, with which man must be brought into reconciliation by a Mediator, lay at the base of all Luther's thoughts. Any man, fixedly meditating upon those thoughts and the results to which they had led, must have asked himself: But who devised this whole scheme of reconciliation and redemption? Who is it that leads men to avail themselves of it? Who is it that determines the operations of their minds, and the consequences to which they shall lead? Such questions had at all times occupied the schools. Augustine, who appeared to have determined them in the same way as Calvin, had ever been regarded as one of their highest oracles. The difference was the same in this case as in the last: the principle that man is to look up to God as the direct source of his acts, and thoughts, and purposes, was presented to the faith of men in the real language of Scripture, and not to the understandings of men in the abstract language of the schools. Those who apprehended their relation to Christ were to speak of themselves as the elect people of God, just as Samuel, or David, or the Israelites did, and to believe that they would have been miserable and accursed if God had not elected them. They were not to trouble themselves with questions about the will, or to seek any other reason for their blessedness than that it was God's good pleasure to give it them. On the other hand, this belief was to be the conclusive barrier against all impostures of Romish priests, those impostures being attempts to persuade men that they must seek by their own efforts to win a position, which ought to be received as the gift of God. This, I think, is the Calvinistic side of Protestantism. To some it may appear that I have given to it, as well as to the doctrine of justification, too little of a scholastic character; that I have spoken of it too much as something that opposed itself to the logical systems of the previous age, whereas Calvin as well as Melanchthon and some of the German Reformers, were remarkable for their devotion to logic. Nevertheless, I believe that I am right. How the scholastic tendencies of the Reformation afterward developed themselves, I may have occasion to explain presently. Here I will only remark that the Reformers who had been trained by the

21

schoolmen would of course preserve many of their characteristics; that men with a strong bias for dialectics may often be those who are led to feel most strongly the want of what is practical and popular, and to seek out a practical and popular language; and that, in fact, those who have commented most, either in the way of praise or blame, upon the scholastic qualitites which appear in the controversial writings of the Reformers, have yet always contended also that the Reformation itself was an appeal to the feelings and sympathies of common men.

3. If then the Lutheran doctrine of justification by faith be the first, and the doctrine of election, as formally asserted by Calvin, the second, I think most persons will agree with me in considering a certain peculiar estimate of the Scriptures the third characteristic of Reformation theology. But there are one or two questions connected with this point. No one acquainted with the writings of the Reformers would say that they were more scrupulous in their treatment of their Canon of Scripture than the doctors who preceded them. Luther's language about the Epistle of St. James and the book of Revelation, though it may have been retracted in his later days, would be conclusive against such an opinion, even if there were nothing similar in the writings of his contemporaries. Neither can it be said that either Luther or Calvin regarded the Bible as a book from which persons without any previous initiation would, as a matter of course, derive light and teaching. They rather looked upon it as a divine witness to men already engaged in a conscious struggle with their evil nature, respecting the character of that struggle, and the means whereby they could obtain deliverance out of it. Such at least, I conceive, was the view most present to the mind of the German Reformer; the Bible was especially the preacher's book, out of which he was to tell men how those of the same flesh and blood with themselves had fought the battle with the world and the flesh and the devil before them, and what manner of strength and help God had vouchsafed them in it. At the same time, it was a fixed and permanent authority, which mounted above all the notions and experiences of particular minds, and enabled them, even in defiance of such notions and experiences, to discover solid grounds of peace and comfort. It is manifest then that veneration for the Bible, high place as it held in Luther's mind, was subordinate to his zeal in asserting the doctrine of Justification. He looked upon the Bible mainly as the witness for that doctrine, and because it was such a witness he loved it with all his heart, and would have given up his life that men might in their own language hear what it said. The same, though in a less degree, must have been true of Calvin; the Bible was the witness to him of the divine Election; on that account mainly it was precious to him, and no diligence that could be employed in studying and expounding it was thrown away. But if the Scripture were valuable as the announcement of one or other of these great ideas or principles, was it not in itself a great idea or principle that there was such a book as a Bible, a book speaking directly to the conscience of men, a fixed and permanent utterance of the divine will? So some (I should think to

22

Zwingli) this seemed the cardinal idea of the Reformation, to which other ideas were subordinate. At all events there was a body which gradually began to be separated by important peculiarities from the other Reformers; and of this body, faith in the Scriptures, with a less distinct reference to the principles taught in them, seems to have been the most striking positive characteristic.

4. These three principles seem to me, in the strictest sense, positive principles. They are not the less so because they were brought forth in opposition to certain popular notions and current practices. On the contrary, here lies the very test and proof of their positive character. There were a number of abominations prevalent when Luther appeared, which Romanists not only now but then abhorred. Some of them were corrected or mitigated at the Council of Trent; some of them disappeared when the infidel temper of Leo and the Roman court of that day gave place to the more earnest spirit of the succeeding popes. But great as this disgust may have been, evident as it was that the disgust had reached to the people of the different countries in Christendom, and that a class had arisen in them which was disposed to assert a position independent alike of the hierarchy and of the aristocracy, it was still a question -- a very solemn question -- with the wiser and better men, how far it was possible to remedy, or safe to denounce, even the most crying abuses. The building is tottering; ought we to touch it under the pretence of repairing it? This was a question which Sir Thomas More, and other men as good as he, may have asked themselves, and for which it may have been out of their power to find a theoretical answer, though they did practically answer it by sitting still. Were they wrong? I would not dare to say so. It seems to me, that looking upon these corruptions merely as the excess of something that was good, they were clearly right. Nay, even if they felt, as I make no doubt they did feel, that the loss of faith was, in some most important sense, the cause of these superstitions -- still more of the contrivances to make them profitable-- yet if they could not perceive that there was some great truth hidden or contradicted by these portions of the popular system, they would evidently have been committing the great hazard -- if we ought not rather to call it the sin -- of taking away something which had a certain hold upon the affections of men without giving them any substitute for it. Which argument must have acquired a great confirmation in the minds of those men who had wisdom and opportunity to remark what kind of change had been taking place in the mind of Europe, and what kind of cravings those were which threatened the Church. The feeling --I do not belong merely to a great Christendom, I have a distinct individual position -- was evidently that which had developed itself in the members of the new class; which made them eager to grasp at novelties, ready to follow particular guides, but impatient of systematic authority. The wise observers, in some countries, might be able to perceive that this feeling was connected with another, which they could allow to be more wholesome and more worthy of encouragement. The tradesman, German or English, along with his Hussite or Lollardite notions, had a sense of

23

belonging to a particular soil, and speaking a particular language, which was often far less strong in the nobleman. But this conviction interfered as much as the other with submission to Church authority, and with an affection for Church ordinances. It gave rise to strange questionings about the dominion of the Roman Bishop, to stories about the spirit with which kings and emperors in former days had resisted him, to a dislike of the universal language. Was it not clear then that the age had a violent inclination towards infidelity and irreverence; that every acknowledgment of an error which had been sanctioned or tolerated by Churchmen, tended to make this inclination irresistible; and that the only duty of men, who wished well to the preservation of society, nay, of truth, was to uphold, as well as they could, the entire system?

It seems to me that the Reformers were led by God's Providence to find the only escape which was possible out of this fearful dilemma. They were led to perceive that certain great moral principles, involved in the very idea of a relation between God and His creatures, say rather that the belief in that relation itself -- were outraged by the existing Roman system. The abuses of that system were not excesses; they were essentially evil; they had their root in a great denial and unbelief. They set at naught great facts concerning man and concerning God -- facts which had been announced by an express revelation from heaven. Here was a standing-point; and I do maintain, and would earnestly press the assertion -- that Protestantism has a standing-point of its own; that it is not merely condemnatory, merely negative; and that so far as it keeps within its own proper and appointed province, it denounces and condemns only that which is itself negative, and which sets at naught something that is needful for the life and being of man.

To the question, what that something is, and what therefore is the appointed province of Protestantism, I have already indicated what seems to me the true answer. The feeling which was most strongly awake at the time Luther appeared, was the feeling in each man that he was an individual man, not merely one of a mass. Luther did not create this thought; it was there. He struggled with it in himself, and would fain have overcome it; but it was too strong for him. He was obliged to find some interpretation of it; he was not at peace till he found one, which told him that the only safe, free, true position of man, is not a position of rebellion, but of allegiance; a position involving the subjection of the whole soul to a righteous and divine government. The clue which led him out of the perplexities of his own mind was that which thousands besides him needed; they received it and rejoiced. To say that he was a minister of sedition, or that he raised up ministers of sedition, is easy, because it is easy to misrepresent history, and to attribute the evil consequences of certain states of mind to those who were God's instruments in preventing them from being universal. But those who look steadily and impartially at the facts, not wishing (and I think I have shewn that I have no wish) to represent them to the disadvantage of those who opposed Protestantism, will, I believe, be

24

more and more convinced, that the Reformers did not call forth the rebellious activity of the period in which they lived, but when it was seeking a refuge in infidelity, taught it to find one in faith.

The three principles of which I have spoken contained the religious satisfaction of that sense of an individual position which the men of the sixteenth century were experiencing.   I have hinted that, closely connected with this, was another -- the sense of a distinct national position. The fourth principle of Protestantism was the recognition of this feeling also as true, and as having a religious basis. The protest against the usurpation of the Bishop of Rome was not mainly grounded upon the idea of its interference with the prerogatives of Christ over the whole Church. I do not say that this idea may not have been often put forward by the Reformers; I do not say that it may not have frequently dawned upon them as the principle which the Papal usurpation invaded. But I do not think it was constantly present to their minds, that it was ever fully developed in them, or that when they used language which implied it, that language conveyed precisely the same meaning to them which it conveys to us.

They may also have alluded, in terms of displeasure or even reprobation, to the assumption by one bishop of an authority over others; but I cannot persuade myself that this was a sin which would have induced them to reject the Papal authority. Their contempt of it arose, as they became more and more convinced that that was true and necessary which an infallible wisdom pronounced to be erroneous and mischievous, and as they observed how it had interfered with the power and functions of the National Sovereigns. By many links the peculiar theology of the Reformation was connected with the assertion of the dignity of this office, and of the national distinctness which it represents; one is very obvious.   The Reformers had resorted to the Scriptures not merely for their authority, but for their practical character. But that practical character is especially exhibited in the Old Testament, and in the Old Testament every truth is brought out in relation to the events of a national history. Their own time interpreted the Scriptures to the Reformers, and the Scriptures in turn interpreted their own time.

SECTION II -- OBJECTIONS TO THE PRINCIPLES OF THE
REFORMATION CONSIDERED

I have already noticed one primary objection against all these doctrines, one which, according to my judgement, would be fatal to them; that they are merely negative -- merely the contradiction of that faith which Romanists hold.

But there are also particular objections against each of them which it is necessary to examine.

1. One charge which is brought against the Lutheran doctrine of justification by faith, belongs especially and characteristically to the Quakers. It is said that justification by faith either means the same thing as the doctrine of the Indwelling Word, or, if it mean something different, that one of them is false. Either (it is contended) the light dwelt with men or it did not: if it did, the following that light is justification; if it did not, the whole doctrine of Fox (which I have defended) is untenable. Men must be justified by the agreement of their minds with a certain inward principle, or by certain outward acts done on their behalf. To say that a man is in his right state with himself and before God when he subjects himself to the Indwelling Word, and that a man is justified in consequence of certain acts which Christ performed as his representative, is impossible. Now I readily admit that the temper of mind, which leads a man vehemently to assert one of these doctrines, is not the same temper of mind which leads him to assert the other; nay, that these tempers are not very often found co-existing in any great strength. The Quaker and the Mystic (to use that word in an indifferent sense, not in the evil sense which I gave to it in my first chapter) habitually contemplate a divine presence in the heart; they associate that presence, very probably, with the life of our Lord; but if they do so, consciously or unconsciously, they affix an import to His acts and words which is different from their obvious historical import. (the Lutheran habitually contemplates a Divine Person, having a real distinct life; rejoices that He entered into ordinary human relations and circumstances; realises his own connexion with Him through those relations and circumstances. Unquestionably anyone who has observed himself, and knows how very different were the feelings which at different times of his life have attracted him in these two directions, will not be slow to confess that Quakerism and Lutheranism have something in their nature which is even curiously antipathetic. But I fancy the same observation will equally incline him to the opinion that each of these doctrines is the complement of the other, and that in spite of their apparent opposition, neither can exist in any real strength if the other be denied.

To explain what I mean, let us consider what were the actual wants and anxieties of the men in the old world, who experienced the struggle between the light and darkness of which Fox has spoken. Must not such thoughts as these have been continually present to their minds: Here are two powers struggling within me, one good, one evil; sometimes one prevails, sometimes the other; sometimes the darkness seems about to be scattered, sometimes the light seems almost quenched: but I, who am I, in the midst of all this awful struggle? Do I belong to the light, or to the darkness? Of which have I a right to call myself the child now; of which shall I be the child for ever? The consciousness of evil, of rebellion against a power continually exerting itself for my good, testifies against me; my belief in the graciousness, in the mightiness of the Being who is on my side, speaks in my favour: but then what awful outward facts seem to corroborate the former conclusion! All the outward sicknesses, sorrows, troubles of the world, seem to be lifting up their voice to condemn me -- to be proving that my unseen friend is either not omnipotent, or that His forbearance with my often repeated disobedience will at last have a limit; -- and what is that limit? May not Death at last decide this struggle? May he not be God's permitted minister, to decide it against me? These thoughts do not imply the least unbelief in a future state; that was not the anxious question of the heathen, as all their mythology proves: but it was, What shall I be, in that state? Some ethereal particle in me may mount up and enter into rest, and even be united to the Divine Essence; -- but will it be myself? I cannot believe that I shall die, in the sense in which all the things about me die. Whenever I feel that I am at all, I feel that I am immortal; I may lose the thought while I am speculating; I can never lose it while I am acting and living. But this is the point -- Shall good or evil, shall light or darkness, be that to which I am united, when all the spiritual energies, by which I seem to have asserted my connexion with something better than myself, shall be as much crushed by pain and weaknesss and death, the great consummation of them, as the energies by which I eat and drink and walk? The Jews were taught to experience precisely the same difficulty, only with still greater power and reality, only with a brighter and better hope as to its solution. They felt in themselves this struggle; but then, taking hold of the covenant, with Abraham, Isaac, and Jacob, they were able to believe that the righteous Lord who revealed Himself to their hearts was indeed their Lord, and would be so for ever and ever; and coming with the appointed sacrifice, at the appointed time, in the appointed place, to the appointed priest, they were able to believe that that covenant had not been destroyed through their iniquity; that they still had an inheritance in the King of their nation; that they should behold His face in righteousness; and that when His glory was manifested to the whole earth they should partake in it. Yet it was a hope still -- still the doubt rested upon their minds, and at times would gain a dreadful ascendency -- Is this evil and accursed nature which belongs to me, my own self? Are not its evils imputed to me? Are not they counted a part of me? Will not Death destroy that nature; and when he destroys it, shall I be spared? These questions must have occupied men, not because they did not possess the light which lighteth every man that cometh into the world, but because they did possess it; -- yea, according to the degree in which that light was revealed to them, or in which they followed it. Surely some answer was needed to them; surely it is a mockery to say that the light itself was the answer. If we accept the doctrine of Luther, the answer is clear and intelligible. The Word was made flesh and dwelt among us; in this flesh He passed through the conflicts and trials of men; He died a real death; He brought back a real body from the grave. This was the voice from heaven replying to the voice from earth. The man asks: "What am I; am I to account myself a child of the light or a child of the darkness?" Christ dying and rising from the dead, declares: "Thy nature is accursed, thy person is justified; married to thy evil nature, thou art sinful and under the curse; claiming thy portion in me, thou art holy, and righteous, and

27

redeemed." Is this merely the doctrine of an Indwelling Word? Does it contradict that doctrine? Or does one prove the necessity and the reality of the other?

It is most true, however, as I have said already, that there is one side or aspect of the Lutheran doctrine, to which there is nothing corresponding in the mystical. The outward acts of our Lord in human flesh, considered as assertions of the right which creatures bearing that flesh have to rise above themselves and claim a portion in Him, have been recognized by many an earnest mystic in his later years, as most needful portions of a spiritual economy. But the feeling which was at the root of all others in Luther's mind, that these acts were mediatorial, propitiatory acts, having for their ultimate object the satisfaction of the will of the Father, has been generally received by persons of this temper with coldness, if not with disgust. It should, I think, be distinctly understood by them at first -- for they must arrive at the discovery sooner or later -- that they cannot hope to connect this faith with, or to reduce it under, any of the ideas which belong properly to mysticism. If those ideas do include all truth, this Lutheran doctrine is not true, for the very assumption upon which it proceeds, and to which everything is referred, that there is an <u>Absolute Will</u> which is the ground of all things, of all being, life, thought, forms no part of mysticism, however mystics may have adopted or grafted it into their faith. The Divine <u>Word</u> is the only real subject of their meditation; a vague gulf of being beyond they may awfully think of, but they dare not speak of it in the forms of human language, or bring it within the region of personality, or dream of it as the ground of human relations. Now that the mystics have most reasonable complaints to make against the systems to which the Lutheran theology has given rise, on this very ground, that they have despoiled the idea of God of its fearfulness and grandeur, and reduced it under human notions and experience, I shall be presently obliged to admit. But the question here at issue is -- Does or does not evidence, similar to that which compelled us to acknowledge the truth of the mystical idea of an Indwelling Word, compel us to acknowledge that there is a truth beside and beyond this, which involves, under some terms or other, the belief of Mediation, Sacrifice, Satisfaction? Supposing, for instance, we attached any value to the discovery, that the doctrine of a Divine Indwelling Word was not merely asserted in certain detached texts of Scripture, but that it imparted a coherency and clearness to the whole course of Scripture history, giving a sense to the word Idolatry, shewing how and why that was treated as <u>the</u> sin of mankind, explaining the lives and language of those who kept themselves free from it -- may we not observe a parallel line of proofs bearing just as strongly in favour of these other principles? Is the Lutheran obliged to depend upon certain words or texts, in order to shew that the idea of human Mediation is contained in Scripture? Is it not worked into the very tissue of the history which the Scripture contains? Is it not involved in the constitution of the Jewish commonwealth, which it treats of? Can less be said concerning the kindred ideas of Propitiation, Atonement,

Sacrifice? May it not be more correctly affirmed, that what gives the sense of continuousness and unity to the books of Scripture, written under so many different circumstances, and at such wide intervals of time, is this fact, that lawgivers, psalmists, prophets, are, one and all, according to their various functions, in obedience to their inward promptings, and to meet the necessities of their respective times, gradually drawing out these ideas which were already embodied in the institutions and life of the Jewish nation?

If, again, it seemed to us a remarkable witness in favour of Fox's principle, that one great portion of Gentile records was scarcely intelligible without it; have we no witness in favour of these principles from another part of those same records? The philosopher discovered a divine light, or wisdom, which he was to cry after and to follow; did not the whole body of the people believe that there was an invisible power, which it was to propitiate, which it was to reach by mediation, to which it must offer sacrifices? Did not the wisest statesmen, even in days when all actual faith had disappeared, still recognize these thoughts as strange and mysterious, which the nation must acknowledge if it were to be a nation, though they might dispense with them, or overlook them? Was philosophy ever able to get above these ideas, or to merge them in that which was peculiarly its own? Many philosophers laboured hard; the best of them felt more strongly than all others, that there was in the popular faith upon these matters, that which contradicted truths which seemed to him most sacred: yet he was the least disposed to attack that faith; the most inclined to recognize it as something which the philosopher needed so much the more, because he was a philosopher.

In this view of the subject he was, as I have hinted before, almost peculiar; nearly all others wished either to extinguish the existing theology by philosophical notions, to translate it into philosophical notions, or to invest philosophy with the mysterious and miraculous character of revealed theology. The records of each experiment are preserved, the more they are studied the better. The fact has survived them all -- these ideas in one form or another have been and are the most characteristic and fundamental ideas of humanity; the very proofs and witnesses that we constitute a Kind. Explain them as you will or as you can, but remember that an explanation is not the thing. If these ideas be not delusions, there is some reality corresponding to them; and that reality, could we know it, might be expected to contain the explanation of them, and also of the partial, false, and mischievous notions which may have encompassed them; if they be delusions, it would seem that all humanity must be a delusion; that there can be no common principles to form the groundwork of it. I cannot think, then, that the mystical objection to the Lutheran doctrine, on whichever side we view it, is a tenable one.

2. Another class of persons, who oppose the doctrine of justification, as it was stated by Luther, maintain that it exaggerates a mere fact or crisis in the history of individuals, into a fixed and permanent law. "At a certain period," they say, "a man, who has been careless of religion, acquires a conviction of his error. He is sensible that he has been leading a faithless, godless life. He has been acting as if there were no Lord and Saviour whom he was meant to trust and to love. He begins to recognize such a Saviour -- to believe in Him. It is unquestionably a new feeling; the beginning of a different class of feelings from any of which he has hitherto been conscious. It is, therefore, invested by him, and rightly, with great sacredness; but it is only the first in a series of spiritual acts. His belief, if it be not stunted by the notion that it is all-sufficient, grows into love and good works. And this it might have done if there had been no such sudden discovery as that to which he gives the name of Justification. From his baptism upward he might have led a faithful and pure life; then that baptism would be just as rightly and reasonably called his justification, as that primary and preliminary act of conscious faith. "Luther," they continue, "was led by his own circumstances, or by those of his age, to dwell with particular delight and emphasis upon the transition-moment of his spiritual history; yet even he speaks frequently of baptism, as if that was entitled to the credit of his justification; it is evident then that there was a confusion in his mind which, though it might not unfit him for an active reformer, certainly must make us suspicious of him when he assumed to be the enunciator of a great principle. And everything in his words, and the history of his doctrine, tends to heighten that suspicion. For why did he dwell so much upon a formal release from guilt, and a formal imputation of righteousness? Surely it is a real deliverance from sin, and a real righteousness that man requires. Give the best form you can to the other notion; strip it of the fictitious character, in which it must be offensive both to God and man; and still it can only point to some feeling on our part of a position offered to us, which we may, if we please, realise; and then to speak of that position as something independent of the realisation, while yet you say that it is a position granted to faith, and that faith is the realising principle, is to give us shadows for substances, a dream of food to satisfy our hunger."

I have stated the argument, I hope, fairly, avoiding only the use of one or two favourite phrases, which have become catchwords, and, I believe, embarrass the minds of all, on either side, who resort to them. I at once acknowledge the great plausibility of the statement, the admirable piety of those, who, in former days or of late, have brought it forward, and the difficulty of shewing why I think the substance of it to be fallacious, without seeming to reject portions of it which I believe to be both true and important. I think, however, that by at once going to the heart of the question, we may be able to relieve it of many of its perplexities. Everyone must have been struck with these words of St. Paul: "That I may be found in him, not having my own righteousness, which is of the law, but that which is by the faith of Christ; the

30

righteousness, that is, of God by or upon faith" ("epi te pistei"). What is remarkable in these words is of course, their connexion. St. Paul is speaking of some very high attainment, some end which was to be the consummation of all his strivings. And this atttainment, this end, is what? Having an individual righteousness? No; but precisely the not having it. The highest perfection this saint and apostle could think of, one which he could not dare to say he had achieved, was the ceasing to be anything in himself, the acknowledgment of his whole moral and spiritual life and being as in another.

* * *

Now let it be remembered, that the especial charge against Luther is, that he mistook the phenomena of a certain crisis in our life for a fixed law applicable to the whole of it. He is blamed for attaching so much importance to this doctrine, as if it were the key to the entire meaning of a man's spiritual existence, when in fact it merely describes the first conscious feeling of such an existence. May we not fairly suggest the thought to the objector, that possibly he may be falling into this very error himself, and mistaking Luther just because he was free from it? May there not be a law which is expressly the law of a man's being; complete conformity to which is his perfection; but which, from the first hour of his life to the last, is his law; which does not depend the least for its reality upon his recognition of it, or his denial of it; which will judge him at the last day; and which must not, therefore, be concealed from him at any time, but be announced to him as that against which he is rebelling? May not this law be, must it not be if St. Paul's words are to be received in their simple sense, the law of union with another, the law of self-renunciation? Suppose then I see a man pursuing an utterly wrong course -- a course of indulgence in the most ordinary sense of the word -- have I not a right to say to him, This is an evil course; and if he ask me why, to answer, Because it is a course of selfishness, and because your were not meant, and your conscience tells you you were not meant, to be selfish. And if he reply to me, as in nine cases out of ten he will -- "But how can I be otherwise? every man is selfish; selfishness is our nature; our necessity; God made us so, we cannot help it." am I hindered from asserting God's ways against man's blasphemy in some such words as these, -- "I care not whether you call selfishness your nature or not; if it be, your nature is a contradiction and a lie, for it makes you do that which you cannot do without being at war with yourself. If that be your nature, then you are not meant to live according to your nature, but to rise out of it -- above it. And there is One who has come to redeem you out of your nature, and to unite you to Himself. In Him you may believe and live; in yourself you cannot?" In saying this, I have preached to this sinful man the Lutheran doctrine of justification. I have told him that there is a state belonging to him, with which he is not living in accordance, but with which he is living at variance. I have said, that union with another is his law; separation from him, his transgression. I have said, that that union is not a natural, but a spiritual one. It is an union which is maintained by faith; unbelief is the renunciation of it: therefore an anomalous sinful condition. There is a fiction here assuredly; it is a fiction to have a state, and not to enjoy it; a fiction to possess the conditions of a spiritual being, and to be acting as if these conditions did not exist. But it is the fiction of an evil world; and I know not how we are to get rid of the fiction but by declaring the fact to which it is opposed.

The dream, that because it is announced as a fact it will be at once received as a fact, that there will not be a fierce conflict with the selfish nature before it can be acknowledged at all, and that these struggles will not be repeated every day of a man's pilgrimage through an evil world, was certainly not Luther's dream. Every page of his writings, like every hour of his life, bears witness to a tremendous struggle. The question which he thought to be all-important, was this -- Is the struggle against the too great proneness of the evil heart to believe and trust, or against its reluctance to believe and trust; against its overeagerness to cleave to its Lord, or against its passion for a selfish independence?

His conviction was, that when he distrusted Christ he was a bad and evil man, with no capacity for doing any right or good act. To trust then must be a duty; a man could not be just or righteous who did not trust; so far as he did trust he must be so. If he were asked whether nothing must precede this trust and give a warrant for it, he would have answered -- Assuredly God's word and promise must precede; the declaration, that this state is yours, must be your warrant for claiming it. The words of the Bible generally, the assurance of baptism to you particularly, give you the right to believe. To seek the right in anything else, in any outward acts or inward feeling of yours, is to commit a contradiction; for these acts and feelings, if they are lawful and right, are acts and feelings which imply trust -- are expressions of trust. A man's repetition of his Credo does not give him a right to trust in God's mercy and forgiveness; but if he repeats it as he should, it is a form of trust and affiance in God. A man's comfortable impressions and feeling are not reasons of confidence; if they are not mere physical sensations, they are the effects of his resting in his true Friend. Faith then, according to him, could not be looked upon as a grace which we may contemplate and reflect upon in ourselves. By its very nature it is the act of going out of self, the act of entering into union with another from whom all our graces are to be derived. That the power of performing such an act is conferred by God, and is therefore a grace, he of course asserted stoutly; but it made an immeasurable difference whether the grace was supposed to be given to a man as so much stock which he might call his own, or whether its effect was to induce him to disclaim all property in himself, and to live entirely in Christ. It was on this account that he resisted so strongly the argument which the Romanists deduced from the relative excellence of faith and love. Love, they said, is a higher grace than faith, by the testimony of your own St. Paul, and yet you make the grace of faith and not of love the ground of justification. I do not, he would answer, make what you call the grace of faith the ground of justification. I do not tell a man that he is to ask himself, how much faith he has, and if he have so much, to call himself justified. What I tell him is precisely that he is not to do this, that this is the very trick which he has been practising upon himself, while he has been under your teaching. He is not to think or speculate about his faith at all. He is to believe, and by believing, to lose sight of himself and to forget himself. And, therefore, I cannot allow that he is justified by his grace of love, though I admit that to be the highest of all graces. Trust is the beginning of love, the way of love. A Being who shews that he cares for me, and in whom all love dwells, proposes himself to me as an object of my trust; I trust him, and so enter into a knowledge and participation of his love. And that love works in me to will and to do of his good pleasure.

* * *

3. When I have mentioned one other objection to this principle, I believe I shall have encountered all those by which persons in this day are likely to be perplexed. Many students are at a loss to discover how the doctrine of justification by faith differs from the general doctrine of atonement, which was as strongly recognized, in words at least, by the Romanists as it could be by Luther.

We can understand, they say, that many practices may have been sanctioned at that time, which interfered with the full acknowledgment of our Lord's sacrifice. We can suppose that it may have been important to reassert the principle strongly for the purpose of protesting against these abuses. But the doctrine was there; the Romanists insisted upon faith in it; what more have we to do? If Protestantism have got rid of any mischievous outgrowths of the elder system, let us be thankful; but why endeavour to maintain this particular mode of expression which was, to all appearance, adopted for a temporary purpose, and has accomplished that purpose?

I think that the statement I have given of Luther's doctrine is, to a certain extent, an answer to this difficulty. He did not call upon men to acknowledge either a new doctrine or an old one, to believe either in a certain opinion concerning justification or in a certain opinion concerning the atonement. He called upon them to believe in God the Father Almighty -- in Jesus Christ His only Son our Lord, and in the Holy Ghost. He said again and again, that the Credo was justification. He told men that union with Christ was deliverance from sin and condemnation; that that union was claimed and maintained by faith; that faith was therefore justification. Such an assertion was true or false. If it were true, it cannot have ceased to be true; all the circumstances and occasions which called it forth may have passed away; but the law which it proclaimed must be as much a law for us as it was for those to whom Tetzel sold his indulgences. And so far from thinking, as those who make this objection seem to think, that we of this day can afford to substitute faith in a certain notion or dogma, for faith in a living person, though the men of the 16th century could not, I rather fancy that this is a temptation to which we have yielded more than even the Romanist did, and from which we almost need a second Reformation to deliver us.

But I do believe that the objector really means this; I suspect that this difficulty about the relation between the idea of justification and the idea of atonement is a very important difficulty indeed; that it is one which did not force itself upon the consideration of the Reformers; that it is one which does force itself upon our consideration; that people are taking various methods of expressing it to themselves -- some of them being very confused methods, tending to increase rather than to remove our perplexity and to rob us of distinctions and principles which with great difficulty have been established for us; but that it must be earnestly considered, and will receive some practical resolution -- a very mischievous if not a satisfactory one. The question is this. Can this doctrine of justification, if it retain its Lutheran meaning, if it be the assertion of a man's personal position and personal duty, if it do not degenerate into the most lifeless of all formulas -- assume the position which it does assume in a great part of our Protestant divinity? Can it be put forward as the truth which lies at the foundation of the Christian Church? Does this view honour the doctrine, or only kiss it, in order to kill? This is a question which we shall have to consider when we inquire into the Protestant systems and their practical workings. Perhaps the reader may be the less unwilling to enter with me upon the examination, if he perceive, as I hope by this time he does, that it is as much my desire as it can be his, to assert the principle in its integrity and fulness.

II. 1. It is evident that the mystics, who oppose themselves mainly to that side of the doctrine of justification which connects it with the idea of the Divine Will, must dislike to see that idea so prominently exhibited as it is in the Calvinistical theology. And it is not difficult to understand, from the style of their previous arguments, what kind of substitute they would be inclined to offer for the doctrine of Election, as it appears in that theology. Each man, they say, stands in a certain relation to the light and to the darkness; following the light, and submitting to the Divine Word, he enters into an elect state; preferring the darkness he becomes reprobate. In the first case he acts according to the purpose of God; in the second he resists it. But because this is the case, man is not therefore to be spoken of as the author of his own salvation; the nature of the act which he performs proves that he is not so; it may be more properly called an act of submission than of choice, though it involve choice; it is the surrender of his own will; whereas the opposite kind of act is emphatically the assertion of his own will, a declaration of independence.

I have already recognized so strongly the principle which this statement embodies, that I am not likely to make any exception against it. I receive it as a satisfactory explanation of the practical conditions under which every man acts; conditions which must remain true, whatever other truth there may be involved in them. The only question is, whether this doctrine, respecting the Divine Word, can set aside, or make unnecessary, the distinct formal belief of a primary, absolute, originant Will? I have already said that I think it cannot. That belief seems to lie deeper than the one respecting our relation to the Divine Word, and to be the necessary ground of it. Take away that ground, and I cannot see that we retain any acknowledgment of God in himself; that we contemplate Him otherwise than in reference to us, or His operations upon us. The mystical doctrine may explain the position and circumstances of man; but these very circumstances, if the doctrine be true, imply a theology, and that theology it seems to me is the very thing which mysticism wants.

2. Again, the class of persons who complain of the Lutheran doctrine of Justification, as leading to the belief of a fictitious righteousness, see in the doctrine of election an arbitrary dispensing with all righteousness. "A person receives eternal life because it is the good pleasure of God that he should receive it. Supposing we grant that the obedience is decreed, as well as the reward of it, yet where is that which is the essence of all obedience that can be acceptable to a perfect Being, freedom? You cannot, therefore, make the doctrine reasonable, except by admitting Divine election to be the foresight of human obedience."

Unquestionably I would admit that proposition, or any other, were it never so startling, rather than acknowledge that great primary contradiction, that the source of all being is self-will. But one contradiction is not the escape from another, and assuredly the idea of an obedience in man, which has no ground to rest upon; which was foreseen by God, but not derived from Him; of something good, therefore, which cannot be traced ultimately to the Fountain of good; nay, which exists independently of it, that is to say, under what are we wont to consider the very condition of evil -- is a most agonizing contradiction. And what need have we of it? Only do not suppose the Being whom you worship to be a mere power; only acknowledge Him to be that in reality which you say in words that He is, the essential truth and goodness; only suppose the absolute will to be a will to good, and how can we imagine that happiness, obedience, freedom, have their origin anywhere but in Him; that misery, disobedience, slavery, mean anything but revolt and separation from Him?

3. The last complaint against this doctrine runs parallel with the last against Luther's. Does not the election mean the election of a body? Has it anything to do with the election of individuals? I would make the same answer here which I made in the other case. Every individual man must be in some state or other. Every individual man ought to know to whom he is to ascribe that state in which he is. The Reformers were especially dealing with the circumstances of individual men. They meant

35

to explain to whom each individual should attribute his election. But what the true state of each man is; in what relation each man stands to a body; whether the election of an individual can be viewed apart from the election of the Church; -- these are questions which are forced upon us at this time, and which it is possible may be resolved in a way in which some of the Reformers and most of their disciples would not have resolved them.

III. 1. The language of the Reformers respecting the BIBLE was probably more offensive to the Quakers and the mystics generally, than even their doctrines of justification and election. The notion of a book to which men, possessing the Inward Light and guided by the Spirit, must defer as an absolute authority, puzzled and confused them. Nevertheless, they were by no means inclined to deny that, the more they were walking in the Light and submitting to the Spirit, the more sympathy they had with the words of this book, the less they were disposed to cavil at them. In this, therefore, as in the two former cases, they were inclined to translate the language of the Reformers into their own, and to affirm that in any other sense except that it was false. The spiritual man had a capacity for discerning spiritual truths under the letter of the Scriptures; to him, therefore, they had a meaning and an exceeding value. But to call them in themselves, as words, as records of facts, divine; to hold them up, in this character, as objects of reverence, was to turn men's eyes away from the true light, and so far as you could to quench it.

The truth of this statement, so far as it describes the faculty which the Scripture addresses, I have already admitted, and have maintained that it is implicitly recognized by those who seem to be most startled by it. That all revelation is to the conscience, to the inner man, and that when that conscience is not awake, when that inner man is buried, the revelation is not really made, most persons, under some form of language or other, are ready to confess. And that the most consistent and intelligible interpretation of this truth is contained in the doctrine that man is created for union with the Living Word, and that except in union with Him he is not in a true living state, I, at least, am most anxious to maintain. But then if this be the state, not for one man but for all men, and if each man, just so far as he enters into his true state, becomes more of a man and less of a mere individual, does it not seem strange that there should be no instrument through which the mind of the Living Word is expressed to the race, and which therefore overreaches the feelings and judgments of each particular mind, while it imparts to these feelings and judgments clearness, purity, and strength? Does not the expectation of such an instrument, a certain conviction that it is necessary and that it will be given, grow up just in proportion as we take in the other idea, and observe how entirely it contradicts the notion that each man is a law to himself? Now, supposing there were such an instrument, of what kind must it be? You say that the same set of facts, words, records, conveys a different meaning to the spiritual enlightened

36

man and to the fleshly ignorant man. Be it so; then what is there to prevent us from believing that the truth which is meant to be conveyed, should be conveyed in facts, records, and words? Why may it not be a spiritual communication, because it is embodied in the ordinary forms of human discourse? Can you imagine how it should be embodied in any other forms? That you may not be able to conjecture what facts and events would be adequate to make known to man the law of his own being, his relation to God, the character of God, I willingly acknowledge. But suppose you were told that a set of men -- a peculiar nation -- had been selected as the organs of a divine communication to the nations generally, and that all their circumstances had been contrived for the purpose of fitting them for such a function, would you say there was an a priori improbability that this would be the method adopted by the Lord of man for speaking to His creatures? Would you not feel there was a singular fitness in it; that there was some difficulty in conjecturing how any other could be equally in accordance with the principle which we have acknowledged?

Whence, then, comes the reluctance of the mystic to receive the reformed doctrine on this subject? It may be traced, I believe, to the same defect which we have observed in him already. He perceives the conditions under which man exists, the relation in which he stands to a divine guide and teacher, but he does not trace that relation up to its ground in an Originating Will. Stopping short of that, he cannot, it seems to me, heartily believe in a Revelation. He thinks of the eye which receives the Light; he cannot steadily reflect that there was a Light before the eye, and that it called into existence the eye which should behold it. I do not say that he does not implicitly acknowledge this truth. But the explicit acknowledgment of it is that which I believe gave the Reformation all its moral strength and grandeur, and above all, which imparted to the Protestant doctrine respecting the Bible all its meaning.

2. The Quaker complains of this doctrine because it subjects the spiritual man to the government of words and letters. A much more popular objection to it is, that it sets particular men, however ill-taught and undisciplined, free from all authority but their own. "Interpretations of Scripture have been compiled by a series of wise, learned, holy men; some of them receiving their lessons immediately from the apostles. Evidently, therefore, there are difficulties, amazing difficulties, about its meaning. Yet the most ignorant mechanic is to be treated as if he could take cognizance of it, and attain to a complete understanding of it."

Now it should be understood or remembered, that however the doctrine of the Reformers respecting the Scriptures may have become identified with the doctrine of private judgment, it did not present itself to them in that form, but in the most dissimilar form imaginable. They expressly proclaimed the Bible to be that book which puts down and

✓ humbles private judgments; which asserts its claim to be heard above them all and in opposition to them all, and which is able to make that claim good. They believe that its words were with power; that when it spoke, man felt that power, and either submitted to it or consciously rebelled against it. I appeal to anyone who has looked at all into the writings of the Reformers, whether this be not the tone which habitually pervades them. Was this notion of theirs absurd or extravagant? Assuredly it might have been justified -- it was justified to the men who lived at what is called the revival of letters -- by the most obvious analogies. Was it the fact that the men and women and children in the Greek isles and on the shores of Asia had heard the Homeric songs from the lips of wandering rhapsodists, and had received them into their memories and their hearts? Was it the fact in the most cultivated period of Athenian life these same songs were listened to, with less of genuine admiration perhaps, but still with delight and a confession of their strange power? Was it the fact that afterwards they became subjects of philosophical speculation to Aristotle, but at the self-same moment stirred the spirit of Alexander to the invasion of the East, without any reference to his master's criticisms upon them? Did English or German schoolboys wait till they had studied Aristotle or Eustathius to feel them -- nay in the best sense to understand them -- in their first dress or in their own tongue? What man in his senses will say that there was any arrogance of private interpretation in all this; that it was the setting up a right to criticise, and not much rather the abandonment of all such right in submission to an influence which could not be resisted? Were the Ionian women and children, the Macedonian prince, the English schoolboys, disparaging the labours of Aristotle or Eustathius? Were they not affording the best justification of them?

All then that the Reformers said when they claimed the Bible for peasants was this -- that if it pleased God to make Himself known to His creatures, and if this book contained the records of His revelation, it was not more strange to expect that His power would go forth to carry the ✓meaning of the book home to those for whom it was meant, and that the words of a human book should be able to make themselves intelligible; it was not more necessary that the peasants of Christendom should wait for a commentary before they opened their ears and hearts to receive the words of the one book, than that the peasants of Greece should wait for a commentary before they opened their ears and hearts to receive the words of the other. This was their notion, which did not, however, require even this process of reasoning for its confirmation; seeing that they had evidence before their eyes that the Bible did speak to poor men, and did make itself heard by them, the more in proportion as it was more directly and livingly set before them. I say livingly, for we must not impute to the Reformers the opinion that the power of the book would be felt by the mere reader of it: they attached, as everyone knows, an importance and sacredness to the office of the preacher which we are apt, and not without reason if the circumstances of our own day are to regulate our belief, to consider extravagant.

38

3. There is however another side to this objection. The doubt recurs here, as in the other cases -- Is this power promised to individuals or a certain body? Are individuals as such to expect that the word of God will reveal itself to their hearts and consciences? And the former answer must be repeated. Unquestionably the Reformers believed that the word was to each man, not to a mere mass of men. They believed that the Bible had its peculiar lesson for everyone, and not merely its general lesson for the world. But to ascertain how the peculiar lesson and the general lesson bear upon each other, and under what circumstances and conditions any given man may hope to profit by either, we must know whether he is in his true state when he is living in a certain body, or when he is standing aloof and asserting his independence. This is, as I have said already, a very important question -- perhaps the question for us in this day to decide. A kind of help to resolving it may perhaps be obtained from the comparison which I first used in defence of the Reformers. The Homeric poems were sung to Greek women and children. They were received and loved by them because they had Greek sympathies: we receive and love them because we, being members of a nation, are able to enter into those sympathies. Whether a set of savages, without any sense of society, could have listened to them with equal rapture, or with any rapture at all, is a point worth considering. But this is merely a hint for reflection; the subject must receive a more full consideration.

IV. I believe it will be more convenient to pass over for the present the objections which are made to the doctrine of the Reformers, respecting National distinctions and the power of Sovereigns. Till we have considered many topics which have not yet come under our notice, the force of these objections could not be appreciated; it would be therefore unfair to attempt a refutation of them. And the omission is of less importance, as we shall find that the systems to which the Reformation has given birth have been but indirectly affected by this particular tenet.

One remark, however, I must make, which is necessary in order to understand the contrast which I have attempted to exhibit between the Quaker tendency and that which characterised the Reformers. I said that the assertion of an Absolute Will was the main peculiarity of the latter, the assertion of a relation between the Divine Word and His creatures of the former. It might seem that this assertion was scarcely consistent with another which I made (and which will be at once admitted as true), that Luther delighted to realise the connexion of our Lord with all human circumstances and relations, and that Fox turned away from such contemplations altogether. But a minute's thought will remove the apparent contradiction. The relation between the heart and spirit of man and its Divine Teacher was the one which the Quaker perceived. To connect ordinary human relations with this seemed to him impossible; it was almost profanation. The Reformer, taking his stand upon the ground of the Divine Will, and looking upon the Bible as

39

containing the revelation of that Will, had no such delicate feeling. The common earth was God's creation. Kings, fathers, and husbands had been appointed by Him and were spoken of in His word; the whole economy of His kingdom had been transacted through their means. The Papists had treated the world as the devil's world, with their "touch not, taste not, handle not;" but there was no safety in such abstinence -- the security was in serving God with a clean heart, and giving Him thanks for His gifts. Such was the Reformation feeling, wherein we must perceive indications of a high truth, which might lead to a deliverance from sensuality or materialism, or might be perverted into them. This was, at all events, the immediate effect of its proclamation. The Teutonic nations, in which family life had always flourished, and in which the King had been able to assert his position as something distinct from that of the premier baron of his realm, and in which there was a tendency towards business and enterprise, became Protestant; the Latin nations, in which there was a lower standard of domestic and national feeling, but more of the feeling and sympathies which dispose to general social intercourse, with more also, as I think, of a tendency to pure contemplation, continued to call themselves Catholic.

SECTION III -- PROTESTANT SYSTEMS

While I have maintained that the Protestant principles are inseparably connected, and that all are implicitly contained in the first, I have hinted also that they presented themselves in quite different aspects and relations to the different Reformers. Justification was the central thought in Luther's mind; Election in Calvin's; the Authority of the Scripture in Zwingli's; the Authority of Sovereigns in all the political patrons of Protestantism, and in some of its theological champions, especially here in England. And as these differences indicated the existence of different, nay, opposite, habits of mind in persons who bore the common name of Protestants (and had a right to that name, not only as being all opposed to Romanism, but as all recognizing the positive doctrines which Romanism denied), so it portended the growth of immediate divisions.

I. The character of the German Reformation is mainly, but not wholly, expressed in Martin Luther. Most students feel that in order to understand it fully we must connect with him, at all events, Philip Melanchthon. It has been a wonder to some that Luther, whose language against the teachers of the Church, not only in his own time but in past times, is probably more vehement than that of any other Protestant, should nevertheless have felt so much syumpathy with the man who was least disposed to commit any act of separation from the old Church, and should have turned away with dislike from those who were labouring to consolidate a Protestant SYSTEM. The circumstance is undoubtedly very curious, and cannot, I think, be explained merely by the influence which a man of calm character and logical intellect is wont to exercise over one of ardent temperament and practical energy. The truth seems to be

40

this -- Luther believed at first, and believed to the end of his life, that the Creed and the Sacraments were the great witnesses for justification -- if it was not proper to call them acts of justification. They were such partly because they were acts of affiance in a person; partly because they, the sacraments at least, were, as he believed, not merely human acts, but acts on the part of God, recognizing and adopting those who would receive them. But everything in the new endeavour to create a Protestant system was drawing men away from this creed and these sacraments. Systematic articles and confessions were beginning to be formed; justification was again taught scholastically as one of a set of dogmas; the very meaning of it was escaping. Now Melanchthon probably was scarcely aware of this danger, for he was an Aristotelian schoolman, and was half disposed to acquiesce in the scholastic theories which Luther abhorred. But his dislike of separation led him to the same result. There was something terrible to him in the thought of leaving the old German Church -- the Church of his fathers. He would have said: "We have made our protest against the abuses of Romanism; possibly we have fulfilled our work." And if he were asked, "But what then becomes of the doctrine of justification?" he would have said, "Has it not been asserted, in a sense, in the Church at all times? The doctors maintain a justification."

For a moment such words may have come with power to Luther's mind; whether they occurred to himself, or were suggested by his friend, they will have derived strength from some Anabaptist atrocity, or some Zwinglian discourse on the Eucharist. But an infamous proceeding of the Romish court will just then have come to light, or a decree will have gone forth from the emperor making reconciliation impossible. Then such thoughts will have been cast away as the suggestions of a fiend. To assert justification, not a justification, but the only real justification, was the business of his life. He who did assert this could have no peace with Rome; he must break all bonds; the name of Catholic itself must be cast away. There must be an Evangelical Church; a Church witnessing for justification by faith, though all Christendom witnessed against it; Germany is to be the seat of such a Church. But it shall not be built upon a mere notion. The Sacraments shall be the great constituents of it. Baptism shall declare to its members their spiritual citizenship. They shall not regard the Eucharist merely as a feast, at which they are to express their own faith and love. The consecrated elements shall not be spoken of as if they were made something by the receiver; they are something in themselves; they are consubstantiated with the Divine Presence. This is the Lutheran system, and of this the Evangelical Church of Germany professes to be the great Conservatrix.

II. It is evident from these remarks, that though the leading Protestant doctrine was meant to be embodied in Lutheranism, we must look, for the purely Protestant system, to Calvinism. It is not necessary to suppose that Calvin, from the first moment that he began to bear witness against Romanism, contemplated a separation from the old

Church. Such a notion would be contrary to all that we know of ecclesiastical history, and of the lives of those who acted in it. But the idea of an Ecclesia, consisting of individuals taken out of the world by Divine Election, was the one which was continually present to his mind, and which gradually subordinated every other to itself. As all the appearances and conditions of the so-called Church outraged in Calvin's apprehension this idea, it must embody itself somewhere else. No self-willed act for the construction of a new body of faithful men might be justifiable. But the circumstances of the time seemed to point out the will and purpose of God; and his position as to Geneva might enable him to carry out that purpose, by planting the seed of a divine society.

That this society should, except in its acknowledgment of a Pope, correspond to that which Calvin did not deny had been once established by God, though it had fallen into so great corruption, would at first have been his wish; that it should feel itself to have some links of connexion with that old stock might be well on some accounts, though on others dangerous. But the main point was, that it should bear witness to the idea of a distinct election. The question, therefore, practically decided itself. The Church was essentially a collection of individuals. Now, an instinct taught Calvin, and his learning helped his instinct, that the existence of Episcopacy involved another idea than this; it was the witness of something besides mere individual association. Episcopacy therefore was, at all events, not necessary; might it not be on the whole rather a perplexing and unintelligible institution?

In some other points Calvin could use language not very different from that which had prevailed among the fathers, and in the Catholic Church. He attached a high importance to Baptism, and a mysterious worth to the Eucharist. Wherein then consisted his difference from them, and even from Luther? The Fathers actually regarded the Incarnation -- Luther wished to regard it -- as the foundation of the Church; Calvin sought for this foundation in individual election. In this difference all others are included. This idea of election involved the idea of a particular redemption; the selection of particular men being regarded merely in the light of a Divine decree; logically implied the reprobation of the rest. Thus the Calvinistic system is formed -- a system essentially distinct from the Calvinistic principle, but necessarily involved in the constitution of the Calvinian Church. To Geneva, as the nucleus of this system, the cradle of this Church, men repaired from other lands for teaching and illumination. Thence came John Knox, and planted that which was destined to be the most vigorous shoot from the Genevan stock. Thence came Englishmen, who had been refugees during the Marian persecution, to lay the foundation of our Puritanism, and of the different nonconformist sects which have issued from it. Of all these bodies, however much they may differ from each other, the Calvinistical doctrine is the animating principle; when that is forgotten, or merged in any other, there ceases to be any meaning in their existence.

III. Luther and Calvin entertained a great reverence for the old Creeds of the Church, and some for the teaching of the Fathers. Those in whom reverence for the Scripture took the place of every other feeling, gradually acquired the habit of disparaging both; but this was not their main or distinguishing characteristic. Looking at the written Word of God, as the declaration of God's will, and as His great gift to man, they became impatient of the value which the other Reformers attached to the Sacraments, especially to the Eucharist. Had not this been the great snare of the Romanists? Had not the belief of sacramental grace made them substitute something else for the great facts of which the Bible is the record? It was well, no doubt, as it was commanded, to keep a memorial feast in remembrance of those facts, or of that which is the most transcendent of them. This was to be the sign and bond of church fellowship in all ages; but the notion that this memorial feast had the virtue which the German, and even the Genevan doctor, was inclined to attribute to it, opened the way to all superstition. These were unquestionably the elements of a peculiar system; but they had not ✓ strength to be the groundwork of a society. The Zwinglians succumbed for a time to the Calvinists; their maxims were not embodied anywhere; but on that very account they were destined to exercise a more powerful influence over the whole Protestant mass.

Another influence of the same kind began to make itself manifest within the century which produced the Reformation; of the same kind in more senses than one, though apparently most unlike the Zwinglian influence, inasmuch as that seemed to contain the very essence of Protestantism, and this to be in direct contradiction to its most remarkable peculiarity. I allude to the doctrines of Arminius and ✓ Grotius. These doctrines looked at on one side bore the distinct impress of the Reformation. They were set up in opposition to all mystical notions; they were presented as the plain, popular, practical view of men's duties and responsibilities; they were deduced from texts of Scripture; they were probably felt by their principal propagators to be much more unlike the sacramental views of the older Church than the Calvinistic views were. But on the other hand, an acknowledgment of the absolute will of God was believed to be -- as we have seen that it was -- the recognition upon which, not one, but all the Protestant doctrines were grounded. Because Calvinism had put forth this acknowledgment more prominently than Lutheranism, Calvinism had become almost identical with Protestantism; it had been believed to be the witness against the self-willed inventions and self-righteous ⟩ doctrines of the Romanists. It was not strange, then, that the vehement Protestants in England and elsewhere should identify Arminianism with Popery, and should believe that the same decisive measures were necessary for extirpating one as the other. They were successful in preventing Arminianism from establishing itself into a rival Church; they were quite unsuccessful in preventing it from leavening the minds of those who adopted the Genevan model, and subscribed the Genevan confessions.

IV. Our last duty in this section would be to consider how far any of these systems became connected with the government of the nations in which they established themselves, or whether any other has arisen to assert the relation between Protestantism and national life. But the last of those questions is closely connected with the history of the English Church; the first will be better considered under our next head.

SECTION IV -- THE PRACTICAL WORKING OF THE PROTESTANT SYSTEMS

I. The character of Luther, like that of most true Teutons, was compounded of hearty joviality and deep sadness. It has often been remarked that the latter element, which was inseparable from his conflicts and his vocation, painfully predominated in his later years, in which one might have hoped there would have been serenity, if not sunshine. Romanists, and many who are not Romanists, have said, that but one inference can be drawn from such a fact; he felt a bitter sense of disappointment in the result of his labours; if pride had permitted him, he would have confessed that he had rashly and sinfully entered upon them. Such observations are very plausible, and very convincing to those who fancy that a man commences a work, like that to which Luther's life was devoted, from some calculations of producing an effect that will redound to his own satisfaction, or profit, or honour, or even to the advantage of the world. He cannot be governed by any such calculations: no one to whom mankind really owes any great gratitude was ever governed by them. A mighty Power which he must obey is urging him forward; at every step there is reluctance; oftentimes he says to himself, "I will speak no more words in His name;" he is ashamed and confounded that one like him should pull down and destroy; but the fire is in his heart, and it must come forth from his heart, whatever it consumes. A man who obeys such an impulse will have much sorrow in himself, and will be little understood by others. All he can say in his own defence is, "I know this was to be done, and that I was to do it." Men will tell him that a knave might use the same language; he will admit it, and will only answer, "Whether I be a knave or no, I do not stand before your tribunal. My judgment is with the Lord, and my work is with my God." It will be time for the Romanists to say that Luther did not accomplish anything which he wished to accomplish, or which his time required, when they are able to explain without reference to him the extraordinary change which took place in the morality and energy of their own hierarchy in the generation following. It will be time for Protestants to sneer at Luther, when they have fully ascertained that every step out of the errors which they deplore in their own systems will not be made most effectually when they understand the spirit in which he acted, and enter into it; and whether every attempt to set aside the principles which he promulgated will not establish the evils of those systems, and strengthen them by the addition of others from which they may have been separated.

44

The fact, however, must not be concealed -- Luther did feel that Protestantism in every form, even that form which he had been the means of establishing, would not be an adequate or faithful witness for√ the truth which he had existed to proclaim. It was not merely that he foresaw a loss of the freshness and fervour by which new converts are wont to be distinguished; he felt -- though he might not be able to find a reason which satisfied him for the feeling -- that there was something in the idea of the Evangelical Church which would involve the necessity of ∨ great practical contradictions. Experience has justified his fears, and, faithfully used, may perhaps assist us in discovering the ground of them.

As soon as a body was expressly established for the purpose of asserting the doctrine of justification by faith, the confessions and formularies which set forth that doctrine began of course to be in the highest esteem. They were the casket which contained the jewel, and the jewel could not be preserved without the casket. It was all very well to say, The Creed contains it; or, as Luther would say, He that can declare, I believe in God the Father, etc., is justified; but the Romanists acknowledge the Creed too, and we are to defend justification against the Romanists. It was still more unsatisfactory to say, The Bible contains the doctrine: the Romanists acknowledge the Bible; the Bible, interpreted in a particular way, or not interpreted in another way, might seem to deny it. Consequently, a certain interpretation of the Creed and of the Bible must be guarded and upheld; these formularies have been carefully worded to include that interpretation, and to exclude every other; to these we must adhere.

* * *

NOTE ON CHAP. II. SECT. IV

When I speak of the final result of the experiment of pure Protestantism, it must be distinctly understood that I do not suppose those who are called Protestants in Germany, in Holland, in Switzerland, to have lost the blessings which they possessed before the Reformation, or those which were claimed for them then. I mean merely, that the systems called Lutheranism, Calvinism, Zwinglianism, have had their day, and that the time of their extinction is at hand. ✓ No persons are ✓ more alive to this fact than Germans. Hence their eagerness to consolidate professors of these systems into an "Evangelical Church;" hence their desire to reconcile the ideas of the Eucharist prevailing among the Lutheran and the "Reformed," by mutual concessions; hence their willingness to tolerate, for a time, subjection to the State, if it will but deliver them from a sectarian position. The existence of such feelings must be a sufficient proof to all who are not themselves spellbound by some system, that the descendants of the Reformers are not deserted by the Head of the Church, and that He may be preparing for them blessings which the great men of the sixteenth century sighed for, but were unable to attain. I will not anticipate the latter portion of my book by explaining what these blessings are, or how they may operate as a cure for the evils under which Germany was groaning long before the Reformers arose to help her and purify her. Still less will I enter upon the practical question, by what means these blessings may be recovered. One thing is clear; those who think and feel the unfortunate ecclesiastical position of Protestant Germany, are also the most determined not to abandon the principles of the Reformation. Some who may have been affected by Austrian or Bavarian influences may dream of recovering the position in which they were before Luther appeared; but all men who are really in earnest, and who know what they mean, will repel such a thought as at once a folly and a sin. The idea that there must be a progress and not a retrogression is one, which the German mind is full of, and which I should be very sorry to drive out of it. The only question is, about the nature of the progress. Beginning in the spirit, the Reformation has, in the most grievous sense, been made perfect in the flesh. Its principles have found no clothing but one of system, which has stifled them; or one of a State organisation, which stifles the minds and energies of those who profess them. The progress Protestants should desire is surely one towards an organisation, which shall not be an artificial but a vital expression of that which is the faith of the nation. If it should be found that the ecclesiastical organisation which Germany once possessed, though corrupted and deadened by the denial of Christ's direct superintendence over it, is of this vital character, the recovery of it will not be less a growth than the acquisition of some newer one would be. Nay, it will be far more a growth; for the one will belong to the proper history of the land; the other will be some fantastic dress, fashioned like the institutions of Napoleon, according to the maxims of an age, and therefore an intolerable burden to all who look beyond it, and feel they have a portion in their fathers and in their posterity. Their Protestantism will make the old Catholicism new and living; the Catholicism which possesses this quickening element will, by degrees, extinguish the Romanist counterfeit of it; the States, which no civil arrangements have been able to consolidate, will become one through their unity of faith, and the words of the poet will be fulfilled, that wherever his tongue is spoken, and God in Heaven praised in it, there the German will find his fatherland.

CHAPTER III

UNITARIANISM

Connexion of Unitarianism with pure Protestantism, with Natural
Philosophy, and with the System of Locke -- Its positive side --
Its negative side -- Final results

I said that the early Quakers acknowledged many of the doctrines
which other Christians acknowledged, but that the sense in which they
received them was determined by the nature of those tenets which were
specifically theirs. It would be incorrect to apply a precisely similar
observation to the Reformers. The doctrines which were not
characteristic of them, but which were professed by their Romanist
opponents, and under certain important modifications by the Eastern as
well as the Western Church -- the doctrines of the Trinity and
Incarnation -- stood prominently forward in the Protestant confessions.
Luther at least looked upon them as the primary doctrines of
Christianity, and upon his own great principle as the link which
connected them with the distinct personality of each man.

But what was not true, or but partially true, of the founders, was
emphatically true or the successors, whether they belonged to the
spiritual or the dogmatic school. The former uniformly spoke of
Election, Justification by faith, the authority of the Written Word, as the
vital, essential truths of Christianity -- those which belonged to personal
religion. When they alluded to the doctrine of the Trinity it was in some
such language as this -- Every true Christian, they said, must needs
recognize a Creator, a Redeemer, and a Sanctifier. These offices were
necessary to the accomplishment of his salvation, and he must attribute
them to distinct agents. Hence the necessity of admitting this principle.
But the thought would present itself: "these offices are undoubtedly
distinct; but does it follow necessarily that there is a distinction of
persons? May not that notion be a mere effort to explain a diversity of
operations, which is capable of being accounted for upon some less
difficult hypothesis?" The suggestion might be repelled by the humble
and pious, but bolder spirits would broach it, and that which was dreaded
by the fathers as a temptation, would be welcomed by the sons as a
discovery.

The Dogmatic school used a different language. They maintained
that this doctrine was taught in Scripture; it formed part of the
confessions, and was just as necessary as any other part. But here
another kind of difficulty presented itself. Were the texts alleged in
behalf of a doctrine so very strange and incomprehensible, adequate to
the support of it? Had not the Romanists done something to keep alive
the belief of it by their traditions? Was it quite consistent with
Protestantism to own such help? These questions were asked, and the

answers to them from the doctors of the Evangelical and of the Reformed Churches became daily more faint and incoherent.

I have shewn already how in the Calvinistical bodies from the first, and in the Lutheran so far as they caught the purely Protestant complexion, the idea of the Incarnation was deposed from the place which it had occupied in the older divinity of the Church. The state and constitution of humanity was determined by the fall; it was only the pure, elect body, which had concern in the redemption; that redemption therefore could only be contemplated as a means devised by God for delivering a certain portion of His creatures from the law of death, to which the race was subjected. In endeavours to explain the mode of this redemption, and to justify the limitation of it, consisted the divinity of the most purely Protestant writers, and for this end they resorted to those arguments from the schools, and illustrations from the market-place, of which I spoke in the last chapter.

Meanwhile a great change had been effected in men's notions upon several subjects not obviously theological. The experimental philosophy in physics held out to students the hope of attaining an actual knowledge of things, by delivering them from the impressions of the senses, and from the notions which the understanding generalises out of those impressions. Already this philosophy had borne its noblest fruits, and the Astonomer had asserted a principle as true, which was the most contradictory to sense and to all conclusions from sense.

But if this experimental philosophy were the great means of leading to such discoveries, did it not follow that Experience was the one source of knowledge? The conviction became stronger and stronger, "There is no other, there can be no other." Then clever men began to explain how many false schemes and systems had their origin in the notion that there was some other foundation of knowledge than this, and each fresh exposure drew from the enlightened and philosophical world a fresh peal of laughter at the absurdities of their forefathers. There were indeed various thoughtful men in different parts of Europe who were struck with the reflection, that the new doctrine, which seemed to have grown up side by side with the great experiments in natural philosophy, had led to exactly the opposite result. Physical science had advanced, or rather had been found to be possible, just so far as it had set itself free from sensible impressions, and the notions deduced out of them. Moral science was advancing, it was believed, to its perfection, by acknowledging these impressions and notions as the only standard of truth. But such suggestions were little heeded at the time. It became the first tenet of philosopical orthodoxy, which it was most dangerous to dispute, that sensible experience is the foundation of all belief and of all knowledge.

The rise of this philosophical theory is historically connected with that of a great political theory, which was also to displace all that had gone before it. In order, it was said, to make men tremble at certain doctrines or notions which contradicted their experience, it was necessary to make them tremble also at the authority by which these notions and doctrines were communicated. A mystery was supposed to attach to the origin of society as well as to the origin of knowledge. The one opinion was a fallacious as the other. As knowledge comes in the simplest and most obvious way through eyes and ears, so society grew up in the simplest way by compacts and conventions. Experience was the root of both. Men either felt the miseries of fighting, or dreamed of the blessings of government; they waived their privilege of being independent units, and either yielded themselves passively to one who was stronger than they, or else entered into stipulations with him to rule them till they should find his rule burdensome.

All these points must be taken into consideration, if we would understand the temper of the last age and the nature of the scheme which obtained so much secret or acknowledged prevalency in it. To suppose that there is nothing positive in Unitarianism, that it derives all the popularity it has ever enjoyed from its denials, is a plausible but serious mistake. It has been embraced by a number of earnest minds, which never could have had any sympathy with a system merely because it rejected what other men believed. I do not say that they may not have felt a certain delight in that peculiarity of their doctrine; that the thought of being different from the vulgar mass may not have been flattering to them, as it is the evil nature of all men; and that the positive and negative elements of their minds, being confounded by their opponents, may not at last have become hopelessly confounded by themselves. But I do maintain, that something deeper and more solid lay beneath their not-belief; that it is very important to know what that was, not only for their sakes but for our own; not only because the only way of extricating any man from a falsehood is to do justice to his truth; but because by this course the history of the Church and the plans of God, so far as we may be allowed to examine into them, become far more intelligible.

1. From the dogmatic tendencies which distinguished one class of Protestant theologians, and from the disposition to exalt and all but deify the modes and experiences of their own minds which belonged to another, the natural philosopher was equally free. But if he were a simple, humble man, if he had been trained in his youth to the habit of worship, if he had been taught to connect deep and holy thoughts with the idea of God's presence, his vocation would certainly not diminish his awe and reverence. It would call such feelings forth; nay, he might easily believe that they were first given to him when the marvellous distinctions and inwoven harmonies of creation revealed themselves to him. At all events he was in a new world, a freer world -- it would seem a more real world -- than that of experiences and notions; one which bore a more immediate and naked witness of a Divine Being. It was only afterwards that this witness came forth in the guise of arguments and demonstrations (the mind of a scientific man naturally enough

endeavouring to clothe all thoughts in the forms to which it was habituated, and recognizing this idea of a God as one of those certainties to which such forms would be applicable); but the heart and conscience had spoken first; the testimony had been received already there where it was needed, before the slow machinery of proofs was constructed to justify the assumption, and the spirit had bowed and worshipped with a mixed fear and joy at hearing in the world without the echoes of a nearer and a deeper voice.

Thus nature spoke to one brought up in a Christian atmosphere, as it was not impossible to suppose it might have spoken to some wondering sage of Greece or India. It seemed to bring the news of a simpler, earlier, more universal faith, which must belong to all, and which all might receive. Other testimonies might be added to this, to confirm it, or to restore it; but no true testimony could set it aside or contradict it. And, therefore, were our Scriptures to be prized to the utter rejection of all Shasters containing the mythologies of the old or new world. The first evidently were affirming and re-establishing this primary testimony; the others were outraging it. The belief of a Being not manifested in outward forms, but manifested in His works; not divided according to the diversity of His operations, but one, was the belief which lay at the root of all their teaching. And since the universality of Christianity had superseded the narrowness of Judaism, it was evident that this belief must be asserted with only greater clearness. It would be strange if the universal religion were more wrapped up in particular notions and opinions, were less expansive, than the ancient which did, however, testify most strongly against idolatry as a limitation of the Divine Presence and a division of His essence; strange if the more perfect religion were to throw us back upon the very notions from which the imperfect had succeeded in emancipating all who faithfully received it. By such feelings and arguments did the idea of the unity of God gradually raise itself up in the last age against the faith which had been recognized in Christendom for seventeen centuries. Where lay the force of these feelings and arguments? Surely in the strong inward conviction which they expressed, that the unity of God is a deep, primary truth, which no words can explain away, no experiences of ten thousand minds make unreal, no dogmas of ten thousand generations turn into a nullity; that it has stood its ground and asserted itself in defiance of all such words, experiences, dogmas; that everything which is true in the teaching which men have received, has tended to bring it into clearer manifestation. With this conviction was associated another, less clearly brought out, but the stronger perhaps for being latent, that this idea of the unity of God must in some way or other be the ground of all unity among men; that if there be a universal religion, this idea must be at the root of it. With such convictions let no man dare to trifle; rather let him labour by all means to draw them forth into great strength and clearness, bringing so far as he can all history, and the history of Unitarianism in the last century most especially, to illustrate them.

2. A natural philosopher, trained to pious and reverent feelings, free from petty vanity, and keeping himself aloof from vulgar excitements, is more likely than most men to have a calm and cheerful temperament. His mind is not turned in upon itself; the evil which is there is not constantly reminding him of its presence; his circumstances do not oblige him to contemplate the sins of the world; he is habitually occupied with objects which are serene and unchangeable. To such a man the lessons which he has received in his childhood respecting a Being of perfect love and purity, will recur with particular delight; every new fact in nature will bring them home to him; the whole face of nature will seem to be beaming with them. But then the thought will occur to him of other lessons received in his childhood, which seemed to contradict these; lessons respecting justice, and vengeance, and schemes for removing or propitiating wrath. Of a Being possessing such attributes, and needing to be approached in such a manner, nature says nothing. There may be tempests and volcanoes, but all her operations, so far as we are able to penetrate them, are subject to fixed, unchangeable laws; these will at last be found to obey a law too, and He to whom we refer all creation and all laws, must needs have a mind perfectly at one with itself, subject to no vicissitudes, the same yesterday, and to-day, and for ever. Here again, see how the pure, original testimony to God's universal love has been darkened by human conceits and systems. But that testimony is reasserted in our Bible, distinguished by this characteristic as much as by its assertion of the divine unity, from all pretended revelations. The heathens are denounced in the Old Testament for setting it aside by their cruel inventions; Jesus Christ, by His words and acts, condemned the Jews because they were not honouring God as the God of mercy and love; His dispensation is one from which every other idea is banished; the beloved disciple affirms in words that God is love; all sacrifices and institutions interfering with that notion are expressly abolished. Such were the feelings and arguments by which thousands in the eighteenth century, either openly or secretly, were led to believe that the idea of Atonement, which had been assumed for seventeen centuries to be the radical idea of Christianity, was a wretched and inconsistent graft upon it from some other stock. Where lay the strength of them? In the conviction, it seems to me, that the idea of the love of God is an absolute primary idea which cannot be reduced under any other; which cannot be explained away by any other; which no records, experiences, dogmas, if they have lasted for a thousand generations, can weaken or contradict; which must be the foundation of all thought, all theology, all human life. With such a conviction I believe it is as dangerous to trifle as with that respecting the divine unity.

3. I have spoken of the natural philosopher as withdrawn from the observation of the evils in the world around him, and to a great extent of his own, and as disposed, by his circumstances, to a benignant view of things. How pleasant to such a man when he came from his closet and his problems, with a mind in a measure fixed and abstracted but not unharmonised, to look round upon his children, and to recollect what he

had been told in his nursery, that He who created the sun and moon was their Father. How pleasant when he had time to think of all the generations which had looked upon the light of this sun and moon, to believe the same of them. But what jarring thoughts derived from the same nursery would intrude themselves! All these children of men, all these generations, have undergone a fall; they are the subjects of a curse! Of only a few, how few if the calculations of different divines are to be admitted, is it possible to think -- "these are God's children;" all the rest we can only speak of as doomed, and not it would seem by their own sin but by an inevitable necessity. Surely this too must be one of the wretched interpolations into the old and simple faith. Nature teaches no such lesson. The same sunshine and rain for all; the whole universe claimed for its Creator. And the Bible does mean this, must mean it, whatever divines may assert to the contrary. In some way or other it does reconcile the existence of man with its witness of God's love; in this way it cannot. By such feelings and arguments was the doctrine of a Fall -- admitted for seventeen centuries by all Christendom, recognized as the central doctrine of Christian divinity by the Protestant sects -- driven out of the hearts of thousands in the eighteenth century.

*　*　*

On the popular supporters of Unitarianism such arguments made no impression. They probably received them with indignation. What! they would have said, Do you suppose we meant a metaphysical unity? we meant to escape from all subtleties -- the Bible is written for simple people. I have hinted already that this language was unfortunate; they appealed unto Caesar -- unto Caesar they must go. They wished to be tried by simple people; it remained to be seen whether there was that in their scheme to which the hearts of simple people responded. But, before that experiment was made, the more thoughtful disciples of Unitarianism began to be struck with another strange contradiction between the principles on which it rested and the system in which they are embodied. The Unitarians were the great assertors of the absolute unqualified love of God, in opposition to all mythologies and theologies which had preceded. And Unitarianism was the first of all theologies or mythologies which denied that the Almighty had, in His own person, by some act of condescension and sacrifice, interfered to redress the evils and miseries of His creatures! Every pagan religion had acknowledged the need of an incarnation; the modern Jew and Mahometan, nominally rejecting it, is yet continually dreaming of it and testifying of its necessity: it was reserved for this religion to make it the greatest evidence and proof of love in a Divine Being, that He merely pardons those who have filled the world with misery; that He has never shared in it; never wrestled with it; never devised any means, save that of sending a wise teacher, for delivering mankind out of it.

Again; to a man who really cherished with earnest affection the thought, "God is a universal Father, His creatures cannot be merely the

52

subjects of a curse," what a strange reflection it must have been -- "And yet, according to those doctrines which I hold, He is not, and cannot be a Father. The word means nothing. It is a lazy inappropriate synonym of Maker, for it is the very glory of my creed to do that which no other has done; first to deny that there is any human bond between men and God; secondly, to deny that they have in themselves any capacity, different from that which an animal has, of receiving impulses from God."

Once more; -- to purify men of their false notions of morality, to establish religion on the basis of morality, and to reveal the existence of another world than the present, were, according to Unitarianism, the objects of Christ's appearance in the world, and the objects which the reformers of His doctrine were to keep steadily in sight. For this end they were to desire the removal of all systems and institutions which had kept alive a false faith and a distorted notion of the character of God. "But who," the disappointed disciple of this school inquired, "who are the great helpers in this work of reformation? -- who shew most longing that it should be accomplished? Are they men of deep thought and high devotion, who have been poring in sadness over the condition of society - -in solitary chambers crying out, Usque quo, Domine? ("how long, O Lord?") Are they even poor men, not aiming at some high standard, but feeling the burden and oppression of the universe, and believing that God could not have meant so many of His creatures to live and die, without comfort or hope? -- or are they not rather men, who for the most part have preserved a quiet decent level tone of mind and character; who belong to the easy, respectable, prosperous classes, and who are actually impatient of anything which disturbs them with the recollection of an elevated supersensual morality, or of a society based upon self-sacrifice?"

Alas! he will have said, and is it for this only that I have parted with all the dreams of my childhood? I thought in my infancy that a kingdom of righteousness, peace, joy, had been set up in the world, and that I was to wait and hope, till that kingdom should rule cver all. It has been the glorious discovery of my manhood, that there is no such kingdom here -- nothing but a world, in which men are to observe certain rules of behaviour towards each other, to restrain themselves within certain rules of prudence for their own sakes, and to cheer themselves with the prospect of a future world -- unknown and undefined -- wherein they shall be rewarded if they have not transgressed social decorums, and be forgiven if they have.

Such a picture of the tendencies and ultimate results of the system, must often have presented itself to those who had embraced it with affection, as a deliverance from the dryness and narrowness of Calvinism, and as a witness for the unity and love of God. But these thoughts would only have stirred powerfully in a few minds if a series of strange movements had not taken place in European society, some of which must have seemed most promising to Unitarians, but which really destroyed the whole credit of their system, depriving it of the patronage of nobles and prelates, and supplying it with no substitute in the sympathies either of the thoughtful or of the poor.

CHAPTER IV

ON THE TENDENCY OF THE RELIGIOUS, PHILOSOPHICAL, AND POLITICAL MOVEMENTS WHICH HAVE TAKEN PLACE IN PROTESTANT BODIES, SINCE THE MIDDLE OF THE LAST CENTURY

SECTION I -- RELIGIOUS MOVEMENTS

Methodism -- Religious Societies -- Search for a Theology

The History of Methodism, in one of its aspects, belongs to the history of the English Church, and does not therefore form a part of the subject I am now considering. But any considerate reader will admit, that as France has been the centre of the political, and Germany of the philosophical movements of the last hundred years, so England has been the centre of all religious movements which have occurred within the same period. It is not necessary to maintain that the first impulse to them was given in England; Wesley may have derived much of his teaching from Zinzendorf, and the different efforts made by him and others to awaken a more earnest religious feeling, may take chronological precedence of those which our countrymen witnessed: still the form which they assumed here was so much more determinate, their influence so much more extensive, that if we wish to investigate their character generally, we shall find that our own soil is the proper place for the experiment.

It is often said, that the Methodist movement had for its object and its effect the revival of the great principles of the Reformation. There is a sense in which this remark is unquestionably true; but if that sense be not carefully noticed and defined, we may, I think, fall into great mistakes. The Unitarianism which formed so large an element in the religious sentiments of the eighteenth century was, as we have seen, essentially impersonal. It was so, even in its best form; for those who felt most deeply and earnestly the necessity that great and wide principles should be asserted respecting the unity and character of God, found no way of connecting these principles with the individual conscience. It came out in direct opposition to Calvinism -- as an escape from it, and yet as what seemed a consistent deduction from some of its maxims; and the more it advanced towards a mere system of denials, the more it was proclaimed as a deliverance from the narrowness of this theology. Above all, Calvinism had maintained, that a set of individual believers constituted the Church, and were to bear witness against the world; the Unitarians affirmed that no warrant existed for any such protest; that an enlightened age or world was far in advance of those who pretended to be in separation from it; that the great object which such an enlightened world should propose to itself, was the extinction of the idea of an Ecclesia, in whatever shape that idea might present itself.

55

It was inevitable that, in any strong revival of religious feeling, these notions should be first attacked; in other words that the personal interest of men in religion, and the distinction of those who felt and acknowledged that interest from those who were indifferent to it, should be asserted. Such convictions are characteristic of any strong awakening in men's consciences; they may be said to be the awakening. But then the vague phrase -- personal interest in religion -- cannot long be adequate to describe the feelings of men who have begun to use it in a real sense. One who knows that he is a person requires a personal object -- an abstraction cannot satisfy him. The doctrine therefore that a man is justified by faith, and lives by faith in Christ, became a principal element in the Methodist, as it had been in the early Lutheran teaching; the doctrine that individual believers constitute a peculiar Ecclesia grew out of that; and the Bible began again to put forth as the poor man's book, which he could receive in its simplicity, though the learned sought to explain it away.

But it is remarkable that the most decided proclamation of these Protestant dogmas grew not out of Methodism itself, but out of a reaction in the minds of those who had been brought, more or less directly, under its influence. The history of the very violent conflicts of the Calvinists, under Toplady and Sir Richard Hill, against Wesley and Fletcher, is abundant evidence of this fact. It is true that the most powerful of the Methodist preachers, Whitfield, joined the opponents of his master and early coadjutor; but it is highly probable that he was led to this step by observing how much his own preaching had tended to stir up affections and feelings in men's minds rather than to give them a firm resting-place, and that he sought in the Calvinistical doctrines for a balance and a counteraction to this danger: at all events it is quite certain that though a far greater influence was attributed to him in his lifetime than to Wesley, he left a comparatively insignificant body of disciples. It must then, I conceive, be admitted, that the revival of these Protestant doctrines, though it might be an inseparable accident, was not the essential distinction of Methodism. There was something in it different from the feelings which worked in the minds of the Reformers -- nay opposite to them, though not therefore incompatible with them.

I think everyone must admit that Luther and Calvin directed men very much more to the invisible object which men are to contemplate, or to the original source of their faith in the Will of God; and the Methodists very much more to the operations of a Divine Spirit upon their own minds. This distinction is so obvious, and was so clearly brought out in the controversies to which I have alluded, by persons who acknowledged that they had once adopted the Methodist peculiarity themselves, and who shewed clearly that they could not divest themselves of it even while they laboured diligently to speak another language, that it needs not to be established by proofs, though it ought to be very carefully noticed. The denial that it was possible for men to be the subjects of a spiritual influence, was the great characteristic of

Unitarianism, and of the age which was imbued with it; the assertion of the reality of such an influence, and of its continual manifestation, was the distinguishing property of the teaching which disturbed and partially subverted the liberal system.

But there were other peculiarities connected with this. Methodism was not, like Quakerism, the proclamation of a law in each man's own mind, or of a power working there. It was expressly addressed to large masses of men; the power was believed to descend upon them, especially when they were met together; and though every individual was, in an important sense, said to be taken apart and brought into debate with his own conscience, it was not denied that the feeling of a united influence had a great tendency to increase the consciousness of it in each one. All that was most fanatical in the Methodists was undoubtedly connected with this belief, and it gave the most plausible, often the most just ground, for the assertion, that the effects said to be produced by their preaching might be traced wholly to contagion and sympathy, and would disappear when the moving cause had ceased. Still we do not get to the meaning of a fact, merely by using the words "contagion and sympathy" to describe it; fanaticism and even consciously dishonest quackery cannot produce any results unless they have some true principle to work with, and it seems as if the principle involved in Methodism might be one which has often been dawning upon us in our previous inquiries, though we have never yet found any satisfactory development of it. We have often been obliged to ask ourselves, whether these distinct individual acts, on which Protestantism dwells so exclusively, may not, must not, depend at last upon some relation in which men stand to their fellows; whether we can take our start from individuals, and form a society out of them; whether the existence of society be not implied in their existence; and whether, consequently, if each man have a spiritual existence, and be subjected to a spiritual government, there must not be somewhere a spiritual body, of which he should account himself a member? The facts of Methodism may offer but few helps for solving this problem, but assuredly they force it upon our attention, and make it more abundantly necessary that we should seek the solution of it somewhere.

There are other points of great importance and interest closely connected with the two to which I have adverted. This proclamation of a spiritual power went forth from men who had been brought up in a university which had the reputation of preserving more of the old Catholic temper than could be found elsewhere, and whose very nickname indicated that they had been more scrupulous and regular than the majority in their devotion to forms and ordinances. Those who are acquainted only with the practices which the Wesleys afterwards tolerated, and which their followers regard as characteristic of their system, would not easily believe how much importance they attached in the outset of their career to the episcopal ordination of ministers. Nevertheless a certain impatience of order -- nay, a conviction that it

57

ought to be broken through -- might be discovered in them from the first. It seemed to them that there was an immense body of human souls, which had no national position, and of which the nation took no account. The upper classes in England cared not much for religious ministrations, but they might have them if they would; the middle class, if they were not particularly well affected to the National Church, had provided for themselves in different organised and tolerated sects; but the class below these, the mob, the canaille, as they were then named by their despisers, the masses, as they are now called by their flatterers, were as little regarded by the churchman who inherited the family living, as by the dissenting minister who received his appointment from the tradesmen of the market town. To these, therefore, the Methodists, like the friars of old, addressed themselves; in them they, like those friars, awakened thoughts and hopes to which their educated countrymen had appeared for a long time to be strangers; in providing for their wants, like the friars, they invaded the privileges of the parochial (both alike would have called them the secular) clergy. I know not in what way Bishop Lavington maintained the position that the enthusiasm of the Methodists and of the Papists had many points in common; but no one who considers these facts, or a hundred others connected with the peculiar superstitions to which they respectively gave currency, will doubt that he may have found very plausible arguments in favour of his opinion. At all events, it must, I think, be admitted, that Methodism had some important peculiarities which it did not derive from Protestantism, and with which a pure exclusive Protestantism can scarcely co-exist.

2. The practical belief of a spiritual operation upon the minds and the hearts of men, may be said to constitute Methodism so far as it is a creed. But as soon as the creed had obtained prevalency, a system developed itself, which, as Mr. Southey has remarked, is a more complete specimen of organisation than any which has been produced in Europe since the days of Loyola. The more this organisation is examined, the less it seems to have to do with any spiritual principle; the more evidently it proves itself to be an invention of human policy. This assertion will scarcely be denied by the Wesleyans themselves; though they are stronger than most in asserting the principle of a divine inspiration in individuals, they have pretended less than almost any that their scheme had a divine origin; they attribute it with scarcely any hesitation to the wisdom and sagacity of their founder and of his successors. In one respect only is there a resemblance between the system and that which called it into existence: the spiritual feelings of the Wesleyans led them to overlook national distinctions; the system of the Methodists is essentially extra-national. It is the effort to establish a powerful government in the heart of a nation, which at no point shall impinge upon, or come into contact with, the government of the nation. It differs from the systems of the old dissenting sects in this important point; the limits of each of them are defined by the profession of some peculiar tenet in which they differ from the others, and from the rest of

Christendom; that of the Wesleyans, professing no tenet which is not recognized or tolerated by the National Church, simply exists to assert their own independence of it, and the importance of such an organisation as theirs for the conversion of mankind.

In this respect Wesleyanism is an indication and specimen of the religious tendencies which prevail in this age very far beyond the immediate circle of its influence. The religious feeling of the last century has given birth to religious societies, between which and their parent one finds it difficult, for some time, to discover a feature of resemblance. The first tended to draw men into themselves; the last throw them altogether out of themselves. The first was grounded upon the acknowledgment of a directly spiritual influence, as the only source of any moral change in the condition of individuals or of the world; the latter are constructed upon the most earthly principles, and seem to attribute all power to them. Accordingly the contrast has been felt, as well by the good men who took part in the movements of the last age and have survived them, as by the younger men who have grown up under their teaching. The first confess, with something of timidity, as if they were afraid of appearing to disparage the fruits of a tree which they believe to have been planted by a divine hand, that the restless turmoil and bustle of a modern religious life is not what they or their fellow-labourers whould have wished to produce; the latter in more open, sometimes in more angry language, complain, that under spiritual words and pretexts there has grown up amongst us a great machinery -- complicated, noisy, but inefficient to produce any great results; acknowledging no law in its workings, save certain vulgar maxims, which are applicable only to trade, if even trade itself does not demand principles of a simpler and nobler kind. Nevertheless we find the very persons who make these complaints confessing that they know not how to dispense with this machinery, for that there must be some method of combined voluntary action, grounded not upon our relations to each other as members of a state, but upon some higher and more universal relation. Here again then we are struck with indications of a Catholic feeling arising out of the very heart of Protestantism.

* * *

SECTION III -- POLITICAL MOVEMENTS

American Revolution -- French Revolution -- Individual Rights -- Individual Will -- Schemes of Universal Society -- Education -- Power of the State

I have had occasion to speak of the theological temper of the United States of North America, as illustrating one stage in the history of Protestantism, and as indicating a desire for something that Protestantism does not supply. But the political change which took palce in these states, when they revolted from the mother country, is, in the same point of view, even more important.

Among the leading characteristics of the Reformation, I noticed an anxiety to assert the rights of national Sovereigns, and, as involved in them, the distinct position of each nation. This feeling, I said, was closely intertwined with that feeling of personal distinctness in each man which is the main spring of Protestantism. But when the Protestant systems had developed themselves, these inseparable twins began to manifest great impatience of each other's company. The monarchs of the reformed States found that the belief in each individual's right to act and think for himself trenched very inconveniently upon their authority, and tended in no degree to the consistency and unity of the nations which they governed. They observed that whenever the religious feeling was strong, it treated all things as subordinate to itself; therefore, unless it could be made to conspire with the objects of their government, it must thwart them. There seemed to be but two expedients: to force the religious feeling into this agreement, or as much as possible to weaken it. The first policy was tried, and failed; afterwards the latter was adopted for a time with better success. The dispositions on the other side of course corresponded to these. The religious bodies became more and more jealous of the sovereign's interference with them; in times of strong excitement they resisted it; but as such times made their terms of communion more strict, these bodies became less and less identical with the nation; therefore it was not difficult to believe, when peace returned, that they had nothing to do with national affairs, that it was their business to be wholly religious, and the business of the monarchs to be wholly secular. This opionion, however, was very slowly adopted by any class of Reformers. The Lutherans thought, and still think, a State tyranny less intolerable then the abandonment of the Reformation principles. The Calvinists, in their palmy days, resolved, that if the State could not be religious with a sovereign, it should be religious without one. The Scotch Covenant affirmed the State to be essentially theocratic; the whole effort of our civil wars was to establish the same principle, and in one strange interlude between the acts of that tragedy, the Scotch tried to create a Presbyterian theocracy in the person of Charles the Second. It was only upon the disappointment of these schemes, that the modern doctrine under its different modifications began to prevail. And in the meantime an experiment was to be made whether religious men, if they could not exercise an influence over the old societies of Europe, might not frame societies for themselves in another world.

The legislation and government of the Puritan colonies bore every mark of their origin. They were, in fact, if the solecism may be pardoned, sect-commonwealths, connected by their religious peculiarities more than by the bonds of a common language, of a common origin, or of subjection to a distant sovereign. Before the time arrived when the last-mentioned of these ties was to be snapt asunder, the colonies had acquired an important position as trading communities. The religious feeling of the early settlers had lost much of its strength, but had left behind it industrious habits, clearness of understanding in common matters, indifference to refinements either physical or intellectual, and a useful pertinacity of character. Of such elements the heroes of the revolution were composed, men who, being exceedingly like the Puritans in these qualities, differed from them in this, that their notions of government and society were unconnected with a spiritual principle, and referred wholly to the condition and circumstances of this world. This change was evident from the Declaration of Independence -- a document in which the old Protestant feeling, that each man is a distinct being possessing distinct privileges and rights, is curiously blended with a vague notion of a general fellowship which was beginning to gain currency in Europe, and which was rather a reaction against Protestantism than the natural result of it. And of this declaration the ultimate consequence was that union of the different independent states, respecting which future history will determine whether it have taken effect by a process of natural fusion, or merely by the decrees and contrivances of legislators.

These events were undoubtedly indications that a strife of principles was at hand, though the scene of it was not to be laid in the land of Franklin and Washington. It was in a country of the old world, a country in which the Protestant doctrine had been stifled two centuries before, a country in which society had been everything and human beings almost nothing, that the most vehement declaration of men's individual rights was to be made, and that the death-struggle between those impulses which lead each person to maintain such rights, and those which lead him to seek communion with his fellows, was to begin.

It has been truly and profoundly observed that the French Revolution could not have been brought about merely by the scepticism of the philosophers, merely by the sins of the civil and ecclesiastical rulers, merely by the starvation of the people, nor by all these combined, if there had not been a certain element of faith to mix with and contradict the scepticism -- to create a kind of moral indignation against the sin -- and to convert the sense of hunger from a dead anguish into a living passion.

***

PART II

OF THE CATHOLIC CHURCH AND THE ROMISH SYSTEM

CHAPTER I

RECAPITULATION

The conclusion to which we have arrived seems to be this -- that the principles asserted by the religious societies which have been formed in Europe since the Reformation are solid and imperishable; that the systems in which those principles have been embodied were faulty in their origin, have been found less and less to fulfil their purpose as they have grown older, and are now exhibiting the most manifest indications of approaching dissolution. Now I have alluded, when speaking of modern philosophical movements, to certain prevalent and popular statements which seem at first sight very closely to resemble those which have been the result of our inquiry. The doctrine that systems, religions, churches, are dying out, but that they have been the clothing of certain important ideas which will survive their extinction, and which it is the business of wise men to note, preserve, and perhaps furnish with a new vesture, is one which I cannot be expected to entertain; nay, to which if this book mean anything I must be directly opposed; nevertheless a conscientious reader may find it difficult to discover what is the point at which this doctrine and mine diverge. It is necessary for the purpose of making the connexion of what has been said with what I am about to say intelligible, that I should relieve him of this embarrassment; and I know no way in which I can do it so effectually as by reminding him of the different points of evidence which have gradually offered themselves to us as we have proceeded.

I. The doctrine which, upon the authority of the old Quaker books, and in opposition to one of their modern teachers, I maintained to be the fundamental one of Quakerism, is, that man is a twofold creature, having inclinations towards sensible things, being united to the divine Word by trusting in whom he may rise above these inclinations and attain to a spiritual life and communion. Of all persons, those who seem the most unlike the primitive Quakers are modern philosophers, artists, and politicians; yet we found that various persons belonging to these different classes had been led by different processes of thought to adopt the maxim which had formed the great obstacle to the belief of Fox's principle. "It cannot be true," said religious people, "because man as such apart from a peculiar religious vocation and impulse is not spiritual;" "It cannot be true," said the philosophers of the last generation, "because he is not susceptible of a religious vocation and impulse at all, he is simply a creature of flesh and blood." Both these opinions would be disowned by those who claim to represent the enlightenment of our time; they would say "man as man has spiritual powers, and is a spiritual creature."

Now it is probable that many of those who use that language would produce it as an instance of the way in which a doctrine has been disencumbered of its ancient form and been reduced to a pure and simple essence. "In the acknowledgment of a spiritual life or existence in man," they would say, "we uphold Fox's meaning, we only take away from it that phraseology with which the religious traditions of former centuries had invested it." My object is not to argue the point whether this be so or not, but to shew that our observations have not led us to this conclusion, but to a most opposite one. It seemed to us that a man believing he has certain spiritual capacities within him, is just the person who is obliged to consider under what conditions these capacities exist; that is was this problem about which Fox was occupied; that the sense of certain upward tendencies within him which were continually restrained and resisted, instead of giving him peace and happiness was the very cause of his torment; that we may talk generally about our spiritual power and existence, but that the moment we practically realise them, amidst all the contradictions under which they exist in this world, they become so involved with awful feelings of responsibility, with the vision of an unknown world, with the certainty of moral evil, that we are glad to escape from them into materialism; that this escape being now impossible we must inquire whence these spiritual desires and impulses have come, by what they are upheld, whither they are tending; that these questions lead directly to the principle which Fox asserted, that it may be omitted or substituted for some other in a system, but that it must be steadily faced and considered by every man who is really engaged in the world's conflict; that modern thinkers are perpetually exhibiting their want of it, especially when they speak of our self-consciousness, the necessity of it, the misery and falsehood of it; that the words, "Not I but Christ in me," are the answer to these perplexities; that we may search heaven and earth before we find any other. And if we are asked on what ground, then, we affirm that the Quaker system has proved inadequate, the answer would be, Precisely on this ground, that it has failed in giving a clear definite expression to the idea of Fox; that it has reduced that idea too nearly into a vague synonym of the notion that we have certain spiritual capacities or feelings within us, that it has not exhibited to men the object on whom Fox affirmed that their spiritual capacities and feelings were to be exercised.

The founder of Quakerism is however not much known to the ordinary philosopher: he would be much more anxious to shew that he had retained all that is really precious in the teaching of the great Reformer. Our mere men of letters, who reverence Leo and believe Erasmus to have protested quite as much as was needful against the abominations of his time, regard Luther, who knew nothing of statues and wrote indifferent Latin, with positive aversion; but the more earnest men among us -- those especially who believe that European society has been making continual progress from darkness to light -- speak of him as one who worked mightily for the overthrow of opinions based upon mere authority and tradition, and prepared the way for the utterance of thoughts which he himself would have rejected with horror. I am not now alluding to the ignorant declaimers who boast of Luther because he exalted the understanding in place of faith; but of those who being really acquainted with his writings, are aware that he as much deserves that

65

praise as Brutus deserved to be canonized by the French sansculotte for the noble plebeian spirit which led him to slay the great aristocrat Julius Caesar; and who would consider it a very ill compliment to anyone to say that he wanted faith himself and wished to destroy it in others. They will cheerfully admit that the assertion, "A man is justified by faith," is more characteristic of Luther than his opposition to popes or masses. They will allow that the different acts of his outward life had all a more or less direct reference to that principle. But then they would say, 'this principle when it is taken out of the swaddling bands of the sixteenth century and allowed to move freely, means just this, that it is the inward state of man and not his performance of certain prescribed acts, or even the worthiness of his outward conduct, which entitles him to be called good, that not what he seems nor even what he does, but what he is, constitutes him a right and true man. This truth had been set at nought by the Church of that day; by the vehemence with which he declared it and compelled men to listen to it, Luther established his chief claim to the gratitude of mankind.'

I am well convinced that his principle had been practically denied by the Romanists, and that Luther was the most powerful of all instruments in re-asserting it. But we have seen reason to believe that George Fox maintained the doctrine of an inward righteousness quite as strongly as the German; and yet that there was a very marked difference between them. The difference seemed to consist in this, that while Fox urged his disciples to exercise their faith in a spiritual Being, the Lord of their spirits, Luther delighted to declare that that Being had actually taken human flesh, had died a human death, and by these acts had redeemed us from a curse and justified us before his Father. If Luther was, as his modern admirers constantly affirm that he was, eminently straightforward and practical, impatient of abstractions, dealing in all plain homely images, -- here, it seemed to us, lay the secret of these qualities. It was no fantastic Being he was speaking of, no mere idea; not even merely an object for spiritual apprehension, though that in the highest degree; it was one who had identified himself with men, had by a series of outward acts -- those which the creed announces -- established his human as well as his divine character. It struck us that this, which is in the strictest sense the Lutheran characteristic, was particularly necessary as a complement of the Quaker doctrine; that this without it soon passes into mere vapour. But be that as it may, it was this peculiarity in Luther's preaching which enabled him to effect the overthrow of existing superstitions, and so to be (as we are told) the precursor of greater deliverances hereafter. No doubt the fact of the Incarnation was fully recognized by the Romanists, but by certain notions about inward and inherent righteousness, and by certain practices which were grounded on these notions, this fact had been deprived of its significance. It had ceased to be a witness to any man of what he was. By affirming the reality of this fact and its significance, Luther got rid of the impositions upon the understanding and conscience, which the practical unbelief of it had made possible. It seemed to us then, judging from these facts, that we do not merely strip Luther of his dress, but that we destroy the man himself when we make him the witness for a principle and not for a fact, that we do not preserve that quality in him which enabled him to be a reformer, and deprive him of that which belonged to him in common with those whom he reformed, but that we take from him that wherein his reforming power consisted, and leave ourselves to the certain peril, if all history be not a delusion, of falling under those sensible tyrannies from which he was permitted to emancipate us. And if I be asked again in this case, what then is my objection to the Lutheran system, I answer this and no other -- that it does not bear witness for the all-importance of that fact which Luther asserted to be all-important; that it teaches us to believe in justification by faith instead of to believe in a Justifier; that it substitutes for Christ a certain notion or scheme of Christianity.

Quakerism and pure Protestantism both belong chiefly, if not entirely, to the region of individual life and experience. Unitarianism we found was of an altogether different character; it took men away from self-reflection to thoughts about nature and God. Nevertheless, it has changed its complexion as men's views about themselves have changed; it applied material standards to the Infinite, so long as it was the habit of the time to consider men as purely material; when that habit ceased, it began to decry the ordinary theological language as too earthly and definite. Here then perhaps we have discovered a system which answered exactly to the philosophers' demand, which readily abandons the dress of one period that it may clothe itself in that of another. But will it be said that this is merely a change of dress? Can those who just now represented the acknowledgment of man's spiritual powers as the very essence of all religion, so entirely alter their note that they look upon it too merely as an accident? According to their shewing Unitarianism has not preserved its identity at all; the alteration of popular opinion has abolished its very nature and substance. But it seemed to us that this was not the case; that it had a principle, that it did contain something which is constantly and invariably true. The hold which it had maintained for a time over earnest minds arose, we thought, from this, that it declared the unity of God, the absolute love of God, the existence of a good and pure state for mankind, to be primary truths which cannot be altered or set aside by any experiences or any dogmas. These were eternal principles not subject to the mutations of costume or fashion; needful for man, needful for him at all times. And the objection which we made to the Unitarian system was, that it did so feebly and miserably represent these truths -- nay, that it practically contradicted them as no other system ever did; a charge which applies to the modern scheme no less than to the old one on grounds even more forcible; for whereas the whole virtue of Unitarianism consisted in its asserting the existence of God as distinct from the thoughts and apprehensions of men, the later teachers are continually approaching nearer and nearer to a confusion between our own spiritual "nature" and the Being whom it acknowledges. The transition from this stage of belief to the worship of the separate feelings and moods of that "spiritual nature," and thence to prostration before them in the shape of idols is very rapid indeed. Surely a strange apotheosis for Unitarianism!

I contend then that the principles of Fox, of Luther, of the Unitarians, are too strong, too vital, to bear the imprisonment to which they have been subjected in the different systems which have been invented for them; but so far from thinking that those principles will be more true and vital when they have lost their religious and personal character, and have been translated into the terms of a philosophical theory, I believe that when they shall suffer that change they will lose all their preciousness, and will attain the perfection of the impotence and insignificance to which hitherto they have been but partially reduced.

II. Seeing, however, that these principles, even in the time of their strength, have shewn a disposition to clothe themselves in some form or other, nay, that it is only in times of great weakness that they can be content to remain merely as notions or opinions for individual minds; we are bound to inquire further what this tendency means, and how it is possible that it may be satisfied when the systems which have owed their existence to it shall satisfy it no longer. To answer this question we must refer to another class of facts which we have been considering. The second distinguishing Quaker tenet was, that there is a spiritual and universal kingdom established in the world. We may conceive, though not without great difficulty, how the doctrine respecting the Indwelling Word might have been received and acknowledged as a doctrine and as nothing more -- at all events might have appeared to Quakers only as the governing law of their own individual lives. But it is obvious that this tenet ceases to be one at all if it is nothing more -- ceases to be a principle for individuals if it be only for them. That there should be such a kingdom, and that an honest man believing it to be should not ask, What are the conditions of citizenship in it? is incredible. To this conviction then we traced the origin of the Quaker society and the Quaker system: by entering the first, disciples of George Fox sought for themselves a place in this kingdom; by adopting the second, they interpreted to themselves and others its nature and its laws. And therefore our main inquiry in reference to the society was, Does it answer to this character? Does it even any longer profess to answer to it? and with respect to the system -- what is there here which may tell us the secret of the failure to which the history of the body bears such a striking witness? I will not now dwell on the answer to this question, farther than to remark that we observed a resolute eschewing of forms to be one of the main characteristics of the Quaker system, and a disposition to formalism one of the most striking characteristics of the Quaker body. But my object at present is rather to remark upon the faith which seemed to make the existence of Quakerism necessary, than upon any of its good or evil features.

Was this faith a new one? was George Fox the first proclaimer of it? We found the acknowledgment of a spiritual kingdom among the Reformers as well as among the Quakers -- a most strong and distinct acknowledgment of it. We found it working so strongly in Luther's mind, connecting itself so closely with his recognition of a divine Person, a divine Man, as the object of all trust and allegiance, as to make him most reluctant to introduce any theory or scheme of doctrine which might eventually become a substitute for it: we found at the same time that it at last urged him and the other Reformers to set up little Churches or kingdoms of their own because they could not imagine or discover how otherwise God's purpose could be accomplished. And we found that it was partly the unspiritual character of these bodies -- their manifest inadequacy to express the idea of Christ's spiritual kingdom, partly the importance which the Reformers and their followers attached to national societies and the confusion that seemed to have arisen between them and the universal body, which led to Fox's protest in the subsequent age.

But though this idea of a spiritual and universal kingdom was not new in the seventeenth century, may it not have become obsolete in the nineteenth? The history of Unitarianism was an important link in the evidence on this subject. We found that in the last century the idea of a spiritual kingdom was distinctly and formally repudiated by those who were most admired for wisdom and enlightenment; man at all events being excluded from any concern in such a kingdom, seeing that he had no faculties wherewith he could take cognizance of it. At the same time the idea of a very comprehensive world, which should include all nations, systems, religions, began at that time to be prevalent, and to be produced in opposition to the different sects of Christendom. Here, then, was one half of the belief which had belonged to other ages, that half which had been apparently least regarded by Protestants -- trying in the eighteenth century to assert itself under new conditions and to the exclusion of the other half. But if the Roman Empire, from Augustus to Diocletian, had not been the sufficient type of this all tolerant all including world, the French Empire which succeeded to and carried out the speculations of the last generation was a fair specimen of what it must be. While this Empire was diffusing philanthropy through Europe, we noticed in different directions the gradual re-appearance of that other element in the idea of a kingdom for mankind, which this philanthropy had cast aside as unnecessary. First, we observed a religious awakening -- men becoming strongly convinced that there is a spiritual power and influence at work among them. The immediate result of this awakening was a greater value for personal religion; then it led to a desire among those who had felt it for combination and fellowship in the promotion of spiritual objects; finally, to the inquiry whether such a combination must not have a spiritual foundation, whether it must not be connected with belief and worship. Then we were struck by various indications among philosophical men of a new habit of thinking in reference to the constitution of our race, of a tendency to

69

look upon man as essentially a spiritual creature, and therefore to conclude that his highest and most important acts and exercises must be of a spiritual kind. Along with this faith, we noticed the growth of another, that there must be a region for those acts and exercises; that they cannot merely turn in upon themselves, though that may be part of their occupation, but that there must be a world adapted to them and formed for them. We could not find any clear account of this world except that it was this universe which surrounds us, and of which our eyes and ears take account; but though this universe be proclaimed as the great possession and inheritance of mankind, we could not learn that more than a few gifted poets and sages had a right of admission to its meanings and mysteries. Another difficulty which these philosophers seemed to experience, arose from the question, whether a distinct spiritual world do exist at all, or whether it be only created out of this common world, by the class which is endued with faculties for that purpose. But this point was peremptorily decided by another set of deep and earnest thinkers, who seemed to have proved the existence of something which man did not create himself, but to which he must in some sort refer all his acts and thoughts, and which must be assumed as the ground of them.

Meanwhile we found the most eager and passionate demands for a universal constitution into which men as men might enter, occupying not religious, not philosophical men, but labourers, handicraftsmen, serfs. The nature of this constitution had been discussed again and again; and the settlement of it had not been left to mere discussions; it had been brought to the most severe practical tests. These inferences seemed to follow from them all: first, that every modern attempt to construct a universal society had been defeated by the determination of men to assert their own wills; secondly, that the true universal society must be one which neither overlooks the existence of those wills, nor considers them as an inconvenient and accidental interruption to its workings, as a friction to be regretted and allowed for, but which assumes them as the very principle and explanation of its existence; thirdly, that it is equally impossible from men to be content with a spiritual society which is not universal, and with a universal society which is not spiritual. This doctrine then, I think, cannot be said to be obsolete, cannot be turned into a mere philosophical notion. Time has added to its strength, not diminished it; there is more necessity now than in any former day, that it should have a practical not a theoretical satisfaction.

III. It would seem from these observations, that the spiritual and universal society must be involved in the very idea of our human constitution, say rather, must be that constitution, by virtue of which we realise that there is a humanity, that we form a kind. 'But supposing this to be the case, may not we suppose that this constitution has been gradually making itself known to men as civilisation has advanced; and that when it has been diffused more widely, each man will feel and understand his place in it -- rightly and harmoniously exercising those

70

spiritual powers which fit him for living in it, and suffering his neighbour without molestation, nay, kindly assisting him to exercise his; that in this way, those strifes and oppositions of opinion which have hindered men from cheerfully co-operating with each other, will gradually cease, and peace and good will become general; and may not one means to this end be the abandonment of those notions which prevailed in the early ages of the world, and which have been kept alive by the different religious sects and systems since -- that the character of this constitution has been revealed to us in an inspired Book; and that it is ruled over in some incredible manner, by a divine Person?" This is the last hint I shall consider. It leads us to notice another class of facts which have passed under our review.

The Quakers, we found, were great disparagers of what they called the outward letter. They were jealous lest reverence for the Bible should interfere with the belief of a Spiritual Invisible Teacher. Nevertheless, it was in the Bible that George Fox learnt clearly the fact that there was such a Teacher; it was from the Bible that he preached of it to others. It was not merely the principle of Justification by Faith which Luther, torn by inward conflicts, learnt from the Bible -- he owed to it still more, the personal form of that doctrine, and the conception of it as a vital truth, not as a scholastic dogma. The belief of Election in its highest, purest form, was received by Calvin from the same source; the Unitarian prized the Bible as the great witness for the Divine Unity, for God's absolute and universal love, for the fact that mankind is under some better condition than that of a curse. Thus, whenever there has been in any man any one of these strong convictions, which seemed to us so precious and important, then he has looked with reverence upon the Scriptures, as the teachers of it and the authority for it; whenever he has been able to carry home that conviction to the minds of his brethren, these have been his instruments. And this fact comes out the more remarkably, when it is set by the side of another, which the study of the different religious systems made known to us -- namely, that just in proportion as any of them has become consolidated, the Bible, even if it has been nominally and formally held up to admiration, nay even to worship, has been deposed from its real dignity. The Quaker, who converts it into a system of conceits and allegories, under pretence of doing reverence to the Spirit, has not really treated it worse than the Lutheran, or the Calvinist, who cuts it up into texts for the confirmation of dogmas, or the mottos of sermons, or than the Unitarian, who would reduce it into a collection of moral maxims. So that, instead of being obliged by our belief of the instability and helplessness of these systems, to suspect the value or underrate the authority of the book to which they all appeal; may we not say boldly, that as it was this book which revealed to each founder of a sect that side or aspect of the spiritual economy which it was his especial vocation to present and elucidate, so it has been a perpetual and most embarrassing witness against the effort to compress that economy within the rules and formulas, which he and his followers have devised for the statement of their opinions?

71

But this is not enough. It is alleged, that whatever may have been the case with religious bodies, the greatest light has, of late especially, been thrown upon the nature of our spiritual constitution, by those who did not derive their knowledge from the Scriptures; nay, who had great doubts about their value and authenticity.

Now, I have not affected to disparage the labours of philosophers, either in these or in past days. I have expressed the highest respect for those who have brought to light what seem to me precious truths respecting certain faculties in us, which have been supposed to have no existence. But I have also intimated an opinion, which I am most anxious should be sifted, and if it be false, exposed, that this is precisely the limit of their doings. They have proved that we have certain faculties which do take cognizance of spiritual transcendental objects: they have not shewn what these spiritual transcendental objects are; they have shewn that we must have a spiritual constitution: they have not shewn what that spiritual constitution is. I do not therefore deny that we have learnt what our forefathers did not know, or did not know nearly as well. I do not deny that it has been the effect of experiments, failures, contradictions, to make us better acquainted with what we are and what we want. I am very thankful, for the sake of mankind, that there have been men who were permitted to make these discoveries, without (obviously, and so far as we know, I mean) seeing the truths which I think answer to them, and which shew that Tantalus is not the one type of humanity. But so far from being led by anything that I see or hear of these writers, to believe that they have discovered any substitute for a Revelation of that which is needful for man's highest necessities, I am well convinced that their teachings honestly received will make his cries for one more passionate; and that it will be seen at last, that the book which has always hitherto met the cravings of its readers, and given them that glimpse of the mysterious world which they required, does contain the full declaration of that state which God has established for us, and which we have been toiling all our lives to find.

The second part of the question is very much involved with the first, and for our purpose is perhaps the most important. 'Is not the idea of a spiritual King, an actual Person, superintending and ordaining the movements of the universal and spiritual society, the dream of a past age? Is it not one which a sensible man, who was also an honest one, and used words in their simple straightforward sense, would be rather reluctant than anxious to bring forward? Is it not obvious, that every step in the progress of thought and discovery has taken us further from such a notion as this, and has bequeathed it, as their proper possession, to old wives and children?' I have perhaps implicitly treated this point already; still, I am so anxious to give it a direct consideration, that I will, at any hazard of repetition and tediousness, recur to my former method of proof.

A belief in a direct spiritual government over the life, thoughts, acts, and words, of those who would submit themselves to it, was, we have seen the third distinguishing peculiarity of Quakerism; the one which produced so many more outward and apparent results than the other two, that in the notions of modern friends it has absorbed them both into itself. The system of the society appears to be expressly devised for the purpose of giving expression to this belief. Did it then seem to us that this system was falling into decay, because it had borne too decisive and consistent a witness to this bygone notion, or had prevented it from undergoing those changes to which, with the increase of light and civilisation, it ought to have been subject? On the contrary, the essential feebleness of Quakerism appeared to lie in this -- that it exhibited the doctrine of spiritual superintendence in an inadequate, inconsistent, and shrivelled form. It testified that sudden thoughts, sudden acts, sudden speeches, oftentimes of the most obviously trifling character, had their origin in divine teaching and inspiration; it virtually excluded what is the most significant, and what Quakers, like all other persons, are obliged to acknowledge as the most significant portion of our life -- that which is occupied with calm, orderly, continuous transactions -- from the spiritual sphere. Education, we saw that the Quakers looked upon as most important; education according to the system of the society could not be a spiritual work.

If we turned from Quakerism to that which is most unlike it, to Calvinism, the same inference was forced upon us in another form. A belief in the will of God as the only spring of Good, Order, Happiness, was, we found, the earnest practical life-giving principle in the minds of Calvin and his disciples; whatever brave acts they had done, whatever good thoughts they had uttered, sprang from this conviction. Had they pushed it too far; had their system riveted the notion of a ruling Will in their minds, and so perpetuated it to an age, when, in the natural course of things, it ought to have been abandoned? We were led to adopt exactly the opposite opinion. Their system, by setting aside the idea of a human will, had left the doctrine of a Divine will barren and unmeaning; the idea of a personal Ruler had disappeared, and those who were most anxious to assert the government of the living God, had been the great instruments of propagating the notion of an atheistical Necessity.

But it may be said, 'Though these Quaker and these Calvinistical opinions, concerning the Spirit which works in man, and the absolute Will of God, may involve or be involved in that idea of an actual King of men to which we are alluding, they are not identical with it. That idea evidently turns upon the doctrine of an Incarnation; it asserts that one who is the Son of Man, as well as the Son of God, is the Lord of the world, and, in some higher sense, of the spiritual Society; and it is this doctrine which seems so connected with the oldest fables of the world, that we cannot but think it must give way before the light of truth.' So the Unitarian of the last century thought, and the question we discussed was -- How did this opinion, which was the root of their system, affect these principles which really formed the faith of the better men among them?

It seemed to us, that the idea of the unity of God was sacrificed, because the person who was acknowledged as the great object and centre of human admiration, was denied to be one with the Father; that the idea of the love of God was sacrificed, because it was denied that He had in His own Person interfered on behalf of His creatures; that the idea of our being children of God was sacrificed, because there was nothing to give the name of Father reality, to shew that it was more than a loose and almost blasphemous figure of speech.

Accordingly, in the new Unitarianism, Jesus of Nazareth is beginning to be recognized as merely one of the world's heroes; he may or may not be the most important and conspicuous one. But this belief, this last and highest discovery of the nineteenth century takes us back to that stage of history, in which universal fellowship was impossible; to the time when there was a Grecian Hercules and an Egyptian Hercules; when he who repealed bad laws was the hero of a country, and he who drained a marsh of a neighbourhood; and when men were crying and sighing for someone who should be the head and prince of all these; who should be indeed the Lord of their race; who should rescue the race from the evils to which, as a race, it was subject; who should connect it with the absolute Being of whom their consciences witnessed. Is not this a strange and melancholy relapse under the name of progression!

We have then a reasonable excuse for inquiring, whether there be on this earth a spiritual and universal kingdom, which the different religious systems have not been able to supersede or destroy; which is likely to make itself manifest when they have all perished; and with which we of the nineteenth century may have fellowship.

And as a preface to this inquiry, it seems not unfitting to consider whether there be any traces of a spiritual constitution in the early ages of the world, and whether the books of Scripture afford us any help in interpreting them.

CHAPTER II

INDICATIONS OF A SPIRITUAL CONSTITUTION

When I was speaking of the Quaker system, I noticed one practical inconsistency which seemed to lie at the root of it, and to affect all its workings. The member of the Society of Friends ought to be the conscious disciple of a Divine Teacher. But every child born to a Quaker is actually considered and treated as a Friend till, by some act of rebellion, he has deprived himself of the title. Something of the same anomaly we have traced in the Protestant systems. Consciusly justified men ought to constitute the Evangelical Church; persons conscious of a divine Election the Reformed: yet neither of these have had the courage to exclude their children from all religious fellowship, to treat them absolutely as heathens. The Anabaptists have made the nearest approach to that practice; but even in them there are very evident indications of timidity and inconsistency.

When we examined the schemes of the world which had been constructed by philosophers, we observed that they had been encountered by a knot, not unlike that which had perplexed the authors of religious sects, and that they had found themselves compelled with more or less of ceremony to cut it. It was next to impossible to organise a universal society, while the distinction of families prevailed. In such a society men must be so many separate units. But there is this glaring fact of family life to prove that they are not units; that they are bound together by a certain law, which may be set at naught, and made almost utterly inefficient, but which cannot be entirely repealed.

I. Now this fact, that men exist in families, which seems so grievously to disturb the inventors of systems, is perhaps the very one which would be most likely to suggest the thought to a plain person, that there must be a moral or spiritual constitution for mankind. We are obliged to speak of every man as being in two conditions. He is in a world of objects which offer themselves to his senses, and which his senses may be fitted to entertain. He is a son, perhaps he is a brother. These two states are equally inevitable; they are also perfectly distinct. You cannot by any artifice reduce them under the same law or name. To describe the one you must speak of what we see, or hear, or handle or smell; to describe the other, you must speak of what we are; "I am a son," "I am a brother." It is impossible therefore to use the word "circumstances" in reference to the one state with the same strictness with which you apply it to the other. All the things which I have to do with, I naturally and rightly call my circumstances -- they stand round me: but that which is necessary in an account of myself, seems to be entitled to another name. We commonly call it a relationship. And this difference soon becomes more conspicuous. We speak of a man having a bad digestion or a bad hearing; we speak of his being a bad brother or a bad son. By both these phrases we imply that there is want of harmony

75

between the man and his condition. But by the one we evidently wish to signify that there need not be this want of harmony, that he is voluntarily acting as if he were not in a relation in which nevertheless he is, and must remain. This inconsistency we describe by the term moral evil, or whatever equivalent phrase we may have invented; for some equivalent, whether we like it or not, we must have.

It might seem to follow from these observations, that the family state is the natural one for man; and accordingly we speak of the affections which correspond to this state, as especially natural affections. But it should be remembered that we use another phrase which is apparently inconsistent with this; we describe the savage condition, that is to say, the one in which man is striving to be independent, as the natural state of society. And though it may be doubtful whether that should be called a state of society, which is the contradiction of all states and of all society, yet there seems a very considerable justification for the application of the word natural to it: seeing that we cannot be acquainted with a family, or be members of a family, without knowing in others, without feeling in ourselves, certain inclinations which tend to the dissolution of its bonds, and to the setting up of that separate independent life, which when exhibited on a large scale we name the savage or wild life. These inclinations are kept down by discipline, and the affections which attract us to the members of our family are called out in opposition to them; surely, therefore, it cannot be a mistake to describe them by the name which we ordinarily apply to plants that spring up in a soil, uncultivated and uncalled for.

We have here some of the indications of a spiritual constitution; that is to say, we have the marks of a state which is designed for a voluntary creature; which is his, whether he approve it or no; against which, he has a nature or inclination to rebel. But still, most persons would mean something more by the phrase than this; they would ask how you could call that spiritual, which had no reference to religion. Now the histories and mythologies of all the people with whom we are acquainted bear unequivocal witness to this fact, that men have connected the ideas of fathers, children, husbands, brothers, sisters, with the beings whom they worshipped. This is the first, rudest observation which we make upon them. But, when we search further, we begin to see that this simple observation has the most intimate connexion with the whole of mythology; that it is not merely a fact in reference to it, but the fact, without which all others which encounter us are unintelligible. You say all kinds of offices are attributed to the gods and goddesses; they rule over this town and that river, they dispense this blessing or send that curse. Be it so; but who are they who exercise these powers? The mythology tells you of relations existing between them; also of relations between them and the objects of their bounty and their enmity. In later ages, when we are studying the differences in the mythology of different nations, it is no wonder that we should notice the character of the soil, the nature of the climate, the beauty or the dreariness of the country, the rains or the inundations which watered it, as circumstances helping to determine the views which the inhabitants entertained of their unseen rulers. And then the transition is very easy to the belief, that by these observations we have accounted for their faith, and that the histories of the gods are merely accidental poetical embellishments. But, if we consider that the worshippers evidently felt that which we call accidental to be essential; that the merging the gods in the objects with which they were connected was merely an artifice of later philosophy; that the circumstances of soil and climate did indeed occasion some important differences between the objects reverenced in various nations, but that the circumstance of their being parents, brothers, and sisters, so far as we know, was common to all, or only wanting in those which were utterly savage, that is, in which the human relations were disregarded; if we observe that those who endeavour to explain mythology by the phenomena of the world, are obliged to beg what they call 'a law of nature,' alleging that we are naturally inclined to inquire into the origin of any great and remarkable objects which we see; if we will notice how utterly inconsistent it is with all experience and observation to attribute such a disposition as this to men whose feelings and faculties have not been by some means previously awakened, how very little a savage is struck by any except the most glaring and alarming phenomena, and how much less he thinks about them: if we will reflect upon these points, we may perhaps be led to adopt the opinion that the simplest method of solving the difficulty is the best; that it is not our being surrounded with a strange world of sensible objects which leads us to think of objects with which we do not sensibly converse, but that these perceptions come to us through our family relationships; that we become more and more merely idolaters when these relationships are lost sight of, and the other facts of our condition only regarded; that a world without family relationships would have no worship, and on the other hand, that without worship all the feelings and affections of family life would have utterly perished.

II. But is there no meaning in that savage wish for independence? Is it merely the dissolution and destruction of those family bonds which are meant for men, or is it the indication that men were meant for other bonds than these, not perhaps of necessity incompatible with them? History seems to decide the question in favour of the latter opinion. It seems to say, that as there is a worse state of society than the patriarchal, there is also a better and more advanced one; it declares that the faculties which are given to man never have had their proper development and expansion, except in a national community. Now if we examine any such community, taking our specimen from the Pagan world, we shall perceive that the member of it had a more distinct feeling of himself, of his own personality, than the mere dweller in a family could have. It may seem to us very puzzling that it should be so; for if we look at Sparta or Rome -- at any commonwealth except Athens -- it seems as if the society were imposing the severest restraints upon each man's own taste, judgment, and will.   Nevertheless, it is the manifestation of energetic purpose in particular leaders, and the assurance we feel that there was the same kind of purpose, though in a less degree, existing in those who composed every rank of their armies, which gives the interest to the better times of these republics; as it is the feeling of a change in this respect -- of the armies having become a body of soldiers merely, not of men, which makes the declining ages of them so mournful. We have evidence, therefore, coming in a way in which it might least be expected, that this personal feeling is connected with the sense of national union.

Of all men the savage has least of the feelings of dignity and personal self-respect; he is most emphatically a mere workman or tool, the habitual slave of his own chance necessities and inclinations, and therefore commonly of other men's also. He who understands the force of the words, 'I am a brother,' has taken a mighty step in advance of this individual man, even in that respect on which he most prides himself; he is more of a person, more of a freeman. But he is not enough of a person, not enough of a freeman. If he will be more, he must be able to say, "I am a citizen;" this is the true onward step; if he aim at freedom by any other, he relapses into an independence which is only another name for slavery. Now, we may observe several facts, too obvious to escape the most careless student of history, except it should be from their very obviousness, which are closely connected with this. One is, that in every organised nation at its commencement, there is a high respect for family relations, that they embody themselves necessarily in the national constitution; another is, that there is a struggle between these relations and the national polity, although they form so great an element in it; the legislator feeling that each brother, husband, father, is a citizen, and that as such, he comes directly under his cognizance.

In Sparta, we see the principle of family life, though distinctly recognized, sacrificed in a great degree to the Laws. In Athens, we see the legislator, in his anxiety to leave men to themselves, allowing the growth of an independence which proved incompatible both with family relations and with national society. In Rome, we see the legislation so exquisitely interwoven with the family principle, that so soon as that became weak, the commonwealth inevitably fell.

These facts lead us to ask what this legislation means, wherein its power lies, and in what way it comes to be so connected with, and yet diverse from, these relationships? In trying to find the answer to this question we are at once struck with this observation -- Law takes each man apart from his fellows; it addresses him with a Thou; it makes him feel that there is an eye fixed upon his doings; that there is a penalty overhanging him. It is therefore, in this point of view, the direct opposite of a relationship by which we are bound to each other, and are made to feel that we cannot exist apart from each other. But, again, we find that the Law denounces those acts which make union and fellowship impossible, those acts which result from the determination of men to live and act as if they were indepencent of each other, as if they might set up themselves and make self-pleasing their end. The Law declares to each man that he is in a fellowship, that he shall not do any act which is inconsistent with that position. That therefore which is the great foe to family relationship, the desire for individuality, is the very thing which Law, even while it deals with men as distinct persons, is threatening and cursing. A nation then, like a family, would seem to possess some of the characteristics of a spiritual constitution. If we take the word spiritual in that sense in which it is used by modern philosophers, we have abundant proofs that where·there is no feeling of national union, there is a most precarious and imperfect exercise of intellectual power. If we take it in the sense of voluntary we find here a constitution evidently meant for creatures which have wills; seeing that it is one which men do not create for themselves, that is one which may be violated, nay, which there is a natural inclination in every man to violate; and that by the words "bad citizen," we express moral reprobation, just as we do when we speak of a bad father of mother. And if we ask whether there are any religious feelings connected with national life, as we found there were with family life, the mythology of the old world is just as decisive in its reply. If the Homeric gods were fathers, brothers, husbands, they were also kings; one character is just as prominent, just as essential as the other. It is possible that the former may have been the most ancient, and this would explain the notion of scholars that traces of an earlier worship are discoverable in the Iliad. In Homer's time the two characters, the domestic and the kingly, were incorporated, and the offices of the gods as connected with nature, though they might be gradually mingling themselves with these characters, and threatening to become identical with them, are nevertheless distinct from them. The princes of Agamemnon's league felt that there must be higher princes than they; they could use no authority, take no counsel, except in that belief. And though they spoke of these rulers as compelling the clouds and winds, they did not look upon this exercise of power as higher or more real, than that of putting wisdom and spirit into Diomed, and arming Hector for the fight. And hence the leaders were always types of the gods in every country which had attained the forms of a national polity. Wherever these existed, invisible rulers were recognized; a class of men interpreted the meaning of their judgments; they were invoked as the guides in battles; sacrifices were offered to avert their displeasure or to claim their protection.

But a time came, when thoughts were awakened in men's minds of something more comprehensive than either this family or this national constitution. The former belonged to all men; yet in another respect it was narrow, separating men from each other. The latter was obviously exclusive; a nation was limited to a small locality; it actually treated all that lay beyond it, and whom it could not subdue to itself, as aliens, if not enemies. If this exclusion were to continue, there was certainly some nation which ought to reign, which had a right to make its polity universal. Great Asiatic monarchies there had been, which had swallowed all tribes and kingdoms into themselves, but these had established a rule of mere physical force.

Might not Greece, the land of intellectual force, shew that it was meant to rule over all? The young hero of Macedon went forth in this hope, and in a few years accomplished his dream. In a few more his empire was broken in pieces; Greece was not to be the lord of the world: still in the Egyptian and Syrian dynasties which she sent forth she asserted a mental supremacy. But a nation which paid no homage to art or to philosophy swallowed up all these dynasties, and with them all that remained of Greece herself. A universal polity was established in the world, and the national life, the family life, of Rome, perished at the very moment in which she established it.

Was there a religion connected with this universal polity as there was with the family and the national? We find that there was. The Emperor was the great God. To him all people and nations and languages were to bow. Subject to this supreme divinity all others might be tolerated and recognized. No form of religion was to be proscribed unless it were absolutely incompatible with the worship of a Tiberius and a Vitellius. It has been suggested already, that this Roman Empire answers exactly to the idea of a universal world. If there is to be anything different from this, if there is to be a universal Church, we ought to know of what elements it is to be composed, we ought to know whether it also sets aside family or national life, or whether it justifies their existence, reconciles them to itself, and interprets the problems of ancient history concerning their mysterious meaning.

80

CHAPTER III

THE SCRIPTURAL VIEW OF THIS CONSTITUTION

It is commonly acknowledged by religious persons, that the Bible is remarkably unsystematic. Sometimes this admission is made thankfully and even triumphantly; it is urged as a proof that the Bible is mainly intended to supply the daily wants, and to meet the ever-changing circumstances of the spiritual man. Sometimes it furnishes the ground of an argument for the necessity of that being done by others which is not done here; by those who lived nearest the age of the Apostles, or at the Reformation, or in a more advanced period of civilisation. Sometimes it is alleged as a reason for denying that there is any book possessing the character which Christians have attributed to this one; for asserting that it is a collection of documents belonging to a particular nation, accidentally strung together, and invested by the superstition of after-times with a fictitious entireness.

All these notions, it seems to me, assume that the words system and method are synonymous, and that if the first is wanting in the Scriptures the last must be wanting also. Now to me these words seem not only not synonymous, but the greatest contraries imaginable: the one indicating that which is most opposed to life, freedom, variety; and the other that without which they cannot exist. If I wished to explain my meaning, I should not resort to a definition; I should take an illustration, and, of all illustrations, I think the most striking is that which is afforded by the Bible itself. While the systematiser is tormented every page he reads with a sense of the refractory and hopeless materials he has to deal with, I am convinced that the person who is determined to read only for his own comfort and profit is haunted with the sense of some harmony, not in the words but in the history, which he ought not to overlook, and without reference to which the meaning of that in which he most delights is not very certain. And, while this sense of a method exists, the fact that these works were written at different periods, in different styles, and by men of totally different characters, increases the impression that there is something most marvellous in the volume they compose. The most skilful and laborious analyst cannot persuade his disciples to abandon the use of the word Bible, he cannot divest himself of the feelings with which it is associated.

I. Perhaps it may be useful for the purpose at which we are aiming, that we should examine a little into this phenomenon. Everyone who reads the Old Testament must perceive that the idea of a covenant of God with a certain people is that which presides in it. In plain history, in lofty prayers and songs, in impassioned denunciations of existing evil, and predictions of coming misery, this idea is still at the root of all others. Take it away, and not merely is there no connexion between the different parts, but each book by itself, however simple in its language or in its details, becomes an incoherent rhapsody. A person, then, who had no higher wish than to understand the character and feelings of that strange people which has preserved its identity through so many generations, would of course begin with examining into the account of this covenant. He would feel that the call of Abraham, the promise made to him and to his seed, and the seal of it which was given him, were the most significant parts of this record. But one thought would strike him above all: This covenant is said to be with a family; with a man doubtless in the first instance, but with a man expressly and emphatically as the head of a family. The very terms of the covenant, and every promise that it held forth, were inseparably associated with the hope of a posterity. It is impossible to look upon the patriarchal character of Abraham as something accidental to his character as the chosen witness and servant of the Most High. These two positions are absolutely inseparable. The fact of his relationship to God is interpreted to him by the feeling of his human relations, and his capacity of fulfilling them arose from his acknowledgment of the higher relation. A little further reflection upon the subordinate parts of the narrative (which, when this fact is felt to be the centre, will all acquire a new value and meaning) must convince us, that sensuality, attended of necessity with sensual worship, was the character of the tribes among which Abraham was dwelling; that in this sensuality and sensual worship was involved the neglect of family bonds; that the witness for an invisible and righteous God, against gods of nature and mere power, was, at the self-same moment and by the same necessity, the witness for the sacredness of these bonds. The notion of a Being exercising power over men, seen in the clouds, and heard in the winds, this was that which the world entertained, and trembled, till utter corruption brought in utter atheism. That there is a God related to men and made known to men through their human relations, this was the faith of Abraham, the beginner of the Church on earth. But this truth could not be exhibited in one individual faithful man; it must be exhibited through a family. The rest of Genesis, therefore, gives us the history of the patriarchs who followed Abraham. But what if these, or any of these, should not be faithful? What if they should not maintain the principle of family relationship, or retain a recollection of the higher principle involved in it? What if the world should find its way into the Church? The historian does not wait for the question to be asked him; his narrative answers it. The great majority of the sons of Jacob were not faithful men, they did not maintain the principle of family life, they did not recollect the Being who had revealed Himself through it. Perhaps then, the Joseph, the true believer, separated himself from his godless brethren, and established a new and distinct fellowship. Had he done so he would have acted upon the principle of Ishmael or Esau; he would nave founded a society which was built upon choice, not upon relationship. The historian declares, that he followed a different course, that he was indeed separated from his brethren, but by their act, not his: that he continued a witness for God's covenant, not with him, but with Abraham, Isaac, and Jacob; not with an individual, but with a family. According then to the Jewish Scriptures, the Abrahamic family, though cut off by their covenant from the other families of the earth, was so cut off expressly that it might bear witness for the true order of the world; for that order against which all sensible idolatry, and all independent choice or self-will, is rebellion; for that order in which alone men can be free, because to abide in it they must sacrifice those inclinations which make them slaves; for that order, in and through which, as we might have guessed from the Gentile records, the idea of God can alone be imparted. The promise of the covenant therefore was, that in the seed of Abraham all the families of the earth should be blessed.

II. But, whatever sentimentalists may say about the patriarchal condition of the world, its essential purity, and the misery of departing from it, the Scriptures give no countenance to such dreams. It was part of the promise that the children of Jacob should enter into another state. They were to possess the Canaanitish nations. They were to become a nation. And although the history, in strict conformity to all experience, describes the middle passage between these two conditions as a grievous one, though the children of Abraham are said to have sunk into moral debasement and actual slavery, yet their redemption is connected with a more awful revelation than any which had been imparted, or, as far as we can see, could have been imparted, to them in their previous state; and leads to new and most wonderful discoveries respecting the relations between men and God. The God of Abraham and Isaac and Jacob declares that He remembers His covenant, and has seen the affliction of His people. But He declares Himself to the appointed guide and deliverer by another name than this -- that name upon which the Jewish covenant stands, which is the foundation of all law, I AM THAT I AM. And as soon as the judgments upon natural worship, and upon a tyranny which set at naught all invisible and righteous government, had been accomplished, and the people had been taught to feel that an unseen Power had delivered them, that awful code was proclaimed amidst thunders and lightnings, which spoke straight to the individual conscience of each man, even while it reminded him in the most direct and solemn manner that he was related to God and his brethren. I will not enter here into an explanation of the manner in which the tribe institutions,those which speak of family relationship, were so embodied in the Jewish constitution that they gave a meaning to this law and yet did not deprive it of its awful personal character. That observation must needs strike everyone who studies with the slightest attention the Jewish institutions, as they are described in the Pentateuch. It is more necessary to notice those which led the thoughts of the Jews above the bonds of family and of law, though they were inseparably intertwined with both; I mean the tabernacle, the priesthood, and sacrifices. That these were the shrines of an undeveloped mystery every thoughtful Jew was conscious; but he was equally certain that this mystery was implied in all his acts, in all his family relations, in the national order, in his legal obedience. That there was an awful self-existent Being from whom all law came, was declared by the commandments: the Tabernacle affirmed that this Being was present among His people, and that it was possible in some awful manner to approach Him. The family covenant bore witness that there was a relation between Him and His worshippers; the Priesthood from generation to generation witnessed that this relation might be actually realised, that it might be realised by the whole people, in a representative. The National Constitution and punishments awakened in each person the feeling of moral evil, and taught them that that evil arose from violating his relations with God and his countrymen, and that the effect of it was a practical exclusion from these blessings; the sacrifices intimated that the relation was restored, when he had personally, and through the priest, given up something, not selected by himself as the most appropriate, or the most precious, but appointed by the law; and when he had given up that self-will which caused the separation. Such thoughts were wrought gradually into the mind of every humble and obedient Jew; they were brought directly home to him by the parting instruction of his great Lawgiver; they were confirmed and illustrated by all his subsequent experience, and by the teachers who shewed him the purpose of it.

The national polity of the Jews was in its essence exclusive. We dwell upon this fact, as if it destroyed all connexion between this polity and that of the Pagans, or of modern Europe. But every nation, as such, is exclusive. Athens was exclusive, Rome was exclusive; nevertheless, we have admitted, all persons admit, that more of humanity came out in the exclusive nations of Athens and of Rome, than ever shewed itself in the savage tribes of the earth, which have never attained to a definite polity. Before we can ascertain whether the exclusiveness of the Jews was an inhuman exclusiveness, we must find out what it excluded; and here the same answer must be given as before. It excluded the worship of sensible, natural things; it excluded the idea of choice and self-will. The covenant with an invisible Being made it treason for men to choose the objects of their worship. This worship of the one Being was the bond of the commonwealt, and, if this were broken, it was dissolved. The covenant with an invisible Being obliged them to look upon all kings as reigning in virtue of His covenant, as representing His dignity, as responsible to Him; upon all other officers, the priestly, the prophetical, the judicial, as in like manner directly receiving their appointments and commissions from Him. By its first protest it affirmed that there are not a set of separate gods over each territory, various according to the peculiarities of soil and of climate; but that there is one Almighty and Invisible Being, who is the Lord of all. The God of Israel is declared to be the God of all the nations of the earth; the Israelites are chosen out to be witnesses of the fact. By the second protest the exclusive Hebrew witnessed, that no king, no priest, no judge, has a right to look upon himself as possessing intrinsic power; that he is exercising office, under a righteous king, a perfect priest, an all-seeing judge; that, in proportion as he preserves that thought, and in the strength of it fulfils his task, the character of that king, and priest, and judge, and the relation in which he stands to men, reveal themselves to him; that these offices are continued from generation to generation, as a witness of His permanence who is Lord of them all, and who abides for ever and ever.

As then in the patriarchal period the Divine Being manifested Himself in the family relations, and by doing so manifested on what these relations depend, how they are upheld, and wherein their worth consists: so in the national period He was manifested to men through all national offices; thereby explaining their meaning and import, how they are upheld, and wherein their worth consists. But we are not to suppose that the family relations had less to do with this stage of the history than with the former. As they were embodied in the national institutions, as the existence of these institutions depended upon them, so their meaning in connexion with national life and national sins, and with a Being of whom both witnessed, became continually more apparent.

I need not point out to anyone who reads the prophets, what is their uniform method of awakening the conscience of the Jew, and of imparting to him the highest truths. I need not say that the Lord is throughout presented in the character of the husband of the nation; that acts of apostasy and false worship are constantly referred to as adulteries; and that the greatest pains are taken to convince us, that these are no poetical flourishes or terms of art, by connecting the actual human relation and human offence with the properly spiritual one. Oftentimes the verbal commentator is at fault, from the apparent confusion of the two. He cannot make up his mind whether it is the infidelity of the nation to her God, or of actual wives to their actual husbands, which the holy man is denouncing. And such perplexity there must needs be in the thoughts of all persons who are determined to separate these two ideas, -- who do not see that it is the main object of the prophet to shew their bearing upon one another, -- who will not enter into his mind, by feeling that human relationships are not artificial types of something divine, but are actually the means and the only means, through which man ascends to any knowledge of the divine; and that every breach of a human relation, as it implies a violation of the higher law, so also is a hindrance and a barrier to the perception of that higher law, -- the drawing a veil between the spirit of a man and his God.

But how did this idea of a human constitution harmonise, or come into collision, with those attempts at universal empire, which appeared to be the necessary consummation or termination of the ancient polities? The Asiatic monarchies have been sometimes called patriarchal, and beyond a doubt the patriarchal feeling -- the belief that the king was a father -- did lie at the foundation of them, and did constitute all that was sound and healthful in the acts of the monarch, or the reverence of the people. But if we are to believe the Bible, the king is not merely a father, he is something more; his position has its ground in the acknowledgment of an unseen absolute Being, whose relations to men lead up to the contemplation of Him in Himself. The effort therefore to make the paternal relation all in all is, according to this shewing, a false effort, one necessarily leading to false results. In this case the result is very apparent. The power of the monarch not having any safe ground to rest upon, soon becomes reverenced merely as power. No conscience of a law, which they ought to obey, is called forth in the minds of the subjects or the monarch; he may have kindly affections towards them which may be reciprocated, but that is all. There is nothing to preserve the existence and sanctity of the family relationship, upon which the sovereign authority is built; nothing to resist the tendency to natural worship, which destroys it; nothing to hinder the monarch from believing that he reigns by his own right. Hence, these so-called patriarchal governments, besides that they awaken neither the energies of the human intellect nor the perception of right and wrong, soon are changed into the direct contraries of that which they profess to be. The father becomes an oppressor of his own people, a conqueror of others; all idea of the invisible is swallowed up in a reverence for him. Ultimately he is looked up to as the God of gods and Lord of lords. It is no false feeling which leads us to rejoice when these patriarchal kings were driven back by the little national bands at Marathon or Plataea. No one who reveres invisible more than visible strength, will restrain his paeans at that discomfiture. It is a hateful and a godless thing to check them, or to stir up our sympathy on behalf of the Eastern tyrant. He who cherishes such a habit of feeling, will not be able to rejoice, whatever he may fancy, when Pharaoh and his host sink like lead into the waters, or when Sisera with his six hundred chariots is put to flight by the prophetess of Israel.

If we look at the history of the Jews, we shall find that their distinct polity was a witness, through all the time it lasted, against these Babel monarchies; that in them the Jew saw that world concentrated in its worst form, out of which the covenant with the Abrahamic family, and with the Israelitish nation, had delivered him. To be like this world, however, to share its splendours, to adopt its worship, was the perpetual tendency of his evil nature, a tendency punished at length by subjection to its tyranny. But it was not merely by punishment that this inclination was resisted. The wish for fellowship with other nations was a true wish inverted; the dream of a human polity was one which the true God had sent to the Jew, though he had been taught how to realise it by an evil spirit. To bring out the true idea of such a polity, to shew how it lay hid in all their own institutions, and how it would at length be brought out into full manifestation, this was the great office of the Hebrew Seer. Side by side with that vision of a Babylonian kingdom, which he taught his countrymen to look upon as based upon a lying principle, the contrary of their own, and as meant to be their scourge if they adopted that principle into their own conduct, rose up another vision of a king who did not judge after the sight of his eyes or the hearing of his ears, but who would rule men in righteousness, and whom the heathen should own. And as each new step in the history of the covenant -- the first call of the patriarch which made them a family, their deliverance under Moses which made them a nation -- was connected with a fresh revelation of

86

the Divine King through these different relations, neither displacing the other but adopting it into itself; this glorious vision would have been utterly imperfect, if it had not involved the prospect of such a discovery as had not been vouchsafed to any former age. The prophet, trained to deep awful meditation in the law, the history of his land, but above all in the mysterious services of the temple, was able by degrees to see, as one sin after another, one judgment after another, shewed him what were the dangers and wants of his nation, that the heir of David's throne must be a MAN, in as strict a sense as David was, capable, not of less but of infinitely greater sympathy with every form of human sorrow than he had been capable of, and yet that in Him, the worshipper must behold GOD less limited by human conceptions, more in His own absoluteness and awfulness, than even in the burning bush, or amidst the lightnings of Sinai. How these two longings could be both accomplished; how idolatry could be abolished by the very manifestation which would bring the object of worship more near to all human thoughts and apprehensions; how the belief of a Being nigh to men, could be reconciled with that of one dwelling in his own perfection; how unceasing action on behalf of His creatures consists with eternal rest; how He could be satisfied with men, and yet be incapable of satisfaction with anything less pure and holy than Himself; these were the awful questions with which the prophet's soul was exercised, and which were answered, not at once, but in glimpses and flashes of light coming across the darkness of his own soul, and of his country's condition, which even now startle us as we read, and make us feel that the words are meant to guide us through our own confusions, and not to give us notions or formulas for disguising them. One part of his teaching must have been derived from that polity which was the great contrast to his own. The universal monarchs, the Sennacheribs and Nebuchadnezzars, were Men-gods. They took to themselves the attributes of the Invisible; and just in proportion as they did so, just in proportion as they hid the view of anything beyond humanity from the eyes of men, just in that proportion did they become inhuman, separate from their kind, dwelling apart in an infernal solitude.

This black ground brought the perfectly clear bright object more distinctly within their view; they felt that the God-man, in whom the fulness and awfulness of Godhead should shine forth, might therefore have perfect sympathy with the poorest and most friendless, and might at the same time enable them to enter into that transcendent region which their spirits had ever been seeking and never been able to penetrate.

III. Now, when we open the first book of the New Testament, the first words of it announce that the subject of it is the Son of David and the Son of Abraham. As we read on, we find that, according to the belief of the writer, this person came into the world to establish a Kingdom. Every act and word which is recorded of Him has reference to this kingdom. A voice is heard crying in the wilderness that a kingdom is at hand. Jesus of Nazareth comes preaching the Gospel of the kingdom.

He goes into a mount to deliver the principles of His kingdom. He speaks parables to the people, nearly every one of which is prefaced with, "The kingdom of heaven is like." He heals the sick; it is that the Jews may know that His kingdom is come nigh to them. His private conferences with His disciples, just as much as His public discourses, relate to the character, the establishment, and the destinies of this kingdom. He is arraigned before Pontius Pilate for claiming to be a king. The superscription on the cross proclaims Him a king.

That there is a difference of character and style in the different Evangelists, and that a hundred different theories may be suggested as to their origin, their coincidences, their varieties, no one will deny. But that this characteristic is common to them all, that the most sweeping doctrine respecting the interpolations which have crept into them could not eliminate it out of them, that it would not be the least affected if the principle and method of their formation were ascertained, is equally true. The kingdom of Christ is under one aspect or other the subject of them all. But this peculiarity, it will be said, is easily accounted for. The writers of the New Testament are Jews; language of this kind is essentially Jewish. It belonged to the idiosyncrasy of the most strange and bigoted of all the people of the earth. To a certain extent, the reader will perceive, these statements exactly tally with mine. I have endeavoured to shew that the habit of thinking, which this perpetual use of a certain phrase indicates, is Jewish, and why it is Jewish. But there is a long step from this admission, to the one which is generally supposed to be involved in it, that this phrase is merely connected with particular accidents and circumstances, and has nothing to do with that which is essential and human. According to my view of the position of the Israelite, he was taken out of all nations expressly to be a witness of that which is unchanging and permanent, of that which is not modal, of the meaning of those relationships which belonged to him in common with the Pagans and with us, and which, as every Pagan felt, and as every peasant among us feels, have a meaning, and of the ground and purpose of national institutions and of law, which the Pagans acknowledged, and which most of us acknowledge, to be the great distinction between men and brutes. And since beneath these relationships, and this national polity, the Pagans believed, and we believe, that some other polity is lying, not limited like the former, not exclusive like the latter, I cannot see why we are to talk of the prejudices and idiosyncrasies of the Jew, because he expresses this universal idea in the words which are the simplest and the aptest to convey it. That, say the Evangelists, which we have been promised, that which we expect, is a Kingdom; this Jesus of Nazareth we believe and affirm to be the King. Either proposition may be denied. It may be said, "Men are not in want of a spiritual and universal society." It may be said, "This person has not the credentials of the character which he assumes." But it must, according to all ordinary rules of criticism, be admitted that this was the idea of the Evangelists, and we ought surely, in studying an author, to seek that we may enter into his idea, before we substitute for it one of our own.

I am aware, however, that the objector would be ready with an answer to this statement, and that it is one which will derive no little countenance from the opinions which are current among religious people, and therefore will have no inconsiderable weight with them. It will be said, 'We have an excuse for this attempt to separate the inward sense of the Gospels from their Jewish accidents, in the inconsistency which we discover in the use of those very phrases to which you allude. Do not the Evangelists constantly represent this kingdom as if it were an outward and visible kingdom, just like that of David and Solomon, nay, that very kingdom restored and extended? as something to supersede the government of Herod, ultimately perhaps that of the Caesars? And do they not at the same time introduce such words as these and attribute them to their Master, "The kingdom of God cometh not with observation," "The kingdom of God is within you," "My kingdom is not of this world" -- words which indicate that He taught (at least commonly) another doctrine, which has become leavened with these coarser and more sensual elements? If so, are we not justified in decomposing the mass and taking out the pure ore?'

I think the reader, who has gone along with me thus far, will not be much staggered by this argument. The kingdom of David, the kingdom of Solomon, was distinguished from the kingdoms of this world. It did not come with observation. It stood upon the principle which other kingdoms set at naught -- the principle that the visible king is the type of the invisible, that he reigns in virtue of a covenant between the invisible king and the nation, that he is subject to a divine law. This principle, which was practically denied in all the great nations of the earth -- denied then especially and emphatically when they became kingdoms (the ordinary, apparently the necessary, consummation of them all) -- the Israelitish kingdom existed to enforce. All through the history, the tendency of the nation and its kings to set at naught the constitutional principle, to forget the covenant, is manifest; but this very tendency proved the truth of the idea against which it warred. If this be so, what contradiction was there in affirming that the new kingdom was the kingdom promised to David, the kingdom of his son, and yet that it was in the highest sense a kingdom not to be observed by the outward eye, a kingdom within, a kingdom not of this world?

Do I mean that there was nothing startling in such announcements to all or to most of those who first heard them? If I did, I should be rejecting the express testimony of the Evangelists. They tell us that the leading members of the Jewish commonwealth, and all the most admired and popular sects which divided it, were continually perplexed and outraged by this language. But they tell us also, that these same persons had lost the family and national character of Hebrews, that they perverted the express commands of God respecting the honouring of fathers and mothers, that they had no feelings of fellowship with Israelites as Israelites, but glorified themselves in their difference from the rest of their countrymen either on the score of righteousness or of wisdom; that individual self-exaltation, on one or the other of these grounds, was their distinguishing characteristic. They tell us, in strict consistency with these observations, that these men were never so scandalised as when Jesus spoke of His Father, of His coming to do His will, of His knowing Him, and being one with Him. The idea of a relation between men and their Maker, which was the idea implied in the Abrahamic covenant, had wholly departed from them; and therefore, the hope of a complete manifestation of the ground upon which this relationship rested, the hope which had sustained every suffering Israelite in every age, which was expressly the hope of Israel, could not be cherished by them. Their idea of God was the heathen one of a Being sitting in the clouds or diffused through the universe, entirely separated from His worshippers, incapable of speaking through men to men, only declaring Himself by signs, like those of the red sky in the morning and the lowering sky in the evening. And therefore the king they expected was the counterpart of the absolute Emperor. It is true that the awful words, "We have no king but Caesar," would not have been uttered at any other moment than the one which called them forth; that it required the most intense hatred and all the other passions which then had possession of their hearts, to induce the priests formally to abandon the dream of Jewish supremacy; and that they probably reserved to themselves a right of maintaining one doctrine in the schools, another in the judgment-hall. Still these words expressed the most inward thought of the speakers; the king of Abraham's seed whom they wanted was a Caesar and nothing else.

But those who amidst much confusion and ignorance had really claimed their position as members of a nation in covenant with God; those who had walked in the ordinances of the Lord blameless, finding in every symbol of the Divine Presence, which seemed to the world a phantom, the deepest reality, and in what the world called realities, the merest phantoms; those who were conscious of their own darkness, but rested upon the promise of a light which should arise and shine upon their land; those who, uniting to public shame a miserable sense of moral evil, looked for a deliverer from both at once; those to whom the sight of the Roman soldier was oppressive, not because it reminded them of their tribute, but because it told them that the national life was gone, or lasted only in their prayers; those who under the fig-tree had besought God that the clouds which hid His countenance from them might be dispersed, that He would remember the poor, and that men might not have the upper hand: these, whether or no they could reconcile in their understandings the idea of a kingdom which should rule over all with one which should be in their hearts, at least acknowledged inwardly that only one to which both descriptions were applicable could meet the cries which they had sent up to heaven. And whatever they saw of Him who was proclaimed the king, whatever they heard Him speak, tended to bring these thoughts into harmony, or at all events to make them feel that each alike was necessary. He exercised power over the elements and over the secret functions of the human body, (of course I am

90

assuming the story of the Evangelists, my object being to shew that the different parts of it are thoroughly consistent when they are viewed in reference to one leading idea,) but this power is exercised for the sake of timid fishermen, of paralytics and lepers. He declares that His kingdom is like unto a grain of mustard-seed, which is indeed the least of all seeds, but which becomes a tree wherein the fowls of the air lodge; He declares also that this seed of the kingdom is scattered over different soils, and that the right soil for it is an honest heart. His acts produce the most obvious outward effects, yet their main effect is to carry the persuasion home to the mind of the prepared observer, that a communion had been opened between the visible and the invisible world, and that the one was under the power of the other. His words were addressed to Israelites as the children of the covenant, yet every one of them tended to awaken in these Israelites a sense of humanity, a feeling that to be Israelites they must be more. And all this general language was preparatory to the discoveries which were made in that last supper when, having loved His own who were in the world, He loved them unto the end, -- to the announcements that they were all united in Him, as the branch is united to the vine, that there was a still more wonderful union between Him and His Father, to the knowledge of which they might through this union attain, and that a Spirit would come to dwell with them and to testify of Him and of the Father. All which discourses to men are gathered up in the amazing prayer, "That they all may be one, as thou, Father, art in me, and I in thee, that they may be one in us."

Either those words contain the essence and meaning of the whole history, or that history must be rejected as being from first to last the wickedest lie and the most awful blasphemy ever palmed upon the world. And if they do contain the meaning of it, that meaning must be embodied in acts. The Evangelists therefore go on to record in words perfectly calm and simple the death of their Master and His resurrection. As events they are related; no comment is made upon them; few hints are given of any effects to follow from them. We are made to feel by the quiet accurate detail, "He certainly died, who, as we believed, was the Son of God, and the King of Israel; He actually rose with His body, and came among us who knew Him, and spake and ate with us: this is the accomplishment of the union between heaven and earth; it is no longer a word, it is a fact." And of this fact, the risen Lord tells His Apostles that they are to go into the world and testify; not merely to testify of it, but to adopt men into a society grounded upon the accomplishment of it. In connexion with that command, and as the ultimate basis of the universal society, a NAME is proclaimed, in which the name that had been revealed to Abraham, and that more awful one which Moses heard in the bush, are combined and reconciled.

To a person who has contemplated the Gospel merely as the case of certain great doctrines or fine moralities, the Acts of the Apostles must be an utterly unintelligible book. For in the specimens of the Apostles' preaching which it gives us, there are comparatively few references to the discourses or the parables of our Lord. They dwell mainly upon the great acts of death and resurrection as evidences that Jesus was the King, as expounding and consummating the previous history of the Jewish people, as justifying and realising the truth which worked in the minds of the heathen, "that we are His offspring." On the other hand, a person who really looks upon the Bible as the history of the establishment of a universal and spiritual kingdom, of that kingdom which God had ever intended for men, and of which the universal kingdom then existing in the world was the formal opposite, will find in this book exactly that without which all the former records would be unmeaning.

The narrator of such transcendent events as the ascension of the Son of Man into the invisible glory, or the descent of the Spirit to take possession of the feelings, thoughts, utterances of mortal men, might have been expected to stand still and wonder at that which with so entire a belief he was recording. But no, he looks upon these events as the necessary consummation of all that went before, the necessary foundations of the existence of the Church. And therefore he can quietly relate any other circumstances, however apparently disproportionate, which were demanded for the outward manifestation and development of that Church, such as the meeting of the Apostles in the upper room, and the completion of their number. If the foundation of this kingdom were the end of all the purposes of God, if it were the kingdom of God among men, the human conditions of it could be no more passed over than the divine; it was as needful to prove that the ladder had its foot upon earth, as that it had come down out of heaven. As we proceed, we find every new step of the story leading us to notice the Church as the child which the Jewish polity had for so many ages been carrying in its womb. Its filial relation is first demonstrated, it is shewn to be an Israelitic not a mundane commonwealth; then it is shewn that, though not mundane, it is essentially human, containing a principle of expansion greater than that which dwelt in the Roman empire.

And here lies the apparent contradiction, the real harmony, of those two aspects in which this kingdom was contemplated by the apostles of the Circumcision and by St. Paul. The one witnessed for the continuity of it, the other for its freedom from all national exclusions. These, we may believe, were their respective offices. Yet, as each fulfilled the one, he was in fact teaching the other truth most effectually. St. Peter and St. James were maintaining the universality of the Church, while they were contending for its Jewish character and derivation. St. Paul was maintaining the national covenant, while he was telling the Gentiles, that if they were circumcised Christ would profit them nothing. Take away the first testimony and the Church becomes an earthly not a spiritual commonwealth, and therefore subject to earthly limitations; take away the second, and the promise to Abraham is unfulfilled. In another sense, as the canon of Scripture shews, St. Paul was more directly carrying our the spirit of the Jewish distinction, by upholding the distinctness of ecclesiastical communities according to tribes and countries, than the Apostles of Jerusalem; and they were carrying out the idea of the universality of the Church more than he did by addressing the members of it as of an entire community dispersed through different parts of the world.

But we must not forget that while this universal society, according to the historical conception of it, grew out of the Jewish family and nation, it is, according to the theological conception of it, the root of both. "That," says Aristotle, "which is first as cause is last in discovery." And this beautiful formula is translated into life and reality in the letter to the Ephesians, when St. Paul tells them that they were created in Christ before all worlds, and when he speaks of the transcendent economy as being gradually revealed to the Apostles and Prophets by the Spirit. In this passage it seems to me lies the key to the whole character of the dispensation, as well as of the books in which it is set forth. If the Gospel be the revelation or unveiling of a mystery hidded from ages and generations; if this mystery be the true constitution of humanity in Christ, so that a man believes and acts a lie who does not claim for himself union with Christ, we can understand why the deepest writings of the New Testament, instead of being digests of doctrine, are epistles, explaining to those who had been admitted into the Church of Christ their own position, bringing out that side of it which had reference to the circumstances in which they were placed or to their most besetting sins, and shewing what life was in consistency, what life at variance, with it. We can understand why the opening of the first of these epistles, of the one which has been supposed to be most like a systematic treatise, announces that the Gospel is concerning Jesus Christ, who was made of the seed of David according to the flesh, and marked out as the Son of God with power, according to the Spirit of holiness, by the resurrection of the dead. The fact of a union between the Godhead and humanity is thus set forth as the one which the Apostle felt himself appointed to proclaim, which was the ground of the message to the Gentiles, and in which all ideas of reconciliation, of a divine life, justification by faith, sanctification by the Spirit, were implicitly contained. We can understand why the great fight of the Apostle with the Corinthians should be because they exalted certain notions, and certain men as the representatives of these notions, into the place of Him who was the Lord of their fellowship, and why pride, sensuality, contempt of others, abuse of ordinances, should be necessarily consequent upon that sin. We can understand why St. Paul curses with such vehemence those false teachers who had denied the Galatians the right to call themselves children of God in Christ in virtue of the new covenant, and had sent them back to the old. We may perceive that those wonderful words in which he addresses the Ephesians, when he tells them that they were sitting in heavenly places in Christ Jesus, are just as real and practical as the exhortations at the end of the same letter, respecting the duties of husbands and wives, fathers and children, and that the second are involved in the first. We may see what connexion there is between the entreaty to the Colossians not to stoop to will-worship and the service of angels, and the assertion of the fact that Christ was in them the hope of glory, and that He is the head in whom dwell all the riches of wisdom and knowledge. We may see how possible it was for some of the Philippian Church to be enemies to the cross of Christ, their god their belly, their glory their shame, not becuse they had not been admitted to the privileges of being members of Christ, but because they had not pressed forward to realise their claim. We may enter a little into the idea of the letters to the Thessalonians, however we may differ about the particular time or times of its accomplishment, that there must be a coeval manifestation of the mystery of iniquity and of the mystery of godliness; that the two kingdoms, being always in conflict, at certain great crises of the world are brought into direct and open collision. We shall not need any evidence of the apostolical derivation of the epistle to the Hebrews, to convince us that it unfolds the relations between the national and universal dispensation, between that which was the shadow and that which was the substance of a Divine humanity; between that which enabled the worshipper to expect a perfect admission into the Divine presence, and that which admitted him to it; between that which revealed God to him as the enemy of evil, and that which revealed Him as the conqueror of it. Nor is it inconsistent with any previous intimation which has been given us, that the writer of this epistle should in every part of it represent the sin of men as consisting in their unbelief of the blessings into which they are received at each stage of the Divine manifestation, and that he should with solemn earnestness, mixed with warnings of a fearful and hopeless apostasy, urge those whom he addressing to believe that the position into which they had been brought was that after which all former ages had been aspiring, and as such, to claim it. From these exhortations and admonitions, the transition is easy to those Catholic epistles which some have found it so hard to reconcile with the doctrine of St. Paul. And doubtless, if the faith which the epistle to the Romans and the epistle to the Hebrews adjured men, by such grand promises and dire threats, to exercise, were not faith in a living Being, who had adopted men into fellowship with himself on purpose that being righteous by virtue of that union they might do righteous acts, that having claimed their place as members of a body the Spirit might work in them to will and to do of his good pleasure, the assertions that faith without works saves, and that faith without works cannot save, are hopelessly irreconcileable. But if the idea of St. Paul, as much of St. James, be, that all worth may be attributed to faith in so far forth as it unites us to an object and raises us out of ourselves, no worth at all, so far as it is contemplated simply as a property in ourselves; if this be the very principle which the whole Bible is developing, one does not well see what either position would be good for, if the other were wanting. If our Lord came among men that He might bring them into a kingdom of righteousness, peace, and joy, because a kingdom grounded upon fellowship with a righteous and perfect Being, the notion that that righteousness can ever belong to any man in himself, and the notion that everyone is not to exhibit the fruits of it in himself, would seem to be equally contradictions. And therefore I believe that without this consideration we shall be as much puzzled by the sketch of a Christian man's life, discipline, and conflicts, in the epistle of St. Peter, and by the doctrine of St. John, that love is the consummation of all God's revelations and all man's strivings, as by any former part of the book. For that men are not to gain a kingdom hereafter, but are put in possession of it now, and that through their chastisements and the oppositions of their evil nature they are to learn its character and enter into its privileges, is surely taught in every verse of the one; and that love has been manifested unto men, that they have been brought into fellowship with it, that by that fellowhip they may rise to the fruition of it, and that this fellowship is for us as members of a family, so that he who loveth God must love his brother also, is affirmed again and again in express words of the other. With such thoughts in our mind, I believe we may venture, with hope of the deepest instruction, upon the study of the last book in the Bible. For though we may not be able to determine which of all the chronological speculations respecting it is the least untenable, though we may not decide confidently whether it speaks to us of the future or of the past, whether it describes a conflict of principles or of persons, of this we shall have no doubt, that it does exhibit at one period or through all periods a real kingdom of heaven upon earth, a kingdom of which the principle must be ever the same, a kingdom to which all kingdoms are meant to be in subjection; a kingdom which is maintaining itself against an opposing tyranny, whereof the ultimate law is brute force or unalloyed selfishness; a kingdom which must prevail because it rests upon a name which expresses the perfect Love, the ineffable Unity, the name of the Father, and of the Son, and of the Holy Ghost.

95

CHAPTER IV

SIGNS OF A SPIRITUAL SOCIETY

We have observed the traces of a spiritual consitution for mankind. We have observed that the two parts of this constitution, which are united by family relationships and by locality, depend upon a third part which is universal. We have observed that there are two possible forms of a universal society, one of which is destructive of the family and national principle, the other the expansion of them. The first of these is that which in Scripture is called THIS WORLD, the latter is that which in Scripture is called THE CHURCH. We have observed that the principles of the world exist in the heart of every family and of every nation; that they are precisely the natural tendencies and inclinations of men; that they are always threatening to become predominant; that when they become predominant there ceases to be any recognition of men as related to a Being above them, any recognition of them as possessing a common humanity. The other body, therefore, the Church, being especially the witness for these facts which it is natural to us to deny, must be a distinct body. In losing its distinctness it loses it meaning, > loses to all intents and purposes, though the words may at first sound paradoxical, its universality. The question then which we have to examine is, Are there any signs in the present day of the existence of a spiritual and universal body upon the earth? Do these signs identify that body with the one spoken of in Scripture? Are they an effectual witness against the world?

SECTION I -- BAPTISM

That there has existed for the last 1800 years, a certain rite called BAPTISM; that it is not derived from the national customs of any of the people among whom it is found; that different tribes of the most different origin and character adopted it, and when they had received it believed themselves to be members of a common society; that this society was supposed to be connected with an invisible world, and with a certain worship and government; that an immense proportion of all the children in Europe are admitted very shortly after their birth to the rite; that it is generally performed by a peculiar class of functionaries; -- these are facts, which it is not necessary to establish by any proof. The only question is whether these facts have a meaning and what that meaning is.

The idea of the Scriptures, so far as we have been able to trace it, is that Jesus Christ came upon earth to reveal a kingdom, which kingdom is founded upon a union established in His person between man and God, between the visible and invisible world, and ultimately upon a revelation of the divine NAME. If then the setting up of this kingdom, and the adoption of men into it, be not connected in the New Testament with the rite of baptism, we may be quite sure that the fact we have just noticed, let its import be what it may, does not concern us. Even though baptism were enjoined as a rite by our Lord Himself, yet if it were appointed in such terms as leave us at liberty to suppose that it was merely accidental to the general purposes of His advent, we cannot prove an identity between the universal society which acknowledges it now and the one which He founded.

Let us then turn to the Gospels that we may see there how far this is the case. One of the first events announced there is contained in these words: "In those days came John the Baptist, preaching in the wilderness of Judea and saying, Repent ye, for the kingdom of heaven is at hand. Then went out to him Jerusalem and all Judea, and were baptized of him in Jordan confessing their sins." This narrative is at least singular: baptism is connected with a spiritual act, that of repentance; with a spiritual promise, that of remission; with the announcement of a kingdom; with an intimation that that kingdom should not merely be composed of the children of Abraham. Supposing it were, as some imagine, a ceremony not known until that time, then it was introduced at the very moment that the kingdom of heaven was to begin; supposing it had been practised, as others say, at the reception of Gentile converts to the privileges of the outer court, then the administration of it to Jews would appear to be a most significant intimation, that they were henceforth to take their stand upon a universal human ground. This baptism then was the preparation for the Gospel. It may, however, for aught that appears at present, have been only a preparation. But Jesus Himself descends into the water, and as He comes out of it, a voice from heaven proclaims Him the well beloved Son, and the Spirit descends upon Him in a bodily shape. The announcement then that the Divine man, the king of men, had really appeared, was, according to the Gospels, connected with Baptism. And this same Baptism they speak of as the beginning of our Lord's public ministry, and of all the acts by which His descent from above was attested. Yet this might have been necessary to mark the leader; it need not have any application to His disciples. But Jesus preached, saying, "Repent, the kingdom of heaven is at hand;" He appoints Apostles to go and declare that kingdom; and these Apostles baptise. The nature of their message may denote, however, that they were only continuing the dispensation of John, that they had nothing directly to do with that higher Baptism of the Holy Ghost and of fire, which John had declared would supersede his own. Out Lord has a conversation with Nicodemus in which He tells him that he must be born again if he would see the kingdom of heaven; because that which is born of the flesh is flesh, and that which is born of the Spirit is spirit; because it was impossible for the fleshly man to understand even earthly things, much more these heavenly things, which He alone could reveal who had come down from heaven, and was in heaven. And this declaration of the transcendental character of the new kingdom is joined to the words, "Except a man be born of water and of the Spirit, he cannot enter into the kingdom of heaven." Yet perhaps even here there may be a reference rather to the spiritual eye in man, which this ordinance, like

98

those earlier ordinances of the Jews, might be the means of opening, than to the actual gift of God's Spirit which was promised; for it is said expressly, "The Spirit was not yet given, becuase that Jesus was not yet glorified." Our Lord appears to His disciples after He had risen from the dead, and He says, "All power is given unto me in heaven and earth, go therefore, and preach the gospel to all nations, baptizing them in the name of the Father, and of the Son, and of the Holy Ghost." This language is certainly strange; for it seems as if it could only look forward to the establishment of a spiritual kingdom. But one other point of evidence is still wanting. Did the Apostles, after the glorification of Christ, after the descent of the Holy Ghost, still baptize with water? St. Peter stood in the midst of the disciples, and said to the Jews, "God hath made this Jesus whom ye crucified, both Lord and Christ; repent therefore, and be baptized, and ye shall receive the gift of the Holy Ghost;" and the same day three thousand were baptized. This evidence may perhaps be enough to shew that the writers of the Gospels and of the Acts believed this to be the sign of admission into Christ's spiritual and universal kingdom, and consequently that every person receiving that sign was ipso facto a member of that kingdom. As the son or servant of the Roman commonwealth entered so soon as he was manumitted upon the rights of a citizen, as all immunities and responsibilities appertaining to this character from that hour became his, the young Christian convert who had derived his instruction from the Scriptures could not doubt, that from the time of his baptism he was free of that brotherhood of which his Lord was the head. He could not doubt that whatever language, be it as lofty as it might, described that brotherhood, described his state; that if Christ came to make men sons of God, he was a son of God; if He came to make them members of His own body, he was a member of that body; if He came to endue men with His Spirit, that Spirit was given to him. His baptism said to him, This is your position; according to the conditions of it you are to live. It will not be an easy life. It will be one of perpetual conflict. You will have a battle not with flesh and blood only, but with principalities and powers, with the rulers of spiritual wickedness in high places. But understnad the nature of the battle. Your foes are not hindering you from obtaining a blessing; they are hindering you from entering into the fruition of one that has been obtained for you; they wil laugh at you for pretending that it is yours; they will tell you that you must not claim it. But in the strength of this covenant you must claim it; otherwise your life will be a lie. I ask anyone calmly to read the epistles, and tell me whether any other sense than this could be put upon Baptism by those who exhorted men, because they were baptized, to count themselves dead unto sin and alive unto God; by those who addressed men, the majority of whom they did not know personally, some of whom they did know to be inconsistent and unholy, as being in Christ, elect, children of God; by those who conjured their disciples not to doubt, not to disbelieve, that they had been admitted into the communion of saints, and told them they would sink into apostasy if they did? But then I must ask also, why, if the kingdom of Christ was declared to be an everlasting kingdom, and this sign was fixed as the admission of men into it at the first, and this sign still exists among us, all we who have received it are not in the same position, have not the same privileges, are not under the same responsibilities, as those who lived eighteen hundred years ago? I ask whether Baptism be not the sign of a spiritual and universal kingdom?

OBJECTIONS -- 1. The Quaker

To this question various answers are given. I will consider first that of the Quakers.

I. It seems to them utterly incredible and monstrous, that a spiritual fact or operation should be denoted by a visible sign. "Either men are livingly united to the Divine Word, or they are not: if they are, the sign is useless; if they are not, it is false. If Christ's kingdom depend upon these outward ceremonies, wherein does it differ from the Jewish? What do the words, that John came baptizing with water but Christ with the Spirit and fire, mean, if both baptisms are equally outward?"

Positions of this kind are so self-evident to the Quaker, that Scripture cannot be suffered to contradict them. It is in vain to allege texts and commandments. These are primary truths which ride over them all, and determine the interpretation of them. If the Apostles did act in opposition to them, the Apostles shewed that they were still ignorant and Judaical. Be it so: if these notions are good for anything, if they do not contradict the leading positive truths of Quakerism, let them be upholden at all risks. But that is the point I wish to examine.

We have seen that Fox did not consider it the work of the Gospel to reveal the fact of men's relation to the Divine Word; that fact, he believed, was intimated both to Heathens and to Jews. To the latter it was intimated by a sign. The Invisible Teacher by this means declared to the children of Abraham that there was a union between themselves and Him, warned them of the tendency there was in their fleshly natures to separate from Him, promised to uphold them against that tendency.

This, I say, Fox acknowledged to be the Divine method in the Jewish dispensation. He never pretended that the union which was made known to the Jew was a material union; if it had been, there would have been no sign, for there would have been nothing to signify. He never pretended that it was a variable union, deriving its existence from certain feelings in the minds of the human creatures who shared in it; if it had been there could have been no sign, for the thing to be signified would have been different each day. So that the appropriateness, the possibility, if I may so speak, of this method, arose from the fact that a certain spiritual and permanent relation was to be made known by it. And yet the reason, according to the Quaker, why this method should be abondoned, is this and this only, that the dispensation of the Gospel has a spiritual and permanent, not a material and transitory, character! Surely

100

this is an inconsistency which needs to be justified by something else than vague declamations about carnal practices, and angry denunciations against the whole of Christendom, from the Apostles downwards, for being guilty of them.

"But it is a false thing to give the sign to anyone who has not the reality." What is meant by the words, has not the reality? Is it meant that the relation is not real? If so, Fox was wrong, for he affirmed that it was real, for all men. Or does the word real refer to the feeling and acknowledgment of the relation? Then this proposition affirms, that it is false to tell a man a truth because he does not believe it. Unquestionably we are guilty of that falsehood; the whole Old Testament dispensation was also guilty of it; Fox and the Quakers themselves are guilty of it.

"But the sign is useless to a man who is truly united to the Divine Word." There are two opinions implied in this language, both of great importance, both very illustrative of Quaker feeling and history. One is that it is nothing to a man that a thing is true, true in itself, true universally, provided he feels it to be true for him; the other is that union with the Divine Word is all which men require. Now every earnest word which Fox spoke was a testimony against both these notions; first (as I have shewn so often), the truth of the thing was the ground upon which he exhorted men to place their feeling of it; secondly, he declared that union with the Divine Word did not satisfy those Heathens or Jews who perceived it, but that it made them long for something more, for a kingdom of Heaven. See here an evidence for Baptism, which all the history of Christendom could not have afforded, frankly offered to us by those who reject it. Their whole preaching is against Judaism, against the old covenant; and yet they are thrown back upon Judaism, they cannot rise above the great doctrine of the old covenant. But neither can they keep that doctrine; they cannot keep the faith that we are related to the Divine Word; they can only substitute for it certain individual feelings and impressions.

And now, having this thought on our minds, let us compare for an instant our interpretation of the words of John the Baptist with theirs. We say that John came baptizing with water unto repentance, for the remission of sins. Here lay the spiritual meaning of his baptism. Our Lord's baptism, we maintain, includes this meaning, but it has a deeper one. His baptism is not only unto repentance; not only intimates that the heart has turned to God, and so turning is delivered from sin: it gives the spirit and power whence repentance and every right act must flow; it brings the subject of it under the discipline of that purifying fire whereby the old and evil nature is to be consumed. This meaning of the passage seems to be literal enough, and it precisely accords with the promises and anticipations of the prophets, with the expositions and retrospections of the Apostles. How does the Quaker improve upon it? He makes it the great characteristic of John, that he did baptize with water, and of Christ, that He would not baptize with water. So that the voice crying in the wilderness said this, "Hear, O Israel! rejoice, O ye Gentiles! the glorious time is at hand, which your fathers expected, which the whole universe has been groaning for --the time when signs are to be abolished. The great Prince and Deliverer is at hand, who will cause that the things of earth shall be no longer pledges and sacraments of a union with Heaven! This is the consummation of all the hopes of mankind, this is what is meant by the Tabernacle of God being with men; by His dwelling with them, and their being His people, and His being their God."

2. The Anti-paedobaptist

II. The Anti-paedobaptist is, in many respects, strongly contrasted with the Quaker. He attaches a very great value to the baptismal sign. He believes that it is intended to be the witness of a spiritual kingdom. In general, he is remarkable for holding the belief firmly, in which the Quaker is deficient, that men are chosen by God to their place in the Divine Economy. But he conceives that the admission of those who have no spiritual consciousness or spiritual capacity to this ordinance, is destructive of its meaning; as it exists in modern Europe it has nothing to do with the Kingdom of Christ.

I should be very careful to answer this objection, for it certainly affects the whole of my argument, if it had not been already so fully considered. The issue to be tried between us and the Anabaptists is not whether the existence of such and such a sign indicates the existence of a kingdom, but what that kingdom is which it should indicate. I have maintained, upon the authority of Scripture, that the Catholic Church is emphatically a kingdom for mankind, a kingdom grounded upon the union which has been established in Christ between God and man. I have maintained that it grew out of a family and a nation, of which social states it proved itself to be the proper and only foundation. Supposing this notion to be altogether false, it may be most reasonable to say that a child, an embryo man, ought to be treated as if he were not a citizen of this kingdom. To one who believes it true, such a doctrine must seem absolutely monstrous. Let us take a member of either of the classes out of which the early Church was formed. First let him be a Heathen. He has been struck with the threatenings of coming judgments which were visible in the sins of the Roman empire, in the divorces, adulteries, incests, parricides of its most conspicuous members. He has felt how little the idea of the gods which was received among his countrymen tended to repress such atrocities. The preaching of some Christian Apostle has awakened him to the fact, that the evil nature from which all these crimes have proceeded is in himself. He hears of a deliverance out of that nature. He hears that God has revealed Himself to men as the enemy of all unrighteousness; that He has also revealed Himself to men as their Father; that His Son has come down to dwell among men; that He has made Himself the brother of our race; that He has claimed

102

the members of it for members of His own body; that He has given them a sign of admission into it; that He has promised them His Spirit. Could he who received this joyful message, and acted upon the command which was involved in it, doubt that he was received into the true human family, that he was taken out of a hateful, anomalous, inhuman world? Could he then dare to say, "This child whom I have begotten belongs to this inhuman anomalous world; he has a human form and countenance, that form and countenance which Christ bore, yet the accursed nature which I have renounced is his proper, his appointed master; the evil society out of which I have fled, is his home; to the evil spirit who I believe has infused his leaven into that nature and that society, I leave him." I am not now reasoning with a person who does not attach any high meaning to Baptism, but with one who believes it to be really the sign of the redeemed covenant family. I ask such a person to consider, what less than this a Christian convert could suppose to be signified, by anyone who told him that he was not to baptize his child, because he could not be sure that it was included in Christ's redemption?

Nor let it be supposed that this is the whole of the contradiction which such a prohibition would involve. Far from it. The idea of the Gospel, as the revelation of truths which are expressed in the forms of family society, and which, to all appearance, are not expressible in any other forms, truths to the apprehension of which he had risen through the feelings which his domestic relations or the consciousness of their violation had called forth, would seem to him utterly destroyed, all links between human relations and Divine at once abolished, if he might not dare to speak of his child as united to him in a spiritual bond. Again, the idea of the Gospel, as the promise of a Spirit who would awaken all consciousness, convictions, and affections, would be equally trifled with, by the doctrine that the existence of these convictions, consciousnesses, affections, was the condition precedent to an admission into the Gospel Covenant.

On this last point, the perplexities of a Hebrew Christian, who was commanded not to baptize his child, must have been still more distressing. His own covenant had been emphatically with children. That which had superseded it was, in all other respects, wider, freer, more directly referring all acts of the creature to the love and good pleasure of the Creator. Yet, without one word of Christ being produced to this effect, I command you not to follow the analogy of God's earlier dispensation, not to suppose that, in my kingdom of grace, infants are accounted human and moral beings as they were under the law - without the record of one sentence to this purpose; with the record of many acts and words which led to just the opposite conclusion, that infants were a most honoured part of that race which He came to seek and save; with the doctrine forming an article of his daily confession, that the Redeemer of humanity had Himself entered into the state of childhood, as well as into that of manhood, the Israelite convert is forced to abandon all the habits of thought and feeling which he had derived from

103

God's own teaching, not because they were too narrow, but because they were too comprehensive for his new position.

The Anti-paedobaptist then, I think, cannot plead, (and this is his only plea,) that the application of Baptism to infants is a strange and perplexing departure from the admitted sense and object of the ordinance. On the contrary, there is some reason, I fancy, for suspecting danger on the other side. It was so reasonable, so inevitable a consequence of the baptismal principle, that infants should be received into the Church -- the law of the Church's propagation was thereby so clearly explained and reconciled with the ordinary laws of God's Providence -- that it would be no wonder if another truth, equally necessary, were lost sight of in the eagerness to enforce that which this practice inculcated. It might be forgotten that we baptize children, not because they are children, but because they are embryo men; that to the complete idea of a spiritual blessing, a receiver is needful as well as a giver; that Baptism is not a momentary act but a perpetual sacrament. Before I finish this section I may have occasion to shew that some or all of these errors have arisen in the Church, and to their prevalency the rise of a sect of Anti-paedobaptists is, no doubt, to be attirbuted. But there is found, side by side with Baptism, in all the countries where it is adopted, an institution which is a far more complete testimony against such perversions, than those have been able to bear who set aside the principle out of which they have grown. This institution, not displacing for superseding Baptism, but confirming, as its name denotes, the authority and pledges of that sacrament, declares to the child that He who has guided it through infancy will be with it in the conscious struggles of manhood, and that it has been made free, not only of a particular congregation, but of the Universal Church.

The doctrine of the Anabaptists then, like that of the Quakers, supplies a strong argument in favour of my position, for it shews that, just so far as the operation of Baptism is restricted, just so far does the belief of a human society become impossible.

3. The Modern Protestant

III. Next to the Anabaptist comes the soi-disant disciple of Luther and Calvin, the modern Protestant or Evangelical. His doctrine is that there are two kingdoms of Christ, one real and spiritual, the other outward and visible. It is highly desirable, perhaps necessary, that young as well as old should be admitted into the latter. Baptism is the appointed mode of admission. What are the privileges of the Gentile court into which, by this ordinance, we are received, they do not precisely determine. Possibly some grace is communicated at Baptism; or if not, the blessings of being permitted to hear preaching, and of obtaining a Christian education, are great, and may be turned to greater use hereafter. But the important point of all is this, to press upon men that till they have been actually and consciously converted they are not members of Christ or children of God. Some disciples of this school believe that these words may be applied to baptized people in a sense; but if you desire to know in what sense, the answers are so vague and indeterminate, as to leave a painful impression upon the mind, that such language is very awful and significant, and yet that it may on certain occasions be sported with or used with a secret reservation.

But those who make these statements say, that they wish to get rid of equivocations, not to invent them. They resort to this hypothesis of a double kingdom, because the plainest observation tells them, that a baptized man may be a very evil man, and because, being evil, they cannot see what he has to do with a kingdom of righteousness, peace, and joy in the Holy Ghost. Again, they say, "Let people make out what theological scheme they please, we know that we, having been baptized in infancy, did in manhood as much pass from death unto life, as any heathen in the first age could have done." It is not, they contend, fair or honest to suppress either of these facts, either that which is obvious to every man's common sense, or that of which they themselves are conscious; but that this is done, and must be done, if we assume Baptism to be what it is sometimes called -- a New Birth -- the actual introduction into a spiritual world.

Now I feel as little disposed to deny the melancholy proposition that Christian men are not living Christian lives; as the Jewish prophet felt to pass over the truth, that the name of God was blasphemed through his countrymen in all lands. The precedents which Holy Scripture furnishes I believe to be strictly applicable to us; that which was the function of the preacher then is his function now; if he who prophesied in Jerusalem was to rebuke men for sin, and to call them to repentance, we in London or Paris are to do the like. The question is, what is the sin which we are to rebuke, what is the repentance to which we are to invite. The Jewish prophet charged his people with forgetting the covenant of their God. He traced up all sins to this sin. He said that the Jew was guilty, because he did not claim the privileges of a Jew, because he did not act as if he was a Jew. Are we to follow this precedent or not? Are we following it when we say, "This covenant is, I will be to you a father, and you shall be to me sons and daughters; you are acting as if you were not in this covenant, you are forgetting it," or when we say, "These titles are not yours, or are yours only in some formal imaginary sense," that is, if we spoke plain English, in no sense at all?

As little do I desire to deny or explain away the other assertion, that baptized men, who have lived without God in the world, are converted to Him by His grace. This is doctrine which I believe was held as strongly by St. Bernard, Tauler, and A Kempis, I might add by Loyola and Xavier, as by any modern Methodist. These eminent persons did not limit their language to cases of open profligacy (though they by no means excluded such cases); they applied it to laymen or priests, who under a respectable exterior had sought the praise of men more than the praise of God. Whether we have a right to restrict the word to a particular act or crisis; whether every act of repentance is not one of conversion or turning to God; whether we are not apt to forget that every such act must be as much attributed to the Spirit of God as the recovery from habitual thoughtlessness and sin, are questions for serious reflection: but the decision of them does not affect the opinion, that there may be an entire change in the feelings and aims of one who has received Christian Baptism. But by what words is such a revolution to be denoted? I believe the answer may be obtained, by comparing different approved records of conversions. We shall find a great difference in them. In some we shall hear a man speaking with great horror and loathing of his past years and of his youthful companions. We shall hear another transferring these expressions of loathing to his evil nature, and to himself for having yielded to it, manifesting the deepest affection for all he has ever been acquainted with, owning them to be more righteous than himself, believing that God cares for them as well as for him, certain that what is true for him, is true also for them. The first talks much of the new start he has taken, of his new heart, of his purified affections; the latter rejoices that having discovered the feebleness of his own heart, he has been led to see that there is another in whom he ought to have trusted before, and may trust now. The first speaks of the grace that has been bestowed upon himself; the other of being taken under the gracious guidance of a Spirit, whom he has resisted too long. Granting that these modes of expression may be sometimes intermingled, that there may be a true feeling in those who chiefly use the former, and that there may be error and confusions in those records wherein the latter predominate, yet does not everyone recognize a characteristic, a most practical, difference between them? Would not any experienced person of the Evangelical school feel, that the one kind of language indicated a much more healthful, genuine state of character than the other? But then ought he not to ask himself whether both of these kinds of language are incompatible with the idea of Baptismal Regeneration, or only one of them; and if only one, whether the false or the true? If the words, "then I was awakened," do now imply "I had been asleep;" if the words, "then I came to the knowledge of the truth," do not imply "that which I knew was true before I knew it;" if the words,"I ceased to strive against the Spirit," do not imply that there had been a previous resistance to the Spirit, they are mere cant words, good for nothing, nay, utterly detestable. But, if they do imply all this, they imply just what the believer in Baptismal Regeneration is charged with fiction and falsehood for maintaining. They presume the existence of a state, which is our state, whether we are conscious of it, whether we are in conformity with it, or no.

It is then not necessary for the vindication of these two facts, that we should adopt the notion that there are two kingdoms, one earthly, formal, fictitious; the other heavenly, spiritual, real. It is not necessary for their vindication, seeing that neither of these facts can be calmly

106

examined, even in the reports of those who insist most upon them, without suggesting the notion, that there must be a heavenly, spiritual, real kingdom, against which all evil men, just in so far forth as they are evil, are rebelling; and into subjection to which all converted men, in so far forth as they are converted, are brought. And therefore, whatever evils have flowed and are flowing from this notion of the two kingdoms, are not justified or compensated for by one practical advantage. How practical the evils are, let the history of Christian Europe since the Reformation attest! I have spoken of the difference between Luther and the Lutherans, even between Calvin and the Calvinists; I have spoken of the way in which Justification by Faith has been turned from a living principle into an empty shibboleth; in which the Divine Election has lost its force, except as an excuse for doubting the existence of our own awful responsibilities. If we trace these miserable fruits to their root, we shall find it, I believe, in this notion. This at least is certain, as I have had occasion again and again to remark, that the doctrine of Baptismal Regeneration was held by Luther not in conjunction with that of Justification by Faith (as he might have held any doctrine which belonged to the natural philosophy of his age), but that he grounded the one on the other. "Believe on the warrant of your Baptism, You are grafted into Christ; claim your position. You have the Spirit, you are children of God; do not live as if you belonged to the devil." This was his invariable language, with this he shook the Seven Hills.

What, I ask, have those done who have abandoned this language, and who, while they talk of Luther, would actually denounce anyone who used it as heretical and papistical? The children of Protestant families are told that they have no right to call themselves children of God. They grow up in that conviction; in maturer years they carry it to its legitimate consequences. They feel that they have no right to use the Lord's Prayer, no right to pray at all; that they have no power near them to keep them from temptation; that they have no bonds of fellowship with any, except on the grounds of liking and taste. Gradually as their understandings ripen and their feelings decay, they begin to regard Protestantism as a halfway house between Popery and Infidelity; and whether they shall go back to the one, or on to the other, depends principally upon their circumstances, and upon the predominance of the fancy or of the intellect in their constitution. I speak of the more courageous; in the majority, dull indifference, which is incapable of either resolve, becomes the ruling habit of mind. Thanks to God, the exceptions to my statement, in all Protestant countries, are innumerable. But I believe it will be found almost universally, that they occur when parents have acted upon the principle which I am maintaining, though in words they have disavowed it; then they have treated their children as if they possessed all Christian titles and privileges, though they did so in utter disregard to their own theory. That, even in such cases, the contradiction has not been innocuous, I think I can affirm with some confidence. A sense of perplexity, of half sincerity, cleaves to the minds of those who most long to keep a clear heart and a free conscience. They do not dare to call themselves by a name which yet they feel they must claim, if they are to serve God or to do any right act. Hence their conduct becomes uncertain, their thoughts are not manly; and, in place of humility, they cultivate a false shame, in which they are conscious that pride is a large ingredient. There are hundreds of young men who will understand my meaning; there are others, I mean ministers of the Gospel, to whom I wish that I could make it intelligible. But at all events, those who feel as I do in this matter, will have bitter cause for self-reproach, if they do not protest in season and out of season, against a notion which, if I be not greatly mistaken, is doing more than all others to undermine the Christianity of the Protestant nations.

4. The Philosopher

IV. Last come our modern Philosophers. Their notions upon this subject are generally indicated by some such language as the following. "Baptism cannot be the sign of a Universal Society, for it excludes Pagans and Mahometans, all but the members of a certain religious sect; Baptism cannot, in any proper sense, be the sign of a Spiritual Society, for it makes no distinction between the most stupid and the most cultivated, the most brutal and the most humane; Baptism, by the very terms in which it is performed, implies the acknowledgment of a doctrine which many Christians deny, few think of, and none understand; Baptism, if we may judge from the words or the ceremonies which everywhere accompany it, presumes the belief of an evil spiritual agency, a belief belonging only to the darkest ages. Baptism was unquestionably a bond of fellowship in certain periods; it did mean something to those who lived in them; but its significance is gone; it is changed into a worthless symbol which may be allowed to last so long as it does not pretend to be anything, but which the moment it endeavours to recover its obsolete importance will be rejected by wise men altogether."

To the first of these objections, that Baptism is exclusive, because merely for those who profess a faith in Christ, I reply, -- As against the theologians who look upon Christ merely as the great teacher, this argument has the greatest force: to baptize men into the name of Christ is, if they be right, to receive them into the sect or school of a certain person who appeared in Palestine 1800 years ago. We may prefer Him to one who appeared in Arabia about 1200 years ago, but our taste, which increased information may change altogether, is surely no true foundation for a human fellowship. But, be it remembered, this is not the idea of Baptism as it is expressed in any one formulary which is recognized in any part of Christendom. That idea assumes Christ to be the Lord of men; it assumes that men are created in Him; that this is the constitution of our race; that therefore all attempts of men to reduce themselves into separate units are contradictory and abortive. Now say, if you please, that this is an utterly false view of things; say that it does not in the least explain the relations of men to each other and the meaning of their history; say that there is no spiritual constitution for mankind or that it cannot be known, or that it is not this. But you cannot say that if it were this, a society founded upon such a principle would be merely one for a party and not for mankind. According to our doctrine we must say to Jews, Pagans, Turks, "There is a fellowship for you as well as for us. We have no right to any spiritual privileges to which you have not as complete, as indefeasible a right. We protest against you, Jews, because you deny this, because you maintain that there is no fellowship for mankind. We protest against you, Pagans, because by giving us different objects of worship, you necessarily divide us according to circumstances, customs, localities. We protest against you, Mahometans, because by affirming the greatest man to be merely a man, you destroy the communication between our race and its Maker; you suppose that communication to exist, if at all, merely for certain sages, not for every human creature. You set up the idea of absoluteness against the idea of relationship; whereas each is involved in the other and depends upon the other; and therefore you make it impossible for the Islamite nations to have any feeling of a humanity, to be anything but slaves."

Again, it is said, that our baptismal fellowship is not spiritual, for that it takes no account of the spiritual differences in men. The dullest clod has the same place in it, as the man who sees furthest into the meaning and life of things. Here, again, it is necessary, that we should recall the objector to the baptismal principle. He may think that we are using a mere phrase, or form of words, when we say that the man or the child is actually adopted into union with a Being above himself, and that the Spirit of Life, of Power, of Wisdom, is given to him.

* * *

Baptism asserts for each man that he is taken into union with a Divine Person, and by virtue of that union is emancipated form his evil Nature. But this assertion rests upon another, that there is a society for mankind which is constituted and held together in that Person, and that he who enters this society is emancipated from the World -- the society which is bound together in the acknowledgment of, and subjection to, the evil selfish tendencies of each man's nature. But, further, it affirms that this unity among men, rests upon a yet more awful and perfect unity, upon that which is expressed in the Name of the Father, the Son, and the Holy Ghost. Lose sight of this last and deepest principle, and both the others perish; for to believe that there is a Truth, a Unity, a Love, existing under certain forms, and not to believe there is an absolute Truth, Unity, Love, from which these forms have derived their excellence and their existence, is impossible, and has been always felt to be impossible.

* * *

I have stated why I look upon Baptism as the first sign of the existence of a Catholic Church or Kingdom of Christ in the world. I have considered the different objections to that view of it. But in the course of these remarks I have alluded to a class of persons who are most earnest in proclaiming the fact that there is such a Church, and equally earnest in maintaining that Baptism is the only induction into it. I have intimated that, nevertheless, I differ most widely with these persons, and believe that the dignity of Baptism was asserted against them by the reformers of the 16th century. I am then, I conceive, bound to consider the doctrine respecting Baptism which is professed by the Romanists, and to give my reasons for not adopting it.

The common phrase that the Romanist regards Baptism as an opus operatum, ("a work having been performed") is one which may be liable to much perversion. An intelligent defender of the system would protest earnestly against some opinions which might seem, at first hearing, to be implied in it. "To suppose," he would say, "from our use of it, that we look upon a baptized person as incapable of falling into sin or losing heaven, would be to contradict monstrously and ridiculously every notion which our doctors have inculcated in their writings or our priests enforced in their practice. The disciples of the Reformation complain of us for our vigilance and self-suspicion. It is our strongest conviction that a dereliction of baptismal privileges is at once most possible and most awful." But having guarded himself by this explanation he would, I think, be most ready to admit the phrase as legitimate, and to unfold, in some such words as these, the sense of it. "By baptism," he would say, "we receive the benefits of the redemption which Christ wrought out for us. We became new and holy creatures. The work is finished; we have received the highest blessing which God can bestow upon us. Henceforth our business is, by the use of all the means which the Church prescribes, to keep ourselves in this state of purity. We shall not preserve it altogether; we shall be committing frequent venial sins, which, after confession and penance, will, we have a right to hope, be forgiven us. But we may, by constantly availing ourselves of the prayers and communion of the Church, preserve ourselves from those mortal sins which would utterly rob us of the Divine blessing. Should a sin of this kind have been committed, or should there be any fear that it has been committed, we may still have just such a hope of restoration as is an encouragement to the most unabated earnestness and diligence in seeking for it by the appointed methods."

Now it will strike the reader at once, that in certain points this explanation corresponds exactly with the one which I have given. First, as to the effect of Baptism. I have contended that Baptism affirms a man to be in a certain state, and affirms the presence of a Spirit with him, who is able and willing to uphold him in that state, and to bring his life into accordance with it. Secondly, as to the sin of men. I have contended that this consists in their voluntarily refusing the blessings of God's covenant. Thirdly, as to the means by which we are most likely to be kept in the right way; I should say, as the Romanist does, by abiding in those ordinances, whereby we maintain a communion with our brethren and with God. Where then does the difference between us begin? I answer, at the threshold of these very statements. A man is brought into a certain state. The point is, what state? I have said, and I know the Romanist would not in words contradict me, into a state of union with Christ. But this state, I have contended, precludes the notion that goodness, purity, holiness, belongs to any creature considered in itself. To be something in himself is man's ambition, man's sin. Baptism is emphatically the renunciation of that pretence. A man does not, therefore, by Baptism, by faith, or by any other process, acquire a new nature, if by nature you mean, as most men do, certain inherent qualities and properties. He does not by Baptism, faith, or by any other process, *identity* become a new creature, if by these words you mean anything else than *relation ship* that he is created anew in Christ Jesus, that he is grafted into Him, that he becomes the inheritor of His life and not of his own. That, being so grafted, he receives the Spirit of Christ, I of course believe. But I contend, that the operation of this Spirit upon him is to draw him continually out of himself, to teach him to disclaim all independent virtue, to bring him into the knowledge and image of the Father and the Son. Upon these grounds, I have maintained, against our modern Protestants, that the sin of a baptized man consists in acting as if he were not in union with Christ, in setting up his own nature and his own will, and in obeying them. That is to say, his sin consists in doing acts which are self-contradictory, in assuming to be that which he is not, and never can be, in denying that he is that which he is and ever must be. What follows? Surely that faith in this union is a duty, the greatest of all duties, and that it can never cease to be a duty. A man has no right to believe a lie. Sin leads him to do it; sin brings him into a condition of mind in which a lie seems truth to him. It may bring him into a condition of mind in which lying becomes the element of his being, in which truth is absolutely closed from his eyes. The possibility of this sort of mortal sin I cannot doubt, either while I meditate upon the awful tendencies of atheism, which there are in every one of us, or while I read the Epistle to the Hebrews. But supposing this awful condition had actually taken place in any man, it could not change the fact in the least degree; it would establish the fact. Is the writer of the Epistle to the Hebrews less earnest in his exhortations to faith than the other writers of the New Testament? Does he less invite men to enter into God's rest? Does he separate these exhortations and invitations from his warnings respecting the peril of apostasy? or does he not make that peril one of his main arguments why every one of those whom he addressed should claim his privileges as a citizen of the New Jerusalem?

For precisely the same reason I attempted to shew that the Evangelical, or modern Protestant, notion made repentance impossible. If we are not allowed to call ourselves children of God, how can we be told to arise and go to our Father? If we are not to do this, what does our repentance mean? It can be nothing but a sinful selfish struggle after the blessings of corn and wine and the fatness of the earth, which we think we have lost; not a humble confession that we have made light of our birthright, and are no more worthy to be called sons. The repentance of the world may be produced by the desire or effort to obtain an assurance that we are members of God's redeemed family; the repentance which leadeth to life must be the confession of the unbelief, ingratitude, hardness of heart, which have led us to slight a love which has been bestowed freely, and which has never ceased to watch over us and to struggle with us.

Now the doctrine of the opus operatum leads, I think, by a more circuitous, but also by a more certain, route to those practical results which seem to me to make our Protestant systems so dangerous and objectionable.

When it is said that a baptized man loses his baptismal state, it is inevitably implied that this state was one of independent holiness and purity. We do not, as I have again and again urged, cease to be children because we are disobedient children. If therefore Baptism were looked upon as the adoption into the state of children, and if its virtue were believed to consist in this, the notion we are considering would be impossible. But it is supposed that the man acquires something for himself in the instant of Baptism, that he is endowed with heavenly virtues, that he is in himself, separately considered, a new creature. By this opinion the Romanist supposes that he exalts Baptism. He seems to me utterly to degrade it and rob it of its meaning. He turns a sacrament into an event. He supposes the redemption of Christ to be exhausted by a certain gift, while the Bible represents it as bringing men into an eternal and indissoluble friendship. He thinks that he promotes a safer, holier, more watchful feeling. It seems to me, that just so far as this opinion becomes the governing one of our lives, it undermines holiness, watchfulness, safety. For it turns the whole of life into a struggle for the recovery of a lost good. If this struggle is pursued honestly, there is no holiness in it, for it is purely selfish, it is not, cannot be, prompted by love. But in most men there arises a cruel sense of contradiction. They are commanded to repent; they feel that they cannot repent, for their consciences tell them that lamentation for the consequences of sin, present or expected, is not repentance; hence a craving for indulgences, a habit of unbelief, a despair of holiness. Which of these conditions of feeling is a safe one for a human creature to be in? But the Romanist thinks that at all events he is honouring the Church by this notion. To me it sseems that he is destroying the very idea of the Church, denying its necessity. For he makes it appear that the blessing of Baptism is not this, that it receives men into the holy Communion of Saints, but that it bestows upon them certain individual blessings, endows them with a certain individual holiness. How then is self-renunciation and fellowship

112

as members of the same body possible?   And if these are impossible, what is the Church?

It will be admitted, I hope, that I have not imputed to Romanists anything which is merely an excess or exaggeration of their creed upon this great subject.   There is a system of which this doctrine forms an integral part.   But do I therefore mean to affirm either that this doctrine is only to be found in Romanist writers, or that the one I have defended is not to be found in them?   I believe that if I brought forward any such propositions I should be easily confuted.   On the one hand it might be proved, by extracts from the Fathers, that the doctrine of an <u>opus operatum</u> did mingle itself in their minds with that of our being grafted into Christ; on the other hand by extracts from Anselm, from Hugo de St. Victor, from Bernard, from Aquinas, nay from eminent Romanists of the present day, that the very idea of which I have endeavoured to express has been unfolded by them, only with infinitely more eloquence and unction. All this I believe most fully. So far from wishing to hinder the theological student from making such observations, I would do my best to force them upon his attention.   I would labour to convince him, that whenever any great spiritual principle has been strongly revealed to men, a material counterfeit of that principle has always appeared also; that they have dwelt together in the minds of the best and wisest men; that if we seek for the one we must turn to their devotional exercises, to the occasions when they were most cultivating fellowship with God and most forgetting themselves, to those parts of their writings therefore which their disciples often study the least; that if we seek for the others we shall find them in elaborate controversial treatises, those which supply the best materials for theorems, the most ready formulas, the most convenient weapons of argument and ridicule against opponents; that the first remain for the delight and consolation of humble Christian people in all ages; that the last gradually shape themselves more and more into a definite system; that they are supposed to be bone of each other's bone, and flesh of each other's flesh, till some great crisis arrives, in which it pleases God to demonstrate the difference of the causes by the difference of the effects, to shew that one had proceeded from Him and the other from the devil. Let the reader then not be dismayed if he find the very highest authorities alleged in support of the doctrine of an <u>opus operatum</u>; let him not be surprised to find it in any age or in any part of the Church, (especially in any which had greatly undervalued sacraments,) reappearing and asserting its claim to be identical with the Scriptural and Catholic idea of it.   Let him not be terrified by being told, when he attempts to discriminate between them, that he is setting up his own judgment aginst the opinion of doctors and the testimony of antiquity.   Let him say boldly, I am doing no such thing; I am simply determining that I will not believe the doctors against themselves; that I will not suffer myself to be cheated of a transcendent truth which they have taught me, a truth which was evidently dear to their inmost hearts, a truth which they felt was derived from the teaching of Christ Himself and bound them to the Apostles and Martyrs of all times, a truth which they acknowledged was contrary to all their carnal apprehensions, and was only preserved to them by the continual teachings of God's Spirit; because they have elsewhere, while arguing with adversaries, while attempting to make a principle tell upon the hopes or fears of men who were incapable of entering into its true meaning, while drawing conclusions from Scripture by their private judgments, while apologizing for some fungus which the maxims of their age had confounded with the tree upon which it grew, produced a plausible explanation of this truth, an explanation forgotten in every moment of higher inspiration, and proving itself the less Divine the more it is tried by its fruits. It is easy to accuse those of wanting humility who have courage to act upon this determination. I believe that the proud system-seeking, system-loving intellect within us, disposes us to embrace the doctrine of the opus operatum; that the humble and contrite heart craves for a deeper principle, and, finding it, is obliged to part with the other for the sake of it.

SECTION II -- THE CREEDS

In the last section I defended my view of Baptism as the sign of admission into a Spiritual and Universal Kingdom, grounded upon our Lord's incarnation, and ultimately resting upon the name of the Father, the Son, and the Holy Spirit, against the different Quaker, Protestant, Philosophical, and Romanist theories, which are current respecting it. But I have very much failed of my purpose, if I have not led the reader to observe that Baptism, according to this idea of it, is also the justification of many of those Quaker, Protestant, Philosophical principles, which were considered in the first part; one step towards satisfaction of that great idea of a Church, one, indivisible, and imperishable, to which the Romanist clings with such honourable tenacity.

That man is a creature prone to sense, rising above it by virtue of a union with an invisible Teacher, is the doctrine of Quakerism. Baptism embodies that doctrine, and converts it, as Fox wished that it should be converted, from a mere doctrine into a living fact. The only foundation, says the Calvinist, for faithful action and for sound hope, is the belief that we are God's elect children. Baptism offers to men that foundation; it tells them that they are chosen of God, and precious. It makes this foundation, what Calvin and all earnest Calvinists have felt that it ought to be, not dependent upon our feelings, apprehensions, and discoveries, but on the will and word of God. At the same time the distinction which it draws between the new and the old man, the man in Christ who alone can be raised and glorified, and the old man which is to be utterly abolished, is a far finer, clearer, more practical distinction than any which the exclusive Calvinist has been able to reach. It denounces the unclean living into which the believer in an absolute separate election for him is in such dnager of falling, as absolutely incompatible with the knowledge and enjoyment of God which is eternal life; and yet it does not treat any living man as lying beyond the pale of God's covenant. Philosophers say that man can only be that or do that which is according to his constitution; he cannot be made by some miraculous process something else then he is; or, if he can, that power must be an injurious one. Baptism declares man's true and right constitution to be that of union with God, and separation from Him to be a violation of that only order according to which, as reason and experience alike shew, he can live. It is a fact that men are living anomalously; it is their own testimony that in doing so they are following their natures. Baptism declares that those who will are taken out of that inconsistent condition to which they are prone, and are taken into a reasonable condition, in which they may live so long as they remember the covenant of God. Finally, Romanism demands that by some direct, visible, permanent token, which all may acknowledge, it shall be felt that God has established the true, Divine, Catholic body upon earth; that it is the same from age to age; that the members are brought under a condition of Divine and spiritual discipline, are invested with mighty privileges, are laid under mighty responsibilities, are trained for a high and glorious condition. Of this demand, Baptism is the accomplishment, in a larger, fuller sense, than the Romanist will at all admit. By this sign we claim him, and hundreds of thousands in the East and West, whom he has anathematized, to be members of the Church and body of Christ; by this sign we protest against him and them, when by any acts or any theories they degrade the spirituality, or narrow the universality, of that fellowship into which they have been admitted, and so (as far as in them lies) make void the covenant and the purpose of God.

I wish now to consider whether there be any other notorious facts which can only be explained on the same principle as this of the existence of Baptism; facts appearing on the face of them to import that there is a spiritual and universal constitution of society for mankind; facts denied to have that significance by a number of warring parties; facts which establish their claim to be what they seem to be, by the help which they afford us in justifying and realising the leading principles of each of these parties, and in reconciling them with each other. The first which presents itself is this: --

There is actually found at this present day, in every Christian country, a certain document called a Creed. It is not necessary to inquire minutely at what time it was formed. Let is be admitted that there is an obscurity over its origin; that we cannot say who put it into that shape in which we now see it. From whatever quarter it may have come, here it is. It has lasted through a great many storms and revolutions. The Roman empire has passed away; modern European society has risen out of its ruins. Political systems have been established and overthrown; religious systems have been established and overthrown. Even the physical world has undergone mighty alterations, and our conception of its laws is altogether changed. The very languages which were spoken in all parts of the world when the Gospel was first preached, have given place to others; but this, "I believe," remains. It is substantially what it was, to say the very least, sixteen hundred years ago. During that time it has not been lying hid in the closet of some antiquarian. It has been repeated by the peasants and children of the different lands into which it has come. It has been given to them as a record of facts with which they had as much to do as any noble. In most parts of Europe it has been repeated publicly every day in the year; and though it has been thus hawked about, and, as men would say, vulgarized, the most earnest and thoughtful men in different countries, different periods, different stages of civilisation, have felt that it connected itself with the most permanent part of their being, that it had to do with each of them personally, and that it was the symbol of that humanity which they shared with their brethren. Reformers who have been engaged in conflict with all the prevailing systems of their age, have gone back to this old form of words, and have said that they lived to reassert the truths which it embodied. Men on sick beds, martyrs at the stake, have said that because they held it fast, they could look death in the face. And, to sink much lower, yet to say what may strike many as far more wonderful, there are many in this day, who, having asked the different philosophers of their own and of past times what they could to in helping them to understand the world, to fight against its evils, to love their fellow-men, are ready to declare that in this child's creed they have found the secret which these philosophers could not give them, and which, by God's grace, they shall not take away from them.

Now a man who has noticed these facts, and has settled it in his mind that, whatever they mean, they must mean something, would certainly wish to inquire into the nature of this document which has been diffused so widely, has lasted so long, and has seemed to so many different persons of so much value. He will find, I think, that is differs from all the digests of doctrines, whether religious or philosophical, which he has ever seen. A man is speaking in it. The form of it is, I believe. That which is believed in is not a certain scheme of divinity, but a name -- a Father, who has made the heaven and the earth: His Son, our Lord, who has been conceived, born, and died, and been buried, and gone down into hell, who has ascended, and is at the right hand of God, who will come to judge the world: a Holy Spirit who has established a holy universal Church, who makes men a communion of saints, who is the witness and power whereby they receive forgiveness of sins, who shall quicken their mortal bodies, who enables them to receive everlasting life. The Creed is evidently an act of allegiance or affiance; and since it has ever been connected with Baptism, one must suppose that from Baptism it derives its interpretation. If by that act we are acknowledged as spiritual creatures, united to a spiritual Being, by this act we claim our spiritual position, we assert our union with that Being. The name into which we are adopted there, is the name we confess here. Those acts which, having been done for all minkind, were the warrant for our particular admission into the covenant, are the acts which we here proclaim to be the warrant of our faith and our fellowship. So far the

116

form is consistent with its apparent object. But is it also consistent with the idea of Christ's kingdom which the Bible develops to us? There we found the primary postulate of such a kingdom to be a condescension of God to man, a cognizance taken of the creature by the Creator; the second, an apprehension of God by men, a recognition of the Creator by the creature. By grace are ye saved; by faith are ye saved. The position is freely given; a position of union and fellowship with another, a position of self-renunciation; the power is given wherewith to claim it: then comes the claim itself. Such seems to be the testimony of Scripture: and the relation in which the Creed stands to Baptism, and their common relation to that name and that kingdom which Scripture is revealing, surely expounds, in a remarkable way, that testimony.

But there is another creed possessing apparently equal authority with the one of which I have spoken, adopted perhaps into earlier use in the Eastern part of Christendom, and recognized by the Western ever since the age of Constantine. If it should be found that these two creeds clash with each other, or that they are not constructed upon the same principle, or that they do not both connect themselves with the idea of which we have spoken, the evidence from the preservation of either would certainly be weakened. Or if, these differences not appearing, it should seem that one could be conveniently substituted for the other, that there is nothing distinct and peculiar in each, one might be puzzled to account for the existence of both, at least as universal symbols. To see whether any of these objections apply, I would urge the reader to a thoughtful comparison of the two documents. First I would ask him whether in reading that which we call the Apostles' Creed, considering it as a declaration of the name into which he is baptized, he do not feel that it is meant to proclaim the distinct personality of the Father, the Son, and the Spirit, as signified by certain relations in which they have been manifested to men? Does not the name express such a relation? Then whether another question do not arise in his mind, which he may perceive from history has arisen also in other men's minds: -- Is there not a more mysterious and awful relation implied and prefigured in these? Does not the name express such a relation? Is not the knowledge of this, as the ground of those relations, part of the revelation which has been vouchsafed to us; one of the deep things which cannot indeed be understood (for who understands the mystery of his own ordinary human relations?) but which lies so immediately beneath those facts which most concern us all, is so needful as the interpretation and reconcilation of those facts, has been so eagerly felt after in all ages, that if it be not disclosed to the heart and reason of man, they will be tormented with such dreams and imaginations concerning it, as must make the acknowledgment of the Divine Unity impossible?

Now the Nicene Creed agrees with the Apostles' altogether in its form and principle. It is still I believe; it is still belief in a name, and not in notions. It differs in this, that it unites with a declaration of the Divine relations to men, a declaration of the relations in the Godhead.

117

To every peasant and child it speaks of this marvellous subject. Certainly a strange fact, doubly strange when one knows how much it has been the tendency of teachers and priests in all ages to believe that only a few initiated persons are fit to know anything which concerns the name and nature of God; and how much this tendency did actually mingle itself with the awe and reverence of those ages by which these creeds have been transmitted to us. That the doctors of the Church should have allowed the Apostles' Creed to be heard in every cottage is strange; that they should not have said that this deeper creed, though embodying the principles and data of the other, was only for theologians, is scarcely credible: yet so it was. Now if it were the purpose of God that His name should be revealed to men; if His name, which seems to most of us to be connected with the highest and most esoteric abstractions, be really the only ground of a universal society, we can interpret these facts. What other explanations have been found for them, I wish now to consider.

OBJECTIONS -- The Quaker

To the Quaker it seems quite evident that the invention of creeds is one manifest symptom of the working of that mystery of iniquity which has been always arising to counterfeit and to destroy the kingdom of Christ. The faith which a Christian man exercises in the Divine Invisible Teacher is entirely of an inward spiritual kind. Here it is thrown outward, turned into propositions, made the language of a whole body or congregation, reduced into a nullity.

One side of this objection I considered when I was speaking of the differences between the Quaker and the Lutheran. It is precisely the objection to the acknowledgment of the manifested Word, and arises from a desire, more or less consciously entertained, to divorce the idea of a spiritual object from that of an actual person.

There is, however, mixed with this radical dislike, a feeling of a most different kind -- a feeling that mere conceptions, opinions, notions, are most inadequate to the wants of a spiritual being, mere pictures and poor pictures of that which is real. To this doctrine I assent most heartily; there is none which I have been so anxious to maintain throughout this book. The problem how we many be delivered from opinions and notions, how we may rise out of them into another region, is the very one which I am investigating. The history of Quakerism I have found most helpful to me in the inquiry, at least in a negative way; for it shews us, I think, that there is no such certain and direct road into mere notionality, as that of rejecting all common and united forms of utterance. The apprehensions and conceits of each man's mind, being those which he regards as alone sacred, become his tyrants; and so far as he is able to give expression to those apprehensions and conceits, they become the tyrants over the minds of others. In no society are there so many traditional phrases which have had a meaning once and have lost it,

118

or are rapidly losing it, as in the Quaker society; in no society is there greater bondage to these phrases, a greater dread of exchanging them for any equivalents. And, therefore, without pressing the point again, that by this means all universaltiy is lost, that a body which professed to be for mankind became in a very few years the narrowest and most peculiar of sects, I maintain that the experiment of dispensing with a Confession as a means of promoting spirituality has been made, and has failed utterly. Once more I claim our strongest opponents as witnesses in our favour. By the character of their arguments, and by the results of their practice, they have increased the probability that if there is to be a kingdom of Christ on earth, a creed, which should present a living object as revealed in living acts to the faith of all men, would be one of the divinely-appointed means of its preservation.

Modern Protestant Objections

But the moment we use the phrase, divinely-appointed means, the modern Protestant, or Evangelical, steps in, and demands how we dare to claim such a dignity as this for a mere human composition, a mere ecclesiastical tradition? The Bible is the Divine document; it is a gross intrusion upon the rights of the Bible to assert that character for any other.

I would beseech the person who proposes this objection, to ask himself whether he seriously believes that the Bible is the only document, the only thing, which has been preserved to men by Divine care and providence? If he will say boldly, "I do think this," all debate is at an end. We are reasoning with a person who is separated by the very narrowest plank from absolute Atheism; a plank so narrow and so fragile, that in a very short time, it will be broken down. For, that he should believe this, and yet continue for any length of time to acknowledge a book which is characterised by nothing so much as its strong assertion, that whatever men possess they are to attribute to God's care and providence, is impossible. But supposing he disclaims, as he no doubt will, very indignantly, any such wicked hypothesis, I would beg him next calmly to consider what assertion of mine it is which offends him. Have I said that the creed is a substitute for the Bible? Have I urged that the creed is necessary, because it supplies information which the Bible does not supply? Have I said that the creed corrects or qualifies anything which the Bible asserts? I have maintained none of these propositions. I have said, "I find a document which has lasted for sixteen centuries or more. It is a document which explains to me the meaning and purpose of the Bible, which shews me that it has done what it proposed to do. As a declaration of the name of God, it proclaims that that which the Bible undertakes to reveal has been revealed; as an act of faith on the part of men, it proclaims that that faith by which the Bible affirms we are saved, can be exercised."

Is the doubt, then, why the creed, seeing that it only affirms the principles and facts of the Bible, should be necesary to those who already possess the Bible? The history of Protestantism gives the answer. The Bible, in the hands of its orthodox teachers, was reduced into a set of dry propositions, about the limitations of which they were perpetually fighting. The Bible, in the hands of its Unitarian and Rationalistic teachers, was reduced into a set of dreary truisms, not worthy to be fought about. You talk about the Bible, and the Bible only; but when you are brought to the proof, you give us, in place of it, dry husks of logic or pompous inanities, dignified with the name of simple truths. We want the Bible as it is, in its life and reality; and experience shews that we shall not have it, if we have not some witness of the principles which it embodies.

Again, the doctrine that faith justifies is, as Protestants affirm, the articulus stantis et cadentis ecclesiae ("article of the standing and falling of the church"). So said Luther, and looked to the creed as the great witness of what he said; as that "confession of the mouth unto salvation," in which "the heart's belief unto righteousness" is expressed and fulfilled. Such language seems to the modern Protestant dry, cold, and carnal; what is the warm, juicy, and spiritual language, which he has substituted for it? History replies, endless controversies about the nature, mode, effect, signs, attributes, qualifications of a living or dead faith; controversies in which nothing is forgotten, save the object of the faith and the person who exercises it; controversies which fill the hearts of humble Christians with bewilderment and despair; controversies with which the exercised dialectician detects on each side great acuteness, admirable ingenuity, but regrets that in both the favourite argumentative figure should be the petitio principii. Am I then wrong in claiming the pure Protestant as a witness that this Catholic creed is an essential sign of the kingdom of Christ?

* * *

THE ROMISH SYSTEM

Anyone who maintains the creed to be an heirloom of the Church, which has been preserved to men by the providence of God, and which each generation of her members is bound to watch over, as an essential sign and necessary safeguard of her existence, may be said to acknowledge the authority and value of a Tradition. He must be, I should think, a rather feeble and cowardly thinker, who is afraid of the name after he has recognized the thing; the creed he believes has been handed down, and that which has been handed down is a tradition. But the Romanist is the great apologist for tradition: how in principle can one who attaches this kind of value to the creed differ from the Romanist?

It is not necesary to inquire to what extent any given Romanist would approve of language like the following: That Scripture is not of

120

itself sufficient to make known all the system which the Church requires; that the notions, opinions, and explanations of the doctors of the Church requires; that the notions, opinions, and explanation of the doctors of the Church, partly as elucidatory of Scripture, partly as supplying that which is deficient and was meant to be deficient in it, are authoritative and necessary; that these together with Scripture constitute the ecclesiastical doctrine. I say I shall not inquire whether any particular Romanist writer may have objected to this statement; it will be allowed, I think, that so far as he did, so far he was rejecting, not certain excesses or exaggerations of the Romanist theory, but a characteristic and integral portion of it.

I think if this statement be compared with the view which I have taken of the creed, it will be seen that they are not exactly the same. It will be admitted that there are points of difference; that at all events I do not choose to use the phrases which Romanists use. But is the difference one of terms only, or is it a vital one, indicating an entirely different conception of the purposes for which this document, and the other documents bequeathed to us by antiquity, exist? I shall reply to this question by translating my words, "The creed is the sign of a spiritual and universal society," into others which I believe to be equivalent -- "The creed is a document which has served as a protection to the meaning of the Scriptures against the tendency which the Church doctors in different ages have exhibited to disturb and mangle them. The creed has served as a protection to the humbler members of the Church against the inclination which the Church doctors of different ages have manifested to rob them of their inheritance, and to appropriate it to themselves."

These propositions I have already illustrated, in reference to the doctors of Reformed bodies. I have maintained that the Bible, left to their mercies, would have been utterly deprived of its significance; and that had we been left to their mercies, we should have been fed with stones rather than with bread. In making these remarks, I speak only of an inclination, at times a most predominating inclination, which has been discernible in these teachers. I do not mean that there have not been many counteracting influences at work both in their own minds and in the minds of those whom they addressed. I have asserted again and again that there have been and are such influences; and that the more we consider the meaning and object of the Reformation, the more we shall discover of them. But I do assert that it is such an inclination as has needed a most strong and Divine power to resist it; and that power which delights to work by humble instruments, has, I believe, been exerted in a great measure through this child's creed. I will now endeavour to shew in what sense and under what limitations I conceive similar remarks are applicable to those early teachers whom the Romanist and we both profess to honour, as well as to the pontifical writers, whom he reverences, and whom we, I trust, do not despise.

It was the great glory of the greatest philosopher of antiquity to affirm, What man wants is a knowledge of that which is; he cannot be content with opinions and notions about that which may be. His being will not rest upon this. Society will not rest upon it. The ground of both must be a reality, an invisible spiritual reality; not any scheme or theory about this matter or that. The first Fathers of the Church had the strongest sympathy with this philosopher, precisely because he affirmed this. They felt that he was asking for the very thing which a revelation, if it were a revelation, ought to give. They felt, We have a revelation not of certain notions and dogmas about certain things, but a revelation of God himself. When I say they felt this, I mean that it was the deepest, strongest conviction of their minds, the one which their admirers have always acknowledged to constitute the great charm of their writings. To know God is eternal life. The Church is that society which rests upon the Name and Unity of God, and through which they are made known to man. I ask any lover of the Fathers, whether he will not fix upon these as the two great principles, which by their words and their lives they are illustrating?

Now, surely, if this be so, the theology of the Fathers must be most precious. They worked their way through infinite confusions into the clear heaven of these truths: God is -- He is one -- and His unity is not a dead material notion, but a unity of life and love, the foundation of all unity among men. If we have no sympathy with them, with those who first saw the light and rejoiced in it, above all, if we dare to mock them, surely we must expect that it will become every hour less clear to us and to our children. And what if these Fathers, having the idea of God ever before them, rather merged those of man and of nature in it, than perceived that each must be distinct, in order that each may preserve its proper relation to the other; may not this very fault of theirs be only an additional help to us, if we will use it humbly and faithfully? Their works are given to students; to them expressly and exclusively. They are committed, then, to men who have a peculiar vocation, a peculiar responsibility; who need nothing so much as to be taught how prone we all are to worship idols of the cave and idols of the forum; to set up the notions which are fashioned by our own peculiar temperaments, or which are popular in our age, in place of great principles, whereof they are the false likenesses; to be taught this in order that they may perceive the glory of that which is free and universal, and be delivered from the preference which our devil-infected nature conceives for that which is esoteric and self-exalting. This lesson, if it be received at all, must be received from the examples of good men, not of bad; of those whose light makes the darkness visible, not of those in whom all is dark. Why then should we deem the Fathers less valuable because they are capable of imparting it?

Alas! students did not make this use of the Fathers; but just that use which they could not have made if they had ever heartily admired that which was most precious in them, or had not lost the admiration of it through the vanity of possessing something in which other men did not share. They extracted notions, opinions, theories, from the writings of those saints who had declared that men are thirsting, not for theories or notions or opinions, but for the living God, and that they must have that thirst satisfied, or perish. Of course, then, the Bible became to the Patristic, as it did to the Protestant, student a mere congeries of notions; of course he also proclaimed, that to ascertain what these notions are was the great problem of human life, the necessary step to the attainment, of everlasting salvation. But this necesary step could not be taken by men generally; they could not find out the true notions. The Fathers must help them. They must interpret the Bible, and supply its deficiencies. Still we are at fault. The Fathers are as unattainable as the Bible. What each of them affirmed, what they agreed in affirming, could be as little ascertained, as what each of the writers of the Bible affirmed, or what they agreed in affirming. There must then be any authority capable of pronouncing on this point, a living authority. Where was it? Was it the whole Church of any given age, or some particular member of it? The first doctrine was plausible, but impracticable; the last, therefore, was adopted. To find the commission was not difficult where the necessity for it was clear. A man was enthroned as the dogmatist of Christendom; he was appointed to say, and could say, what men ought to think. Thus was another stone added -- not perhaps, the key-stone -- to the Romish system. But the system was not all that existed in the ages which gave it birth, and brought it to maturity. There was another element at work. Men still repeated their Paternosters and Credos; eminent men felt, "Here lies the deepest wisdom; no decrees and dogmas can reach the sense of the Scriptures, the sense of the Fathers, like this infantine lore." And so through the very heart of school divinity there ran a stream of simple faith, a silent acknowledgment that the truth had been revealed, and that the infinite complications of our minds, the various forms under which we are capable of beholding it, need not hinder us from knowing it and loving it. By degrees this faith became more and more obscured; opinion became all in all; then corruptions and infidelity grew and flourished by the side of increasing superstition and slavery. Still, there were holy and brave men, even in the later schools, who sought for a truth beyond opinions. The mystical writers spoke of beholding God, and dwelling in God. Ficinus and the Platonists, at the revival of letters, declared that there was a method of seeking the substantial and the real. But the "I believe" changed the glorious hope of the one, the philosophical idea of the other, into a fact for men. Then it became necessary for Pope Pius IV. to do that openly which had so long been done covertly -- to set antiquity at defiance, and to invent a creed of his own. Thanks be to God, he could not do this work effectually! In the nations which acknowledge his infallibility, not his creed, but the Apostles', is still repeated by mothers and nurses to their infants, still lisped by them in their own language, still taught them by their priests. The words, surely, are not always dead sounds; at all events they may start, some day, into life. Protestants may discover that there is in them the very heart of that Reformation

123

doctrine which the systems of Protestantism have been setting at naught; the Churches which seek for a centre of unity by crouching to Rome, may find in them at once the bond of their fellowship and the charter of their liberation; the Greeks may wake up to the conviction that centuries of alienation have been unable to deprive them and the West of these common symbols, it cannot be God's will that they should be divided. What a day will that be for the Catholic Church! what a day for the Romish system!

SECTION III -- FORMS OF WORSHIP

Every traveller is ready to testify how different the modes of worship are in the countries which he has visited. They vary, he says, with every degree of latitude. Within the same district he notices a persistency in certain practices and in the acknowledgment of the traditions which have given rise to them. Nevertheless the effects of Time may, he remarks, be traced almost as visibly as those of Locality. If through an invasion, or by any other fortunate accident, the habits of a more cultivated people are brought to bear upon an inferior one, the old customs acquire a more reasonable character; by-and-by, if the cultivation spread, and a particular class do not acquire the power of narrowing it to a certain point, a scepticism respecting old traditions becomes general. On the other hand, if a people be left to itself, without any of these influences, their minds become daily grosser, and the old superstitions lose all traces of the meaning and worth which they might have once possessed.

These remarks, which must be familiar to every modern reader, are undoubtedly derived from a true observation. Nor is their application at all limited to Pagan or Mahometan countries. I believe that where Christianity is found, the influence of locality and of periods is far more noticeable than elsewhere. There is a more strongly marked nationality in the different countries of modern Europe than in all the rest of the world at any moment of its existence; and that one century differs more from another in them than in the East, is a truism which it is almost foolish to utter. It is equally certain (as liberal writers so continually assure us) that the effect of this nationality and these changes in society upon religious opinion is most striking, and that there is no parallel to it in China or Hindostan.

But if it be so, is it not remarkable that certain forms of worship, actually of worship, have subsisted through all the revolutions to which Christendom has been subjected; have defied the restraints of national customs and languages; have stood their ground against all the varieties of opinion in reference to subjects human and Divine?

Is it not a strange thing, to take an example, that we in England in this nineteenth century should be using forms of prayer which were written by Greeks in the third and fourth? nay, that the whole conception of our liturgy from beginning to end; the assignment of particular services to particular seasons of the year; the use of Psalms; the ascriptions; the acts of confession, thanksgiving, adoration, should have been taught us by nations from which, by taste, by feelings, by political institutions, by the progress of civilisation, by religious antipathies, we are divided? Think only of our northern character, our cloudy skies, our Teutonic independence, our vehement nationality, and then recollect that we are using, perhaps every day, certainly every week in the year, at the times which we believe to be most solemn, words which we owe to Hebrews and Greeks and Latins; and that in these words the simple folk of England, in spite of their narrow notions and local customs, are able to find solace and delight.

Now if the meaning of Baptism be that we are brought into God's family, and that we become therefore capable, with one mind and one mouth, of glorifying His name; if the creed be teaching us, as children of that family, severally and unitedly to acknowledge that name, and how it is related to us; we must feel that acts of worship should be, of all acts, those which most belong to our position, and in which our fellowship is most entirely realised. And this feeling is surely one which must be wrought out in us the more we read the Bible and enter into the sense of it. That all division comes through idolatry; that all union comes throught the adoration of the one living and true God; these are the two texts of the Bible, which, from the record of the dispersion at Babel, where men would build a tower whose top should reach to heaven, for the worship of natural things, down to the day of Pentecost, when the little band of Apostles in the temple were heard by the multitudes, each in their own tongue, magnifying God, it is illustrating and inculcating. If anything is to break down the barriers of space and time, it must be the worship of Him who is, and who was, and who is to come, whom the heaven of heavens cannot contain, and whose dwelling is with the humble and contrite heart; if anything is to bring those at one whom these accidents of our mortality are separating, this must be the means. That men have turned worship to precisely the opposite use; that they have made it the slave of their circumstances, the badge of their divisions, the instrument of their hatred, I have confessed. The question is whether there be any witness in the world against this tendency; whether God has given us any sign that these separations are the effects of our choice, not of His will. I say that these forms of worship, preserved through so many generations, adapted to every locality, are such a sign; I say, that using these, I have a right to believe that the blessings of the day of Pentecost have been given once, and never withdrawn; that in the deepest and most practical sense there is a community which the distinction of tongues and the succession of ages cannot break.

OBJECTIONS -- The Quaker

Against this conclusion the Quaker protests vehemently. Forms of worship are not only no signs of the existence of a spiritual commonwealth; they are positively incompatible with it. The Spirit bloweth where it listeth. Prayer is given by the Spirit. By these prepared forms we make it the utterance of the will and the reason of man.

Nothing can be truer than the last assertion. We do make prayer the utterance of the will and reason of man. We consider it their highest and most perfect utterance; that in which, and in which alone, they fully realise themselves. What the human Will is we can understand from no terms and definitions of logic. They can only express one half of its meaning, for they can only describe it by its intrinsic properties; whereas its essential characteristic is, that it is ever going out of itself. They can only describe it at rest; whereas it only is while it acts. But in prayer we can know truly and safely what the will is; prayer expounds to us its inmost nature; prayer substantiates it, and proves that to be the greatest reality which seems in language to be the greatest contradiction. The will gives itself up that it may be itself. It dies that it may enjoy life. In acknowledging another will as the only will, it attains its own freedom; even as in trying to have a being of its own, it becomes a slave. "Father, not my will, but thine." Where do we behold the human will in such perfection,in such distinctness of life and power, as in these awful words? And it is the same with that organ which beholds as with that which determines, with that which is the seat of wisdom as with that which is the source of action. This only knows itself when it forgets itself; this only sees while the sense of sight is lost in the object of it. Accordingly the Reason also finds its deepest meaning and expression in worship.

But do we therefore deny that the Spirit of God is the author of prayer, or, in Barclay's words,that all prayer is spurious which does not proceed from Him? No; but in affirming the one proposition we affirm the other. We believe that the Spirit of God is the awakener, the only awakener, of the spirit in man; that the will and reason not called forth by Him must remain for ever the torpid helpless victims of nature and sense. We believe that unless the Spirit of God give these powers their direction, they will only minister to that which they are meant to rule, only rivet the bondage which it is their privilege to break. We believe that whoever in past ages, either in heathen or Jewish lands, used them aright, was taught and enabled so to use them, and in proportion as he used them aright, confessed the inspiration. We believe that it is our privilege to exercise them as they could not be exercised by heathens, or even by Jews, because it is our privilege to know that there is a living Person actuating and governing them; and to know what manner of person He is, of whom He is the Spirit, from whom He proceeds, with whom He dwells. We believe that this knowledge is far more deep and awful than that which anyone possessed who merely felt that he was the subject of an inspiration; but that being deep and awful, it is incompatible with excitement, with any distortions of manner or of voice, with the notion that we are merely the unconscious animal

126

utterers of certain sounds which are imparted to us, instead of the living, conscious, voluntary, rational agents of One who, when He promised the Spirit to His disciples, said: "Henceforth I call you not servants, but I have called you friends, for the servant knoweth not what his Lord doeth; but whatsoever I have heard and learned of the Father, I have made known unto you." We believe that we must attribute every act of our minds, every exercise of our affections, every energy of our will, to this Spirit; if the purpose to which we direct them be wrong, still the gift and power are His, that purpose only ours; if it be right, we shall own that of it also He is the author. We believe again that every operation in nature, the growth of every tree, the budding of every flower, should be referred to the influence of Him who first moved upon the face of the waters; but we do not call this a spiritual influence, because, though wrought by a spiritual being, it is wrought upon unspiritual subjects, upon things, and not upon persons.

Such are some of the inferences which follow directly from the idea of Baptism as a new birth, and of the Creed as the proper act of the new-born creature. That which is born of the Spirit is spirit, and seeks its spiritual home and Father, refers all its acts and movements to His inspiration, and thereby attains its own proper distinctness and freedom. That which is born of the flesh is flesh, and seeks the earth from which it came, acknowledging no influence and attraction but that. The contradiction of humanity is this -- when the human spirit glorifies itself, and, as the necessary consequence and punishment of that sin, abdicates its own proper rights and throne, and sinks into the slave of the flesh, impregnating it with its own sin. The glory of humanity is this -- when the human spirit renounces itself, and as its reward attains a knowledge of Him from whom it came, a victory over the flesh, and the power of communication to it its own life.

The objection, then which the Quaker makes to forms of prayer, that they proceed from man's reason and will, and not from the Divine Spirit, is one which involves a denial of the very nature and possibility of prayer. And this denial has been of the most practical king. He aknowledges prayer to be a necesary act, at once the sign of moral health and the instrument in producing it. Yet he dares not pray unless he have a sensible impulse urging him to the exercise. I will not dwell upon the Quaker use of the word "sensible," though it seems to me very significant, indicating that those who most abhor all appeals to the senses in worship, who think that the sights and sounds with which God has filled the universe cannot be redeemed by the redeemed spirit to his service, do yet grossly confound impressions on the spirit with impressions on the sense. But the important point is that the idea of our life as a conflict, an idea continually present, one would suppose, to Fox's mind, is thus set at naught. If the Quakers understood that the true will and real self was ever at war with the mere sensible impulse, they would surely have believed that the reluctance of the natural man towards an act which we know to be good, and feel to be necessary, is one of the best proofs that it is prompted and encouraged by the Divine Spirit. But the truth is, that the idea of a constant living personal presence has practically deserted those who seemed at one time to make this belief the whole of their religion; that the notion of an influence, an inspiration, visiting certain persons at certain seasons, which is common to Christianity with Paganism, is nearly all that they have preserved. Is it wonderful, then, that they should be unable to understand how the Spirit should have taught men in distant generations to express their deepest wants in the same words, or how through these words they should enjoy secret and awful communion with each other, and with the Most High? But, if so, what better proof do I want that these forms are one of the clear and indispensable signs of a spiritual and universal fellowship?

The Pure Protestant

The pure Protestants who have rejected the use of Liturgies sympathize but little in the Quaker's objections to them. They have no disposition to deny the voluntary nature of prayer or of any religious act. Because it has this character, they say forms are an intolerable bondage. "Each man should be able to express his own wants in his own way. In his chamber each man does or should lay bare his own feelings and wishes before God. This is the proper rule and standard of prayer according to our Lord's words, 'When thou prayest, enter into thy closet.' But since the minister, who is or should be chosen by the congregation, has a knowledge of the different circumstance of its members, and is looked up to by them as a person fit to preach the Gospel of Christ to them, it is very right that he should offer up prayers for himself and them, suggested by the feelings of the moment, probably a preparation for the sermon he is about to deliver, and therefore full of earnestness and unction. Forms of prayers are manifestly unsuitable for both these purposes; they cannot be adapted to changes of circumstances; they cannot be connected with the feelings either of the pastor or of the people; they are the impositions of another age, affronting to the understanding and painful to the conscience of those who use them."

Prayer to God is assumed in this statement to be, according to the primary notion of it, individual. A particular man wants to obtain certain blessings; he therefore asks them of Him who be believes can bestow them. To many persons this propostion seems self-evident; whoever doubts it is an enemy of common sense. Nevertheless it is, I believe, at war with the experience of every religious man. He learns soon that passionate eagerness to get some good thing for himself -- be it fine weather for the sake of his crops, or the salvation of his soul -- is not a help to prayer, but the greatest possible hindrance to it. Explain the fact as you will, but a fact it is, confessed by persons of different sentiments in different forms of language, continually presenting itself afresh to those who visit dying beds. The selfish object which we seek floats before our minds -- if it be an earthly object, palpably; if an invisible unknown object, in hazy images, having more in them of terror

128

than of beauty -- but the object, He to whom our prayer is addressed, is afar off; of Him there is scarcely the least discernment. He is regarded as a Being who can inflict evil and may choose to confer a blessing; or if, through the teachings of our childhood, we have some better knowledge, the consciousness of self-seeking perverts it, and we rise up feeling that the sacrifice is not accepted; "we are very wroth, and our countenance falls." And how is it that this kind of prayer, so natural to every man, is changed for any other? "When thou enterest into thy closet," these are the words of our Lord to which the pure Protestant appeals, say, "Our Father which art in heaven, hallowed be thy name." O wonderful teaching! not how the selfishness of the closet may be carried into the temple, but how the breadth and universality of spirit which belong to the temple may be attained in the closet.

When thou art most alone thou must still, if thou wouldest pray, be in the midst of a family; thou must call upon a Father; thou must not dare to say my, but our. Dost thou desire to be very holy? Yet this must not be thy petition; thou must say, "Hallowed be thy name." Dost thou wish for some assurance of a heaven for thyself? Yet this must be thy language: "Thy kingdom come." Dost thou wish to get some favourite project accomplished? It must be sought in this manner: "Thy will be done on earth as it is in heaven." Dost thou want a supply of thy necessities, bodily or spiritual? Then thou must desire the same for all thy brethren, as well as for thyself: "Give us this day our daily bread." Dost thou want forgiveness for thy individual sins? The prayer is still, "Forgive us our trespasses," and the gift is only received when it is circulated, "as we forgive them that trespass against us." Do you feel that your fellow-creatures are your tempters? Yet you must acknowledge their temptations and yours to be the same; you must ask that they may not be led into the very temptations which they cause, else you will be their tempter as well as your own. And this because the evil from which you must pray to be delivered is a common evil, an evil which is the same in root and principle, though it may take innumerable forms; that very evil of selfishness, of individuality, which we are disposed to make our very prayers a means of seeking, and which will encompass us and possess us, if we do not learn to join in the ascription: "Thine is the kingdom and the power and the glory."

I do not mean that many objectors to forms may not have preserved these truths, and with heart and soul entered into them; but I must maintain, that just so far as they have done so, the reason of their complaint ceases. If the individual prayer is not the highest and most essential prayer, but rather is no prayer at all, then the prayer of the congregation is not an aggregate of such individual prayers, but the prayer of a body, each member of which professes to have renounced his own selfish position, that he may come as one of a family to seek the Father of it.

129

In what sense, then, can extempore utterances be said to be most declaratory of our wants? Of what wants? Do the members of the congregation feel that they have sinned, and do they wish to confess their sins? Is this a local feeling, a feeling belonging to one set of circumstances, or to one period of time? Or is it a human feeling, belonging to men as men? "But each man has his own particular sin; his own burden, of which he himself is conscious." Undoubtedly; and is not his sin and burden just this, that he has chosen a scheme of his own, that he has followed certain tastes and inclinations of his own, and so that he has forgotten his Father in heaven and his brethren on earth? Does not each particular sin spring from this root? And is it not this which interprets that sense of the individual character of sin, and the personal responsibility for it, upon which so much stress is -- so rightly -- laid? The load lies on the separate conscience of each man. It is the very nature and law of the conscience that it singles out each man, severs him from his fellow, makes him feel that the participation of the whole universe in his guilt does not make it less to him. But then the conscience reproves us for this very thing; for having chosen to be divided when we were meant to be one. And since it has reproved men for this sin ever since Adam's fall, and since it has taught every Christian man that this was emphatically and most awfully his sin ever since Christ died that we might be all one, as He is with the Father; there seems no reason why the language of one generation, in confessing this sin, should not be the language of all. No reason why it should not be; the greatest blessing, if by any means it could be; since by this means the sense of sonship and brotherhood would be realised and revived in the very act of acknowledging disobedience and selfishness.

Or does some member of the congregation desire to give thanks for a blessing which has been vouchsafed to him particularly -- must this be a local temporary feeling, because it is called forth by a local temporary occasion? Does it not cease to be a true feeling if it is? If from the particular blessing the heart do not gain enlargement, be not drawn out into a contemplation of other blessings; if it be not led to dwell most upon those which are common and permanent, as being the greatest, though perhaps only observed when they are taken away or when some startling novelty brings them into notice, the purpose of God in bestowing that good thing is surely not accomplished; the man has not really profited by it. But if he have, his feelings become human feelings; they do not want a specific, self-chosen mode of expression; he can find them in the Psalms of David; he can utter them in the language of Christian men who lived in other climes and periods. He can give thanks for creation, preservation, redemption; for gifts enabling him to enjoy this life and another, which are bestowed upon his race as well as himself; he can ask that they as well he may have, above all other good things, a thankful spirit; his own special mercies will then be understood and appreciated.

Or does a particular member of the congregation long for some means, not of declaring his own sins, or his own thankfulness, but of praising the name of God, of glorifying Him for His great glory? Is this a specific, local, temporary, individual emotion? Can it have a specific, local, temporary, individual expression? Is it too humiliating, too limiting to the largeness of a modern intellect, that it should use the words of other days, and say, "We praise Thee, O God; we acknowledge Thee to be the Lord!" or, "Glory be to the Father, and to the Son, and to the Holy Ghost: As it was in the beginning, is now, and ever shall be, world without end"?

Or, lastly, does the same particular member of the congregation feel his need of mercies spiritual and temporal, and desire to ask for them? We have seen by the Lord's prayer how he ought to ask them, if he be alone in his chamber; how necessary it is that he should not look for them as meant for him, otherwise than as the child of a Father, as one of many brethren. Are they temporal, the blesings of food and raiment? Does he dare to seek for these with a desire to appropriate them exclusively? Then his prayer becomes a sin. Are they spiritual? Then the blessing itself is that of more intimate communion with his Father, a larger communion with the family. Is it necessary that he should limit these by the particular notions and phrases of his own time? Is it a great hardship and bondage to be obliged to use a more general, and therefore, one would fancy, a more becoming language?

If it be said, "Every prayer must be composed in some age, why do you suppose that those which have come down from another time must possess those qualities which you attribute to prayer more than those which are composed in our own?" I answer, I do not say that they must be better, or why they must be better, I have merely been contending with those who say, because they come down to us from another time, they cannot be fit for our use. I do believe, however, that the prayers written in the first ages of Christianity are in general more free, more reverent, more universal, than those which have been poured forth since. I do not think the opinion is a singular one; and I would rather its soundness were tried by the feelings and sympathies of religious men in different periods and circumstances, but especially of men in times of great suffering, than by any theories or arguments of mine. Still I do not find it harder to explain to myself why this should be so, than why there should be a fresher, truer feeling respecting nature and the outward transactions of men in Homer, than in the poetry of the seventeenth or eighteenth centuries. If there were that feeling respecting God, as the source of all things and the end of all things, which I attributed in the last section to the age of the Fathers, it cannot be strange, I think, that their devotional outpourings should have been simpler, purer, more human, than those of men who were occupied, and, as I conceive, were by the order of Providence meant to be occupied, in subtle questions respecting the operations of their own minds, or with inquiries into the law and course of nature. Whether the succession and order of devotional acts may not have much to do with the history and circumstances of man, as well as with the nature and plans of God; and whether, therefore, other ages may not have thrown a light upon this subject, which the first did not possess, I will not say. To those who deny all order in devotion, who think it little less than a sin that offices of confession should be laid down as preparatory to offices of thanksgiving, these again to offices of prayer, and these to the higher communion, it can seem no great derogation from the honour of the primitive times, if we should admit that the apprehension of this spiritual sequence may only in part have belonged to them. And if such persons still require a further reason why we think that the particular acts of praise and prayer were more congenial to older times than to modern, the considerations which have been occupying us under this head involve the reply. There has been a constant tendency for several centuries towards greater individuality of thought and feeling. There is a true ground for this tendency, though it may have led to the most false results. But it is in itself, when unsustained by another tendency, unfavourable to the worship of God, as well as to fellowship among men. A vehement reaction against this tendency has begun in all parts of Europe. One of the fruits of it will certainly be an aversion from all those utterances which modern Protestants have dignified with the name of devotion; if another consequence of it be not a return to the old forms and a delight in them, we must expect a reign of atheism.

The Philosopher

When the modern philosopher makes any objection to forms of worship, it is chiefly because they substantiate and perpetuate two mischievous superstitions. One is that a Being, who by His idea and law is unchangeable and perfect, can be swayed or led into better acts and purposes than His own by our petitions; the other is that it can please Him to receive the praises or commendations of His creatures. These complaints are usually put forth with most breadth and precision by disciples of the Utilitarian school. But it is evident that they are practically adopted, though with some varieties of expression, and in connexion with a different anthropological theory, by a large section of Rationalists.

Now in one phrase or another both these parties acknowledge, by every word which they speak, and every act which they do, either as philosophers or as ordinary men, that evil exists, and that it ought to be and may be by some means diminished. The Utilitarian traces it all to bad systems of government; the Rationalist refers it directly to man's ignorance of himself and his own powers. Each looks forward to his own Avatar, and to a millennial period of the species which shall follow. Each then does acknowledge an Ideal, with which men should be in agreement, with which they are not in agreement, into agreement with which they may by some process be brought. Wherein, then, do we and they differ? Not in the acknowledgment of actual inconsistency and contradiction: this has nothing to do with either of us; we simply own what we cannot deny. But in this, that our Ideal is a living Being; that we believe Him to have given all things their right type and order; that we believe them when in their relation to Him to be still very good; that we believe their disturbance and incoherency to be the result of a voluntary renunciation of allegiance to Him, by the only creature which could commit such an act; that we believe all disturbance and incoherency to be contrary to His will; that we believe the restoration to begin in the submission of those who have brought about the confusion. The submission consists in the confession that His will is the good will; one of the main acts and exercises of it is that of entering into His will, and beseeching that it may be put forth for the removal of those curses whereof the evil will has been the cause. This is the rationale -- in cold and miserable words -- of those ancient litanies which express to this day the thoughts and longings of the most earnest people in different corners of the earth. They are not founded on the notion that any thing is mutable in God. They are cries for the vindication and preservation of His immutable order. They are confessions that every act of His providence, from the first hour of the world, has had for its end the making this immutable order manifest, and the bringing the universe into conformity with it. But they are not founded upon the lying fancy that the world is right; that persons are fulfilling their proper relations to each other; that things are not discomposed and made evil by the sin of those who are meant to direct them. Man, they assume, is God's minister, acting for Him, able to perform His intentions towards His involuntary creatures; able, because he has a will, to set them at naught. His proper condition, in whatever place he were, would be that of dependence, of doing the will of another. His proper way of fulfillling that condition here, is by crying out for the rectification of that which is independent, which has lost its centre, which is struggling to stand by itself, and which therefore cannot stand at all; for the rectification of this, and therefore of whatever else has through this cause suffered decay and ruin.

But if it be said, "This supposes that a restoration has taken place already. These prayers are unmeaning, unless those who offer them believe themselves, on some pretext or other, to be in a better condition than those about whom they pray --" I answer, "Unquestionably; it is the very point which I have been pressing, that prayer does suppose a restoration; that the idea of prayer and the idea of a Church can never be separated, each implying the other; and that a Church which is not built upon the confession of a restored humanity is a contradition in terms." But, observe, a restored humanity; and therefore those who offer their prayers do not put forth any claim of superiority to their race, nay, not to the worst member of their race. The very essence of their prayers is this -- a cry that those sins which they feel in themselves, under which they are groaning, which they have committed, may not be, as they have been, their masters, and the masters of the universe. They who pray do not feel this less than other men, but more;

they do not reject evils from themselves to cast them upon their neighbours, more than other men do; on the contrary, they identify their neighbours' sins with their own; they feel that they have them, and are responsible for them. Only as members of a redeemed race and family can they vindicate the privilege, which has been asserted for them, of being new creatures, of casting off the slough of their selfish natures, of disclaiming that misery which by their rebellion they have made their own, of entering into that blessedness which their Master by His obedience has obtained for all who will have their portion in Him. So that the Philosopher says well and truly, that this superstition of prayer, if it be one, has been maintained by forms, and without forms would be likely to die out. Not as if the sense and necessity of prayer could ever die out in man, but because the only condition under which it can be a true and reasonable service, that of its being presented by men, as members of a body or family, which continues the same from generation to generation, and which converts the notion of a human race from a dream into a reality, is in these forms embodied, and wheresoever they are neglected is nearly lost.

I have still to speak on the subject of praise, which seems to the Philosopher a thing so unworthy of men to offer or of God to receive. The ground of this conclusion is that the words praise and flattery are convertible: and that since flattery is offensive to an imperfect being, so far as he has right feelings, and is only so far tolerable as he is weak and vain, it must to a perfect Being, if He took cognizance of such folly, be altogether odious. Now I join issue with them upon all these points. Suppose praise to be offered to a fellow-man which he does not deserve, it is abominable because it is false; suppose that, being deserved, it is offered to him with the view of bribing him to bestow future favours, it is offensive, because it is mean; suppose him to deserve it, and that it is offered with no unworthy motive, it may be wrong, because it is imprudent; for men, through their imperfections, are made vain, by hearing themselves even rightly commended. But if we could suppose these circumstances absent, I confidently affirm, that there is not any occupation so elevating and delightful to man, as that of praising and thanking his brethren. Generous men, in all ages and nations, have felt it so; when the motives of self-interest have been farthest from them, even respect for the object of their admiration, and fear of doing him hurt, have not availed to restrain them from expressing their sense of the favours which he has bestowed on them, or their delight in the beauty and harmony of his character. With no ignoble aim, these outpourings of the heart have often been directed to kings and great men; because the thankful and humble heart has felt their acts as a condescension, and has perceived a kind of special propriety and suitableness in their virtues. But they have been directed also to suffering friends, and poor scholars, and persecuted saints, and especially to the dead, from whom nothing could ever be expected, and to whom they could not be dangerous. Wherefore the true and obvious analogy from human experience is, --that if God have none of the imperfection which could make Him obnoxious to the mischievousness of praise; and if there have proceeded from Him all the benefits which all His creatures have received; and if there be in Him all the goodness and truth, of which the goodness and truth in man are the reflection, -- there can be no act so entirely suitable to man, so thoroughly joyful, as that of thanking and blessing Him. In which act if anyone discovers a low and cringing desire to win some good from the Being thus magnified, let him know that whoever enters upon the work in this spirit, and with this object, will be soon so struck with its utter ridiculousness and incongruity, or else so wearied with the heartless and hypocritical effort, that no pains he can use will enable him to persevere in it; or, at any rate, to persuade himself that he is doing more than repeating a set of incoherent, unintelligible sounds. In the loss of self, in the escape from self, consists the freedom and enjoyment of that act. The worshipper has found that object to which the eyes of himself and of all creatures were meant to be directed, in beholding which they attain the perfection of their being, while they lose all the feeling of selfish appropriation which is incompatible with perfection. They gaze upon Him who is the all-embracing Love, with whom no selfishness can dwell, the all-clear and distinguishing Truth, from which darkness and falsehood flee away; and they are changed into the same image, and their praises are only the responses to the joy with which He looks upon His redeemed creation and declares it very good.

* * *

THE ROMISH SYSTEM

But still these old Liturgies are in some sense Popish. The prayers in them have reached any modern nations which may have adopted them through Popish hands; they have received a Popish imprimatur. Nay, portions of them may be actually the composition of Bishops of Rome, or of persons who acknowledge their supremacy. What can be said to rebut this charge? Can it be pretended that there is an exact chronological line, at which what we please to call Catholicism ends and what we call Popery begins? Would we reject a prayer of Bernard's as passing the limit? If not, may there not by possibility be one by A Kempis or even by Pascal, which we would not utterly disown?

To these questions I answer precisely as I did in the former case; I want no chronological lines. I am quite ready to use a prayer of A Kempis or of Pascal or of many a person less commonly tolerated among us. Why I conceive the older prayers are in general likely to be better than those which have been composed in any part of Europe for several centuries I have explained; but that explanation has no direct connexion with the question before us. If there be no clearer and more palpable distinction between the forms of the Catholic Church and those to which the Romish system has given birth, than that which is arrived at by special pleadings about the date of the birth or the degree of the

135

soundness of particular men, I at least would rather leave the question unresolved.

But if the main and characteristic glory of the Church be precisely this, that it is brought into the Holiest of the Holies, not into the figure of the true, but into the presence of God Himself; if this be the grand point of separation between older forms and the cold efforts of modern devotions, that with holy fear and confidence they claim this privilege; if ascriptions to the name of the Father, the Son, and the Holy Ghost are continually on the lips, always in the hearts, of those who wrote them, giving at once the essence and the body to their supplications; if each individual member of the Church be in these forms supposed to join with the whole of it in every act of confession, of petition, or of thanksgiving; if this union of each with all be involved in the fact that these prayers are offered up for the merits and mediation of the one Lord of the whole body; if it is on the ground of these merits and this mediation that the poorest member of the flock may join with saints and angels about the throne because the virtue and life of both are in Him; if to these same causes is owing the freedom of the older prayers from those fetters of time and locality which mankind in the person of its King has shaken off; if therefore in these qualities consists their Catholicity, we have another, a more righteous and a more safe measure, for determining the value of the system which takes to itself the Catholic name. For that this system does in its mildest form embody the doctrine that men who are members of Christ's Church and body <u>cannot</u> enter into the Holiest of the Holies, <u>cannot</u> present themselves before God, <u>cannot</u> ascend up where Christ has gone before them, unless they approach through intervening mediators; that this notion is practically and constantly embodied in those forms which would be recognized by all as truly and properly Romish; that the mediators are not merely ideals of human excellence and beauty, but also the helpers and heroes of particular towns, professions, individuals; thus much will not be denied even by those who are most eager to disclaim the charge of positive idolatry. Now, more than this I do not want. I do not care to dwell upon those practical results which seem to me to have followed quite inevitably, and by a far stronger necessity than a mere logical one, though by that also, from these premises; I do not care to establish the fact, which seems to me written with sunbeams on the history of Europe, that a continually downward progress from Divine worship to hero-worship, from hero-worship to natural, must be the consequence, when that first fatal step is taken of doubting or denying that the communion between God and His creatures is really established in the incarnate Son, that the union of men with their Lord has been completed and cemented in Him. I simply take my stand upon this ground. I say, "By these acts you Romanists have set aside so far as in you lies, the very meaning and end of the Church's existence; have destroyed the very principle of its union and fellowship; you have reduced it into a set of incoherent fragments held together by no Divine law, and therefore needing some wretched human law to give it consistency." I repeat is, <u>as far as in you lay</u>, for you have

136

not done the work. A mightier power has been traversing your schemes and preparing the way for their ultimate confusion and discomfiture. Not without you but within you has there been a seed of life with which these seeds of corruption and death have been seeking to amalgamate, because they could not destroy it. These old, holy, reverent forms have been mocking your inventions as no vulgar Protestant scoffer was ever able to mock them, mocking them by witnessing that the blessings which those inventions offered were not too great for men to dream of, but too poor and pitiful for them not to trample under their feet when once they know out of what curse they have been delivered and to what height they have been raised.

These forms witness to us of holy men whom we are to remember, and with whose special graces we may sympathize, just because we are united like them to Him of whose fulness all have received, and grace for grace. Let them be multiplied if you will, let each age contribute its quota to the goodly company, let all the blessings which through them Christ has bestowed upon His flock or upon any the least portion of it (for blessings to a part are blessings to the whole) be thankfully commemorated. The forms bear no protest against such recollections; rather teach how it is possible rightly to entertain them. But the moment any one of these holy men is so regarded, that his translation out of this world shall not be a sign to the poorest man who stays in it of his own fellowship with an unseen Lord, but shall rather be a restraint upon his spirit, a fleshly impediment to communion, an earthly dream to obscure the vision of a heavenly reality, that moment the principle of these forms is assaulted, and any new language which may be introduced into them sanctioning such an inversion or denial of the doctrine of the communion of saints stands out in the most broad and palpable contradiction to the living words in which they have embodied it.

These forms invite us on certain days to remember our Lord's acts, condescension, humiliation, triumph. They teach us that if we forget the days, we shall be in danger of forgetting that of which they speak, and therefore of sinking back into that dark, idolatrous, divided state, out of which by Christ's work we have been brought. For there is not and cannot be any return to the state of Jewish outlooking and hope; denying the fulfilment, we lose also the expectation; we lose everything but a confused dream of a possible blessing. But if through any degrading sensualization of this testimony men shall come to fancy that the Church is not really redeemed, justified, and glorified in Christ, but that by the keeping of these days, or by any observances whereby they preserve their own fellowship with the Church, these yet unobtained blessings are to be purchased, then the forms which commemorate these days, as the great signs and trophies of Christ's accomplished work, do far more by anticipation to refute such a shameful and ignominious delusion, than all the words which can be devised after it has become prevalent. These forms authorise certain days and seasons, during which the members of Christ's body may enter into His humiliation, and chasten themselves with His stripes, that so they may keep down the evil inclinations which separate them from their brethren, may sympathize in the sorrows of mankind, may realise the blessings which are given to the whole Church. But, it any selfish and lying spirit should go forth proclaiming that by these fasts and penances for subduing the flesh that blessing is to be obtained which is given without money and price, that by them the individual man who performs them is put into a higher individual condition, and has a right to claim something for himself on that score which as an ordinary Churchman is not his, then these forms of humiliation do pour such contempt upon that godless and uncatholic pride, as no one who thinks all restraints upon self-indulgence vain and childish has ever been able to express.

I might go on through a number of other cases, but these will suffice as hints. They prove, I think, that there lies hid in these ancient forms of worship, something of that power which I attributed to Baptism and the Creed; a power before which all human systems, and therefore the Romish, the most complete of them all, must at last shrink and quail.

SECTION IV -- THE EUCHARIST

In all those old forms of worship of which we have been speaking, there is one service which is supposed to be of a higher character than all the rest, and to give them their worth and their interpretation. This is the service which belongs to a feast, called sometimes the Lord's Supper, sometimes the Eucharist, sometimes the Communion.

This feast does exist at this day in every part of Europe, in various districts of Asia, of America, of Africa. It has existed for 1800 years. It has survived, therefore, all those changes of which we spoke when we were considering Baptism and the Creed; it has been the most holy symbol to nations, between which race, political institutions, acquired habits, had established the most seemingly impassable barriers. In each of these nations, during that course of years, there have been endless conflicts between rich and poor, nobles and plebeians. Nevertheless this feast, during the time when these conflicts were the greatest, was acknowledged as the highest gift to the great, and yet as one in which the lowest were intended to share. During the same period the boundary line between the untaught and the scholar was even stronger and more marked than that which was made by wealth or honours. The baron might need the help of the serf; the student seemed to dwell in a region altogether his own, yet he acknowledged that in this feast he found the deepest, most unfathomable subject for his thoughts and speculations, and that the most unlearned might possess its blessings as much as himself. When the Reformation came it may be supposed that one at least of these phenomena ceased; that this feast was no longer regarded as the centre round which religious and philosophical meditations naturally revolved. Unquestionably there was change in this respect; it was the effort of the Reformation to detach itself from this centre; to a

138

certain extent the different reformed bodies succeeded in discovering each a separate centre for itself. But it is equally true, that in spite of this effort the Reformers were compelled to make their views respecting this feast the characteristic and distinguishing feature of their systems. Because they could not agree respecting its character and validity, all the terrors of a common enemy, all the sympathies which attracted them to each other, were insufficient to bind them together.

Through the seventeenth century the strife continued; new religious and philosophical systems were completed or established; still the Eucharist, in Protestant no less than in Romish countries, was a strange remnant of the past, which could not be passed over, which it was most hard to compress into any of the systems, and yet which must be brought into them, seeing that it was continually asserting its power in defiance of them. The eighteenth century came, and the same processes which were used for shutting out the invisible in every other direction, were applied also in this. And yet tens of thousands of men and women in every part of Europe, would in that day have rather parted with their lives, or with anything more dear to them, than with this feast. And now in this nineteenth century there are not a few persons, who, meditating on these different experiments, have arrived at this deep and inward conviction, that the question whether Christianity shall be a practical principle and truth in the hearts of men, or shall be exchanged for a set of intellectual notions or generalisations, depends mainly on the question whether the Eucharist shall or shall not be acknowledged and received as the bond of a universal life, and the means whereby men become partakers of it.

Supposing this notion to be utterly extravagant and false, yet it must be interesting to know what the institution is which seems to have obtained so many willing and so many reluctant testimonies to its importance. Now to describe its nature may be difficult, without entering on some of the points upon which these parties are disagreed. But its origin is not a matter of dispute. Protestants, Romanists, Greeks, all who receive it, refer it to the same period of time, and practise it in obedience to the same authority. All would say, "The night before the crucifixion of Jesus Christ, when He was keeping the passover with His disciples, He took bread and wine, and blessed them, saying, 'This is my body, this is my blood; do this in remembrance of me.' This is the meaning of our custom; we continue it in subjection to this command."

Now these words were addressed to a little band of disciples; to them, and only to them. There was no multitude present, as in the case of many of our Lord's discourses; no distant bystanders to whom the sentence might apply: "What I say unto you, I say unto all." Neither is there any express language affirming that the command given to these poor fishermen on that night was meant to extend to other ages. They might only signify that a person who had been deeply beloved was leaving with the friends from whom he was about to be separated a token and memorial of his intercourse with them. The words, indeed, "This is my body, this is my blood," might sound strange and hyperbolical, especially in a moment of what seemed final separation, for then the utterances of such a friend would be especially simple and awful, as we know that His other utterances were; but yet they might only signify, This will remind you of my person, and this of the blood which is about to be so unrighteously shed. Such an explanation, however embarrassing, would be the easiest, nay, it would be the only possible one, unless there were some circumstances connected with the whole character of Him who spake the words, with His other acts and purposes, with the time when they were spoken, which determined them to a different sense.

Suppose now that the person who spoke these words was the Son of man and the Son of God; suppose at the very time He spoke them He had been declaring Himself to be the way through which men must come to the unseen Father, to be the truth, to be the life, to be in that relation to His disciples in which the vine is to its branches, to be about to bestow upon them a Spirit who should guide them into the knowledge of the Father and of the Son; suppose Him to have told His disciples that they were the appointed messengers of these truths to men; suppose Him to have prayed that not only they, but all who should believe in Him through their word might be one in Him as He and the Father were one; suppose Him to have connected all these mysterious words with the giving up of Himself to death; suppose death to have been felt in all ages and in all countries to be the great barrier between the visible and the invisible world; suppose sacrifice, or the giving up of certain animals to death, and the offering them to some unseen Ruler, had been felt in all countries which attained to anything like national fellowship and consistency to be the means whereby they could approach that Ruler's presence, obtain His favour, remove His wrath; suppose sacrifices to have been the most essential part of the Jewish institutions, the most important element in their worship, the only way whereby they could draw nigh, as members of a nation, to the God of their nation; suppose them, however, to have been taught, both by the law which appointed those sacrifices and by the prophets who expounded it, that they were not valuable for their own sakes, but were accepted when they were performed by God's appointment, through His priests, as a confession on the part of the offerer, that he had violated his relation to the head of the commonwealth and to its members, as a submission of the will, as a prayer to be restored to that position which through self-will had been lost, or else as a means of expressing that entire self-surrender, which was implied in the fact of belonging to the Divine society; suppose that the feast which the disciples were keeping with their Master was the most purely national and strictly sacrificial of all the feasts, that one which celebrated the first deliverance and establishment of the nation, and which recalled the fact that it was a nation based upon sacrifices in which every Jew realised the blessings of his covenant, rejoiced that God was his King, knew that he was indeed an Israelite! -- suppose all this,

140

and then consider whether that which seemed the only possible interpretation of Christ's words, though a most difficult and perplexing one, do not become actually irrational and monstrous!

Consider whether anyone who believed what we know the Apostles did believe respecting their Master, His Person, His kingdom, could attach any but the very highest significance to language concerning His body and blood. Consider whether any persons who believed what we know they believed respecting their own office and work, could imagine that this significance was limited and temporary. Consider whether persons who connected, as we know they did connect, the kingdom whereof they were ministers with the earlier dispensations, could believe otherwise than that, by the same simple, wonderful method which had been used in all countries, and had been appointed, as they believed, by the authority of God Himself in their own, by the method which had enabled the Jews to enter into the fruition of their covenant and its privileges, and the neglect of which had again and again cheated them of it, He meant to put them in possession of all the substantial good things which He came to bestow upon mankind. Could they doubt that when they ate this bread and drank this wine, He meant that they should have the fullest participation of that sacrifice with which God had declared Himself well pleased, that they should really enter into that Presence, into which the Forerunner had for them entered, that they should really receive in that communion all the spiritual blessings which, through the union of the Godhead with human flesh, the heirs of this flesh might inherit? Could they doubt that the state of individual death which they had claimed for themselves in Baptism, was here to be practically attained by fellowship with Christ's death; that the new life which they had claimed for themselves, as members of Christ's body, was here to be attained through the communication of His life? Could they doubt that if their spirits were to be raised up to behold the infinite and absolute glory, here they were admitted into that blessedness; that if their hearts and affections desired a manifested and embodied king, here they became united to Him; that if spirit, soul, and body were to be subjected to the government of God's Spirit, that each might be delivered from its own corruption, receive its own quickening, and exert its own living powers, here each received that strength and renewal by which it was enabled to do its appointed work, to overcome its peculiar temptations, to be fitted for its future perfection? Could they doubt that if they were baptized into the name of the Father, the Son, and the Holy Ghost, and if this deepest unity were the foundation of such a union among men as no barrier of time, or space, or death, could break, here they were actually received into communion with that awful name, and into communion with all the saints who live by beholding it and delighting in it? Could they doubt that here the partial views and one-sided words and opposing thoughts of men, found their meeting-point and complete reconciliation; that here lay the clear vital expression of those distinctions which in verbal theology become dry, hard, dogmatic oppositions; that here it is apprehended how faith alone justifies, and how faith without works is dead; how it is we that act, and yet not we, but Christ in us; how he that is born of God cannot commit sin, and yet if we say we have no sin we deceive ourselves; how we may be persuaded that neither life nor death, nor things present, nor things to come, shall separate us from the love of God which is in Christ, yet may tremble lest we should be castaways? Could they doubt that it was their office to present Christianity in its different aspects to the different wants and circumstances of their own age and of ages to come; that it was the office of this sacrament to exhibit it as a whole truth, at once transcedent and practical, surpassing men's thoughts, not dependent on men's faith and opinions, and yet essentially belonging to man, the governing law of his being, the actuating power of this life? Could they doubt that they were to lay the foundation of the Church on earth, and that this sacrament was to give it permanency, coherency, vitality throughout all generations? And if this were their fatih, why, I ask, is it not to be ours? What has happened to rob this sacrament of its meaning, or to make that meaning less applicable to us of the nineteenth century than it was to those who lived in the first, less necessary for us than it was for them? The answers to these questions are various.

OBJECTIONS -- The Quaker

In this case, as in that of Baptism, the Quaker believes that we have adhered dangerously to Jewish precedent, have preserved signs when they should have been abolished, have followed shadows when the spiritual substance was that which we should have apprehended. But here the sin is more flagrant. The essence of Christianity lies in the reality of the sacrifice which we, after the example and by the power of Christ, are able to offer up. For the surrender of ourselves, the true self-annihiliation, this ceremony is substituted, a ceremony clothed with great names and fictitious attributes, in order that we may excuse ourselves from the necessity of any practical sacrifice.

I am not unwilling to incur the charge of tautology, for the sake of noticing again the first and more general of these complaints. For they receive a new and most valuable illustration from the special arguments which are connected with them. It will be remembered that the difference between us and the Quakers in the other instance seemed to be this. They suppose that the Christian Covenant, because it is spiritual, dispenses with that method which was sanctioned by divine authority in the earlier dispensation. We believe that the Christian Covenant, because it is more spiritual than the Jewish, requires another application of the same method in order that the difference may be perceived. Having the sign of the lower covenant to compare with the sign of the higher, I can understand wherein the one surpasses the other; the Quaker, being unable to make any such comparison, only talks of the distinction, cannot apprehend it in fact, cannot even express it in language: while he rates the old far below its true value, he yet continually in his thoughts reduces the new to a level with it, in his practice makes the perfect spirituality of the latter to consist merely in the absence of a characteristic which the degree of spirituality possessed by the former made necessary. Thus much with reference to the preliminary act or condition of the covenant. Applying the same rule to the results, privileges, and enjoyments of it, the Quaker asserts that the Jew realised the blessings of his covenant in a sacrificial feast; that the blessings of ours being spiritual, such a method is, in our case, impossible. We affirm, that the privileges which the Jews realised in their festivals were spiritual privileges; that the privilege of looking up to an invisible Guide and King and Friend, and rejoicing in Him, was a spiritual privilege; that the privilege of feeling themselves a nation was a spiritual privilege; that these are emphatically the privileges which the spirit of man craves for; that God gave them to the Jews in a most simple, reasonable method; and that when we understand what the things given were, it becomes difficult to imagine how by any other method they could have been received. We affirm again that our privileges are higher than those of the Jews, but higher only as being the perfection of what they had imperfectly. They are the privileges still of fellowship with God, of fellowship with our brethren; but of fellowship with God as with a Being who has entered into a direct union with our race in the Person of His Son; of fellowship with a Race in its Head, not merely with a particular Nation. Now we want to know what there is in the character of these blessings which makes a united festival unsuitable for the realisation of them? It was suitable, nay, actually necessary for the realisation of the others; shew us in some other way than by merely repeating the words, carnal and spiritual, how the change has taken place?

We grant most freely that there must be a change in the nature of the institution appropriate to a change in the nature of that which it expresses. We grant that Christianity is nothing, if it be not the actualization and substantiation of a union which was before to a great extent prophetical and ideal. We grant that a mere shadow, a pictorial feast, would be more inconsistent with the nature of the Gospel, than even of the Law -- though inconsistent with either, seeing that in each case the feast ought to put the receivers of it into actual possession of that which at the time they were capable of possessing. But admitting all this, the questions recur, "Can there be no feast, which is applicable to the position of Christians, as the feast of the Passover was to that of the Jews? Have those who deny the existence of such a feast, stigmatizing it as a mere ceremony and phantasm, shewn that they retain the substance of Christianity?"

To examine this last point, let us consider why it is that the Quaker protests against this particular institution. The Christian sacrifice, he says, ought to be real; the giving up of a man's own self to death according to the example of our Lord and Saviour. Our Lord's death in itself was most real, carried into every act which He performed and every word which He spoke, how can we think that we manifest that death in a service less actual, individual, continuous? From this statement it will be seen at once, that the end of Christianity, according to the Quakers, is individual self-denial or self-sacrifice. Christ perfectly sacrificed Himself; by Christ's power in us we may do the like; this is their habitual language. Now that Christianity involves this, that there is no meaning in it if the principle of self-sacrifice be not at the root of it, I believe I acknowledge as strongly as he can. But as we both agree that our Lord's example is the one by which we are to shape ourselves, that the type of sacrifice is in Him, I must inquire whether He referred to sacrifice as the object of His life, or only as the indispensable condition of it. The answer which He gives on this point seems to me very express. He declares that He came to glorify His Father's Name, to do His Father's Will. He declares that He came to die for the sheep. Because He glorified His Father's Name and would not glorify His own; because He would not be an individual man but would identify Himself with the lowest condition of those whom He was not ashamed to call His brethren, therefore do we see in Him the perfect example of self-sacrifice. The whole idea of His life is lost the moment we forget this. Imagine Him coming into the world not to manifest God, but to exhibit a specimen of glorious heroic self-sacrifice; not to die for men, but to shew how He could die, and the example perishes. We have an object presented to us which no man who has been used to contemplate his Lord with anything of love or devotion, could bear to look at. And yet if we believe that the end we are to keep in view in our own lives is this of self-annihilation, we either must make this change in the image we profess to copy, or else forget it altogether and fix our eyes only upon ourselves.

Nor is this all, as the history of the Quakers has proved. This doctrine of self-sacrifice and self-annihilation, when it has not led them into conscious self-righteousness and self-glorification, has occasioned a miserable confusion respecting their own lives and duties. If the Spirit of Christ, they have said to themselves, be leading us to entire crucifixion, shall we not be resisting Him if we keep alive any peculiar affection or faculty? And yet the same conscience which seemed to enjoin self-sacrifice, said also, How dare you crush those powers, energies, and affections which God has given you, and of which you are to render an account to Him? The difficulty is most practical, the contradiction most agonizing. And the fruits of it to those who have witnessed it, have been as distressing as to those who have been exercised by it: one part of them, thinking that such feelings must be the consequence of a dark supersition, fly to infidelity or indifference; another, more earnest and sincere, seeing that the sacrifice of Christ has been lost sight of in these efforts after self-sacrifice, have violently denounced all such efforts as godless and vain, and adopting sound language respecting the all-sufficiency of the one sacrifice, have made it a foundation for Antinomian doctrine and practice.

But if we kept this thought steadily before us, that the hallowing of God's name is the end for which our Lord lived and for which we are to live; that to give Him thanks and praise for that which He is and for that which He had done, and so to enter into the perception and apprehension of that which He is and that which He has done, is the highest felicity which we can attain; that our Lord who was one with the Father did in all the acts of His life exhibit this perfect sympathy with Him and delight in Him, and submission to Him; that the voluntary sacrifice of His body to death was the final and consummate act of sympathy, delight, submission; that as self-will and disobedience are the obstacles to the communion of men with their Creator, so are they obstacles to communion with each other; that the same act therefore which removed the only obstacle to the one communion removed also the obstacle to the other; that the cross of Christ is the centre point of all fellowship; that while we seek our fellowship there, affirming ourselves to exist only as members of Christ's body, and to derive our life from Him, we may find strength habitually to deny ourselves according to His example -- we surely obtain an idea of Christianity altogether different from the other, and yet one which includes all the practical truth of it, and which must have hovered as we know it did hover before the minds of the early Quakers, in order that they might be able to conceive their own narrow and fragmentary notion. A person who lives in the light of this truth must look upon the sacrifice of Christ as <u>distinct</u> from all other sacrifices, because it is only by means of it that we are brought into the presence of God or are made one body. He cannot look upon the sacrifice of Christ as <u>separate</u> from any other sacrifice, because he conceives all sacrifices to derive their worth and meaning from it. He must regard self-sacrifice as the necessary element of a Christian life. He cannot permit it to assume a self-conscious and therefore contradictory character by regarding it as the means of procuring a blessing, when it is in fact the fruit and the fruition of a blessing already procured. He must consider every Christian obliged to mortify his selfish nature, in order that he may offer an acceptable sacrifice to God. He cannot confound the mortification of the evil nature with the destruction or weakening of a single faculty which God has bestowed. For those faculties are imparied and ruined by the dominion of the evil nature; they are strongest when it is most subdued. They must be kept strong because God requires them as a sacrifice; and the more they are sacrificed to Him the more strength do they acquire.

We have seen yet another instance in which the Quaker, refusing to maintain what he calls a mere form, has utterly perverted or lost a principle. I do not charge it upon him as a special sin that he has inverted the notion of sacrifice, has substituted means for ends, has introduced self-righteousness under the name of self-forgetfulness. These tendencies are common to all ages, they are precisely the tendencies of our individualizing natures. In this respect the Quakers are not different from the rest of men. The sin which I do charge them with is this: that when Christ had, of His love and mercy to mankind, provided them with a simple and wonderful testimony against these narrow notions and dividing tendencies; when He had embodied in a living feast the complete idea of His kingdom, which we, looking at things partially, from different sides, through the prejudices and false colourings of particular times and places, are continually reducing under some name, notion, or formula of ours; when He had made this feast effectual for imparting to men a faith far above the level of their ordinary theories and speculations; when He had given it as a bond to all peoples and languages and generations -- they chose to fancy that His ordinance signified nothing, that they had a much better storehouse for His truths in their own fine thoughts and spiritual apprehensions. Of this sin I maintain that they are suffering the punishment in the almost entire loss of that Spirituality and that Universality which they hoped by these means to attain.

2. <u>The Zwinglian, the Calvinist, the Lutheran</u>

1. There is one objection to my statements on this subject in which pure Protestants would in general agree. They would say that when I call the Eucharist a sacrificial feast I am using dangerous language, incompatible with the full recognition of Christ's finished sacrifice upon the cross. "If it be sacrificial it must be propitiatory; the words are convertible; then what becomes of the doctrine of the Atonement as it was held by the Reformers?"

Starting from this negative point of agreement our opponents soon divide themselves into several classes. To the first the Eucharist appears a mere memorial of a past transaction. When I treat it as a substantial feast, as in some strange way identified with the spiritual things of which it speaks, and as being a channel through which actual blessings are received, I am using phrases, they say, for which Scripture gives no warrant, and which are contrary to plain sense and experience.

The second class think differently. According to them the true believer does realise in the Sacrament an actual mysterious blessing. He not only recollects a past good; he is conscious of a present good; Christ is with him in the feast. The mistake I have committed consists in supposing the good to exist in the Sacrament apart from the faith of the receiver. Such a doctrine unsettles the very foundation of Protestant Christianity.

The third party by no means agree in this opinion. They think that the Sacrament has a reality in it which it does not receive from the mind of the partaker. Christ is actually consubstantiated with the elements. The error of the principle I have maintained consists in this, that is supposes us to be brought into a holy and Divine Presence, and yet offers no explanation of the way in which so wonderful a transaction takes place.

146

Before I consider the first objection, in which Zwinglians, Lutherans, and Calvinists agree, let me remind my readers of the remarks which I made under the last head. I affirmed that Quaker history had proved the incredible danger which results from supposing that our Lord's sacrifice is merely a pattern or example of our sacrifices, or merely the power by which these sacrifices are effected. It must have an entirely distinct character; otherwise it is of no worth as an example or as a power. And I maintained further that this distinct character, in virtue of which it is an example and a power, is exhibited in this Sacrament, and that by losing this Sacrament the Quakers have lost the sense of it. I think these assertions hardly bear out the suspicion that I confound the sacramental act, -- an act performed by men and therefore their act, by the hypothesis one of our sacrifices, -- with the sacrifice of Christ; or suppose that the necessity of the one proves the other incomplete. Every word I have used leads to precisely the opposite conclusion. I have maintained that because the sacrifice had once for all accomplished the object of bringing our race, constituted and redeemed in Christ, into a state of acceptance and union with God, therefore it was most fitting that there should be an act whereby we are admitted into the blessings thus claimed and secured to us. And because those blessings were not given to the generation which lived in the days of our Lord's incarnation and death, but to all generations, therefore is it fitting that this act sould be renewed through all generations; and because those blessings do not belong to one moment of our existence but to every moment, therefore is it fitting that the act by which we receive them should continually be renewed by us during our pilgrimage on earth. When we say then that our feast, like that of the Passover, is sacrificial, we do not mean that it does not commemorate a blessing which has been fully obtained and realised; if we did we should violate the analogy in the very moment of applying it; for the Passover did commemorate a complete deliverance and the establishment of a national state in consequence of that deliverance. But as that deliverance was accompanied with a sacrificial act, and by a sacrifical act accomplished, and yet in this Passover the act was perpetually renewed; because in this way the nation understood that by sacrifice it subsisted and consisted; and because by such a renewal its members realised the permanent and living character of the good that had been bestowed upon them, so it is here. The sacrifice of Christ is that with which alone God can be satisfied and in the sight of which alone He can contemplate our race; it is therefore the only meeting-point of communion with Him; but this communion being established, it must be by presenting the finished sacrifice before God that we both bear witness what our position is and realise the glory of it; otherwise we have a name without a reality, and with the words "finished and complete" are robbing ourselves of the very thing which makes it so important that we should prize them and preserve them.

Why these considerations have been overlooked by Protestants I think will be evident from the remarks which were made in the former part. The worth of Protestantism consisted in this, that it asserted the distinct position of each man, affirming that he was a person and not merely one of a mass. This truth had been working itself out into clearness for many centuries, but the process was a strange and painful one. The conscience is that which tells each man he is a person, making him feel that which he has done in past time to be his own, giving him an awful assurance of identity, responsibility, permanence. Overburdened with the sense of evil, it sought for a remedy; it was commanded to perform certain services in the hope of finding one; with each attempt the sense of moral evil increased. The Reformers found that the whole scheme was a delusion. The services presumed that freedom of conscience which men sought to acquire by them; without it they were not true godly services. The emancipation of the conscience was therefore that which they sought as the step to all good; they declared that by faith in Christ, grounded upon acts of complete redemption done on their behalf, they could alone obtain it.

How true this language was, what a curse had come upon the Church through the denial of it, how necessary it was that, at that time especially but also at all times, it should be proclaimed, I have contended again and again. But it is equally certain that as the Quakers believe self-sacrifice, so the Reformers believed the emancipation of the conscience, to be not a necessary condition of our moral being but the end of it. Whatever contributed to this end was necessary, whatever did not contribute to it was worthless. The belief of Christ's sacrifice upon the cross was that which had given peace to their consciences; that it had any purpose save that of giving peace to the conscience was more and more forgotten. And therefore it became necessary to explain how it accomplished this purpose. Then began all the theories about sacrifice, satisfaction, and imputation, which I spoke of as at once so fatal to the principles of the Reformation and to the practical life of Christianity, as affording no comfort to the humble heart, as leading to all disputes and separations, as preparing the way for the infidelity of the eighteenth century. These hungry notions of the understanding being substituted for the clear, simple belief of the Reformers that we are adopted into Christ by Baptism and are therefore children of God, and may draw nigh to Him in all duties and services, confessing the sins which have polluted us and separated us from Him, turned everything into confusion. Men knew that they were not approaching God with pure consciences; the Reformers said that if they did not, the service was a mockery; they therefore sought hither and thither for some better kind of faith which could give them relief; not finding it, they deemed the whole Gospel to be a dream and fable.

2. But that which lay beneath all these dark imaginations and sad results was, I believe, the imperfect apprehension which the Reformers themselves had of the nature of the Communion. This feast, says the Zwinglian, is nothing but the memorial of a past transaction. That it is the memorial of a past transaction is of course assumed in every word I

have said. If it were not it could have no pretence to the name of Eucharist; it would bear no analogy to the Passover. But the Passover had not merely reference to the past. The Jew had been brought out of Pharaoh's government and brought under God's government. In commemorating the past emancipation of his nation he claimed for himself a privilege which belonged to it then. It would, I think, be insulting the Zwinglian to suppose that he thought the Christian ordinance, in this respect, different from its predecessor. He is particularly practical and rational; he must therefore know well that no men ever did or ever could celebrate with the least heartiness and affectionateness an event which they did not suppose in some sense to be the cause or the commencement of an improved condition of things, that condition of things being one with which they were in some way connected. The Zwinglian then cannot mean by his words "Simple memorial" that there is nothing of present continuous interest in it; if he did he would suppose, contrary to all his professions, that our Lord's religion imposes, as a test of obedience, a most dry, dreary, unmeaning ceremony. But if he allows, as of course he will, that certain effects have followed from our Lord's death, in which we are partakers, and that these effects, and not merely the cause which produced them, are recalled to us by this feast, then the question immediately occurs, What are these effects? The great effect which we believe to have proceeded from it, that in which every other is included, is that thereby we are made capable of entering into the presence of God; that a mercy-seat is revealed to mankind, where his Maker may meet with him. Supposing this were so, this must surely be one of the effects which is brought to our recollection by the Eucharist. I do not object to the word recollection; there is nothing in it which is not applicable to a Living Actual Presence. What I plead for is the duty of recollecting that presence in the Eucharist, because it is there.

But the Zwinglian will ask, Why there, and not elsewhere? The question may bear two constructions. It may mean, Why may we not feed upon the sacrifice of Christ at all times, and thus enter into the presence of Him who perfectly delights in that sacrifice? Or it may mean, God is omnipresent; why then are we not always in His presence? Evidently these two thoughts are of the most different kind, and originate in most different states of feeling. The first suggests to us the highest standard of perfection which a Christian can propose to himself, and yet a standard which, if what I have said be true, must be a most real and reasonable one: for that the Church is brought into the presence of God, is the first principle of the New Dispensation, the one which is especially involved in this sacrament; and if every one of us ought to consider himself a member of the Church, this wonderful privilege belongs to us, not in proportion as we raise ourselves to some individual excellence, but in proportion as we renounce all such distinctions, and yield ourselves to the Spirit who dwells in the whole body. What then I should say, in reference to this view of the case, is precisely what I have said in reference to the Quaker doctrine. If we

149

acknowledge that the light is somewhere concentrated, that it reveals itself to us in some way which it has chosen; that the revelation is not for us only, but for all; if we make this acknowledgment practically, we are at least in the right road to the realisation of that blessing which it is so truly affirmed that we ought to seek. Otherwise we shall fancy that we produce this presence by our acts of meditation or faith; we glorify ourselves for these acts, and for a reality we get a dream; then we gladly betake ourselves to the other doctrine, which comes forth with the boast that it asserts "the Omnipresence of the Deity."

So I believe it has happened with the Zwinglians. An early disciple of the school, attaching an almost superstitious veneration to the Bible, would at once have rejected this phrase as incompatible alike with its letter and its spirit. He would have asked how it could be reconciled with the words of the Book of Genesis, which speak of God as meeting Adam in the garden, as coming down to see the tower which men had builded, as appearing to Abraham at the tent-door? A Zwinglian of the next century would have learnt perhaps to use the phrases, "figures," "eastern allegories," and such like, in reference to these passages. Still he would have said to himself, "Honest men use allegories and figures for some purpose; they mean something by them; it is a truth which they wish to convey. But if I admit these phrases, 'ubiquity,' 'omnipresence,' in their ordinary sense, I must suppose the Word of God less honest and true than the word of men; for these stories, instead of implying or hinting a truth, involve the direct contradiction of one." But a Zwinglian of the third century will have mastered all these difficulties. He will at once dispose of these scriptural expressions, by calling them "anthropomorphic," or indications of a low state of civilisation; or with less honesty he will pass them over altogether, only assuming that the phrase, "Omnipresence of the Deity," must be good and true, whatever else, either in the early thoughts and feelings of men, or in the revelations to which these have been leading, should happen to be false.

Let us consider then for a moment the philosophy of this phrase. It has been adopted to convey the impression that the limits of space are not applicable to a Divine and absolute Being. But does it convey this impression to anyone who is capable ot reflecting upon his own thoughts? Is "everywhere" less a word of space then "somewhere"? Did the ancients less imprison the Divine Essence in forms, when they spoke of it as inhabiting every tree and flower, than when they viewed it in the person of a Jupiter sitting on the Thessalian mount? No! in proportion as they attached personal qualities to their Jupiter, in proportion as they believed that He was capable of loving and hating, and that He had the feelings of a father, they were conceiving of Him infinitely less under the limits of space (and of time also) than when they were translating His name by "the air," and regarding Him as a subtle fluid diffused through every portion of the universe. In the one case they were dreaming of a SPIRIT with whom men might converse; a Spirit indeed mixed of good and ill -- their own image -- but still to be apprehended

150

by that which is spiritual in man: in the other case their thoughts were wholly physical; not the less so for being rarefied and subtilized; or if there was any thing else in them, it was what they derived from the older faith.

In strict conformity with this principle is that passage of our Lord's teaching which is so often quoted to prove a very different doctrine. He told the woman of Samaria that a time was coming when neither on Mount Gerizim nor at Jerusalem should men worship the Father. He does not give as the reason, "God is everywhere;" but He rises at once to the higher level; He says "God is a Spirit, and they that worship Him must worship Him in spirit and in truth." And He connects with these words what would seem to modern thinkers the most direct contradiction of them: "We know what we worship, for salvation is of the Jews." Unquestionably such language would have been utterly inconsistent with the Omnipresent doctrine; it was no wise inconsistent with the doctrine, "God is a Spirit." Every step in the Jewish revelation and history had presumed that truth, and had been preparing the way for the full manifestation of it. Every step of it had been more fully bringing out the idea of God as the Holy One, as the Moral Being, the object of trust and awe and reverence. And in nothing had this idea been more expressed, than in those arrangements which seemed to localize the Divine Presence. Because He was the Holy One, He must not be worshipped in all the forms of nature and visible things; He must be viewed as distinct, personal; He must be approached, in the temple, through the priest with the sacrifice. By all these means, now regarded as so sensual, men were taught that it was not with their senses that they were to apprehend God; that it was that in them which desires truth and holiness which must seek Him, which by a wonderful method He was drawing towards Himself. And therefore, though simple people who had sought God without the law, might be far better prepared to welcome Him who brought their sins to their mind, and told them all things that ever they did, than the proud idolater of the law could ever be; yet those who had profited by the law, those who were Israelites indeed, and without guile, those who had served God day and night in the temple, and waited for the consolation of Israel, were far better prepared than any others could be to see the glory of God in the man Christ Jesus; to feel that there was no contradiction in the perfectly Holy One inhabiting a body of human clay; that it was a low, carnal, sensual notion of the Godhead, one which really identified Him with physical things, and therefore subjected Him practically to the laws of space, which made it seem to be a contradiction.

I maintain, then, that the highest, clearest, most spiritual, most universal idea of God which any creature can attain to, is not that which he receives from a dream about the attribute of omnipresence, but that into which he enters when he contemplates the fulness of truth and holiness and love, the absolute and perfect Being pleasing to identify Himself with a human soul and body, to suffer with them, to raise them out of death, to raise them to glory. We have not here an attempt to merge complete spirituality and distinct locality -- each of which is demanded by man's reason, each of which is necessary to the other -- in a wretched abstraction called ubiquity, a notion vacant of all substance and reality, only serving to puff up the mind with the vague consciousness of possessing a great idea, which it really needs but has missed altogether. I should be scrupulous about the use of such language as this, in reference to a phrase which is so prevalent among religious people, and which may therefore have some sacred associations connected with it, if I did not see that it had been the means of perplexing the minds of little children, of making moral and Christian education almost impossible, of introducing infinite vagueness and weakness into our pulpit discourses, of preparing men's minds for a settled and hopeless pantheism. That it has also been the means of lowering and confounding our feelings about the Eucharistic feast, is implied in all its other effects. But here it has met with an enemy able to cope with it. The impression that this sacrament is a reality, in spite of all men's attempts to prove it and make it a fiction, has kept alive the belief that the presence of God is a truth and not a dream; and that we may enter into it in a better and truer way than be fancying ourselves in it, when we are only indulging pleasant sensations and high conceits.

But if I maintain so strongly that it is only with the spirit that we can hold communion with a spiritual Being, how do I differ from the Calvinists, who admit that there is a Presence in the sacrament to those who believe? I do not think that I differ from them except when they differ from themselves. I no more suppose that our spirits can perceive a spiritual object without faith, than that our eyes can perceive a natural object if they be blind. Faith is as much that exercise in which the spirit is and lives, as sight is the exercise in which the eye is and lives. What more does the Calvinist require? He requires that we should suppose there is no object present, unless there be something which perceives it; and having got into this contradiction, the next step is to suppose that faith is not a receptive, but a creative power; that it makes the thing which it believes. We have seen what a tendency to this belief there has been among all Protestants; but we have seen also that there were characteristics in the creed of the Calvinist which ought especially to have delivered him from it. His principle is to refer every thing to the will of God, to suppose that nothing originates with the creature. How then has he fallen into an hypothesis apparently so foreign from his deepest convictions? He has been driven into it by his habit of resolving his belief of the Divine Will into his doctrine of individual election. He cannot suppose that God has any higher end in His manifestations than the redemption and sanctification of particular men; the idea, therefore, of the God-Manhood, of God manifesting Himself in the person of His Son, shrinks and dwindles into a mere expedient for accomplishing His objects of mercy towards the favoured members of the race, and by necessary consequence the belief that He has devised a means whereby men, as members of a body, may apprehend Him who is the Head of the

152

body, loses itself in this strange attempt to conceive a presence which is not a presence till we make it so. Still it is a curious and interesting fact, that the form and principle of Calvin's doctrine, as distinguished from his system, was mainly upheld by his faith in this sacrament; and that when his followers approximated, as of necessity they did, more and more nearly to the Zwinglian doctrine on this subject, the system became more and more prominent and exclusive.

It is a great transition to go from either of these views to the Lutheran, wherein the actual presence of Christ as the ground of faith, and not as grounded upon it, is so unequivocally asserted. It might seem that in doing so I must change the character of my statements; that whereas I have hitherto been endeavouring to assert this presence against those who deny it, I must now, if I discover any difference with this class of Protestants, point out the danger of carrying a true principle to its extreme. But I shall make no such change, and I see no such danger. I complain of the Lutheran, as I do of the Zwinglian and the Calvinist, for seeking the deliverance of the individual conscience as an ultimate end; and therefore for failing to acknowledge the completeness and integrity of the blessing which Christ has bestowed upon his Church. Whatever logical perplexity the Lutheran has fallen into; whatever violence he has done to the understanding by his theory; whatever of confusion he has introduced between the sensible and the spiritual world, is, as I conceive, the consequence of his not taking the language of our Lord and of His Apostles in a sufficiently plain and literal sense. Our Lord says: "This is my body." St. Paul addresses the Ephesian converts as sitting in the heavenly places with Christ. He tells the Philippians that their bodies shall be made like unto Christ's glorious body. Surely this is Christianity. It is the Gospel of the deliverance of the spirit and soul and body from all the fetters by which they are held down, and prevented from fulfilling each its own proper function -- from maintaining their right relations to each other. And this emancipation is connected with and consequent upon, our union, as members of one body, with Christ, the crucified, the risen, the glorified Lord of our race. Now, if these be the privileges of Christian men, and if these privileges, whatever they be, are in this sacrament asserted and realised, what a low notion it is, that we are invited to hold communion, not with Christ as He is, not with His body exalted at the right hand of God, but with a body consubstantiated in the elements.

Think only of the freedom, the fellowship of hope -- not only compatible with, but inseparable from , humiliation and fear -- implied in intercourse with the Prince and Forerunner who has actually broken through the barriers of space and time, whose body has been subjected to the events and sufferings of mortality, and who is now glorified with the glory which He had with the Father before the worlds were, and hereafter to be manifested in the sight of quick and dead. Bring these thoughts before you in connexion with the words: "This is my body," and with the command that we should shew forth His death till He come; and then reflect, if you can, upon the logical dogma of Consubstantiation, the notion that all these blessings do in some way dwell in the bread and wine. Surely what we need is, that they should be made a perfectly transparent medium through which His glory may be manifested, that nothing should be really beheld by the spirit of the worshippers but He into whose presence they are brought. For this end the elements require a solemn consecration from the priest, through whom Christ distributes them to His flock; not that they may be clothed with some new and peculiar attributes; not that they may acquire some essential and miraculous virtue, but that they may be diverted from their ordinary uses, that they may become purely sacramental. No doubt the world is full of sacraments. Morning and evening, the kind looks and parting words of friends, the laugh of childhood, daily bread, sickness and death; all have a holy sacramental meaning, and should as such be viewed by us. But then they have another meaning, which keeps this out of sight. If we would have them translated to us, we need some pure untroubled element, which has no significancy, except as the organ through which the voice of God speaks to man, and through which he may answer: "Thy servant heareth." Such we believe are this bread and wine when redeemed to his service: let us not deprive them of their ethereal whiteness and clearness by the colours of our fancy or the clouds of our intellect.

Rationalistic Objections

* * *

For what is the spirit of the age, as it exhibits itself in those philosophers whose objections we are now considering? I have endeavoured, in a former part of this work, to shew that no persons are so disposed as they are to confound God with the world -- to look at this visible universe, with its mysterious powers and properties, as the real Being, or at least at the greatest manifestation of the real Being. This pantheistic tendency is especially our tendency at this time; and this has been in all past times the source of that confusion between the permanent and the tranistory, the essential and the accidental, which we are told, and rightly told, to beware of. And therefore Christian priests will not be the only galvanizers. It is to the philosophers of the age following the promulgation of Christianity, to Plotinus and Porphyry and Jamblichus, that we are indebted for the most remarkable galvanic experiments on record. They tried to reproduce the old Pagan forms, expressly as a means of giving a body to their philosophy, which otherwise they felt that it had not, and as a means to resisting the progress of the new kingdom. There are symptoms of the same inclination among us now. We shall see more and more of them. Pantheism never has existed, and never will exist, in that naked essential character which it affects. It will beget idolatries, and since the imagination of man has well-nigh exhausted itself in that kind of production, these idolatries will not be new, but old. How may they be

154

withstood? I believe in no way so effectually as by the simple putting forth of this sacrament, not clothed with a number of fantastic rites and emblems, but in its own dreadful grandeur, as the bond of a communion between heaven and earth, -- as a witness that man is not a creature of this world, but has his home, his citizenship in another, -- as a witness that his spirit is not the function or creature of his body, and has not therefore need to make out its enjoyments from the things which the eye sees, and the ear hears; but that this body is the attendant and minister of his spirit, is to be exalted by it, is to bring all visible things under it, -- as a witness that the Son of man is set down at the right hand of the Throne of God, and that those who believe in Him, and suffer with Him, are meant to live and reign with Him there. The forms of nature, the forms of the understanding, have striven to reduce this sacrament to their own level; it remains as a mighty power in God's hands, to raise man above these forms, into communion with Himself.

THE ROMISH SYSTEM

After the remarks under the last head, it may seem scarcely needful that I should vindicate my statements respecting this sacrament from the charge of Romanism; but since I have maintained that the character of the Eucharistic feast is sacrificial, that Christ is really present in it, and that the words of institution are to be taken literally; since it is very evidently implied in what I have said, that a certain order of persons first received the sacramental elements, and that a certain order ought to administer them now: it may be advisable to shew, even at the risk of some repetition, wherein I am opposed to the Romish theory upon each of these points.

1. I need only ask the reader to compare the observations which were made respecting the difference between the Catholic and the Romish idea of Baptism, and the Catholic and Romish forms of worship, with those which have been made in this section respecting the question of sacrifice; in order that he may perceive the principle which governs all three cases. I complained that the baptized man, according to the Romish theory, only receives a momentary gift, and is not admitted into a permanent state; and that the worshipper, according to the Romish notion, is purchasing some future benefit by his acts of devotion, not claiming a blessing which has been already purchased for him. It is impossible that he should not act in strict conformity to these maxims when he is dealing with the sacrifice which is the foundation of the Christian's state, and the consummation of the Christian's worship. The Eucharistic sacrifice is of course regarded by him as the means of obtaining those advantages and blessings which Christ's sacrifice has not fully procured for us, or which we through our sins and negligence have lost. Such, I need hardly say, is the view commonly presented of it by Romish writers, and such is the view against which all the attacks of the Reformers were directed; consequently the doctrine which I have put forward, that this feast derives its peculiarity, derives its sacrificail

character, from the fact that a complete sacrifice has been offered up for man, is far more formally and practically opposed to Romanism than that which is prevalent in our day. There is no formal opposition between the doctrine which denies the very existence of a Eucharistic sacrifice, and that which affirms it to be the carrying out of an incomplete sacrifice made for us by Christ. The two opinions contradict each other, but they cannot be brought into comparison; each is continually gaining strength from the denial which is contained in the other: but what each asserts, or to what test they can be brought, the supporters of them are constantly puzzled to discover. Neither is there a practical opposition, for the Protestants are constantly losing sight of the finished sacrifice of Christ, in their anxiety to assert the importance of human faith; and the Romanists are constantly trying, through a violent effort of recollection, assisted by visible images and presentations, to bring back the very event of our Lord's crucifixion, and all the circumstances attending it: so that there is an unconscious confession on the part of the one, that there must be acts of ours in which the blessing of the sacrifice is realised; on the part of the other, that it is that one sacrifice, and not any repetition of it by us, in which all virtue dwells. I maintain that the sacrament being acknowledged as the sacrificial feast of the new dispensation, realises and harmonises these two truths, satisfies the meaning which the Romanist feels that he cannot part with, and so enables him to cast aside, as degrading, dangerous, and antichristian,that doctrine which has been one of the greatest barriers between him and his Protestant brethren.

2. To the same habit of mind which introduced this view of the Eucharistic sacrifice, we must attribute the entertainment which was given by the Church, after some hard struggles, to the doctrine respecting the transubstantiation of the elements. I have discovered the intellectual origin of this dogma in the scholastic philosophy; but that philosophy could never have given it currency, if there had not been a moral predisposition in men's minds to receive it. The cry for some signal proof of condescension to our low estate, the sense of a weakness which could only be met by a mightly act of Divine humiliation, -- these feelings characterised the Middle Ages, and constituted their strength. The belief that by these acts the spirit of man was to be raised out of its grave of sense, was to be made capable of actual communion with the invisible and the absolute; this belief hovered about many minds, was conveyed in many emblems and enigmas, was actually grasped by some earnest and thoughtful men, but never really entered into the practical life of the period. To shew forth acts of bravery, condescension, sacrifice, and so to glorify God, was the desire of a number; to inspire others with the same ambition, the aim of a few. But everywhere one may trace the wish to see the likeness of God in visible things, and under earthly conditions, rather than the craving to see Him as He is. I have no need to inquire how far good or evil preponderated in this temper of mind. That it was a very imperfect one, most will be ready to acknowledge; and that its imperfection laid it open to invasions of gross

sensuality, is only questioned by resolutely one-sided or one-eyed inquirers. In such a state of mind it was impossible that the thought of communion with Christ where He is, should be as distinctly presented to the best men in their best moments, as it may now be presented to indifferent men who may very little realise their own vision. The discovery, therefore, of a substitute for this faith, of a way in which Christ might be believed to be present by a fresh act of descent and condescension into the circumstances of human nature, was naturally and eagerly welcomed -- the obstacles which the understanding opposed to the opinion readily swept away. What sensuality and death grew out of this notion, were fostered by it, and helped to keep it alive; what profaneness mingled in the speculations to which it gave rise, how it connected itself with every other shape of idolatry, I think all ecclesiastical history demonstrates. But I have no belief that the demonstration will be heeded, that facts will not be perverted and explained away, that the natural results of a system will not be treated as if they might be condemned without any reference to the system itself, unless men be led to perceive that there is a spiritual truth which this doctrine has been counterfeiting and keeping out of sight, and to which it is in far more direct antipathy than it ever can be to the different Protestant and infidel notions which have been set up against it.

3. It is evident from these remarks, and from all which I have said in this section, that I do not seek to get rid of the papal notion respecting a real Presence, merely by saying that what is spiritual is also most real. I do indeed look upon that proposition as nearly the most important one which a theological student can think of or remember, and also as the one which Romanism is most habitually denying. But I have maintained, that in order to the full acknowledgment of Christ's spiritual presence, we must distinctly acknowledge that He is clothed with a body; that if we lose this belief, we adopt a vague pantheistic notion of a presence hovering about us somewhere in the air, in place of a clear spiritual apprehension of a Person in whom all truth and love dwell; that the spiritual organ therefore does demand an actual body for its nourishment; that through that spiritual organ our bodies themselves are meant to be purified and glorified; that this sacrament meets and satisfies the needs both of the human spirit which is redeemed, and of the body which is waiting for its redemption. But all these admissions only bring out the difference with the Romanist into stronger relief. To enter into fellowship with Christ as He is, ascended at the right hand of God, in a body of glory and not of humiliation, this must be the desire of a Christian man, if he seek the presence of a real, not an imaginary object, if he desire his body as well as his spirit to be raised and exalted. On this ground then he must reject all theories which involve the imagination of a descent into the elements; on this ground, also, he must feel that the intellectual contradiction which such theories contain, and even boast of, is the counterpart of a spiritual contradiction still more gross and dangerous.

157

4. I must say a few words before I conclude upon the difference between my views and those of the Romanists, respecting those who administer this sacrament. The pure Protestant expresses his differences in such words as these. The Romanist, he says, unhappily connecting the idea of sacrifice with the Eucharist, necessarily supposes that the Christian Church must have its priests as well as the Jewish; we rejecting the first idea, of course reject the second. Now as I have so carefully connected the idea of sacrifice with the Eucharist, it follows from this statement, that if I suppose it to be administered by human hands at all, I must suppose those hands to be, in some sense of the word, sacerdotal. Nay, it would seem to follow by almost necessary inference, that if I suppose the Jewish sacrifice to have passed into something higher, I must suppose the Jewish priesthood to have passed into something higher. And this in fact is my belief. I do think that a Melchisedec priesthood has succeeded to an Aaronical priesthood, even as the power of an endless life has succeeded to the law of a carnal commandment. I do think that he who presents the perfect sacrifice before God, and himself and his people as redeemed by that sacrifice, has a higher function than he had who presented the daily offering, or made the yearly atonement before God. I do think that he who is permitted to feed the people with this bread and wine has a higher work to do than he who came out of the holy place to bless the people in God's name. And I complain of the Romanists for lowering this office, for depriving it of its spiritual and Catholic character, for reducing it to the level or below the level of that which existed before the incarnation. No honour which is put upon the person of the priest can make amends to him for the degradation which he suffers by being treated as if he were without the veil, pleading for admission into the presence of God, not claiming the privilege for himself and his people of being admitted into it. No emblems which exhibit his own mysterious glory and beauty can be any compensation for the loss of the belief that he is permitted with open face to behold the glory of his Lord. Above all, the differences which are made between him and his flock, especially that most gross and offensive one, by whatever arguments it may be palliated, of permitting him alone to receive the sacramental wine, do but shew that he is not like his Lord, that he is not one of many brethren, but has only the melancholy delight of fancying that there are blessings reserved for him in which other men are not sharers. Herein he is far below the Jew. The high priest believed that he was one of a kingdom of priests; that he received his garments of beauty and his holy mitre because he was their representative. A Jew would have answered to the complaint of Korah, "Ye take too much upon you, seeing that all the congregation are holy, every one of them," -- 'We take this upon us which has been put upon us, because the congregation is holy, and because it would not be holy if we were not consecrated to be witnesses and preservers of its holiness.' A Jew could see that the oil upon Aaron's head went down to the skirts of his garments. It is not surely for Christians and Catholics to set up an office in the Church against the Church itself, to set at naught the ascription which they are appointed to offer up in the name of the whole

158

body: "Unto Him that loved us and washed us from our sins in His own blood, and hath made us kings and priests unto God and His Father; to Him be glory and dominion for ever and ever." But I am intruding upon the subject of the next section.

SECTION V -- THE MINISTRY

It is commonly observed, that a sacerdotal caste has three invariable characteristics. It assumes a lofty dominion over the minds as well as the bodies of man, it imposes a very heavy yoke upon both, it is opposed to every thing humane and expansive.

How much warrant there is for these accusations, everyone who reads history must perceive. And assuredly these evil tendencies have not been confined to one set of circumstances or one form of religion; they have manifested themselves in Judea and Christendom as well as in Hindostan. They may therefore be fairly considered as belonging to human nature, and as being especialy likely to assail anyone who anywhere and under any conditions, assumes the office of a religious guide and authority.

That this institution has not been merely fruitful of evil, the impartial inquirer, especially in the most modern times, is ready to acknowledge. But he rightly observes, that we must not restrict the advantages it has produced to any particular system. Much has been done for civilisation by Memphis, and Delphi, and by the Brahmins of the East. And it remains, he says, to be proved, that the idea of the priesthood does not involve tyranny and narrowness, though at certain periods the tyranny may have been useful, the narrowness common to all classes.

Undoubtedly this is the real question. If we should find upon inquiry that the fundamental principles of a sacerdotal caste, amidst all its outward varieties, are those we have just set down, it ought to be got rid of as soon as possible; and it will disappear as soon as truth and honesty have gained the victory, which we at least are bound to believe they will ultimately gain, over fraud and falsehood. If on the other hand it should be found that an idea of the priesthood, curiously and exactly opposite to that which presumes dominion, restraint upon the human spirit, confinement of men within certain districts and habits of thought, to be its objects, is embodied in the forms and language of the Christian Church, we may perhaps ask ourselves whether this may not be the idea after which men in all ages and in all religions have been feeling; whether the good which is attributed to them have not been the consequence of their attaining to some apprehension of it, the evil they have done, the consequence of their losing sight of it or contradicting it; whether therefore the triumph of truth over falsehood may not be exhibited in the full accomplishment of this idea, not in the destruction of the institution which has witnessed for it and preserved it.

Now these facts are indisputable, 1. The whole sacerdotal caste in Christendom has the name of <u>ministers</u> or <u>servants</u>. From the Bishop of Rome down to the founder fo the last new sect in the United States of America, everyone who deals with the Gospel at all, or pretends in any sense to have a Divine commission, assumes this name as the description of his office. 2. The most remarkable power which these ministers have claimed, and that on account of which the greatest homage has been paid to them, is the power of <u>absolving</u> or <u>setting free</u>. This claim has in a manner been universal. Luther believed that he was to absolve as much as Tetzel. Every person who says that the sole office of a minister is to preach the Gospel, says so because he believes this is the way to absolve. There are most serious differences about the nature of the power and the mode in which it is to be exercised, none at all about the existence of it, and about its connexion in some way or other with the Christian ministry. 3. The third fact is this. In Christian Europe, ever since it became Christian, the most conspicuous order of ministers has been one which assumed to itself a universal character. The overseers or Bishops of the Christian Church have felt themselves to be emphatically the bonds of communicaton between different parts of the earth. The jurisdiction of each has been confined within a certain district; but, by the very nature of their office, they have held fellowship; and been obliged to hold fellowship, with those who lived in other districts, who spoke different languages, who were bound together by different notions and customs. Now though such an order may be very far more dangerous, and may have been felt by the rulers of particular countries to be far more dangerous than that kind of priesthood which confines itself within a particular region, yet it is evidently of an entirely different kind. Whatever this institution may have effected, it seems to aim at establishing a more extended commerce and fellowship among men. Looking at it superficially, one would say that this ecclesiastical order imported something more comprehensive, more diffusive, than any civil order which one can think of, unless it should be some one which attempts universal conquest, and destroys its character as an order by the attempt. And yet this episcopacy has not been merely an accidental addition to, or overgrowth upon other forms of priesthood. In those countries where it is recognized, it has been the root of all other forms, and has been supposed to contain them within it. It has been believed, as a necessary consequence of the importance attached to the Eucharist, that an order of men must exist in the Christian Church corresponding to the priests of the old dispensation, with the difference that the sacrifice in the one case was anticipatory, in the other commemorative. This office has been associated with that absolving power of which I spoke just now. Yet it has been always supposed to be included in that of the Bishop; and where it is assigned to a distinct class of persons, that class receives its authority from him. In like manner there has been acknowledged in the Church an order whose functions are evidently distinct from either of these; whose main object is to provide for the bodily wants of men, or only to announce to them spiritual truths. Yet even this office has been understood to be only a delegation of certain powers inhering in the Bishop, which he has not leisure to discharge, and no person can undertake it, in the countries which recognize episcopacy, without such a delegation. So that an office implying an attention so very remote from that which the word priest ordinarily suggests to us, would seem to have been the characteristic one in the Christian Church, that which includes all others, and out of which they arise.

But I have used the phrase, "the countries in which episcopacy is recognized." It is important, that we should consider what these countries are, lest we should be drawing an inference respecting the nature of this institution which facts do not warrant. Let, then, the reader call to mind, first of all, the circumstances of the Eastern Church for the last fifteen or sixteen hundred years. Let him think of it at the time when Constantinople was in its glory, of the different sects which broke from it, of the horrible contentions which took place between those sects and their common mother. Let him remember the degradation which every part of this Church, and every one of these sects, has suffered from the Ottoman power, and let him then reflect that in whatever countries they may have dwelt, to whatever circumstances of good or evil fortune they may have been exposed, whatever strifes may have gone on amongst them, this institution has been preserved by them all. Let him next consider the different circumstances under which Christianity was preached and adopted in the different nations of the West, the different influences to which it has been subjected, the different characters of the different races which compose it; and let him then remember that all these nations, under all these influences, amidst all their conflicts with the eastern part of Christendom, did, without one clearly established exception, preserve this institution till the sixteenth century. Let him consider the circumstances of the Reformation leading to the separation of the nations, to a violent conflict with the old system of Europe, to an excessive magnifying of individual faith, and then reflect that this universal institution was preserved in all the Latin nations -- among the Teutonic nations, in England, in Denmark, and in Sweden; that it was rejected, and that not without great reluctance, in certain parts of Germany, in Holland, in Switzerland, and in Scotland; that in each of these countries some witness of its existence as been preserved; that in at least one of them there are those who think that it is more necessary now than in any past time. Let it be remembered, further, that this institution has passed over to the continent of America; that it has established itself in a set of colonies founded by Puritans and Quakers; that it grew up after the influence of England had ceased in those colonies; that without the least state patronage it is making itself an instrument for diffusing the Gospel from those colonies to many parts of the world. These are the pretensions which episcopacy makes to the character of a Catholic institution.

It is implied in what I have said, that this institution has a character of permanence as well as of universality. It is implied also that this permanence is something different from the permanence of a custom which has first derived its significance from some local accident, and then has perpetuated itself by the care of some body especially created for its conservation. For we have seen this institution maintaining itself amidst the oppositions and contradictions of bodies differing most vehemently with each other; we have seen it reappearing when all local habits and customs were adverse to it. How then has it been preserved or seemed to be preserved? It has been preserved by an act of consecration performed through the agency of three existing Bishops; signifying, according to the faith of all the nations and ages which have retained it, that the person newly entering upon the function receives the same kind of authority and the same kind of gifts as those who were first endowed with it.

It must be quite evident to the reader, that the facts which we have now been considering touch the very heart of the questions which I have been discussing in this work. These questions have been, Is there any meaning in the words Kingdom of Christ? Do the words mean what they seem to mean? Are there any facts in the history of the world which seem to shew that they denote that which is really and actually existing? Now we have found a series of facts, all, it seemed to us, bearing to the same point, all proving the existence of a universal and spiritual society; a society maintaining its existence amidst the greatest perplexities and contradictions; a society of which all the conditions are inexplicable unless we suppose it to be connected with, and upheld by, an unseen power. But as all these signs which we have considered hitherto exist for the sake of men, so also they imply the agency of men. And upon the character of this agency must depend the whole character of the kingdom itself. It may be something else, but it is not a commonwealth, not a kingdom according to any admitted sense of the word, if it have not certain magistrates or officers. Practially these exist even in those societes which boast most of their self-government; they have officers, whatever be the tenure of their office. And, therefore, we must either give up all that we have previously maintained as untenable, or we must steadily consider this question -- What kind of officers would be consistent with the character of such a kingdom as those other signs speak of? It would seem clear that as all these signs pointed to an invisible presence, and were intended to admit men into it, these officers must be constituted with a view to the same end. They must be intended to bring before men the fact that they are subject to an invisible and universal Ruler.

And if so, it would seem also necessary that they should exhibit Him to men in that character and in those offices which He actually came to perform. If He came not to be ministered unto but to minister, if His exercise of power was a ministry, theirs must be so too. They can look upon themselves in no other light than as ministers; they cannot suppose their power diminished by this acknowledgement; they cannot suppose that their power will be real, if not exercised with a continual

162

recollection of it. If one chief part of His work in the world was to absolve men from past evil, from the power of present evil, from the danger of future evil; and if there be a continual necessity for all men who come into the world, that they should have this absolution, and if He exercise His powers or make Himself manifest in any way through men, one must suppose that they would be called especially to represent Him in the office of Absolver. If His greatest purpose was to bind men together in one family, if the office on which he entered when He ascended on high, was that of Head and overseer of this family; if all His other acts and service to men are implied and presupposed in this, one must conceive the highest office of His servants would be to exhibit Him in this character, and so to make it known that His kingdom was a real kingdom, and one that ruleth over all. If, finally, Jesus himself when upon earth received a formal and outward designation to the office which He had undertaken, that it might be signified to men on what terms He held it -- not as a separate independent Being, but as one with the Father, and honouring Him in all His words and acts -- it would seem reasonable to expect that an equally formal and visible designation would bear witness to men, that those offices which are fulfilled for their sakes, by creatures of their own flesh and blood, are not held in virtue of any qualities or merits in those creatures, but are held from Christ and under Christ by persons who can exhibit His character truly only just so far as they perform their work faithfully.

But is there anything in the language of the New Testament which accords with these anticipations and explains these facts? One would think that this language, like that which refers to the institution of Baptism, must lie on the very surface of the record, and yet must connect itself with all its deepest announcements; otherwise it can be no authority for institutions which pretend to embody the whole character of the new dispensation. A few casual hints could never suffice as the warrant for fallible men to suppose that they were meant to be the ministers of Christ and to present Him before men. Still less could such hints be an excuse for sinful men who should take upon them, in God's name, to absolve their brethren. Least of all could they justify the existence of an order, which assumes such a singular position , and claims such high functions as the Episcopal. The mere appearance of such an office, even in the time immediately following our Lord's departure from the world, ought not, I think, to be looked upon as a sufficient reason for its claiming to be an estate of His kingdom, if He did not expressly and formally institute it Himself.

We turn, then, to the Gospels for the purpose of inquiring whether they offer any guidance upon the subject; and we are immediately encountered by the history of the selection and appointment of a set of men who were emphatically distinct from all classes which had existed in the Jewish polity. They are, indeed, carefully connected with that polity; their number shews that they were meant to remind the Jews of the tribes into which their nation had been distributed. They were all Jews,

163

and their first commission was strictly confined to the house of Israel. But these circumstances only make the peculiarity of their office more remarkable. The most evident indications were given to them, even from the first, even at the time when they were least capable of understanding the nature of their service, that it was meant to transcend national limitations. At the same time, even while they were falling into the greatest confusions respecting the place which they were to occupy in the world, even while they had need to be reminded continually that the kings of the Gentiles exercised dominion over them, but that it was not so to be in the Church; they were still assured, in the strongest language, that they were to perform a wonderful work, and to be endued with wonderful powers; that he who received them would receive their Master; that they were sent forth by Him, even as He was sent forth by the Father.

Everyone must perceive that these intimations are not scattered carelessly through the Gospels, that they form a part of their very substance and tissue. It was in teaching the disciples that those who became as little children were greatest in the kingdom of heaven, that their rule was to be a service, it was in the acts which accompanied these teachings, that our Lord's own life and image are most distinctly brought before us. Evidently He never separates the thought of training them in their office from that of performing His own. As evidently He is training them to an office; He is not teaching them to be great saints, to keep up a high tone of personal holiness as if that were the end of their lives. But He is teaching them that they have a work to do even as He has; that He is straitened till he can accomplish His; that they must be straitened till they can accomplish theirs; and that in trying to accomplish it, they will most find that they are lights of the world, and that they must derive their light continually from Him. So that if we called the four Gospels 'The Institution of a Christian Ministry,' we might not go very far wrong, or lose sight of many of their essential qualities. Above all, one would not lose sight of the different crises in our Lord's life, and of their connexion with different discoveries of grace and truth to man. Before the resurrection there was merely the general commission, "Go and preach the Kingdom of God. Heal the sick. Cast out devils. Freely ye have received, freely give." Far deeper views of their office were brought out in those conversations which our Lord had with them the night before His Passion; views all connecting themselves with the awful facts of which they were to be witnesses, and with the mysterious service which they had been performing. But it was not till our Lord came back from the grave, with the witness and the power of a new life for man, that He breathed upon His disciples and said, "Receive ye the Holy Ghost. Whosoever sins ye remit, they are remitted; whosoever sins ye retain, they are retained." It was not till He was just leaving them that the commission was given, "Go ye into all nations," and the promise, "Lo I am with you always, even unto the end of the world." And it was not till He had ascended on high that the powers for fulfilling this commission were confirmed, that a sign was given of the existence of a union which the distinctions of nations and language could not break, that they were declared to be the pillars of a universal Church.

Now these poor fishermen could not doubt for a moment that these powers belonged to them officially, and not personally; and therefore the chief question to be considered is this: Did they suppose this kingdom was to die with them, or that they were to perpetuate its existence? Were they to perpetuate it in the manner in which our Lord Himself had established it, or in some other manner? Was the change which the new circumstances of the Church necessarily occasioned in the position of those who were to be its ministers, to be a change in the nature of their office and institution, or only a change in their numbers and in the circumstances of their jurisdiction? Supposing the latter to be the case, were those who succeeded to the Apostolic office to reckon that they derived their powers less immediately from Christ, that they were less witnesses of His permanent government, than those who received their first commission from Him while He was dwelling upon earth? If these questions be answered in one way, those nations which have preserved the episcopal institution have a right to believe that they have preserved one of the appointed and indispensable signs of a spiritual and universal society. If they are answered in the other way, it seems difficult to understand how such a universal society can exist at all.

The Quaker

* * *

The Son of God selects His chosen servants, the heralds of His kingdom, from the fishermen of Galilee. With them He converses for three years, teaching them to apprehend mysteries which had been kept hid from generations; telling them that they were permitted to see that which Kings and Prophets had not seen; in all His intercourse with them, still treating them as men destined for a work -- not merely imparting to them a knowledge of truth, but a method of communicating it. But, after the call which these disciples had received; after the wonderful discipline by which He had so long prepared them; after He had reappeared to them in His risen form, and breathed on them, saying "Receive ye the Holy Ghost;" still He told them that they were to tarry in Jerusalem to receive the promise of the Father; and that then, and then only, should they have power from on high to perform their work. As I have remarked before, they were met, not as individuals, but as a college; they had formally completed their number when this promise was fulfilled. And what was the fulfilment? The deep mystery of it, I have contended before (herein following the Church, which has fixed Trinity Sunday to follow next upon Whitsunday), consisted in the formal declaration of the Holy Spirit as a Person, the assertion of the Divine Unity of the Father and the Son in Him, and in the establishment of a Universal Church. But this is inseparably connected in Scripture with

165

the conferring of powers on a set of men previously marked out to be Ministers of Christ. The call of Christ was not sufficient; here was a formal endowment with the gifts which Christ had designed for them when He bade them leave their nets, and which He had now received for them on high.

Signs, we know, accompanied the first great declaration of this Divine Presence in the Church. Those signs were like the twig or clod of earth which in ancient feoffments attested the delivery of a portion of land to a certain person and his heirs for ever. We should as little expect them to be continually repeated, as that the twig or clod should be solemnly presented to the new possessor, whenever he performed a fresh act of ownership. But the principle asserted by these signs, we affirm to be perpetual. The Spirit of God, by a wonderful demonstration, declares that He is dwelling among men; that an organised body of men has been provided for His habitation; that through this body His blessings are to be transmitted to the world; that through a portion of this body, His blessings are to be transmitted to the rest. Everything on this great day of spiritual inspiration speaks of preparation, order, distinction, unity. No chance or casual moment is selected, but the period of an ancient festival; no secret place, but an upper chamber in the temple; no chance individual, but men who have been for years openly preparing for the work. Whatever system, then, teaches that a minister is not publicly, and openly, and once for all endowed with certain powers and faculties for his work, these powers being sustained within him by the constant presence of Him who bestows them; whatever system conveys the notion, that the minister, being such by virture of his inward call, is either then invested with the requisite gifts, or receives them afterwards, from time to time, by sudden movements and inspirations, we affirm is essentially an Old Testament system. And the consequences of such a system must infallibly be these: -- The mere spiritual faculty, which is awakened in him by the voice of the Spirit of God, will be confounded with that Spirit himself; His personality will be forgotten in His operations; there will be a fearful confusion between the human speaker and the invisible power which speaks in him, alternating with a continual attempt to separate them; the intellectual faculties and endowments will first be despised because they are supposed to have no connexion with the Spirit; and then will be confounded with the faculty which is truly Divine and spiritual in man, when both are found to proceed from the same source, and the former to be the means of evoking the latter. I say, if we considered wherein the Old Testament system was defective, and how the blanks are filled up in the New; and then heard of a scheme in which these blanks were restored, without, however, a restoration of those other portions of the old system, which prevented that which was necessarily imperfect from being evil, we should look for all these mischiefs as the fruits of it. And the actual history of the Quakers fulfils every one of these predictions. The belief in the Personality of the Spirit, in His difference from the spiritual life which He originates, has been that truth which they have found it most difficult to realise, and which has been continually slipping away from them. Their ministers, even in the best age of their society, were almost idolized. They have veered continually between contempt for the intellectual powers generally, and a vast over-appreciation of them, when they seemed to be under spiritual guidance. And all these contradictions are now reaching a head, and threatening the extinction of their body.

The Presbyterian

We pass to those whose objections are principally and expressly against Episcopacy. Some of these turn upon the idea of the Church, some are derived from the letter of Scripture, and some are founded upon experience. The first take this form -- 'Christ is the only Bishop of His Church. All attempts to substitute another overseership, for His, are founded upon a misconception of our relation to Him. The words, "Call no man your father upon earth, for one is your Father which is in heaven," though they do not interfere with the acknowledgment of spiritual fathers in some sense, for St. Paul constantly calls himself one, do assuredly confound all such pretensions to fatherhood as the Bishops by the very nature of their office put forth. Assumption and domination, the very opposite qualities to those which should appear in a ministry, are applied in the conception of this function. And secondly, it is not borne out by the least warrant of revelation. That the word episkopos is to be found in the Acts of the Apostles, no one will dispute. But it is found in such connexions as shew that the officer whom it denotes was not distinguished from the Presbyter -- that the Apostles, at all events, did not look upon the distinction as in any wise connected with the being of the Church. If, then, we would have a Church upon a scriptural platform, framed according to Apostolical precedent, there seems little doubt that Bishops would find no place, or a very unimportant place in it. But, thirdly, it may be said that we cannot return strictly to those precedents, that the Church has a principle of life and authority in itself, and that we are to consider the way in which institutions have actually developed themselves. Very well; then look at all the cruelty, usurpation, pride, secularity, which have been manifested by these spiritual fathers. And then say, whether the history of the Church be not as conclusive a witness against them as the words of inspiration.'

It is evident that the objection which is founded upon the constitution of the Church, does not merely affect the principle of Episcopacy. Its application is very wide indeed. Presbyterians in general have perceived that it strikes at the notion of any human priesthood. If the fact that Christ is the universal Bishop, interfere with the existence of earthly Bishops, the fact that He is the Priest of His Church, of course makes it impossible that any inferior person should usurp that name. Probably the last case will be felt to be stronger than the first; at all events, many persons are found to denounce the use of the words 'iereus and and Sacerdos in the Divine economy, who will contend stoutly for the importance of Bishops. Now I wish it might be considered, that if

167

these phrases be on this ground denied to the ministers of the Church, they must on the same ground be denied to the members of it. The words, "We are made Kings and Priests unto God," which are so often quoted to confute the pretensions of a particular caste or ministry, are themselves profane and dangerous words. They are appropriating to the servants the acts and offices which, according to this doctrine, exclusively appertain to the Lord. Nor can the argument stop here. There must be a careful weeding out in theological books, and above all, in the Book of Revelation, of every phrase which, being first used to describe the head of the body, is afterwards applied to the body itself, or to any of its members. I beseech anyone calmly and seriously to reflect upon the effect which such a change must produce -- I do not say in the dialect of Christianity, but -- in its deepest and most essential principles. For surely, if it have one principle which more essentially belongs to it than another, this is the one, that the language which makes Christ known to us, is the only language which can fitly make the Church known to us. Not merely Catholic divinity, but Puritan divinity, recognizes the identification of offices in Christ and in His faithful members, as involved in the very idea of the Gospel. Where, I ask, is the line to be drawn?

Whence arises the propriety of the doctrine, that the state of the whole Church, and of each member of the Church, is the image of His state who has redeemed it; and the impropriety of the doctrine, that every office in the Church is the image of some office performed by Christ in His own person -- is the means by which that office is presented to men, and made effectual for them through all time?

I have no more earnest desire than that the proposition which I have put forward: 'If the Incarnation mean anything if the Church be not a dream, all offices exercised by her on behalf of humanity must be offices first exercised by Christ,' should be set side by side with the Presbyterian proposition, 'It is profane and wicked to apply to ordinary human creatures, the names which designate the works and offices of Christ,' that each should be pushed to its furthest consequences, and that each should be submitted to the judgment of the holiest men among those whose educational prejudices would lead them to reject Episcopacy. I have no fear as the the result; and I am quite sure that a great collateral advantage would follow from this method of considering the subject. We are constantly asked how we dare to lay so much stress upon an outward ordinance, as if it had anything to do with the great essential truths of the Gospel. Is it not at best a mere outwork of Christianity? Our answer is derived from this great Presbyterian argument. That cannot be a trifle which involves the most opposite conception of the whole order of the Church and of human society. If the objection we have been considering be a true one, the language which the most earnestly religious men have been using, at the times when they were most religious, when they were striving to express the most spiritual and fundamental truths, is inconsistent language, and must be abandoned. If, on the other hand, our principle be a true one, it must be a question of the highest practical moment, whether the idea of Christ's Episcopacy or of His Priesthood can be preserved among men, when that, which upon this hypothesis is the Divine method for preserving them, has been rejected.

2. 'But this view, however it may be defended by theories, receives no justification from Scripture.' I admit at once, that if the Acts of the Apostles were set before me, and I were desired to make out from them alone what the office of the Overseer was, as distinguished from that of the Presbyter, I should decline the task as hopeless. Nor do I think, that if I were allowed to add to the hints which this book supplies, all that I could gather with respect to these particular names from the Epistles, I should be much nearer to satisfaction. My difficulty, I confess, is to understand how, from these scattered notices, the Presbyterian has been able to arrive at the clear and satisfying conclusion, that the whole Church for thirteen centuries, and the greater part of the Church for sixteen centuries, has been utterly wrong in believing that such an officer as the one who is understood by the word Bishop is meant to exist in it. I should be sorry upon such evidence to condemn the very paltriest ceremony which could allege a similar prescription in its favour. Of course, therefore, I should be equally sorry to put in such evidence as supplying the original title-deed of the institution. For, were there no other, I should scarcely know how to state the question which is to be settled. The Presbyterian would not allow me to word it thus: 'Did there exist in the time of the Apostles an order of priests distinct from that of Bishops?' for he does not admit that there is an order of priests any more than one of Bishops, nor should I be at all anxious to ascertain how soon the functions which I attribute to the priest became separated from those which I suppose belong to the Bishop. The only point, therefore, which could be brought into debate, would be whether the word episkopos always means, in the language of the New Testament, the pastor of a number of congregations, and the word presbyteros always means, in the same language, the pastor of one; a question which I should be inclined to answer in the negative. But when I turn again to these Acts and these Epistles, I find a name which puzzles me much more than either of these; one which meets me at every turn, one which is implied in every sentence of them, one of which I must get a solution somewhere if I can. What manner of people are these Apostles whose acts are recorded in the work of St. Luke, whose letters are preserved for the perpetual instruction of the Church? It may be answered, 'They were the persons selected by our Lord to be with Him in His temptations while He was upon earth, and to bear witness of His resurrection after He had left the world.' No doubt these were the functions of the first twelve disciples. The Incarnation of Christ was to be the ground of the new kingdom; it was needful that there should be persons who had seen and handled the Word of life. About this matter there is no dispute. The question is, first, whether the fruits of the Incarnation ceased with the time when our Lord left the world, or whether they only then began to shew

themselves; next, whether the form which Christ Himself gave to the infant kingdom, was the form which it was to retain through all the future circumstances of its development; and therefore, 3rdly, whether the office of the Apostles was to be defunct when the particular circumstances which made the name appropriate had ceased to exist. If the apostleship were inseparably connected with its first accidents, it would seem strange that St. Paul, whose calling was of an altogether different kind from that of the twelve, who had not been with our Lord during His stay upon earth, who was expressly a witness of that state of glory in which we believe that Christ is now, as much as when He stopped the persecutor on the way to Damascus, should have so eagerly asserted for himself the position and the powers of an Apostle. It would seem strange, too, that those powers, in virtue of which the other Apostles were able to go forth witnessing of their Master's resurrection, were not those which they derived from Him while He was upon earth, not those even which they received from Him immediately after His resurrection, but were those which came upon them after He had gone out of the sight of men, and was ascended on high that He might fill all things. The question, therefore, to be decided when this evidence is brought before us, is simply whether there was or was not to be continued in the Church, any office corresponding in its essential characteristics to that one which we judge from the New Testament to be the distinguishing one of the Church at its foundation. The common opinion is, that by the perpetuation of this office the Church has been perpetuated; the connexion of different ages with each other realised; the wholeness and unity of the body declared. The changes which have taken place in the condition of this office we suppose to be changes as to name, as to the number of the persons filling it, as to the limits of their government; changes, some of them presupposed in the very existence of a body which was to have an unlimited expansion; none of them affecting its nature or its object. The Presbyterian says that no institution of the kind does exist in the Church; that is to say, that the platform of the Church in the present day is not the apostolic platform. Yet he says this in the same breath with which he protests against our departure from the simplicity of the New Testament practice, and calls upon us to abandon all ecclesiastical precedents for the sake of conforming to it.

3. One of the main reasons which he gives for this exhortation, is the gross corruption and secularity which have been the result of the Episcopal system wherever it has been established. I neither meet this charge by saying that there is no foundation for it, nor by explaining away the instances which are brought forward in support of it; nor by resorting to the seldom satisfactory common-place, that the abuse of an institution is no argument against its use. I might with far more reason and success produce the facts, which prove that in nearly every case in which the Church has enlarged her borders, in which the commission, "Go ye into all nations," has been really acted out, Bishops have been the instruments of fulfilling the command and obeying the promise. But I would rather place the argument on another ground: I would undertake

to shew, and I would go through all ecclesiastical history in support of the position, that the secularity of Bishops has been in all cases the effect of their not believing in the dignity and divinity of their own ordination; that the assumption of any particular Bishop has always been the effect of his denying the dignity and effect of his brethren's ordination. You shew me a Bishop who is in all respects a splendid feudal lord, with his hounds and his falcons, his sumptuous table, his armed retainers. Well! I see a man who feels about his office, just as you do, that it carries with it no Divine authority; that he is under no responsibility for the exercise of it except to the class in which he moves, and to the civil power which has added certain honours to it. My wish is to cure him of the habit of feeling which you would rivet in him. But you will say, perhaps, 'Were he a Christian minister he would not be tempted to this secularity.' -- What do you mean by such words? Do you mean that he would not be tempted to any secularity -- that the parochial clergyman, comfortably settled in his manse, has not the temptation to sink into the habits of an ordinary member of the middle class; that the mendicant friar, or the itinerant Protestant preacher, is not liable to be infected by the set to whom he ministers, and by whom he obtains his livelihood? You cannot say this without outraging the authority of Scripture and the witness of experience. Secularity of some kind (of what kind the character of the age, of the man, of his company, determines) has assailed, and must always assail every man in this world; and I believe there is no deliverance from it for any man, but in the belief that he has a vocation. Whether it is in accordance or not with the order of Providence, that the ministers of Christ's flock should be also ministers of the nation, and that each class of the nation should feel the influence of some one of its classes, I shall consider in a future section. On the subject of Episcopal assumption, I need only refer to the history of popes and patriarchs for a proof, that the occasion of it is ever an exaltation of some advantage of place or circumstance connected with the order above the order itself.

Objections to an Absolving Power in Ministers

I have said that the main principle of the Presbyterian argument is as directly opposed to the idea of a priesthood as it is to the idea of Episcopacy. In dealing with the one question, then, I have implicitly discussed the other. Moreover, the doctrine of a priesthood is so much involved with the doctrine of sacrifice, that my last section may be looked upon as a sufficient statement of my views respecting it. Still there is so much horror in many minds of that absolving power which I have attributed to the Christian bishop and to those whom he endows with it, and their complaints involve consequences of so practical a character, that I think I should be wrong not to give them a separate consideration. I do not class them under the head of Presbyterian objections, because there are many Episcopalians who appear to share in them. They may be expressed thus:

171

'According to St. Paul, those who believe in Christ are justified from all things from which they could not be justified by the Law of Moses. Ambassadors are sent forth to declare Christ's Gospel to men, in order that they may not be prevented from believing by the want of hearing; in order that if they believe they may receive this justification and freedom of the conscience. This is the true office of the minister; all others are accidental and subordinate to it. He may own orders and governments in the Church, Presbyterian, Episcopal, Apostolical, what you will; but the preaching of Christ is his true and essential function: his commission is to do this, this first, this above all things. When he pretends that he has some other way of relieving the conscience than this; when he says that he has the power of pardoning and absolving, -- that he may pronounce men free from their sins, -- he is not only committing a fearful usurpation upon the rights of Christ, he is actually misunderstanding and denying the true character of his office. He deprives himself of his true power, in his eagerness to grasp a power which has never been given him by God, and can never be of the least use to man.'

There is one point which is very important to take notice of in reference to this subject. According to the idea which has always existed in the Christian Church, the same person to whom the function of absolving is committed has also the function of administering the Eucharist. These two duties never have been separated, and it is most needful that they should be contemplated in their relation to each other; for if the Eucharist be that act in which the worshipper is especially brought into direct communion with his Lord, that act in which the mere human and visible agent is most entirely lost and forgotten, or only contemplated as one who bears witness that He whom he serves is a living and actual person, we must suppose that this is a key to the whole character of the office, in whatever way it may be exercised. If, again, the Eucharist involve at once a confession of sins on the part of the receivers, a thankful acknowledgment of a state of fellowship and blessedness with their Lord, into which they have been brought, though they may have walked most unworthily of it, the acceptance of a pledge of forgiveness for the past, strength for the present, a strength only to be realised by union with the invisible Lord, a promise of future blessings, to be attained in the same way and in no other, this would seem to determine the nature of that particular function which the minister presumes to exercise when he pronounces absolution. His whole object is to present Christ to men and men to Christ really and practically. Suppose him in the congregation, he is there to represent its unity, to offer it before God as a whole body, to confess the sins which its members have committed by separating themselves from the body. Then he is a witness of Christ's continual intercession for the entire church. Suppose him alone, with any particular member of the congregation, he is with him to preserve him in the unity of the Church, to present before God his tears and contrition for having lived unworthy of his position in it. Then he is a witness of Christ's distinct intercession

172

for every member of his flock. But still this can be but half his duty. The incarnation means very little, the kingdom of God is a mere delusion, if there be not a voice speaking from heaven as well as one crying from earth: if the one be not an answer to the other, if the minister may not say to the congregation, 'God has heard your petitions, rise up as pardoned men, with strength to offer up praises and prayers, with strength to do your work,' the confession is but half real, the Gospel is not real at all. And if he may not say in like manner to the sick and solitary penitent, God accepts thy tears and pardons thy sin, I do not see what he means by saying that he has authority to <u>preach</u> forgiveness of sins. He preaches forgiveness to those who will accept it, understanding its nature and purpose; receiving it not as a licence to the conscience, but as a deliverance of it. He delivers forgiveness under precisely the same conditions. How many of the congregation are in a state of mind to claim their fellowship with Christ and each other, and so to take the mercy which is freely given them, whether the individual man can do this, God only knows. The absolver at all events has spoken the truth; he has acted out his commission; the rest he must leave. His public preaching, his private exhortations, are all intended to remove some stumbling-block out of the way of those to whom he has been sent; to explain to them the meaning of their confession and of his absolution; to prevent their offering the one or receiving the other in vain; to hinder them from turning either to an evil account.

Supposing this to be the case, it would seem that there is no greater peril in this doctrine, than in the one which makes preaching the main work and office of a minister. As to misconstruction, there is, at all events, no greater likelihood of it in the case of words which are not our own, which are spoken in the name of God, and on the most solemn occasion, than in the case of words, which, under whatever teaching from above, we have composed, which must be mixed with our own peculiar modes of expression and habits of thought. So much I think must be admitted by everyone who considers the subject without prejudice. And the question which such a person might be inclined to ask, would perhaps be this: 'Where is the great difference? You mean by your absolving power just what others mean by preaching the Gospel. Let this be clearly understood, and then no Christian would object to your statements any longer.' My answer is, I cannot make this explanation, because it would not be a true one. I do conceive, there is very great difference between the notion that the act of absolution which the minister pronounces in the name of the Church is that act which interprets the object of his preaching, and the notion that he is sent to preach, and that because he preaches, he may, in a certain sense, absolve. The difference seems to me to be this: in the former case the minister presents Christ actually and personally to his congregation. His office is a witness of Christ's presence among them, of Christ's relation to them. It is grounded on the acknowledgment of an actual union between the body and its Head. In the other case there is much speech -- it may be eloquent, it may be true speech -- about Christ, his work, and his offices. But it is

> a painted ship
> Upon a painted ocean;

a description of what is very good and beautiful, and what man wants, but not the thing itself, not the reality. I appeal to the history of modern preaching whether this be not the case, and to the complaints of men in all directions, whether it is not felt to be the case. And if so, it must be a serious question in what way those ends may be best accomplished, which I fully believe that the objectors I am now addressing sincerely desire, the end of bringing men more directly in contact with the true and unseen Absolver; the end of making His ministers understand that they are nothing except as representatives of Him, that they do nothing, except as they lead men to the knowledge of Him. Let it be considered patiently and calmly, whether a priest, who habitually believes, that as he may confess in the people's name, so he may absolve in Christ's name, must not have a humbler sense of his own insignificance, a greater confidence in an invisible kingdom, a more serious conviction that all men are meant to be members of it, than one who believes that he has ever so many gifts, merely bestowed for the purpose of enabling him to announce the message of salvation. And do we not find, in fact, that the best of those men, whose education and theories would induce them to adopt the latter opinion, have been led in practical life, in the conduct and discipline of their flocks, in their intercourse with them as well as in their discourses to them, to act upon the former?

* * *

The Romish System

It remains that I should explain wherein the views I have expressed on the subject of the Christian ministry differ from those of the Romanists. It will be obvious at once, that on some most important points, I must be in agreement with them. For I have spoken of ministers as representing Christ to men; I have maintained that the absolving power is not a nominal but a real one; I have maintained that the Apostolic functions and authority still exist in the Church; I have admitted that the Judaical institutions have their counterparts in the new dispensation. Let us inquire under each of these four heads, what points of similarity there are between that which I have asserted to be the Catholic principle, and that which is acknowledged be the Romish one.

First, I have spoken of ministers as representing Christ to men. Long before there was the assertion of a supreme vicar of Christ upon earth, there was a feeling in men's minds, that the office of the priest is vicarial, that ministers are deputed by our Lord to do that work now which He did Himself while He was upon earth. This notion has gone into the heart of the Romish system. I believe it has created the system. Now those who laugh at the notion of a man like Athanasius contending to the death about an iota, will, of course, be much amused by my affecting to discover an important difference of signification in the words representative and vicarial. And, certainly, if the difference between the Nicene Fathers and the Arians was a difference about a word and not about a reality, those who contended upon either side were very weak and vain men. And if I suppose any charm to reside in these two words, so that the one which I reject might not be used in a good sense, and the one which I adopt in an evil one, I shall be exhibiting a less pardonable instance of folly. But I will endeavour to shew that the difference to which I allude, whether it be rightly or improperly expressed by these particular phrases, is as essential and practical a one as it is possible to conceive of. In the word vicarial, the Romanist means to embody his notion that the priest is doing the work of one who is absent, and who, only at certain times and under certain conditions, presents himself to men. By the word representative, I mean to express the truth that the minister sets forth Christ to men as present in His Church at all times, as exercising those functions Himself upon which He entered when He ascended on high. Now it must be felt, I think, that this is a radical difference, not about a word, but about the most solemn question upon which the mind of man can be occupied. And it will be seen that it is no isolated difference. It stands in the closest connexion with all those which we have been taking notice of in former sections. The principle of the Catholic Church which I have endeavoured to develop in reference to Baptism, the Eucharist, the Creed, the Forms of Worship, is the principle of a direct, real, and practical union between men and their Lord. The doctrine of the Romish system, which we have discovered in each and all of these cases, is that the veil between us and the invisible world is not yet withdrawn; that offices and ordinances are not the organs through which men converse with their Lord and He with them, but are mere outward things, which He has stamped with a certain authority and virtue, or mere pictures which exhibit Him to the imagination. Happily, this system has never fully realised itself; there seems an impossibility in the nature of things that it should. The moment it becomes or nearly becomes that which it is always striving to be, it so entirely loses its meaning, it becomes such a merely oppressive phantom, that the judgments of God, and the faith as well as the infidelity of man, appear together to confound it.

2. It follows from what I have said, that the absolving power which I claim for the Catholic priest is altogether a different one from that which is claimed by the Romish priest. I do not say that it is a less power, it seems to me a much greater one. He who can, in Christ's name, declare to a man that the state of union with Christ, which was assured to him in baptism, is his state still; that he has committed evil by living inconsistently with it; that this evil shall not be imputed to him,

175

though it may perchance be sorely punished for his good, if he turn to God and claim the better life which is his, in his Lord; that he shall have strength from Him to be His servant and do His will; that he shall know Him, and that this knowledge shall make him free: he who can pronounce these words confidently, because they are true and because he has received a commission to declare them to such and such men -- neither their truth nor his commission being in the slightest degree affected by the unbelief and the consequent unrepentance of those to whom they are addressed -- has a power of absolution affecting the past, the present, and the future, which he would be sorry indeed to exchange for any which have ever been exercised by those who claim it vicarially as their own, not representatively as their Lord's. For he must perceive, if he know anything of history, that this vicarial power has been one which did not absolve the human spirit, but bound it with heavy chains, giving it no sense of the glorious liberty which Christ has purchased for it; not only leaving it but teaching it to grovel when God has provided wings wherewith it may soar. How could penances ever have been translated from their proper and legitimate use, as means whereby those evil habits may be subdued which make the spirit proud, and hinder it from being free, into heavy shackles and torments of the conscience, into checks upon all holy and thankful devotion, into instruments of pride and self-exaltation, if those who enjoined them had really felt that they were acting on behalf of the great Redeemer and Absolver; if they had not said within their hearts, "The Lord delayeth His Coming," and therefore had thought themselves privileged to beat the men-servants and the maid-servants, while they themselves ate and drank and were drunken? How could the monstrous thought of indulgences ever have crept into the minds of men who had not lost the sense of their direct subjection to an invisible Lord, and therefore of necessity had become the slaves of those whom they professed to rule, obliged to cater to their fleshly and worldly appetites, in order that they might keep them in bondage? These may be very old stories, but they are written legibly upon the history of the world, not to be exaggerated, doubtless, for the sake of establishing Protestant conclusions, but also not to be erased by any chicanery of another kind; not to be overlooked, because we may choose to fancy that other facts of an opposite kind concern us more nearly. Facts cannot contradict each other. The records of the miseries which the Romish system has produced, cannot contradict those which prove even to the satisfaction of the most thoughtful Liberals of our day, that the Catholic Church has conferred innumerable blessings upon mankind. If we only understand both they must confirm and illustrate each other. What we want to discover is the point of their connexion.

3. This point, I believe, is found in that Romanist application of the vicarial doctrine which has reference to the episcopal or apostolic authority. According to the representative doctrine all ministers exhibit Christ in that office to which they are called. The whole body of bishops -- each bishop in his own sphere -- present him to men as the bishop or overseer of the Church. Once make ministers vicarial, and it is

evident that we have the seed of an entirely new scheme. The oneness and universality of Christ's office of course distinguishes Him from each one of His representatives, and from the whole body of His representatives. But this oneness and this universality are utterly lost to the world, they are merely dreams -- if Christ be absent from His Church. They must, therefore, be imaged somewhere, since they have lost their virtue as realities. Ministers must not only be vicars of Christ, but there must be a vicar of Christ; one who absorbs into himself, and exhibits in himself, his one and universal episcopacy. Here is the POPEDOM, an idea which may have been most gradual in its development, which could not come forth into actual manifestation as a Church idea, while one so very like it was openly realised as the idea of the World in the persons of the Roman emperors: but which, nevertheless, was latent in the minds of all ministers who assumed to themselves a vicarial character, in the minds of all laymen who acknowledged them in that character. The conception of an apostolical primacy in St. Peter, upon which it appears to rest, is evidently a mere creature of this idea, a harmless, it may be a legitimate, historical theory when considered in itself; but when it has received the vicarial virus, capable of supporting one of the greatest denials and contradictions recorded in the annals of the universe. Fot this view of the Popedom is not merely that which came under our notice, when we were considering how men had been led to look for a great dogmatist to give them right and safe opinions; this is that other aspect of the office, its kingly aspect, that in which it presents itself either as the true law of Christ's kingdom, or as the flagrant transgression and violation of it. If Christ be really in His Church, if all the offices of the Church be declaring Him to men, then is the existence of a Pope the most frightful of all anomalies, then is his existence a key to all the other anomalies in the history of Christianity. If Christ be not really in His Church, if there be no real connexion between Him and those who speak in His name, or if that connexion be merely an individual one, and there be no spiritual constitution among men, then I own I do not see how the popish system can fail to commend itself to us as the most comprehensive, the most effective, the most practical, religious organisation ever conceived of. Nor will this conviction be materially weakened by any display of the evils which the system may have produced. All these will be described as excesses. We shall be asked, what is so good or so Divine, that it is not exposed to corruption from the corruption of the human will? We shall be asked, how we can account for the good that flowed in the Middle Ages, not from a certain idea of Christianity merely, but from that idea as expressed in the organisation of the Church? I think we are able to answer, as we have answered before, 'This papal system is itself, in its simplest, best form, that result of the corrupt human will which you speak of. It is itself not the excess but the counterfeit of the Church constitution, the violation indeed of an idea, but also of the organisation in which that idea is embodied. Because it could not destroy that idea or that organisation the Church Catholic was able to diffuse some of those blessings which God meant it to diffuse. Just so far as the system prevailed, just so far as it did not contradict itself by asserting the principles it sets at naught, it has hindered God's mercies from reaching the world, it has turned them into curses.' Such language as this craves to be tried by Scripture, by history, by the conscience of papists themselves, by the truths which they profess, and which some of them, I am convinced, hold most dear. The other language which supposes that there is no spiritual constitution of Christ's ministry, has, I believe, done more, and is, at this present time, doing more to promote and establish Popery than all its own most diligent efforts.

4. I must still allude briefly to the connexion which I suppose, and which the Romanist supposes, to exist between the Jewish and the Christian economy. We are agreed so far as this -- we both believe the connexion to be a real one, we both believe that it has to do with an ecclesiastical economy, we both believe that the forms of the Jewish Commonwealth, so far as they were not merely national or oriental, were translated into corresponding forms, and not merely into spiritual notions. Wherein then do we differ? In this all-important point, that we look upon the Incarnation, the Resurrection, and the Ascension of our Lord, as declaring Him to be really and actually, not nominally or fantastically, head of the universal kingdom as the mortal High Priest had been of the peculiar kingdom, all the Jewish history being a preparation for the substitution of the one for the other. They believe that this High Priest has been succeeded in the new dispensation by one mortal and sinful as himself; that he is to preserve the doctrines of the Creed to the Church, while he practically and in his own person declares that those doctrines do not mean what they seem to mean; that a real connexion has not been established between man and God in the person of the Mediator; that the Church is not what her Creed affirms her to be, united to Him in His victory as well as in His humiliation. Again, then, we contend, and with so much more conviction and earnestness, as we approach nearer to the heart of the subject, that the Romish system and the Catholic Church, instead of being identical, instead of having any natural affinity for each other, are deadly opposites, one of which must perish if the other is to survive.

SECTION VI -- THE SCRIPTURES

In a preceeding chapter I inquired into the meaning of certain indications of a spiritual and universal constitution which offered themselves to us while we were studying the actual phenomena of the world and its past history. We wanted some help to explain these to us, and to tell us how they should exist, and yet the acknowledgment of this constitution by men should seem to be the exception rather than the rule. We found this help in the documents which compose our Bible. These documents profess to reveal a constitution, which is declared to be the Divine constitution for man. It is revealed first to a particular family, then to a particular nation, then, through that family and nation, to mankind. But this revelation is a history. The acts of this family and this nation, and the acts by which their possession becomes a universal one, embody the discovery. The oppositions which arise without and within this family and nation to the principle upon which they are founded, explain to us the contradiction between the will of man and the order in which he is placed. They make us conscious of the existence of two societies, one formed in accordance with the order of God, the other based upon self-will.

Now, as the Bible declares that the constitution which it affirms to be the true one should last for ever, and as it speaks of a society grounded upon that constitution which is to last for ever, we wished to inquire what signs there are of such a society in the world at this present moment. We have discovered some, which seem to import the existence of it; we have inquired whether they correspond with the signs of it which we found set down in Scripture. Thus we have referred to the Bible, not only to clear up our difficulties respecting the meaning of God in His universe, but also to tell us how far that meaning is effectual for us at this day, not only to make known the nature of the order in which we are placed, but also the outward shape of the body in which that order is expressed.

It may seem, then, that the purpose and character of the Scriptures have been already investigated as much at large as the limits of a book like this can permit, especially as the subject has already come before us in another shape, while we were discussing the opinions of different religious bodies. But it can hardly escape the observation of any reader, that if there be such a book as the Bible has seemed to us to be, it must not only interpret to us the signs of a spiritual and universal kingdom, but must be itself one of the most remarkable of those signs. And if so, we may, perhaps, by considering its relation to the other signs of which we have spoken, obtain a solution of some difficulties which much embarrass the modern student.

I. (1.) This view of the general intent of the Scriptures seems to shew how particular books may have been ascertained to form a part of them, or to have no claims of admission to them. To conceive the possibility of a canon of Scripture is the same thing as to conceive the possibility of Scripture itself. If one be necessary, the other is necessary. If one be supposed to be formed by human agency, there is no difficulty in supposing that human agency should have been most proper for the other. Regard the Bible merely as an isolated thing, and it is no doubt hard to understand how such an authority as that of fixing what it is, should have been exercised by any persons who were not employed in the writing of it. Look upon it as the witness of a permanent kingdom, believe that it is a part of the plan of God for the establishment and building up of that kingdom, and there is surely no difficulty in supposing that wisdom adequate to the work of determining, with all necessary practical exactness, what books did and what did not contain the authentic history of this kingdom, should have been imparted to men, whose offices proclaimed that they could not fulfil their most ordinary tasks by any wisdom of their own.

(2.) By looking at the Scriptures as the sign of a spiritual and universal kingdom, we seem able to reconcile several methods or schemes for interpreting them, which often present themselves to us as contradictory and exclusive. For instance, it has been one well-known tendency of men to look for a mystical character in them, to supose that beneath the letter some secret cabbala must be lurking. It has been the tendency of another class to maintain the strictness and sufficiency of the letter, and indignantly to repudiate every recondite meaning as inconsistent with the simplicity of a revelation. Now every sign of this kingdom which we have considered hitherto has partaken of this double character; it has pointed to a relation which is invisible, mystical, transcendent; it has been in itself plain, definite, visible. The relation which it expressed was real and permanent; here lay the necessity of a sign which had nothing in it of a fluctuating character, which did not derive its strength from the notions and apprehensions of men, which spoke to all. One would certainly expect to find the same principle holding good in the case of this other sign; one would think that the more simple, accurate, and historical the outward clothing was, the more it would be felt to embody some higher principle.

Again; it has been a great controversy whether each part of these records should be taken to have a distinct definite meaning, applicable to some particular event and crisis, or whether it may have a remote application to some other crisis, or even to a series of yet undeveloped events. Now supposing the Bible to be the history of the gradual development and manifestation of a kingdom fixed upon certain permanent principles, it seems the most natural supposition, that it would always exhibit these principles in reference to some present or approaching contingency, yet that it would explain similar contingencies and circumstances to the end of time. Refusing to acknowledge the first event, we lose the principle; determined to restrict it to some other event of our own selection, we compel ourselves to depart from the letter without gaining anything for the spirit. We may be right in our feeling that the particular event we have fixed upon does fall under the law which this part of Scripture makes known to us; we are almost sure to be wrong when we restrain the application of the law to that given event. These conclusions proceeded naturally from the belief that the Scriptures are not to be looked upon apart from the spiritual kingdom.

(3.) Hence also we seem to obtain the solution of another, and what strikes many as a more difficult problem, Where are the interpreters of this book to be found? How is it at once to be a lawgiver, and yet to be subject to the maxims and rules of interpretation of those who are its subjects? The difficulty is the same as in all previous cases. Take the Bible as a solitary fact, speak of it simply as the Word of God addressing itself to man, without inquiring what this Word of God affirms man to be, what kind of order it says that he is placed in; and there must be endless puzzles to ascertain in what position of simple acquiescence of earnest inquiry such utterances are to be received, whether each man is to grasp them for himself, or whether his fellows are in any wise helping him to grasp them.

But let it be supposed that the words speak as they seem to speak, of men being placed in a certain Divine order -- of God, as addressing them in that order -- it would seem plain enough that the words will be realised just so far as we avail ourselves of our position, missed just so far as we reject it. The difficulty of understanding how, through the help of Christ's minsiters, we may attain to a practical insight into the facts and principles which this book makes known, how, choosing to dispense with that help, we shall be most likely to go astray, is precisely the difficulty which is supposed in all education; or, would it not be more correct to say, that here we find the key to the puzzles of ordinary education, because we arrive at a point, where we find God proclaiming Himself as the Educator, and marking out those through whom He will educate? The difficulty which arises from the discovery that these ministers may forget their task, and instead of calling out the personal life and apprehension of their disciples, stifle them with mere words and notions, is still the same problem of daily life repeated, only that we perceive more clearly against whom the sin is committed, and what the responsibility for it is. The difficulty of comprehending how men should teach out of a book, which they acknowledge to overreach themselves, and to be above them, is but the difficulty of every magistrate and judge who is set for the purpose of bringing out into light and clearness the meaning of the Law which he both administers and obeys, who may, doubtless, put himself in the place of it, may read himself into it, may choose to keep it from men instead of guiding them into an intelligent submission to it, but who acts in this way at his peril, bringing himself under the sentence, if of no earthly superior, of One who yet, in this spiritual kingdom, holds His constant and acknowledged court of appeal.

II. These questions are debated between those who are agreed in acknowledging the Scriptures as possessing Divine authority. Let us now consider the objections of those who either reject the notion of a Bible altogether, or who see no special reason why the books which we hold sacred should usurp the name.

These objections may be stated in this way. 'Ever since the critical spirit and knowledge of modern Europe have been brought to bear upon these documents, it has been found more and more difficult to maintain the claims which are put forth on their behalf by the elder Church as well as by the Reformers. Supposing the doctrine of their inspiration, of their paramount authority to all other books, of their fixed and peculiar character, to be true, the detection of any unauthentic record amongst them, of any report which will not bear sifting, even of any considerable error in the reading of a text which had been used to support some opinion, must be sufficient to shake the credit of the whole scheme. It was, therefore, unquestionably honest in those early critics who wished to assert the general authority of the book, that they ventured to commence these fatal inroads. But if they were not stopped at first, they certainly cannot be stopped now. The principle of criticism, which has been admitted as to a part, must be applied to the whole. Whatever maxim has been thought just, and has stood the test of inquiry in reference to other books, must be brought to bear upon these. And little help will be derived in our day from those evidences, which in the last century were thought so conclusive. The credit of the book was supposed to be sustained by the miracles which are recorded in it, by the consistency of the facts with the general testimony of antiquity, by the admirable character of the four narratives which form the centre of it, by its ideal truth and consistency. Now those miracles are the very stories which we require should be accounted for. The testimony of antiquity has been proved only to establish the existence of certain habits of thought and feeling in different nations, which will themselves account for what has been supposed to be peculiar in these records. The four narratives have been subjected to a severe analysis, and it has been found most difficult to understand either their internal history or their relation to outward events. Finally, the supposed ideal consistency has been examined of the whole record, and has been shewn, indeed, to be an explanation of the phenomena of Christianity, but in a way most unsatisfactory to those who regard it as embodied in a series of facts.'

This is a statement, I hope it is a fair statement, of the objections which are now current in all parts of society, and which, when they do not appear as a complete system of arguments, are only the more effectual, because they suggest the thought that much has been left unsaid which would be quite conclusive if it might safely be uttered.

I begin, then, with admitting that I do not see how it is possible for those who look upon the Scriptures merely as a set of documents contrived for the instruction of individual men, merely as a witness to them of what has been done for them, of what the plans and purposes of God respecting them are, to encounter some of these arguments. I do not mean that they may not encounter them practically, in what seems to me a most honest and effectual method. If they will resolutely hold fast that which they have felt and ascertained in their own lives to be true; it they will say, 'This we have learnt and received; the Bible taught it us, and we cannot give it up for any arguments;' I believe their position is a safe and impregnable one. It is not a position of prejudice, it is a reasonable and sound position; it is founded upon the first and wisest maxim of ethical philosophy, Keep what thou hast; add to it if thou canst; but if thou wishest to realise more, never let anything which thou hast realised be snatched away from thee. My fear is that few people in our day are likely to be content with this position. They well be going out of it with their arguments and their evidences, with their attempts to prove how and why a book having the character which they impute to the Bible, must be Divine and perfect.   Here I think they will be discomfited.   This logic is not a part of their realised truths, it is something altogether extraneous to them.   And what is worse, they do not yet know what it is they are arguing about; for they may have derived these individual facts from the Bible; but the Bible itself evidently assumes to be something else; it assumes to be a collection of historical documents, and the question is, how this assumption is connected with that quality of it which they have discovered and recognized.

Are we, then, to hope that those who are willing to consider it principally as a collection of historical documents, and as such to defend it, will be able to maintain their position?   I think writers of this class will bring forward much that is very valuable, much that their opponents cannot without great difficulty and without some dishonesty reply to; I think they will do more than this; they will be enabled to leave an impression upon thoughtful and sincere minds, that there are facts existing in the world now, and that there has been a series of such facts, of which these books may offer the explanation.   But here again, the difficulty is to find how these facts cohere, how it is that they are related to the doctrines and principles which these books embody; why it is necessary to suppose any Divine oversight in the arrangement and preservation of them.

Are we then to say, as the objector affirms we must say, that criticism is wholly inapplicable to this particular set of records; that they must taken for granted upon some authority or other, be it that of primitive antiquity, or of the Church in the present day; and that, being so taken for granted, all further inquiry respecting them is to be discarded?   Every one will see that there is a plausibility in this opinion; nay, there is more than plausibility, there is a truth hidden in it which we must not deny.   As long as we receive the Scriptures at all, as long as we do not determine absolutely to reject them, we must in the education of our own minds, in the education of our children's minds, take them for granted.   We cannot begin with being critics, or with making them critics.   If we do, we and they will assuredly be most miserable critics, and as certainly we and they shall be nothing else.   But do we not in this respect deal with the Scriptures as we deal with other books?   We take them for granted too; we do not in merely reading or in teaching them, enter into a criticism of the sources whence they are derived or of the conditions of their authority.   There comes a time, however, when other books are subjected to this trial; it has been the will of God that the book which we consider pre-eminently His should be subjected to the same.   It is a solemn inquiry for us, whether we shall dare to pretend that we will take better care of His book than He has taken of it; whether we shall affirm that it cannot bear the application of tests, which we believe that ordinary literature will bear.

And this brings us to the main question which I wish to place before the reader, What has been the character of that criticism to which the Scriptures have been for the most part subjected during the last century and a half? I do not ask whether it has been sound criticism, learned criticism, devout criticism. It may have had any or all of these characters. But what has been its object? The safest answer with respect to the last century may be obtained from a consideration of what was the object of all criticism, whether it referred to the human body or the human soul, to the universe or to the creatures who lived in it. Nearly every philosopher of that day thought it was the business of his life to analyze; he was to analyze the operations of the mind, to analyze himself, to analyze his fellow-creatures, to analyze the being of his Maker. Do I say that all this labour was wasted, that nothing came out of the inquiries and dissections of that period? I say no such thing; I believe much was learnt from them; that many false notions and phantoms, which men had transferred from themselves to the objects of their study, were got rid of; many idols thrown down, broken in pieces, and trampled upon, which had beset the caves of thoughtful men or the market-places of busy men. But the great lesson of all which this method of study bequeathed to us, was the lesson of its own utter incapacity to lead into the apprehension of any truth, though it might avail for the discomfiture of some error. Hence every step that has been taken in our day towards real profitable inquiry, whether in physics or metaphysics, has been a step out of this method, a step towards the investigation of the powers and principles of things as they exist; not an attempt, except for certain subordinate purposes, to reduce them into their elements. Above all, this change has been effected in reference to literature. Here the analytical spirit of the last age displayed itself in its full power; every book was to be cut up into its elements, and whatever elements did not please the critic to be cast out as worthless; nothing whatever was done in the study of a book as a whole, nothing towards the discovery of the purpose which actuated and informed it. The Scriptures were treated in the same manner. The fact of their constituting a whole, which had been felt as a whole by innumerable minds for many centuries, was more and more overlooked as utterly unimportant to the critic and the philosopher. He could not deny that they had a common name, but his business was to shew what separate items went to the composition of this name, and then to pursue his inquiries with as little reference as possible to it. Of course it was part of the ordinary philosophy at the period, that everything in this book, which spoke of invisible powers, should be explained away. The object was to discover how many of its elements might be preserved, without infringing upon the ordinary maxims of the time in reference to physics, metaphysics, and ethics.

Now I would say, in reference to these inquiries, just as I said in reference to all others undertaken at the same period, that I do not believe they were useless, or will ultimately be mischievous. If the student of the physics of the seventeenth century perceives that there were a multitude of strange theories and supersitions then accumulated and accumulating, which had need by some whirlwind to be swept away; the student of theology must equally confess that a number of hard, dogmatical abstractions respecting spiritual objects, and, not least, respecting the books which treat of these objects, were darkening the face of the heavens, and making men's path along their common earth less clear. That some fiery process would be necessary for the destruction of these, we might conjecture. Of what kind it should be, we could not be judges. God ordained that it should be this destructive analysis. We cannot doubt that what He appointed was best. Many obstructions to the perception of that which is real and substantial have been removed out of the path of the young theologian; it is his own fault if he seeks for them again. He may, if he will, be less entangled with the abstractions and conceits of the intellect than his forefathers were. And in this case, as in the others I have mentioned, the analysts have conferred this great blessing on us -- they have proved the inadequacy and feebleness of their method to explain any one living fact, or to lead us onward to any one important discovery.

When, therefore, the objectors of whom we are speaking, say that the Bible ought to be tried by the same rules as other books, we can perhaps go a great way with them, provided we understand what they mean. It always, I believe, will be tried by the same standard as other books; that is to say, the habits of mind which we cultivate in regard to one, we shall cultivate in regard to the other. When all books are merely cut up into their elements, the Bible will be dealt with in like manner. When other books, and the whole series of books which constitute the literature of a nation, are contemplated in reference to their principle or idea, it is utterly impossible but that these should be studied upon the same principle. And the question arises, what is this principle or idea? We have had occasion to consider that view of it, so prevalent in our day, which tries to separate the idea from the event, to exhibit the one as common to all ages, the other as its mere accidental temporary clothing. I have endeavoured to shew how inadequate this doctrine is to account for the phenomena which present themselves to us in the history of the world; how it turns living ideas into mere notions and apprehensions of our minds, and so legalizes and stamps with authority the very superstitions from which is seeks to deliver us; how it confounds the permanent and the transitory in the very attempt to distinguish them; how it destroys human progress in the very attempt to assert it. If, indeed, it were possible entirely to separate this modern idealism from the old analytical method which it professes to supersede and to despise, we might easily prove the insufficiency of either. The chief strength of each lies in a vague notion of the one being the expansion and full development of the other; in a loose impression that the belief of inspiration, of miracles, of a Gospel history, which had been partially subverted by the one, has been completely subverted by the other.

The facts, in recent German history especially, which prove that the ideal system could not have been produced at all, if it had not been preceded by a vehement religious protest against the analysts, are not known or not heeded; and we are asked what hope there can be of maintaining our obsolete notions respecting a Divine order and a Divine book, when each age has furnished its own peculiar and appropriate refutation of them. Our answer is, 'No hope at all, if what you call our notions be not something more than notions, if they be not founded on eternal principles and truths. But, on the other hand, the belief that they have this foundation is strengthened not weakened, by the history of these different attempts to confute them; strengthened not weakened by the fact, that no adequate answer has been offered to the particular charges against the Bible, except by those who are willing to speak of the Bible in the way it seems to speak of itself, as the revelation of a Divine kingdom.'

1. Looking at it is this light, I would inquire, first, what difficulties there are in the old notion that the writers of the book were inspired men? According to the principle of a spiritual kingdom, as we have considered it, inspiration is not a strange anomalous fact; it is the proper law and order of the world; no man ought to write, or speak, or think, except under the acknowledgment of an inspiration; no man can speak, or write, or think if he have not really an inspiration. Is, then, the constant habitual confession of Divine teaching, the reference of everything to God by the writers of this Bible, something which stamps them with the character of impostors? Would not this seem to be the characteristic of true men? But still you say 'it is the characteristic of fanatics,' of those who are not true men; where do you draw the line?' I draw it in this way: -- I say, according to the principle of a spiritual kingdom, every man who is doing the work he is set to do, may believe that he is inspired with a power to do that work; every man who is doing some other work which he is not set to do may, indeed, say that he is using powers which he has received from above; but he is violating the purposes for which those powers have been given him; his will is obeying an impulse contrary to the will of the Being who bestowed the power. Here is fanaticism, here is confusion. The question, therefore, is not really, Were these men who wrote the Scriptures inspired by God? but, Were they in a certain position and appointed to a certain work? So that we are driven by this argument, as we are driven by the book itself, from that which we read to that which we read of. Was there such a society as that which this book speaks of? was there such a nation as the Jews? had they a history? was there a meaning in the history? does this book explain to us their history and its meaning? The question of inspiration belongs to these questions -- cannot be viewed apart from them. If there be no spiritual kingdom in the world, no kings, priests, prophets appointed by God, then assuredly I cannot make out that the Scriptures had a right to describe such kings, and priests, and prophets. If there were such men, I have as great difficulty in understanding how we can dispense with such a record, or how any Being, except Him who formed

the society for the sake of His own glory and for the good of His creatures, can have caused that book to be written.

But it will be answered: 'This is evading the difficulty. It is not merely the men, but the words, which, according to the common theory, are inspired. And though less extravagant theories may have been invented and received among Christians, yet none which denies a verbal inspiration or dictation is consistent with itself, is anything but a subterfuge.' Two words are used here as synonymous, which seem to involve the most different significations. When you speak to me of verbal inspiration, though I do not like the phrase, though it seems to me to involve a violent -- a scarcely grammatical -- ellipsis, yet I subscribe most unequivocally to the meaning which I suppose is latent in it. I have no notion of inspired thoughts which do not find for themselves a suitable clothing of words. I can scarcely, even in my mind, separate the language of a writer from his meaning. And I certainly find this difficulty greater in studying a book of the Bible than in studying any other book. The peculiarities of its language seem to me strangely significant. And yet its greatest peculiarity of all, if I may be pardoned the solecism, is its universality, its capacity of translation into any dialect which has a living and human quality, which is not merely the echo of passing impressions and the utterance of animal necessities. But just because I see this link between the inbreathed thought and the spoken word, I must reject as monstrous and heretical the notion of a dictation. I call it monstrous and heretical, for I know none more directly at variance with the letter and spirit of Scripture. If the hint of it is to be found anywhere, it is certainly in the history of the giving of the divine Code. That was, of course, a formal literal document, and therefore is signified to proceed formally and literally from its Author. Yet mark how carefully we are warned against the notion, so natural to the sensual and idolatrous heart of man, that Moses was a mere mechanical utterer or tanscriber. Why are we told that he went into the thick darkness? why do we hear of his awful communion for forty days? why have we the records of his deep sympathy with his people, of his prayers, his meditations, his murmurings, if not that we may be exalted to understand something of the human privilege of spiritual intercourse, and that we may consider this the great privilege of the most honoured seer? And this surely is the object of all Scripture, if it have any object at all, to withdraw us from outward sensual impressions of the Divine Majesty, to make us feel the reality of the relation between Him and His creatures, to make us understand that it is a spiritual relation, and that, therefore, it can manifest itself in outward words and acts. It is, then, no concession to the Rationalist, but a necessity of our own faith, that we should utterly reject and abhor this theory of dictation.

* * *

THE ROMISH SYSTEM

I have contended, then, that a Bible without a Church is inconceivable, that the appointed ministers of the Church are the appointed ministers of the Church are the appointed instruments for guiding men into a knowledge of the Bible, that the notion of private judgment is a false notion, that Inspiration belongs to the Church, and not merely to the writers of the Bible, that the miracles of the New Testament were the introduction of a new dispensation, and were not merely a set of strange acts belonging to a particular time; lastly, that the Gospel narratives must be received as parts of the necessary furniture of the Church. Now is there not a manifest tendency towards Romanism in these positions? Do they not one and all belong to the system which I have denounced?

Let us consider:

1st. I have supposed the Bible and the Church to be mutual interpreters of each other. The Church exists as a fact, the Bible shews what that fact means. The Bible is a fact, the Church shews what that fact means. Now, what I complain of in Romanism, is that it has entirely overlooked the relation of these two parts of God's scheme to each other. It has concealed the Bible from men on purpose that the Church might be exalted. And it has proved that the Church could not be exalted while the Bible was hidden, that while there was no book to explain to the whole body of the Church its own position, that position of necessity became unintelligible. Men did not know what it was to be Churchmen, because they could not learn it from this book, and because no other was able to tell them.

2ndly. Hence we see, wherein my notion of the powers of ministers differs from that of the Romanist. He thinks that the minister has a power and commission to hide the Bible from the laity. I think he has a power and commission to lay it open to the laity. I think that everyone has an appointed work to do; that when we refuse our own appointed work, or do not acknowledge the different appointment of another, we necessarily miss some good which was intended for us. And therefore I do not think that the laity, rejecting the teachings of their appointed ministers, will understand the Bible. And I do not think, on the other hand, that the minister, putting himself in place of the Bible, and not encouraging the laity to read it, and digest it, can be a true teacher, can exercise the powers which God has committed to him.

3rdly. I believe, as I have said, that the Bible and the Church were intended to raise men out of their private judgments, and to guide each man who will be guided, into the truth which is meant for all. The Romanist claims an authority for the Church in opposition to private judgments. But it is not an authority to call forth the spirits of men -- to draw them out of the little narrow circle of private experiences and

188

conclusions; but an authority to crush the exercise of their spirits, to hinder them from obtaining freedom. And therefore this authority has itself become the tool of private judgments. Half the inventions of Romanism are the inventions of private judgment, the fruits of a condescension on the part of the priest to the narrow-minded feelings and judgments of his subjects, or else the creations of his own judgment, both alike manifesting the need of that universal law and standard by which both ought to have been tried.

4thly. The presence of that Spirit who is the source of all inspiration, in the whole body of the Church, and in each of its members that he may fulfil his own appointed position, -- this is involved in the idea of our baptism; disbelieving this, we acknowledge no Church at all. In virtue of this gift, we are to believe that every member of the Church has a capacity for understanding the high privileges which have been obtained for him; in virtue of this gift, we believe that the ministers of the Church can educate their flocks into the apprehension of them. Our complaint aginst the Romish system is, that it does not allow us to act upon the faith of this inspiration. It supposes inspiration to be communicated to certain persons at certain periods, for the sake of certain startling effects. If supposes an inspiration to reside somewhere in the Church, for the purpose of determinig what men are, and what they are not, to hold, for the purposes of keeping down questioning, and giving a sense to Scripture. But an abiding Spirit, one who will guide into all truth, and can tolerate no falsehood, one who can unfold the Scriptures to different ages according to their different wants, such a Spirit, such an inspiration, it will not allow us to recognize.

5thly. And, therefore, our difference on the subject of miracles is also very intelligible. If you recognize miracles, as connected with the idea of a spiritual kingdom, and not merely belonging to a certain book, why, the Romanist asks, will you not recognize the miracles in which we believe? why not suppose that they may occur in the nineteenth century as well as in the first? I answer, I neither affirm nor deny anything as to the question how often in the history of the Church or in what periods of it God may have been pleased to suspend the operations of intermediate agents, for the purpose of shewing that He is at all times the Author and Mover of them. This question must be determined by a careful study of historical evidence; upon the result of such a study I should be very sorry to dogmatize. Those who believe that miracles are for the assertion of order, and not for the violation of it, for the sake of proving the constant presence of a spiritual power, and not for the sake of shewing that it interferes occasionally with the affairs of the world, will be the least inclined to expect the frequent repetitions of such signs, for they hold, that being recorded as facts in the former ages of the world, they become laws in ours, that we are to own Him who healed the sick of the palsy in every cure which is wrought by the ordinary physician, Him who stilled the storm on the lake of Gennesareth, in the guidance and preservation of every ship which crosses the ocean; and that this effect would be lost, if we were led to put any contempt upon that which is daily and habitual. Still, I should think it very presumptuous to say, that it has never been needful, in the modern history of the world, to break the idols of sense and experience by the same method which was sanctioned in the days of old. Far less should I be inclined to underrate the piety and criticise the wisdom or honesty of those men who, missing or overlooking intermediate powers, of which they knew little, at once referred the acts and events they witnessed to their primary source.

But these admissions only compel me the more solemnly to reject at least nineteen-twentieths of all the miracles recorded in Romanist books in later times. In reference to these, we are not bound to go into a careful collation of evidences. In general there is very little to collate, but where there is apparently the best and most respectable, there is a grand preliminary objection. I dare not believe such miracles as these, because I believe the miracles of the New Testament. I am expressly told in Scripture that there are miracles which I am not to believe, which are to produce no impression upon me whatever. I do not want to go into the question of the honesty or the dishonesty of persons who report them, that is a question between their own consciences and their Creator; they best know whether they are or are not lying for God. But it is the character of the miracle which determines my judgment of it. Is it to lead me into the worship of the Visible or the Invisible? Is it to deliver me from sensible things, or to make me a slave of sensible things?

Does the Romanist advocate say that I have no right to ask these questions? I know he says so and I will tell him why he says so. He says so because there is a secret root of unbelief in his mind, a secret doubt whether anything is true, which finds refuge in the thought that everything may be true. This is a very prevailing tendency in our day; it is the natural reaction against the scepticism of the last century. A number of men in France and Germany, and perhaps quite as many in England as in either, have passed or are passing, not through any gradual stages, but per saltum ("through a leap") from universal doubt to universal credence. And they are able to carry the same habits of mind into both professions; they are able to say to themselves with great complacency, and with no little truth, 'we are not really changed, we do not acknowledge any standard now more than before; the only difference is, that we have substituted the new pourquoi non ("why not") for the old pourquoi.' It does not the least surprise us to hear such men, men who twenty years ago would have laughed us to scorn for believing in the resurrection of Lazarus, now indulging in fierce denunciations of all who doubt the miracles in the Tyrol. The logic, 'where are you to stop short?' was that which they used in their contemptuous manhood, and which still seems to them perfectly conclusive, in their not less contemptuous nor less really sceptical old age. We can only repeat, we stop short when we find ourselves arrived at the exact contradiction of that which we have believed. We have received our Lord as the Great Deliverer, who has led captive our captivity to sense; we stop short when we meet with persons who would bring us into that captivity again.

The Bible, we believe, is meant to cultivate in us a habit of distinguishing; faithfully and humbly used, it has that effect. If you, who have not used it or believed in it, shew that you have not acquired that habit, we have only another reason for giving thanks, that God has been pleased not to hide the blessing from us or from our children.

6thly. These last considerations apply very remarkbly to the case of the Gospel narratives. It is said, "The Church has preserved to us these histories of our Lord's life; you receive them upon the authority of the Church. You know very little about the persons who wrote them, you accept them because they are given to you as parts of the canon. Well, but the Church has put its sanction upon many histories of the saints; she deems them also profitable for her children. Granted that they refer to inferior persons, that they never can be as important as the Gospels, yet where do you draw the line? You have admitted Church authority in one case, the highest case of all, why not admit it also in a lower case?" I answer, By the care of God's providence through His Church, these records of its Lord and Head have been preserved. They have been preserved, no doubt, for many great and solemn purposes, but for this especially, that there may be a standard in the world, by which all other acts and lives may be tried. Exclude the Gospels from our canon, let there be nothing there but epistles setting forth spiritual principles, and not only do those principles lose their meaning for want of a true personal object to which they may refer; but this end is wholly lost -- there is no character set before men, which exhibits to them the image after which they were formed in connexion with the life of this earth. Now if the Church have preserved for me these books, and have told me the object for which they were preserved, I am not obeying her when I lose sight of this object; I am not obeying her when I am not bringing all other books and lives to this standard. I am not, indeed, to do this for the sake of condemning them, not for the sake of seeing what is wrong in them -- I have no commission or powers for that purpose -- but certainly for the sake of seeing how far I may safely follow them. If, then, I find records of different men, all professedly acknowledging this type or image as the one to which they should be conformed, I am bound thankfully to admire every feature of their lives which has been caught by reflection from it. I may very often go wrong in my judgement of these features; I may mistake a bad copy for a good one, or disown a true one because I have not sufficient spiritual cultivation to understand the circumstances of its form and colouring. Still, the more I study the original under such guidance as is given to me, the more I must believe and hope that the faculty will be cultivated in me, whereby I may discern the true from the counterfeit. And I must look to the Church to help me in this work, to be continually teaching me how to observe the traces of the Divine model in the human imitation, how to see what in it was produced merely by the accidents of the time, or by human self-will and frailness.

Such help I believe the Church, holding the Bible in her hand, is able to furnish to her faithful disciples; and my charge against the Romish system is, that it has hindered the Church from exercising this prerogative, and forced her to exercise a most different one. What I mean will be best understood by the use which has been made in this system of the word 'Saint.'

The Gospels teach me, the Church in all ages teaches me, to acknowledge our Lord as one who perfectly identified himself with humanity, with all its sorrows and sufferings, yea, with its sins; because He was without sin, He was able to bear the sins of all men. This character of essential humanity, is so much the character which we feel to belong to our Lord, so much the character which did manifest, and which alone could manifest, His divinity, that it may be said to be the grand object of the Church, in her Advents, her Epiphanies, her Lents, her Passion Weeks, her Easter-Days, her Ascension-Days, to exhibit it. And it has been the feeling of every true saint in the world's history, that this was the character which our Lord would especially seek to produce in His disciples. A largeness of heart, a sympathy with all our race, a fellowship in its sufferings, grief for the sins which hold it down, these assuredly are qualities which the most conspicuous saints of the Romish calendar acknowledge as most high and Divine. Along with these are associated humiliation, suffering, indifference to good or evil report. But now comes in the counterfeit system: 'What a great and glorious thing it is to be a saint, to be above the rest of men, to be unlike them! What a fine thing it is to be humble, self-denying, submitting to persecution and shame! What glory do those get who can eclipse one another in this race! What an honour it is to be enrolled in this calendar; what fame we get here, what rewards in the life to come!' Who does not feel instinctively that we have here introduced a new image, the very opposite to that we were just considering? It has come in one knows not how, under the very names and words which seemed so sacred and beautiful; but see how frightful and deformed it is! Yet will anyone dare to say that there has not been a system, that there is not a system now, which sanctions this image, puts honour upon it, holds it up to imitation and idolatry?

We are not bound to say of any particular person, He has given himself up to this system, he has caught this image. We may believe, and rejoice to believe, that there have been multitudes in every age of the Church, that there are numbers in every country in Europe at this day, who, be their outward professions and symbols what they may, do in their hearts confess the true image, do in their lives conform to it. Such persons belong to the Catholic Church, they are witnesses of her permanence, and that she will one day come out bright and beautiful from all her corruptions, as a bride adorned for her husband. But the

192

existence of such persons only makes us see more clearly and hate more fervently the system which has assumed the name and affected the powers of the Church; only makes us believe more surely, that it will be destroyed by the brightness of His coming, who is the true and only Pope and Potentate, the real King of Saints.

CHAPTER V

OF THE RELATIONS OF THE CHURCH WITH NATIONAL BODIES

SECTION I

The Old Testament -- Ancient Pagan History -- History of Modern
Europe -- General Inferences

* * *

Now anyone who considers these Ten Commandments, must perceive that they are definitive and conservative, not creative or constitutive. They presume the existence of certain facts, principles, and institutions, and it is the violation or forgetfulness of these which they denounce. The first presumes that the Jews had been brought out of Egypt by an unseen Being. He is their deliverer and Lord; as such they are to acknowledge Him. The second presumes the existence of Worship, a tendency in men to create the objects of it for themselves out of the things which they see and handle; a relation between the worshippers and the Invisible Lord; a government exercised by Him from generation to generation. The third presumes the practice of appealing to the Name of God, of invoking Him as one who knows whether a man be guilty or innocent. The fourth assumes the institution of the Week; explains whereof it is the sign; gives warnings against the forgetfulness of the distinction between the six days and the seventh day. The fifth presumes the existence of the Paternal Relation, and treats the respect for it as the condition of abiding in the land given to the nation. The sixth presumes the existence of a community which is interested in the Life of each of its members. The seventh presumes the institution of Marriage. The eighth presumes the institution of Property. The ninth presumes the existence of Tribunals, before which one may give witness respecting another. The tenth affirms the existence of a bond of Neighbourhood -- the same bond which is supposed in all the rest -- and declares that even the coveting of that which is a neighbour's is a violation of it.

That these facts, institutions, and principles, had a very close connexion with the life and being of that nation which was brought out of Egypt, most readers will acknowledge: but if they turn to ancient history, they find that some of them had a very close connexion with the being and life of every nation which it speaks of. The Greeks and Romans were remarkably distinguished from each other. But they were both alike distinguished from the slaves and barbarians, of whose existence we become aware chiefly through them. Wherein lay the difference? Apart from all intellectual superiority, (though it is hardly right to say, apart, the one characteristic was so involved in the other,) it is quite evident that they had a clear sense of certain great landmarks and boundaries in human society, the violation of which was an evil; that they believed these landmarks to have been fixed by an awful Unseen

Power, and to be preserved by that Power: that among the chief of these landmarks they reckoned the sacredness of life, of the paternal relation, of marriage, of property, of appeals to the Divine name, of tribunals for rectifying wrong; the law of neighbourhood as binding those who acknowledged a common ancestry, and were living in the same locality; the majesty of law as preserved by the majesty of worship.

But two of the Commandments have no counterparts in the legislation of Greece or Rome. There was, I have said, a distinct recognition of an unseen Majesty from which it proceeded, and by which it was upheld; there was not the prohibition of confounding the unseen Majesty with things visible. There was the recognition of different sacred seasons connected with the course of the sun and moon: there was not the recognition of a Week; a division of time depending upon some other law then the astronomical; defining human life, by its two great principles of action and rest; connecting these two principles with the life and being of God; teaching that His rest and action are the patterns of ours, and yet that He is ever at rest while we are working, and ever at work on our behalf while we are resting; incorporating the Divine with the common, and yet hallowing the distinction between them; signifying that the palace and the hut, nay, the master and his cattle, are subject to the same government; making each nightly slumber the image of the final repose of the spirit and soul and body, each in its proper and appointed object. Let anyone consider how the political life of these nations was affected by the sensual tendencies of their worship; let him meditate upon the difficulty which every philosopher experienced in his endeavour to reconcile the idea of a living, acting God, with one continually resting in his own beatitude, the still greater difficulty of finding any point of sympathy between his own thoughts and those of common men who felt that the God they feared must interfere in all their transactions, and then let him say whether the second or the fourth Commandments do not receive as much illustration and confirmation from the human feeling and conscience of the old world as the sixth or the seventh.

Be that as it may, not only some of these institutions, but all of them, exist among ourselves. The Jewish order of time, so far as the week is concerned, has become as much a part of the institutions of modern Europe as marriage or property. All three may be regarded in different places with more or less of reverence; but they are recognized by every nation of Christendom, and incorporated with their daily transactions.

* * *

PART III

THE ENGLISH CHURCH AND THE SYSTEMS WHICH DIVIDE IT

CHAPTER I

HOW FAR THIS SUBJECT IS CONNECTED WITH THOSE PREVIOUSLY DISCUSSED

Are these principles applicable to our circumstances as Englishmen? If not, we may be sure that there is some flaw in them which we have not yet detected. If they are, the question how to apply them must be, above all others, important to us.

I think the young English ecclesiastical student is very apt to be perplexed with questions of this kind. 'Is our National Church, as I have often been told it is, the best in the world? Supposing it is not, why may I not go in search of a better! It is easy to talk of acquiescence in the state which Providence has assigned us. But surely there are circumstances in which a Christian must regard acquiescence as a sin. How do I know that mine are not these circumstances?'

Now were the principles which have seemed to prove themselves to us in other cases appropriate to this one, the reader will perceive at once that there is a fallacy in the statement of these questions. We have maintained that there is a spiritual and universal society in the world: that there are also national societies in the world: that the Universal Society and the National Society cannot, according to the scheme of Providence, be separated from each other, that when they are brought into conjunction, that form of character which is intended for each nation is gradually developed in it by means of the spiritual body. Can we then be called upon to prove either -- (1), that there is some constitution for the Universal Society as it exists in England, which does not belong to it elsewhere, and which makes it better here than elsewhere; or (2), that the principles which unite the Universal Society with the National Society among us are not the same principles which unite it elsewhere, and that we are better for this difference; or (3), that what is peculiarly our National character, ought to be the character of every other nation? Evidently, no one who has any real affection for his Church or his land, will put forth such claims as these on its behalf. He will inquire whether it does or does not recognize that constitution which belongs to all mankind; whether this constitution be or be not so recognized here, as to be compatible with the distinct National Constitution; what character it is which is intended for Englishmen; how that character may be realised in its perfection, or depraved. But putting the inquiry into this form, one does not see what acquiescence can be demanded of us, which is inconsistent with the position of militant Christians. Have we lost that Universal Constitution or any element of it? We must labour by all means to recover it. Have we lost our distinct National position? We must seek it again. Are we living inconsistently with the one or the other? We must inquire where the evil is, and commence at once the work of personal reformation. The subject then upon which I propose now to enter will divide itself in the way which I have indicated. As we take for granted the previous steps of our discussion, it will not, I hope, occupy us long.

SECTION I -- DO THE SIGNS OF A UNIVERSAL AND SPIRITUAL CONSTITUTION EXIST IN ENGLAND?

There is no difficulty in giving a direct answer to this question. Supposing these signs to be Baptism, the Creeds, Forms of Worship, the Eucharist, the Ministerial Orders, the Scriptures, no one will deny that a society has existed in England for the last twelve hundred years, of which these are constituent elements. Under all changes in the outward circumstances of the country, in its national policy, in its religious opinions, a body has dwelt in this land, which has acknowledged not one or two but all of these signs, which has acknowledged them as the conditions of its own subsistence.

But is this the only point to be considered? Ought we not to inquire whether the same import has in all times, or what import has at any particular time been attached to these signs, by the body which acknowledged them? And again, may there not be two bodies existing at the same time in this country, differing with each other, and yet both acknowledging all these signs? In that case how are we to determine which does and which does not represent the Universal Society?

I. In reference to the first question I answer, If you mean that I am to take the votes of the members of the English Church now, or at any period since it was established, for the purpose of ascertaining what the majority think or have thought about any or all of these signs, I should decline the task, not merely on the ground of its impossibility, but because, if it were possible, I should be violating all the principles which I have put forward in this book, by undertaking it. I have said, that the members of a Church will be continually losing sight of the grounds of the society to which they belong, and that permanent institutions are given us for the purpose of witnessing against our tendencies to degeneracy, and of enabling us to obtain, in each successive age, a clearer view of the Divine purpose and order. On the same grounds, I must protest against any attempt to ascertain the principles of the English Church, by comparing or balancing the opinions of its most eminent writers. For I have urged, that permanent creeds and institutions are our preservatives against the particular judgments and prepossessions of these writers. But if there be among these signs any one which has so far a peculiar character, is so far distinctively English, that is may be taken as expressive of the mind of the English Church itself, by that I am most willing it shall be tried. Now a Liturgy is of this kind. I have shewn how remarkably it is the sign of a universal society. Yet it is equally true that each nation has always had its own Liturgies. To this, therefore, there is a fair appeal. But how shall the appeal be made? Why may I not read my own opinions into the Liturgy as well as into any other book? Undoubtedly I may. And therefore, the fairer way of getting at its meaning is to receive it from others, especially from those who have attacked it. Let us try this course.

1. Again and again the English Dissenters have complained of our formularies, because they assert in what seems to them such plain and direct language, so solemnly, so habitually, the principle that a baptized man is to regard himself as regenerate, a child of God, an heir of the blessings of the New Covenant. 'It is idle,' say these Dissenters, 'to pretend that by leaving out a few words in your form of baptism, you would remove this dreadful plague-spot from your Church. Supposing that were possible, think what a monstrous delusion you have been propagating in such solemn moments for so many generations. What, thrust out such words privily in this nineteenth century! They ought to be extirpated amidst groans and confessions of sin, for having mocked God and ruined the souls of men. But if you did thrust out the words, the spirit of them goes through all your other services. You tell the same story to the children whom you are catechising; you declare to them that they are members of Christ and children of God. Nay, every confession and every prayer in which you call upon adults old in sin to engage, turns upon the same principle. You invite them to confess and to pray, as if they were children of God, and as if the Spirit were still with them.'

That these charges are constantly preferred against us everyone knows. I ask, are they not true? Has any apologist of the Liturgy, who agreed with the Dissenters in their theological principle, been able to refute them? And is it not very painful to think that we should be using equivocations and double meanings, at a time when we are professing to address the most awful prayers to Him who is Truth? I may affirm then, not from any conclusions of my own, but on the authority of those who are most opposed to me, that the idea of Baptismal Regeneration is the idea of our Liturgy.

But is this connected with the idea of an opus operatum? I think the question has already been answered. The Dissenter perceives, everyone who thinks perceives, that the whole of our Liturgy is constructed upon the principle that the men who engage in it have not lost their baptismal privileges; that the sin which they confess is the sin of not having owned God as their Father, of not having remembered His covenant, and therefore, of not having walked in His ways; that they ask to be restored to the enjoyment of a position with which their lives need not have been and have been at variance; in one word, that the sacrament is not believed to have conferred on men a temporary blessing, but to have admitted them into a permanent state, which is at all times theirs, which they are bound at all times to claim, and by which they will be judged.

I know that we have apologists who can defend us from this imputation as well as the other, by dint of ingenious special pleading. They say, 'All this language presumes the existence of discipline; we have undoubtedly lost our discipline, but we are not therefore to lose our prayers.' How, not to lose our prayers? We had better lose anything than go on in direct mockery of God. If the want of discipline makes the prayers false, if there are not half a dozen persons in any congregation who would dare to say they have not lost their baptismal purity; and if those nine or ten be the very persons, who one may be sure cannot join in these prayers, of in any prayer but that of the Pharisee, how can we have courage to practise such profaneness, because, at some time or other, we hope to get a discipline which shall cut off the majority of those who now call themselves Churchmen? But does our Liturgy give the slightest sanction to the notion, that the most complete restoration of discipline would make these prayers more true than they are now? Why then in her 'Commination Service' does she not announce the doctrine of the <u>opus operatum</u>? Why does she not say, there, 'You have been made members of Christ once, but the privilege is gone, the blessing is exhausted; you have resisted the Spirit, He is striving no more with you; recover the gift, if possible, by penitence and prayer'? Why in this service, as much as in all the rest, are men called to repent, on the ground of their being children, though rebellious children; on the ground of the will of God, that they should turn from their wickedness and live?

2. Thus far I have spoken of Baptism. The view which the Liturgy takes of the Creeds, is sufficiently evident from the mode of their introduction into it. They are made parts of our worship; acts of allegiance, declarations by the whole congregation of the Name into which each one has been baptized; preparations for prayer; steps to communion. The notion of them as mere collections of dogmas is never once insinuated, is refuted by the whole order of the services.

3. In speaking of the Eucharist, it is safer again to refer to the language of opponents. Again and again we have been told that the idea of a Real Presence is distinctly implied in our Communion Service; that at all events the words must convey this impression to any ordinary person; that they are such as could not have been written by anyone who held the simple Zwinglian dogma, and cannot be used with comfort, nay, without a sense of pain and contradiction, by anyone who feels it to be the true one. And yet, though there may be constant admonitions respecting the spirit in which this sacrament is to be received, the faith and repentance which are the preparations for it, the danger of a careless and unworthy treatment of such mysteries, is it not evident at the same time, from the earnest exhortations to partake of it, that it is looked upon as a common blessing, as one to which all men have a claim, as one from which it is a perilous responsibility to exclude any, whose open sins do not shew that they have excluded themselves? The English Dissenter regarding this ordinance as the right of a few who can give an account of their feelings, and experiences, and change of mind, is continually denouncing our service for its manifest departure from the maxims upon which he acts. On the one hand the Eucharist is spoken of in such awful language, as it seems to him must have been borrowed

from periods of pure superstition; on the other hand, there is the strangest notion of it, as if it were a bond of fellowship for the whole universe. 'One would suppose', he says, 'from the phrases you use, that you look upon this sacrament as the very opening of the kingdom of heaven, and yet you treat it as the proper preparation for the most vulgar and earthly employments. Sometimes you seem to fancy it possible, that men should eat the flesh and drink the blood of the Son of Man by partaking of these elements, and yet you can admit persons to be partakers of it who would have very great difficulty in explaining themselves respecting the most ordinary propositions of the Christian system. By your carefulness in restraining the administration of the sacrament to a particular class, one would suppose that you regarded it as a Jewish sacrifice, or as something yet more wonderful. And yet you speak, at the same time, of the sacrifice of Christ, once made upon the cross, as full, and sufficient, and satisfactory.'

Meantime, it is not pretended by any person, be he friend or foe, that a single passage exists in thie service which favours the notion that the presence of Christ is connected with a change in the elements. Whoever adopts that notion instantly becomes dissatisfied with the eucharistic part of our liturgy, proclaims it to be cold, heartless, dead, &c. In like manner, whoever believes the Eucharist to be a sacrifice in any sense which implies that the sacrifice of Christ upon the cross is less complete and finished for all mankind than it has been supposed to be by the strongest Lutheran or Calvinist, also denounces our Liturgy as departing from that idea which the Mass, in other portions of the Latin Church, embodies. By the confession, then, of all it regards the feast as the highest Christian privilege, as the most complete reality; not because it works a change in our Christian state and position; not because it brings one before us who is habitually absent from us, but because it enables us to enter into the fulness of our Church life, into that truly human and divine fellowship, which Christ, by His incarnation, His death, and His ascension, has claimed for all whom He is not ashamed to call His brethren.

4. This being the case, the communion service in our liturgy interprets the rest of our worship. Throughout, it is the worship of a body, of a family. It is open, and has been subject, to all the objections which the defenders of extempore prayer can raise against any form as belonging to mankind in general, and not to our nation and our family, to our particular circumstances, except so far as we can connect them with the knowledge of God and of His purposes to our race. On the other hand, it is open, and has been subject, to the objections of those who think that worship is cold and dead, if it lead us from the visible to the invisible, if it claim the privilege of approaching at once through the one Mediator the throne of the Absolute and the Infinite. It proscribes nothing; it does not affirm how much or how little of the sensible may be useful in assisting us to reach that which is beyond our senses. Human agency and help it distinctly recognizes as the appointed and ordinary

channel through which the blessings of Him who was made flesh descend upon his Church, and through which the prayers and praises of His Church ascend as a united sacrifice to Him. But it does affirm, that all sensible helps, and all human agency, lose their meaning and become positively evil when they are converted into ends, or when they impair the belief that the whole Church is admitted into the holiest place.

5. It is impossible to separate this subject from that of ministerial orders, as it is expounded to us in our ordination and consecration services. Part of the complaint against these had been considered already. Only those who have received presbyteral ordination are allowed to administer the Eucharist or to pronounce absolution. 'Now,' argue the Dissenters, 'you may say if you will, that the words presbyteros and 'iereus are different; and that you affix the former, not the latter, to the second rank of your ministers. But is not the refusal of these particular offices to the lower order a distinct and significant recognition of the principle, though you may not express it by a name? If your Church felt as we do about the sin of appropriating these names to men, would she have dared to approach so very closely in her acts to such an assumption? Would she have proceeded habitually upon a maxim, which must at least convey the impression, that she thinks it no assumption at all?' I leave those who please to answer these arguments; to me they seem irresistible. Nor am I better able to clear our services of the charge of distinctly and formally connecting the gift of spiritual powers with ordination; of distinctly encouraging and urging her ministers to believe that they have the Holy Spirit committed to them for the work of the ministry. I do not complain of anyone who performs the office of a minister in our Church, and yet believes that he possesses no such power. I should no more wish to exclude him from his office on that account, than I should wish to depose a magistrate who did not understand the extent of the powers which the laws invested him with. Each may be using that which he does believe is his, very far more honestly than I am using that which I believe is mine. Each is far more honest than he would be if he merely acknowledged the words without attaching a meaning to them. But still the words are there; and I think he cannot complain of me for taking them in their plain sense; for saying that, little as I enter into their force, little as my conduct corresponds with them, there are very few which I have ever heard, that I could bear less to part with, or that I more feel I must learn to understand by acting upon the conviction of their truth.

With the continual allegation of Dissenters, that in spite of many tendencies to the contrary opinion in some of our divines, ancient as well as modern, our Liturgy recognizes the Episcopate as the root of all the other orders, and supposes it to contain them all within itself, I can as little quarrel as with either of the former. They seem to me to have made their point good. And I cannot find that any answers which have been made to them amount to more than awkward though ingenious evasions.

But where are we to find the doctrine of the vicarial powers of ministers in any part of these services? Where are we to find one single hint that the Presbyter absolves or administers the Eucharist, that the Bishop exercises his own functions or that he ordains others, as the minister and delegate of one who is absent from his Church? Those who adopt this opinion begin at once to exclaim against our services, as containing the most cold and unsatisfactory recognition of the mighty authority with which the Priest and Bishop of the New Testament are endowed. They feel it absolutely necessary that he should clothe himself with other attributes, in another mystery, than any which the English Church recognizes in him. The self-same language which offends the Dissenter as containing such high and profane assertions of a perpetually derived and renewing power, is that which contradicts this notion of an inherent power.

6. Lastly, we come to the Scriptures. Here the intention of the Liturgy seems remarkably evident. The Scripture is adopted into our worship, the service explains the lessons, the lessons explain the service. The Bible is read partly as a continuous history, the history of God's revelation, and of the Church's growth and expansion; partly in connexion with our communion -- the epistles of the New Testament expounding to us the law of the Spirit of life, the Gospels, the image after which the Spirit would form us. This is precisely that relation between the Scriptures and the Church, which I endeavoured to set forth in the former part of this book. The Protestant Dissenter says that we set aside the Bible, though we read more of it in any one month in one of our Churches than he reads in two years in any of his meetings; and though our reading of it is continuous, his casual and arbitrary. The Romanist says that we set aside the authority of the Church in the interpretation of Scripture, though we make it a formal and habitual part of the services, in which the mind of the Church is expressed.

II. 1. I think, then, I have answered the question as to the meaning which the English Church puts upon the signs which it has in common with other Churches, fairly and legitimately. Another question was, how we can determine between two bodies, both existing in this country, and both possessing these signs, which may and which may not fairly call itself Catholic. If our previous statements have been true, this question is also settled. A body acknowledging itself connected with the Church in all previous ages by the bond of sacraments, of creeds, of worship, of ministerial succession, has the prima facie marks of Catholicity. Should any other body standing aloof from it put in a claim upon the same grounds to be Catholic, it is bound to shew the reasons of its own pretension, and the reasons upon which it rejects the former pretension. Those reasons must be the same which we have considered already. We are not Catholic in the opinion of the Romish body which resides in this country, because we do not acknowlegdge the opus operatum in Baptism, the new creeds of Popes, Transubstantiation in the Eucharist, the existence of an intermediate agency between Christ and His members on earth, the vicarial authority of ministers, the existence of a Universal mortal Bishop, the right of the Church to hide the Scriptures from the Laity; in one word, because we do not acknowledge that system which appeared to us, before we entered upon English ground at all, to be anti-Catholic. The Church in every land exists under the condition, either of professing this system, or of protesting against it. Its existence is not denoted by the Profession or by the Protest, but by the Signs to which the profession and the protest refer. If the Romish body say that it stands in certain notions <u>about</u> sacraments and about orders, and not in its sacraments and in the orders themselves, that declaration is a practical renunciation of its claims to be a Church. We say that we protest against these notions, because they are incompatible with the acknowledgment of Christ's Spiritual and Universal kingdom.

2. But since we have seen that the confessions in different Protestant bodies have (contrary to the intentions of their compilers) greatly interfered with the simple recognition of the facts contained in the creed, and that the Romish confessions sanctioned by the Council of Trent, and by Pope Pius IV, interfere with it yet more; we are bound to shew whether there is anything corresponding to these in the Church of England, any addition made upon its own authority to the admitted formularies of the whole Church. Till we are satisfied on this point we cannot, I conceive, rightly understand our own position in reference to the other portions of the Church.

Now it appears that in the sixteenth century, we as well as the Protestants and Romanists on the Continent, drew up a set of dogmatic articles, and that these have continued to be the test of orthodoxy for those who take orders in our Church and for those who are studying in at least one of our universities, ever since. Seeing then that there were different systems at that time in vogue, and that the object of different religious bodies in making confessions, was to identify themselves with one or other of these systems, -- for example, the Genevan body thus identified itself with the Calvinistic system, the Romanist bodies with the Tridentine system, -- we must desire to know how far these articles of ours identify us with any of them. One remark has been made respecting them, which is not unimportant for our present purpose, that they carefully avoid any intrusion upon the ground occupied by the old creeds. They do not take the living forms of the creeds, they constitute a set of distinct dogmatic propositions; they would be ridiculous if introduced into worship; they are not intended for the majority of the laity; they belong exclusively to the student. But these observations respecting them would be of little worth, if it appeared that they inculcate upon the teacher a certain theological system alien from the spirit and temper of the creeds; for this system he will communicate to those who hear him.

How stands the case? We have seen that there is one main characteristic of the Calvinistic system as a system. It makes the fall of man the central point of its divinity: it treats the incarnation, and all the facts which manifest the Son of God to men, as merely growing out of this, and necessary in consequence of it. On this principle that very spirited confession which was drawn up by the Scotch preachers for the use of the Kirk in the sixteenth century, is constructed. The first Article is on the Trinity; the second, on the Fall; then comes the explanation of the existence of the Church or Kirk, as grounded upon the predestination of certain individuals in this fallen race to eternal life. There cannot be a finer or better model of a purely Calvinistical confession than this one; nor any which illustrates more completely the direct opposition between the idea of the Genevan system and the idea of the old Catholic Creeds. We have seen again that the Lutheran had a very different conception of Christianity from this, a great desire to make the incarnation of Christ the centre of all his thoughts, and to use the Apostles' Creed as his symbol: of such a disposition the Augsburg confession is a satisfactory testimony. But we have seen, also, that in his eagerness to assert conscious Justification as the one great principle of divinity, he was driven back upon the same ground as the Calvinist; he was forced to start from the evil root, in order that he might explain the process of restoration. And thus, as I remarked before, systematic Protestantism became identical with Calvinism, until the Arminian form of it was developed, which is little more than a contradiction of Calvinism, little more than a denial of the principle that the will of God is the originating cause of all good in man.

Now if anyone will turn to our Thirty-nine Articles, he will perceive that the first Article being upon the Trinity, the second is upon the Incarnation, and that the first eight Articles relate to truths directly connected with the being of God, to His manifestations of Himself, to the Scriptures as expounding them, to the Creeds as illustrating and interpreting the Scriptures. When this Catholic foundation has been laid, we proceed in the ninth Article to the fall of man, and then to all those questions concerning free-will, justification and election, which were occupying men's minds in the sixteenth century. On all these points it seems to me the language of the Articles is as distinct and definite as it can be. The Calvinistic and Lutheran principles are plainly and distinctly asserted, there is no hint or prophecy of Arminianism; the Romish system in every point wherein it is opposed to the distinct affirmations of the Reformers, on the subject of God's will and man's faith, is repudiated; that is to say, the system of Romanism is rejected in the Articles from the ninth to the nineteenth, just as the system of Calvinism, or pure Protestantism, had been repudiated by the Articles from the first to the eighth. The principles of the Reformation are asserted in the one division, not as necessary qualifications, but as indispensable conditions, of the great Catholic truths which had been asserted in the other. And so, to whatever cause we owe it, this has been the result of these Articles; they have been thorns in the side of those who have wished to establish an English theological system, fashioned out of the materials which either Romanism or Calvinism

206

supplies; they have encouraged persons of all sects and schools to hope that their principles, in some sense or other, might be contained in them, or by some process or other extracted out of them, or, at all events, not positively denied by them; and yet there is no sect or school, when speaking its sect or school language, which, if it were honest, would not confess that there are clauses and passages in them which it would be glad to be rid of; that a small omission, or addition, of a 'not' would often be very acceptable to it; that it would like exceedingly, if not to remodel them, at least to subjoin to them on all occasions a commentary of its own.

I conclude this head with remarking, that if our observations respecting the true meaning of Quakerism, of Calvinism, of Lutheranism, of Unitarianism, be accurate, the ideas and principles of each of these bodies are expressed in the forms of our English Church; only the systems which they have grafted upon these, and which have separated them from each other, are rejected. The idea of man as constituted in the divine Word, of a Kingdom based upon that constitution, of a Spirit working to bring him into conformity with it, of a perpetual struggle with an evil and sensual nature; this is the idea of Quakerism, and it is the idea of our Liturgy in every one of its forms and services. The idea of a divine Will going before all acts of the human will, the primary source of all that is in eternity, and all that becomes in time, to which everything is meant to be in subjection, which can alone bring that which has rebelled into subjection, to which every creature must attribute all the motions to good which he finds within him, the primary direction of his thoughts, the power of perseverance; this is the idea of Calvinism, and it is the idea which is implied in all the prayers of our Litany, which is formally set forth in the words of our Articles. The idea of man struggling with his own evil nature, discovering in it nothing but a bottomless pit of evil, grasping at a deliverer, finding that in union with him only is his life; that he is strong only in his strength, righteous only in his righteousness; this is the idea of Lutheranism, and it is the idea which is involved in all our prayers and Creeds, which our Articles reassert in logical terms. The idea of a unity which lies beneath all other unity, of a love which is the ground of all other love, of Humanity as connected with that love, regarded by it, comprehended in it; this is the idea which has hovered about the mind of the Unitarian, and which he has vainly attempted to comprehend in his system of contradictions and denials: this idea is the basis of our Liturgy, our Articles, our Church.

SECTION II --   DOES THE UNIVERSAL SOCIETY IN ENGLAND EXIST
                APART FROM ITS CIVIL INSTITUTIONS, OR IN UNION
                WITH THEM?

To this question the answer is unanimous.

The English dissenter affirms that the Church is embodied in the State; it is an Act of Parliament Church. The modern civil Ruler says, that the State is impeded in all its operations by the Church; the Sovereign is crowned by the Archbishop, the Bishops as a body taking part in the deliberations of Parliament; above all, the greater part of the education of the land is ecclesiastical. The Romanist affirms that the Church has no pretensions to be called a Catholic body; it is a national body. There can be no doubt, then, that the ecclesiastical and civil institutions are united, and this by bonds which it must require some violence to break. But when did this union take place? How was it brought to pass? Who were the contracting parties to it? On all these questions history preserves a profound silence. It records no meeting of Sovereigns and Bishops to adjust the terms of the fellowship; it fixes no date at which the Church began to say it would acknowledge the State, or at which the State said it would acknowledge the Church. So soon as we find the Church in the land, we find her doing homage to the civil powers, such as they were, which ruled the land. So soon as the Church begins to exercise its own peculiar influence, the civil power begins to feel that influence, and to be moulded by it. Then indeed we meet with records of transactions between these two bodies, each of which is perceived to have its distinct representative, and its peculiar object, though neither the representatives nor the objects are defined by any formal line of separation. But these transactions are not for the purpose of establishing a covenant on the part of the State, that it will protect the Church, or on the part of the Church, that it will do certain services for the State; far rather they are attempts by each, either to reclaim a portion of its own province which it supposes that the other has invaded, or to conquer a portion of that province of which the other has hitherto had peaceable possession. They are such transactions as presuppose a real, though a yet imperfectly understood relation, not such as could have been produced by a compact, or had the least tendency to create one. The Church affirms that it has a right to assign the powers and jurisdiction of its own Bishops; the State maintains that Bishops as well as the rest of its subjects must acknowledge its paramount authority. The Church affirms that it has a spiritual government altogether distinct from the civil government. The State says that the minister of the Church must submit like other men to its laws and its tribunals. Every impartial and thoughtful reader of our history feels that there is a right and wrong in each of these pretensions; that Becket must have been contending for a principle, that Henry must have been contending for a principle. The resolution of our annalists generally to choose favourites, and to nickname opponents, the eagerness of young readers to arrive at a positive conclusion about every matter in dispute, the obvious injustice of those (so called) fair critics, who try both parties by the standards of their own time, and of course condemn both, acquitting and exalting only themselves and their own wisdom, may hinder us from acknowledging at once and in terms, that we are under deep obligations to these opposing champions, and that a higher power was working out its ends by the help of both; but we all feel inwardly, that this is the case; we all unconsciously express our conviction that it is so in one set of phrases or another. And we feel also in a remarkable way, that the history of these struggles is, if not the history of England, yet the heart and centre of it, whence more light is thrown upon the records of the conflicts between Kings and Barons, Normans and Saxons, the old orders and the new, than they throw back upon it. Those who have learnt that the science of politics is not comprehended in the theory of representation, that in order to understand what representation means, we must first know what there is to represent, have perceived that in these civil and ecclesiastical disputes lies the inward secret which we have need to investigate before we can trace its working on the surface and in the external machinery of Society.

So it was before the Reformation. And what was the Reformation itself? Its opponents of both classes say, that it was merely a national movement. 'Henry not Cranmer was at the root of it. There was more of politics in it than of religion.' I should not use such language; I do not understand their distinction between politics and religion. But I believe that in their meaning they are right. The most obvious peculiarity of the English Reformation seems to be this, that it was a movement originating with the Sovereign and not with Theologians. And therefore it was not a new movement, but one of a series of movements. Not only the Constitutions of Clarendon, made in the days of a rebellious Sovereign, but the statues of praemunire, passed in the time of some of the most orthodox, some of the greatest persecutors of Lollardism, had attempted to cut off the correspondence of the Church of Rome. The difference in the reign of Henry VIII was simply this, that a large body of the Bishops and Clergy had been led by their religious feelings to desire that this correspondence should be broken off; to feel that the English Church could not maintain its own position unless it became strictly national; unless it abandoned that subjection to a foreign bishop, which the State had always wished it to abandon.

And what has been the state of things since the Reformation? It is this: a number of bodies or sects have gradually grown up in the country, which have affirmed that the principles of Protestantism were not asserted with sufficient boldness at our Reformation. We stopped short, is is said, at a certain point. We retain much of the papal system, which the other Protestant nations have thrown off. On the other hand, the Romanists have felt that the English Reformation was more fatal to the maxim upon which they were habitually acting than the Reformation in any other quarter had been. There was a hope that men might renounce a new system of opinions and adopt an old one. But a Church which had affirmed the principle of nationality, which had come to an understanding with the Sovereign of its own land, was, to all appearance, utterly incorrigible. The most earnest and intelligent Jesuits who came perceived that this was a condition of things, which must be changed, not merely by preaching, but by plotting; many of them believed that the best hope of the restoration of the papal power lay in the triumph of those sects which professed a more vehement Protestantism. Another curious point deserves to be noticed: the Puritan body was, as I have said before, essentially Calvinistical. Calvinism was the principle of its life. It was the feeling that the English Church was not founded upon the Calvinistical idea which gave occasion to the earliest Puritan movements. And yet we imported the anti-Calvinistical doctrine, which the Puritans afterwards identified with popery, from one of the purely Protestant countries of the Continent. Nay, further, it was not till we had a Scottish King upon the throne, a King bred under Presbyterian preachers, that we had any connexion with this Arminian system at all. It is to this King that we owe a very marked change in our position. Elizabeth had troubled herself as little as possible about systems of opinion; she had merely endeavoured to assert her position as a national Sovereign. James could only look upon every question as a schoolman and a pedant. He had, indeed, one living practical feeling; he had been disgusted with the Presbyterian preachers, and had found that their power practically interfered with his. But he had no sense of sympathy or connexion with our Church; he only wished that the Episcopalian system should prevail against the Presbyterian. And this system, with whatever belonged to it, was to be established in Scotland, and maintained here, by the efforts of the State. Both in Scotland, therfore, and in England, the feeling that there is a spiritual power distinct from and higher than the mere State power, was called forth. In Scotland this spiritual feeling connected itself with the national feeling. The people revolted against the notion of a prelacy which was imposed upon them by England. Here, the mixture of spiritual with national feelings in the Puritan produced some strange anomalies. The body in the Commons' House which had most sympathy with Puritanism were occupied in maintaining the old forms of the national constitution against the royal prerogative. The Puritan clergy were raising their voices against old national and ecclesiastical forms, and maintaining the rights of the spiritual man. Mixed with these assertions, however, one can perceive in them from the first a desire for a more formal and systematic divinity than had ever existed in England before. At length they triumph, and it is their business to realise as well as they can their three objects, of upholding the liberty of the subject, which had been asserted by the Long Parliament; the superiority of Christians to outward forms, which had been maintained by their preachers against Laud and the Bishops; and, lastly, the all-importance of a peculiar theological system. The first attempt issued in the establishment of a military despotism; the second led to the rise and independence of the different sects which revolted from the stern Presbyterian government and sought to maintain freedom of conscience; the last effort was embodied in the deliberations, decrees, catechisms, committees of triers, of the Westminster Assembly. It is a grievous thing that English Churchmen should, from their prejudices and partialities, refuse to study the history of this remarkable period simply and fairly, looking at it from all sides and all points of view, and labouring to do justice to the feelings of all the parties who were concerned in it. For it is when thus considered, and not when warped into an apology for some ecclesiastical hero, or into a sentence of condemnation upon his opponents, that it illustrates and makes manifest the essential relation between spiritual and civil life, and the impossibility of destroying that relation by any efforts of ours, however unfriendly and uncomfortable we may make it.

The Westminster Assembly had done their best to establish an uniformity of opinions; that wherein they had left their ministers free, was in their modes of worship. The opposite principle had been the one hitherto recognized in England. The bond of national fellowship had been supposed to be the bond of worship; men who had books and leisure might occupy themselves with the study of opinions. I do not know how far the Episcopal clergy at the Restoration were aware that this was the question at issue between them and their opponents; possibly they looked upon it merely as a question whether the nation should adopt a more or less comprehensive system. But if so, their old habits were stronger than their theories; the State felt that it could not trouble itself about shades of opinion, but that old forms of worship were practical and general, and there was One over us who saw further than either statesmen or churchmen. At all events, this was the result. The Act of Uniformity in Worship was the substitute for the efforts at a dogmatic uniformity which belonged to the genius of Presbyterianism. The immediate effect of that measure was the separation of the Puritan clegy from that which was now again recognized as the national Church. Then began various stupid efforts on the part of the State to silence them, or to coerce them into a union, mixed with various royal experiments at a general liberty of conscience which should include Romanist as well as Protestant Dissenters. The resistance to these marks the strong sense of the people and of the Parliament that Romanism was something anti-national. This feeling was strong in the minds of the seven Bishops who refused to read James's declaration. They believed that the act of the King was, as it proved to be, suicidal. Several of them could not, however, follow out that principle to what seems to me its legitimate consequence; that when the King did commit his act of legal suicide by deserting the country, he was as one lying under a sentence of deposition from God Himself, for having violated the covenant by which he held his power. The Convention Parliament took that pious view of the matter, and accordingly inquired, not what person they might by their own power or in conformity with the people's will choose into his place, but who seemed to be designated to the office by the providence of God. At no period, I think, was the religious character of the English State more distinctly asserted than at this; and at no time was it more important that it should be asserted. For now was beginning that change in the habits and feelings of men, here as well as elsewhere, to which I adverted in Part I; the change, I mean, from the notion of government as grounded upon deep mysterious principles, to the notion of it as the result of mere commercial arrangements -- of some imaginary artificial compact. That this change has been productive of very mischievous effects to the Church and the nation of England, I shall have occasion presently to remark. That it has led to any legislative Acts which involve a formal or a virtual violation of the union between the ecclesiastical and the civil bodies, I believe is a notion which could only have become prevalent through this very habit of mind. We have supposed the Church and the State to be knit together by some material outward terms of agreement: we do not know what they are; they may be that the State shall not recognize any persons as its subjects who are not Churchmen; in other words, that it shoud ignore facts; they may therefore be violated by Acts of toleration, repeals of test laws, emancipation of Romanists. I do not express any opinion about the policy of one or other of these measures; some of them may have been inexpedient measures; they were all, I should conceive, defended as well as attacked by many feeble and imperfect arguments. But I do think that it requires something far deeper and more subtle than any such measures, to destroy a union which has cemented itself by no human contrivances, and which exists in the very nature of things. By carelessness, ignorance, faithlessness, immorality, we may undermine our national life, and to these perils it is continually exposed. But the Acts of our legislators when they are evil, are in general but reflexes of something which is evil in the national mind, and which legislators cannot correct. And in general they are better than could at all be expected from the tempers of those who passed them, or of us who criticise them. Oftentimes the very errors which are in them, and the mischievous consequences to which they lead, may become our teachers, and may be far more profitable to us than the success of our opposition to them could have been . And therefore I am naturally led from the consideration of this subject, to that which I proposed next to consider.

SECTION III -- WHAT IS THE FORM OF CHARACTER WHICH
        BELONGS ESPECIALLY TO ENGLISHMEN? TO WHAT
        KIND OF DEPRAVATON IS IT LIABLE?

From what I have said already, it will be evident to the reader that I believe the first thoughts of men upon this subject to be well founded. 'You Englishmen are such mere politicians,' this is the ordinary complaint which foreigners make of us. 'Alas! how exclusively we are devoted to politics,' this is our continual groan concerning ourselves. The proofs of the position are manifold -- none more striking than those which are supplied by men who are determined that they will at all events be exempt from the national disease; that they will be artists, philosophers, mystics -- anything but politicians. Watch them well, and you will see how utterly impossible it is for them to realise their dream; how continually some speculation about the organisation of society, some practical effort to remodel it, mixes with their high and serene contemplations; how fierce and restless the contemplators become, from the very effort to keep themselves from all contact with the fever and restlessness which they suppose to be inherent in the English character, and which they know are in their own. Other cases there are, of another kind, which confirm the same fact still more remarkably. I have known

212

persons who possessed no practical talent whatever, all whose attempts at action were of the most ludicrously and painfully abortive kind, who, if they tried to realise some fine conception of their own, were sure either to render it contemptible by their failure, or else very soon to run into one of the old ruts from which they had been labouring with all their might to extricate themselves. And yet such Englishmen as these, who, if they have any gifts at all, seem to be exclusively endowed with those which are most un-English, feel themselves just as much compelled to be political and practical as their countrymen. They find it impossible to think unless they can in some way or other connect their thoughts with action, and despairing of any such alliance in their own persons, they try whether they may not at least be able to point out a method of action to others...

* * *

But though these arguments are very decisive, I cannot but think that there are others which are more cheering. Why do we turn to the literature of the reign of Queen Elizabeth as to that which most represents the genius of our nation, as that which most shews of what we are capable? Why but because in every department it was more historical, more political, than it has been at any time since. Look at our drama, how it draws its highest inspirations from the old records of our national life. See how needful it was even for the allegorical poet, the singer of 'Fairy Land,' when dealing with his twelve moral virtues, and the battles of the inner man, to interweave a history of Prince Arthur, and to confound the image of Gloriana with that of Queen Elizabeth. With all their dreams about poetry, and scholarship, and philosophy, how evident it is that the deepest and most earnest thoughts of Sidney and Raleigh were occupied with policy and politics! What nation may not be able to shew profounder works in exegetical or dogmatical divinity than we? Who can hold our countrymen pace, when they fashion their minds to the consideration of the laws according to which God has formed heavenly, and human, and natural creatures?

Hooker's work is the specimen of a class, though certainly the highest specimen. And when one considers it, and the whole life and character of the man who wrote it, I think we must feel how very little excuse lies in that habit of mind which God has bestowed upon us, for any defect in meekness and gentleness, in superiority to the low notions and cannons of this world, in converse with the hierarchies of heaven. I do not wish to exalt this form of character above every other; I cannot tell whether it is better or worse than that which belongs to Frenchmen or Germans; I know only that it is ours, and that it is capable of being expanded into that which is most noble, as well as sinking into that which is most base.

We ought to contemplate it in both conditions, that we may not separate hope from humiliation, that we may know both our responsibilities and our temptations, and that we may be able to honour the good when it is mixed with the evil which lies nearest to it. Of that charity we have need in every part of our history. It is impossible not to observe a tendency in the English Reformers of the sixteenth century to a kind of diplomacy which one does not like to perceive in holy men, and which it is very easy to represent as pervading the whole of their characters, and explaining the meaning of their acts. Presently after you find them suffering with a constancy worthy, their detractors say, of heroes, we have been used to believe and think, of martyrs. The political bias of their mind did not, I fancy, tend on the whole to lower the tone of it, to bring them more helplessly into contact with outward things, or to give them less faith in the invisible. Its main effect was to lead then to think of Christ's Church, as a Kingdom rather than as a system: in the dust and bustle of affairs their strong conviction that this kingdom was a reality and not a metaphor may have led them to forget that it is the type of all kingdoms, and is not moulded after the maxims of any even of those which confess it, and do homage to it. But in silence and suffering, this thought gave a fixedness and substantiality to their faith, which even the most devout schoolmen are seldom able to attain. They knew that it was a Person in whom they they were believing; in the hour of trial and death they looked directly to Him, and not to any dogma or system of dogmas, for strength and consolation.

That this way of considering the Church is an eminently English one, became evident in the time of the civil wars. It might be said to characterise every class of thinkers. It was at first less marked in those among whom one would expect most of it, I mean among the Episcopalians; for the systematic tendency had become very prevalent through the influence of James I, and Laud especially seems to have contracted it. His faults were far more those of a schoolmaster or a collegian, than of an arrogant and usurping politician. And these faults made him especially unable to deal with the energetic national impulses of that period. But the sense of the Church as a kingdom returned to the Episcopalians in their hour of humiliation. It is this which prevailed in the mind of Jeremy Taylor, above all other views. In spite of his learning and his fondness for casuistry, he could not bear to contemplate Christianity as a system. He would look upon it as a life, but then it was a life connecting itself with an order, and realised in that kind of dependence which a subject pays to his sovereign, rather than that which a pupil renders to his master. Therefore one may trace a curious point of sympathy between him and the most extreme mystics and spiritualists of that age; all spoke of a divine kingdom, none could be content with any language which did not import it, or with any acts which did not endeavour to realise it. Even Milton, who was as a star, and dwelt apart, was in the last age of his life as much as in the first, dreaming of a polity. All men might be kings and priests in his commonwealth, but kings and priests they were to be, not professors and doctors.

But we must look at another side of the picture. When the feeling of spiritual life and spiritual government decayed, as we saw it did decay, in the latter part of the seventeenth and the beginning of the eighteenth century, one may fancy what an effect must have been produced upon a people, whose political feelings were the deepest which they had. Our literature could not separate itself from our social life. It was a mere mockery and pretence when it tried to throw itself into some Arcadian condition of things. It had always been real and homely, and such it must continue to be. But if all realities had become conventions, if what was homely had become base, we need be at no loss to understand the necessary limitations of our best, and the fearful debasement of our worst literature during the period between the Revolution in England and that in France. The degradation of our professed statesmen, the loss of all high ends in their policy, the maxims and practices which have made Sir Robert Walpole's name and administration immortal, are all equally explicable. Still there were indications of English strength, and of the direction which that strength naturally takes. In the physical world, men are busy, either about the mechanism of actual things, or about God's laws and order. Either study was most fitted to the truest and noblest part of our character, and here therefore there were true and worthy results.

But the commercial activities and the scientific discoveries of this age were gradually concentrating an immense population of human beings in our cities. Who were caring for these? The church possessed some prelates of high and even comprehensive views, many humble and sincere pastors in its rural districts; many men capable of thinking vigorously respecting the moral constitution of individuals and of society. In general however, its habit of mind was too well expressed in the theory of Warburton respecting the alliance of the Church and State; in the practice of sending bishops to Ireland for the sake of supporting the English interest. It apparently possessed the means of influencing the aristocracy; but the aristocracy was commonly infidel. It should have been able through its less exalted members to have reached the heart of the trading classes, but they were chiefly under the influence of dissent; it seemed not to be aware that the new class of poor men was coming into existence. Undoubtedly they were members of the National Church who first went forth to evangelise the mining and manufacturing districts; but their movements were regarded with anything but sympathy by the rulers of the Church; no pains were taken to give them a right direction. Humble and quiet men in country parishes disliked them because they were opposed to the order and regularity which had been always associated in their minds with the idea of religion; to others they were odious because they appealed to feelings which were dormant in themselves, but which were found to exist in their flocks. Then came the French Revolution, with its terrors and warnings. The clergy began to feel themselves less mere parts of an obsolete machinery existing for some unintelligible purposes; more necessary to the being of the commonwealth. The aristocracy began to acknowledge them in that character. Their scepticism vanished, and they spoke of religion and its teachers with much respect, as exerting those influences of fear and hope, which could alone make property and government secure. Such was the new tone which the character and patronage of George III, and the dread of French disorganisation, rendered popular. One cannot call it a very elevated tone. So long as the war lasted, it was mixed with much that was generous and patriotic in the upper classes of laymen; the portion of the clergy who shared in it became active magistrates, careful of their domestic and relative duties, zealous in defence of that which seemed to them old and English. With these useful dispositions were connected a tendency to maintain customs and practices, simply because they did exist, and could allege some moderate prescription in their favour; an acquiescence in the maxims of society even when they seemed to be at variance with the higher morality; a great impatience of enthusiasm and mysticism, and all that cannot be at once brought under the rules of existing convention or obvious expediency; a suspicion of any great efforts of active virtue and self-sacrifice; a feeling that the Church is bound to sympathize with the aristocracy, and to overlook its sins, for the sake of preserving good order among the people; a strong sense of the service which subjects owe to their rulers, without any corresponding sense of the service which rulers owe to their subjects; an inclination to assert the privileges of clergymen, chiefly by treating it as a rudeness that any infidel notions should be broached in their presence; great anxiety for a State encouragement of religion on the ground that otherwise it was not likely to thrive, or to enlist fashion and the opinion of the world on its side; a vehement dislike of dissenters, as disturbing the quietness and regularity of society, and as introducing something of vulgarity into religion; a certain anger and restlessness at the discovery of any new doubts respecting the English Church or Christianity, which could not at once be removed by an application of the arguments used on behalf of Establishments in Paley's Moral Philosophy, and of the Gospel in his Evidences.

Now the spirit of this State Churchmanship was evidently the spirit of an age of our national Church, not of the Church itself. That continued to express itself in the Liturgy; and when it required a dogmatical language, in the Articles. The younger and more active members of the Church soon became conscious of the contradiction. They began to seek for some SYSTEM which should be a refuge from the dreariness of political Anglicanism. What they have found is our next inquiry.

CHAPTER II

MODERN ENGLISH SYSTEMS

SECTION I - THE LIBERAL SYSTEM: THE EVANGELICAL SYSTEM: THE HIGH CHURCH OR CATHOLIC SYSTEM

1. 'See!' exclaims the Liberal, taking his view of this English orthodoxy from that side on which it presents itself as the antagonist of change and improvement, 'see what a hopeless class of people these old pillars of the Church are! How can it stand if it is to be supported by such maxims as these? Is not everything moving about us, and can we determine to remain stationary? Opinions upon every subject are undergoing revolution, and we think that our Articles and Formularies can be kept as they are? How can you be so foolish as not to perceive that the Dissenters will grow upon us, and ultimately overwhelm us, unless we discover some scheme for comprehending them? And then there is that body of Romanists in the midst of us; why are you determined to look upon them as if they belonged to the days of Gregory the Seventh or Innocent the Third? Whey not make them your friends, by assuming that they are so? Why not throw overboard your prejudices, and enter at once and heartily into the spirit of the age?'

2. In quite other language did the Evangelical complain of the spirit which animated the members of old school; 'They have lost sight of all spiritual influences and realities: a dry notion of human merit is at the bottom of all their thoughts and teachings. They expect men to get to heaven by being baptized, and by leading good and respectable lives; the principle of faith is forgotten altogether. The power of the Gospel, as a message of peace to man, is not felt or regarded. Another bond of union than that of spiritual fellowship with Christ is set up; hence holy Dissenters are denounced, ungodly Churchmen fraternized with. Restore the doctrines of our Articles; preach the Gospel in season and out of season; this is the only way to improve the condition of things among us, to remedy the mischiefs whcih the indifference of the last age has produced.'

3. 'Alas!' cry those members of the English Church who wish to be called Catholics, 'miserable comforters are ye all. It is true that our English orthodoxy is very bad; you Liberals and Evangelicals will introduce something which is a thousandfold worse. The error of those whom you attack is, that they thought they were members of a nation rather than members of a Church; that they were to follow the maxims of their own day, and not recall the maxims of better days; that they were to look up to the State as their guide and authority, instead of feeling that the State has an object altogether different from ours, that at certain happy moments under some godly princes, it may conform itself to our teachings, but that habitually, and at this time above all others, it is our jealous foe, and aspires to be our tyrant. The Church is

a body which may combine with a State, or rather, submit to it, but which has no natural connexion with it. It has divine sacraments, an apostolic order, a power of binding and loosing; the practice and rules of the age of the Fathers are her model; to these she must be ever seeking to adapt herself. She must reject communion with the Dissenters in this country, not because they want the privileges of the State, but because they have cut themselves off from the universal Church; renouncing her orders, counterfeiting her sacraments. She must, in like manner, repudiate those Protestants abroad who have separated from and abandoned their succession; she must aspire after union with the orthodox Greeks and Latins, but must be content to wait till we or they are prepared for this union. At home we must labour to assert the worth of sacraments, to introduce discipline for the purpose of preserving baptismal purity in our children, and giving repentance to those who have lost it; of cutting off those who hold schismatical or heretical notions under the garb of Churchmen. We must stir men up to a more exact and religious life, encourage them to do good works, and to expect heavenly rewards for them. We must urge our disciples to retirement from the world, to penances and mortifications; we must preach repentance as the only way of recovering the privileges of Churchmen, which were given once, but which most men lose through sin; we must discountenance every exercise of private judgment, except in the matter of choosing teachers; we must advise out disciples to be content with probable conclusions as all that faith requires, and bid them leave certainties to men of science.'

SECTION II - REFLECTIONS ON THESE SYSTEMS, AND ON OUR POSITION GENERALLY

These are the main outlines of the three systems which offer themselves to the deliberation of the young English theologian in the present day. He is told by the supporters of each that he must embrace one or other of them. All his attempts to incorporate them into each other have been very vain. It seems prodigious arrogance to invent a scheme of his own. He feels that he cannot fall back upon the old State Churchmanship.

This fear of arrogance is surely one which we ought to encourage in ourselves, and in every other person. If we had had more humility, we should probably have much fewer difficulties to encounter than we have. And therefore I would say, if I had any chance of being heard, let us try by all means to be humble. And that we may not be otherwise, do not let us hastily set ourselves up to condemn any of these systems, or those who propound them. Our consciences, I believe, have told us from time to time that there is something in each of them which we ought not to reject. Let us not reject it. But we may find, that there is a divine harmony, of which the living principle in each of these systems forms one note, of which the systems themselves are a disturbance and a violation. This seemed to be the case in our previous inquiries respecting

Protestant bodies and the Catholic Church; let us see whether our own national Church presents an exception to the rule, or an illustration of it.

1. How much does every true heart respond to that assertion of the Liberal, that if our Church be indeed a living body, it cannot be tied down by the system of a particular age; it must have an expansive power; it must breathe and move; it must be able to throw off the results of partial experiences; it must be able to profit by all new experiences! With what sympathy do we listen to him, when he says that the Church is meant to comprehend and not to exclude; that neither Protestant Dissenters not Romish Dissenters should be out of the range of its sympathies, or should be prohibited from sharing in any portion of its benefits! And, now, how would he accomplish his beautiful conception? He proposes to us that we should abandon the prayers which we have derived from ages gone by, and the Articles which have come down to us from the Reformation; or he would have us adapt these to the maxims of our own time. But what if those Prayers should be the very means by which we have been preserved from the bondage to particular modes and habits of feeling, when they have been threatening to hold us fast? What if those Articles have kept us from sinking into a particular theological system, and have compelled us to feel that there were two sides of truth, neither of which could be asserted to the exclusion of the other? What if the abondonment either of the Prayers or the Articles, or the reduction of them to our own present standards of thought, should bring the Church into the most flat and hopeless monotony, should so level her to the superstitions of the nineteenth century, so divorce her from the past and the future, that all expansion would for ever be impossible? Again, how would he accomplish his projects of comprehension? He would take away this and that thing about which we and the Dissenters differ, till at last he discovered a few common principles upon which we might all agree. But what if the peculiar doctrines and practices of each class of Dissenters be those in which their most living feelings are expressed? What if all plans of comprehension have failed just because the best and most earnest men were those who saw most the importance of that which was to be given up? If these suppositions should be true, we must look somewhere else than to a liberal system, to produce the effects which Liberals have dreamed of.

2. With that truth and power do the words of the Evangelicals come home to us; -- that the loss of faith was the great misery of the last age; that outward acts usurped the place of life-giving principles; and that, therefore, outward acts were poor and dead; that if a vital glow was restored to any part of the Church at the close of the last century, it came from the feeling that God had interfered on behalf of His creatures, and was interfering on behalf of them still; that there is a real relation between the creature and the Creator; that there is a real power coming forth from the Creator to succour His creatures, and to enable them to do His will! What mighty words are these! How

important it must be, as the Evangelical says, that all men should hear them, and be brought to act upon the conviction of their truth!

And how is this hope to be realised? Go forth and tell men that their baptism is <u>not</u> an admission into the privileges of God's spiritual Church; that they are <u>not</u> to take this sign as a warrant of their right to call themselves members of Christ, and to pray to God as their Father in Him. Go and tell them that they are not in a real relation with God, but only in a nominal one; go and tell them that if they are ever to enter into that relation they must bring themselves into it by an act of faith, or else wait till an angel comes down and troubles the waters; go and tell them that the Eucharist is not a real bond between Christ and His members, but only a picture or likeness, which, by a violent act of our will, we may turn into a reality; go and make these comfortable declarations to men, and mix them well with denunciations of other men for not preaching the Gospel; thus you will reform a corrupt and sinful land.

3. What a charm lies in the words of the propounders of the Catholic system; -- that there is indeed a Church in the world, which God himself has established; that He has not left it to the faith and feelings and notions of men; that He has given us permanent signs of its existence; that He has not left us to find our way into it, but has Himself taken us into it; that being in it we are under His own guidance and discipline; that we are not bound to prove ourselves members of it, by tests which exclude others who share the same privileges with us; that we are not bound to form ourselves into circles and parties and coteries; that we belong to the Communion of Saints, and need not ask for another! What good tidings, amidst all the confusions of our political parties, to hear that we are not the slaves of any of them; that we can do without the State's money, or the State's sword; that we have powers of our own, which the State did not give nor can take away!

And as to practical matters, how evidently true we feel the assertion to be, that men ought to be called to repentance, and to do good works, and to restrain themselves, and to offer sacrifices to God! How clear it seems, that the Evangelicals, though they may wish most heartily to press these duties upon their flocks, are practically unable to do so; that they cannot bid the members of their congregations generally, 'Arise and go to their Father,' because they will only allow that a portion of them may call God their Father; and because that portion of them, according to their doctrine, has already repented and turned to God; that they cannot call the members of their congregation generally to do holy acts from holy principles, because they do not believe that the majority of them have received the Spirit, from whom all holy desires and just works must proceed!

But how great then must be our confusion and dismay, when we discover that the preaching of repentance and of good works, is just as

220

impossible, upon the Catholic system, as upon the Evangelical; that the congregations of the one are to be treated practically as if they had lost their baptismal rights, just as the congregations of the other are to be treated as if they had never obtained them; that repentance and moral discipline are to be held forth as the possible means of recovering a treasure, not as the fruit of shame for the past, and precaution against the future abuse of it; that exhortations to good works, therefore, must of necessity take a selfish form, and be confirmed by selfish sanctions! After all those splendid assurances, that the Church really exists, and that it is endowed with such mighty powers, how grievous it is to find the most strange uncertainty about the terms under which she exists; whether only as a splendid dream, whereof the record is preserved in the writings of the Fathers, and which may some day be realised; or as a potentiality, which was made a fact during the Middle Ages by the supremacy of the Pope; or, lastly, as an invisible equatorial line between Romanism and Protestantism; a line, of which some dim traces may, from time to time, be discovered, with the help of powerful glasses, in our English history, but which has gradually been lost in the dark ground upon one side of it. And, finally, to men who have left the intolerable pride, and the real slavery, of those notions about private judgment, which have been of late current among us, how painful is the discovery, that these Catholic denouncers of it do in fact justify the most extravagant, self-conceited, and unreasonable use which has ever been made of it; and only condemn it when it has lost its evil character, and is actually exercised under moral discipline and government! For what can be more subversive of all order and government, what so direct an outrage upon fact, as the assertion, that men in general are left to choose their teachers? And what so subversive of the very idea of a teacher, as the notion that he is not to cultivate the mind and judgment of his pupil, but only to pour into him certain notions of his own? The very arrogance from which we wish to deliver men, is the notion that they are not to receive the teachers, the parents, judges, pastors, whom God has set over them. The very hope we wish to encourage in them is, that if they receive humbly the light which is vouchsafed to them, it will be increased to them more and more, till they are brought into the perfect day.

And, lastly, the dogma respecting probable evidence, which the Catholic school make the foundation of their intellectual, as the dogma of baptismal purity is the foundation of their moral teaching, seems to contain the very virus of that scepticism which they denounce in the Liberal. The Liberal says, 'Nothing is certain in morals; one opinion may be less mischievous or more plausible than another; but, as to the thing which dogmatists call truth, sensible men, who know anything of history, have discarded the dream of it altogether.' And what says our English Catholic? -- 'We admit nothing is certain in morals; but then we do not want certainty. We are so faithful and submissive that we are content with appearances and likelihoods; we receive what we are told by the authority which we have determined to be on the whole the best. God has not willed that we should have more light.' I appeal to the conscience of mankind against this language. Do we not mean when we use the awful name of God, 'THE BEING, He who is'? If there be no certainty, how dare we take that name into our lips? Are not the very words, 'I believe in God the Father Almighty,' an assertion that there is something fixed and eternal upon which the pillars of the universe rest? Do not the next words mean, 'He who Is has revealed Himself to us? We are not to live upon probabilities and plausibilities. He who is Truth does wish that we should know the truth, and that the truth should make us free?' I do therefore say, that this system, so far as it stands upon the doctrine of probabilities, begins in scepticism, and that in scepticism it must terminate.

It will be observed that I have not charged the authors of these systems with the tendencies which they commonly impute to each other. I have not said that the Liberal wishes to substitute Rationalism for Orthodoxy; that the Evangelical wishes to establish the principle of Dissent; that the Catholic systematiser wishes to introduce Popery. My charge against each is, that he defeats his own object. As to the question how far these different accusations are true, I should feel obliged in many cases to give a double answer in order to make myself intelligible. I can quite understand that each of these prties believes the clear and strong assertion of its own principle to be the best preservative against the very evil which it is supposed to favour. And I think this is a true and reasonable opinion. I think the Liberal has a right to say, 'Recognize the idea of Rationalism in the Church, and it will not assert itself out of the Church in the form of Infidelity.' That the Evangelical has a right to say, 'Recognize the idea of personal faith as the condition of Christian fellowship in the Church, and it will not assert itself in the form of Dissent out of the Church.' I think the Catholic has a right to way, 'Recognize the idea of Chtholicism in your Church, and it will not assert itself out of the Church in the form of Romanism.' But while I acknowledge this, and therefore can enter into the feelings of disappointment and indignation which each in turn experiences when he finds that his purpose it not understood, I must say also, that it seems to me evident both from facts and reason, that each of these principles, when it is worked into a system, does become fairly obnoxious to the complaint of those who denounce it most vehemently. I cannot see what Church Liberalism reduced to a system is but the denial of anything as given to men either in the shape of Tradition or Revelation; what Church Evangelicism reduced to a system is but the denial of the very idea of Church fellowship or Unity, and the substitution for it of a combination of individual units; what Catholicism reduced to a system is but Romanism; that is to say, the direct denial of the distinction of National Churches, and the implicit denial of the Church as a spiritual body holding a spiritual Head. And it seems to me a false way of speaking to say that each of these systems is good in moderation, but when pushed to its extreme is bad. I do not think the system is the extension or expansion of the principle, but its limitation and contradiction. I do not see how the principle can be carried too far. I do not see how anything can be done towards the formation of the system, without introducing a seed of evil which must germinate till it produces all its natural fruits.

I have written very much in vain, if I have not yet explained why I suppose this must be the case. These systems, Protestant, Romish, English, seem to me each to bear witness of the existence of a <u>Divine Order</u>; each to be a miserable, partial, human substitute for it. In every country, therefore, I should desire to see men emancipated from the chains which they have made for themselves, and entering into the freedom of God's Church. But it seems to me, that in England we have a clearer witness than there is anywhere of our right to this emancipation, and of the way in which it may be effected. This system-building is not natural to us. We have evils which are natural to us, and against which we have to be continually on our guard. But <u>this</u> is an exotic product: one of the charges which the Liberal and Evangelical and Catholic systematisers make against our native English divines is, that they have little understanding of any systems; that they go on in a blind mechanical course, merely caring to keep their places and do their work. And yet the members of all these parties are continually giving proof, when they are not occupied with actual controversies, that they feel this maxim of "keeping their places, and doing their work," to be not a low or grovelling one; but one which their consciences testify in favour of, and to which they would wish, if they could, to conform themselves. As they become more aged and holy, more disciplined by affliction, more apprehensive of God's will and of the ends which they are to seek, it would seem as if this old-fashioned notion, which struck them as so vulgar and earthly in their youth, is more and more acknowledged to be one high in its origin, and difficult in its realisation. An old systematiser in England is a very rare spectacle indeed. There is either a gravitation into some lower region, or an ascent into some higher one; either a fall out of the middle air of speculations to our mother clods; or a clear perception that the heavenly things are substantial, and that in the solid earth and not in the clouds we are to find the images of them. I should be very presumptuous if I spoke to such men, except in the language of deference and humility, beseeching them not to make us that which they have ceased to be themselves; not to let us fancy from their words that they belong to schools and parties, when we know that in their closets and in their lives they must be renouncing them all. It is from the ranks of young men that these parties will be recruited. They want, as they say, principles and ideas. They cannot move on in the line of mere practical business and exertion. They must know why they act and what is the end of action, or they will not act at all. I think I am as sensible of this necessity as they can be; and sensible, too, how little their elders are able to sympathize in the want, or to satisfy it. Nay, I think I can see further, that unless we who are younger do earnestly seek after principles and grounds of action, we must sink into the monotony of the last century, or into a far worse state than that. I believe the great principles, which each of these systems has developed, have been made known to us for he wisest purposes. But then I think that they are the sap which is to invigorate and restore the oak trunk which has been standing for so many ages on our soil, and that the seedlings which they themselves have sent forth, are of a poor, weak, tortuous growth, not capable of resisting any tempest. I do not urge the young English student to make light of these principles; I say he cannot with safety make light of any one of them. All belong to him, he has need of them all; but I beseech him to consider solemnly, and as in the presence of God, whether he may lawfully do any acts which imply that he adopts one of the systems in which these principles are buried, and whether he dares to fraternize with any parties, as parties, which profess them.

He will be told, of course, that to stand aloof from them is practically impossible; that to attempt it is an act of self-conceit and self-will; that he is an Eclectic or a Syncretist; that in a short time if he perseveres in his determination he will throw off his faith altogether. To the first charge he may reply, that it cannot be impossible for an Englishman to be that which it is the natural bias of an Englishman, not under some peculiar influence, to be. To the second he will answer, that instead of rejecting the instructions of his parents and teachers, he is seeking to hold them fast. Possibly they belong to a particular school. His first impulse on beginning to think, is to emancipate himself from their notions, to choose new teachers, to adopt the system which is most opposite to that of his education. Those who beseech him not to join a party say, 'By no means do this; the notions which you have learnt must not be abandoned. There is a truth in them which you must have; never let them go till you have made yourself master of it; when you are master of it, do what you like with the system; you will love those who taught it you more than you ever did; you will only not suffer their teachings to keep you separate from men whom you ought also to love.' The accusation of Eclecticism or Syncretism it is better not to notice at all; nine out of ten persons who use the words, do not know what they mean; they are merely bugbears to frighten children with; the tenth man who does know will understand that he who endeavours to substitute a Church for systems, must regard with most dread and suspicion the attempt at a complete, all-comprehending system. Hating all systems, he hates those most which are most perfect, because in them there are the fewest crannies and crevices through which the light and air of heaven may enter. He hates the Romish system more than all Protestant systems, becuase the latter are inconsistent and fragmentary, the former is all-embracing and satisfactory, therefore more lifeless, inhuman, godless. As to the fear of his losing his faith, when he has thrown down the party walls which have been raised for the defence of it, he may venture to stand the risk. If his faith be in the doctrines of men and not in the wisdom of God, the sooner it falls the better. If it be in Him whose name is Truth, to Him be the care of it committed. We believe that His sentence has gone forth against systems and parties; we do not believe that He has recalled the words, 'None who trusteth in Me shall be confounded.'

I am sure our responsibility in this matter is becoming more weighty every day. I have said that these systems are not natural to us. But I do not mean that they are not able to assimilate themselves with our most characteristic tendencies. (Elsewhere the defenders of a system may merely form a school. In England, because by constitution we are politicians and not systematisers, they must form a party. The moment we have adopted a peculiar theory we begin to organise.) We have our flags and our watchwords, our chiefs and our subordinates. All the generous feelings of sympathy and courage, of readiness to support a friend, of unwillingness to desert him when he has done some unpopular act, bind us to one and another maxim which our leaders or allies have put forth, even though there is nothing in our own minds which answers to it; we throw the feelings befitting men of action and soldiers, into the defence of propostions which have been worked out by the most dry school logic. Thus personality necessarily enters into all our solemnest discussions. A noble symptom of what we ought to be! a miserable effect when we are striving to make ourselves something else! The respectable champions on each side ask, and ask again, why they should be treated with harshness and malignity, for maintaining principles which they believe in their hearts to be charitable and true. Immediately after, their Newspapers and Reviews are seen generously striving that no other party shall have the stigma of being more unfair and libellous than their own. What seems to me worse and more grievous still -- all, whether they are capable of understanding systems or not, are expected to enlist in one of these parties, and to bear its name. The poor must be instructed in penny tracts to call such a man a Papist, or such a man a Low Churchman. Our children must become polemics before they can repeat their catechism; and the members of that sex which exists to pacify and harmonise society, to be a witnesss against our cold logical habits of thought, to teach us the worth of things above words, must talk about opinions, imitate our discords, pollute their minds if not their lips with the ribaldry which we think it a part of our Christian duty and profession to indulge against those who are called by the same name and partake of the same sacraments with us. Surely such a state of things must bring down heavy judgments upon our Church and land, and therefore everyone ought to consider whether he will make himself an accessory to the sin, whether he can do nothing to avert the punishment.

I am aware how much pains the defenders of party have taken, to engage the practical feelings of Englishmen on their side. They have said, 'Let theorists talk what they will, the moment we begin to act, we must associate with some men or other, and this association will assume a party character. To bid us abandon parties and systems, is only another way of bidding us hang down our hands in stupid indolence. Those who wish to do anything must be content to take things as they find them.' Yes, this is undoubtedly the right test; I rejoice that we should be brought to it. I leave it then to the defenders of systems and parties, to explain what they are doing with them. They cannot complain that their machinery is not in active operation. It may occasionally

225

meet with a little obstruction from a certain vague impression in men's minds, that they have been commanded to love their neighbours as themselves; still they cannot be so ungrateful as not to acknowledge that it has been brought to very tolerable perfection, and of course, to very great efficiency, in this nineteenth century in our English towns and villages. Any description of its results from an opponent could not be a fair one. I will therefore confine myself to a short statement of certain modes of action which I believe are open to a person who does not avail himself of this machinery, but is content with the powers which he believes God has bestowed upon him, as a minister of His Kingdom.

1. Does such a person find himself among the members of different sects and parties -- a Quaker here, a Baptist there, a Unitarian on his right, a Plymouth Christian on his left? He believes that he is a member of a polity which recognizes the truth contained in each of these sytems; but they have made a system out of some principle which they have torn apart from the rest; that they have destroyed that principle by its separation. He believes that there are earnest men in these sects who are feeling this to be the case, who are catching at all schemes of union because they feel it, who are angry with us because we do not enter into their sense of the necessity of a union and therefore fraternize with them; who are proclaiming the very principle upon which the Catholic Church stands, that all unity is to be in Christ, and that intellectual notions and opinions ought not to divide men from Him. There is therefore a practical renunciation of the sect principle, as something which is no longer tenable. There is at the same time a very furious desire to maintain it as against the national Church. The reasons will seem to him to be these. First, the Church has put itself forth merely as an English Church. Its character as a Catholic body, as a kingdom set up in the world for all nations, has been kept out of sight. Secondly, in the reaction against this tendency, it has taken a negative, i.e. a sectarian, form. The idea of the Church, as a united body, has been put forth, chiefly to shew the wickedness of those who have separated from it. Its episcopacy and its sacraments have been looked upon chiefly as exclusive of those who have them not. Above all, the spiritual character of the Church as deriving its life from its head, a character which the Dissenters are especially disposed by their profession to recognize, has been disjoined from the institutions which embody it. Men have been asked to receive these institutions merely as such, and then to hope for spiritual life through them. Little attempt has been made to prove to them that the institutions are themselves living portions of the divine kingdom. A person therefore who has entered into these convictions himself, will not despair of seeing all the true hearty Dissenters gradually receiving them also. He will not be impatient to force any notions of his own upon them. His desires will be to meet their feelings and to enter into them. He will be most anxious not to destroy anything which they have received or learnt; to confirm them in their feelings of affection and reverence for their fathers; to strengthen in them by all means the hereditary affections, which their

doctrines respecting private judgment so much impair. He wishes to preserve all the faith which they have from the destruction which is threatening it; to unite their faith with that of those from whom they are separated; to make them integral members of the body from which they fancy that it is the object of our pride and selfishness to exclude them. What the result of such a method may be, is in God's hands, not ours. At all events other methods have been tried and have failed; this has not been tried.

2. Or does the Churchman I am supposing find himself in one of our awful manufacturing districts? Of course, the sense of his own utter inadequacy to deal with the mass of evil which he meets there is the first which will take hold of him, and will grow stronger every day. Yet he is there, and he knows that there is One who cares for this mass of living beings infinitely more than he does. Nay, his own coldness and heartlessness will continually remind him that if he is to care for them at all, the feeling must be communicated to him by Him who often seems to these unhappy creatures utterly heedless of their sorrows and complainings. And then he has the consolation which the Athenian orator found when he reflected on the reverses of his countrymen, and the resistless march of Philip. "If we had done such and such things and they had failed, we might despair; we have not done them, therefore let us hope.' A Church which was looked upon, and almost looked upon itself, as a tool of the aristocracy, which compared its own orders with the ranks in civil society, and forgot that it existed to testify that man as man is the object of his Creator's sympathy; such a Church had no voice which could reach the hearts of these multitudes. The Liberal proclamation which says, 'Teach them; impart to them a few of the things that we know,' was more genial and humane. But there are thoughts ever at work in these Englishmen, in these human beings, thoughts quickened by hunger and suffering, which such instruction could not appease. More impressive far was the speech of the Methodist and the Evangelical: 'You have immortal souls, they are perishing; oh! ask how they may be saved.' Such words spoken with true earnestness are very mighty. But they are not enough; men feel that they are not merely lost creatures; they look up to heaven above them, and ask whether it can be true that this is the whole account of their condition; that their sense of right and wrong, their cravings for fellowship, their consciousness of being creatures having powers which no other creatures possess, are all nothing. If religion, they say, will give us no explanation of these feelings, if it can only tell us about a fall for the whole race, and an escape for a few individuals of it, then our wants must be satisfied without religion. Then begin Chartism and Socialism, and whatever schemes make rich men tremble. Surely, what the modern assertors of a Church system say about the duty of administering active charity to these sufferers, of shewing that we do not merely regard them as pensioners on the national bounty, but as fellow-men for whom we are to make sacrifices -- surely this language is far more to the purpose. Surely if acted upon even imperfectly, it must produce most happy

227

effects. But how would the proclamation to our Chartists and Socialists, that they had baptismal purity once, and that they have lost it now; that they must recover their ground by repentance, by prayer and fasting; that they must submit to discipline, and be deprived of privileges which they never exercised nor cared for; how can such a proclamation as this meet any of the confused, disorderly notions which are stirring in their minds, or set them right?

On the other hand, if the new and unwonted proclamation were to go forth,' God has cared for you, you are indeed His children; His Son has redeemed you, His Spirit is striving with you; there is a fellowship larger, more irrespective of outward distinctions, more democratical, than any which you can create; but it is a fellowship of mutual love, not mutual selfishness, in which the chief of all is the servant of all' -- may not one think that a result would follow as great as that which attended the preaching of any Franciscan friar in the twelfth century, or any Methodist preacher in the eighteenth? For these are true words, everlasting words, and yet words which belong especially to our time; they are words which interpret, and must be interpreted by, that regular charity, that ministerial holiness, those sacraments, prayers, discipline, of which the Catholic speaks. They connect his words about repentance with those of the Evangelical, making it manifest, that nothing but an accursed nature and a depraved will could have robbed any of the blessings which God has bestowed upon us all. They translate into meaning and life all the liberal plans for the education of adults and children; they enable us to fulfil the notion, which statesmen have entertained, that the Church is to be the supporter of the existing orders, by making her a teacher and example to those orders respecting their duties and responsibilities; by removing the hatred which their forgetfullness of those duties and responsibilities is threatening to create in the minds of the lower classes.

3. But a Churchman, such as I have supposed, would be both compelled by his curcumstances, and urged by his principles, to change these convictions into action, by enlisting all the wealthier inhabitants of his parish in different services and occupations for the benefit of their inferiors. I am unwilling to enlarge upon this subject; first, because my practical ignorance makes me unfit to offer any suggestions upon it; and, secondly, because I am certain that our English political wisdom, guided by Catholic feeling, is already doing much in many parts of this land, in the accomplishment of such a design. I must, however, refer to it for the purpose of remarking, how the notion, that party organisation is necessary, is at once explained and refuted the moment we aim at an ecclesiastical organisation. It is explained when the truth, that no man is meant to work alone, which is the truth that is implied in this strange maxim, is made the principle of our action. It is refuted; for we find how infinitely freer from friction a society is which is held together by sacramental bonds, and is moving under the direction of an appointed pastor, than all societies constructed upon a party model, or

228

acknowledging a party motive, ever have been or ever can be. For the one seeks to preserve all existing ranks and relations, the other sets them all aside. The one is continually endeavouring to understand how the middle classes may be brought most to act upon the lower, so as to be their guides and not their tyrants; how the upper classes may be brought to act upon the middle, so as not to be their fawning slaves and at the same time the betrayers of their consciences at elections, cold and distant and the objects of their servile imitation at other times; how each portion of the community may preserve its proper position to the rest, and may be fused together by the spiritual power which exists for each, the minister of all, the creature of none. The other confounds all orders, and yet does not the least diminish their mutual repulsion, or make them feel that they have a common object. Above all, the Churchman is ever longing to discover how the handmaidens of the Church may be brought to do her the services which they alone can do, without departing for a moment from their own true estate, as wives, as sisters, as mothers; how the whole sex may be an order of Sisters of Charity; and how, in each particular neighbourhood, this order may be at work in lowliness and meekness, softening and healing the sorrows of the world. The partisan acknowledges no difference of vocation in man and woman; all are to be equally feverish and restless; careful about many things, unfit alike for quiet contemplation or regular activity.

4. Again, let us suppose our Churchman in Ireland, amidst a population, the majority of which acknowledge no relation to the body of which he is a member; how would he feel, and how would he desire to act? Would he not think thus within himself? -- 'When Anselm came over from his Norman convent to be Archbishop of Canterbury, and his victorious countrymen thought that he of course would look upon the old Saxons of the soil as they did; he told them plainly, that a Churchman acknowledged no distinctions of race, and that his vocation was to be the friend of the poor and distressed wherever he met with them.' And these principles, of course with great exceptions and deviations, were acted upon by a large portion of the Norman bishops and clergy. What was the effect? We grew up to be an English nation. The Saxon serf felt that he had a portion and a right in the soil; he recollected the sounds of his native language; he began to speak it; in due time the conquerors and the conquered became one. If our Churchmen had but acted upon this principle in Ireland; if they had but said to the English settlers, -- We will have nothing to do with your Orange lodges and your hell-fire clubs, except to discipline and restrain those who belong to them; we are come over as protectors of these Celts; we are to raise them out of barbarism; to speak to their Church feelings and their national feelings; to call forth both together: -- if these had been our maxims, how many problems, which perplex the statesman at this day, might have been solved long ago! But that phrase, The English interest, was continually present to the minds of the statesmen who sent out our Bishops, and though they might often stumble by mistake upon a noble rebel to their commands, they sought diligently for men who should forward their own narrow

229

policy. What has been the consequence? The national feeling in Ireland has strangely and unnaturally associated itself with that Romanism which is the foe of all national feeling. The Irish look upon our Church as a Saxon Church, and they actually fly to Rome to give them an Irish Church. But even now at the eleventh hour, if better and truer feelings of our position are rising in the minds of statesmen, may not the Church be the means of carrying them out? We have tried what the mere preaching of Protestantism will do in Ireland, and so far as it has been earnest and sincere, it has not been in vain. But still it has not touched the hearts of Irishmen; there has been a resistance to it, not merely in their bad feelings but in their good. State liberality has been tried. So far as it has been the token of kindness and sympathy, perhaps this too has not been in vain. Still all must acknowledge that it has done very little; most men think that a fair proportion of evil has been mingled with the good. But if there be a sympathy between the Catholic and National principle, if they cannot really exist apart, why may we not begin to speak to the national sympathies of Irishmen; to speak to them as members of an Irish Catholic Church; to declare that every Irishman ought to look upon himself as a member of such a Church, and not of any other Church, Saxon or Romish; to make it manifest by acts, that we hold our revenues for the good of the whole land, and that it would not gain anything but misery by the confiscation of them, or by the extirpation of those who possessed them?' Such thoughts, I say, are likely to arise in the mind of an Irish Churchman, who enters into the principles I have endeavoured to develop. They may be very crude, but still they may be the germs of acts which neither the State nor the Church will have reason to complain of.

5. To one who feels the importance of the Protestant principle, and that its true home is in the Catholic Church, it must needs seem a strange providence in respect to England, that she should have on one side of her a nation in which Protestantism has tried to exist nakedly and exclusively; on the other side, a nation which wishes to be Catholic by being Romanist. Each experiment is, I think, very decisive, but each is connected with sins which we have need to confess and deplore. The utter insufficiency of Presbyterianism to support a national life has been surely proved by the example of Scotland. But we began with setting up our episcopacy as if it were an English thing. We gave the Scotch people the notion, that their own kings were coming back to reduce them into an ecclesiastical province of England, and the religious as well as the national spirit rose against such a pretension. Now, it would seem as if the episcopalian body in Scotland had the opportunity of shewing, that they are neither members of a religious sect nor tools of England. They have existed for many years without any State patronage; their chief fault has been, that they have not sympathized with the feelings of the people, that they have stood too much upon their ecclesiastical dignity, that they have seemed too much mere anti-presbyterians. But if, in the present crisis of Scotland, they will consider earnestly, that they exist as witnesses, not of a system but of a Church, not of certain notions about

230

episcopacy, but of episcopacy as part of the constitution of Christ's spiritual kingdom; they will find, I think, that they may exercise a quiet and soothing influence over that ferment of Scotch feelings, which all State contrivances have been so utterly ineffectual to allay. They will not, I hope, look with proud aristocratical contempt upon the earnest cry which the people have sent forth to be freed from civil dominion. They will not, I hope, indulge in mocking allusions to the proud language in which Presbyterianism used to assert that it was free of this control. They will acknowledge that spiritual freedom is most essential to the life of a nation. They will labour to shew, that the Church, rightly and truly constituted, is able to humble the lofty and to exalt the lowly; that the tyranny which Presbyterianism granted to its aristocracy at the time of the Reformation, is the tyranny against which its sons are groaning now; that its boast of being a Church for the poor has ended in a sadder separation between the poor and the rich than has almost ever existed in any country. Here again I am suggesting no projects or plans to Scotch Churchmen. I am merely urging them to consider seriously the indications of God's will, and to desire that they may act in accordance with it.

6. The lessons which we have derived from the history of our connexion with Scotland and Ireland (I have spoken before of those which are suggested by the circumstances of our old colonies in North America) cannot surely be lost upon us when we go forth to plant new settlements on the other side of the globe, or when we are inquiring how we are to deal with those which we possess already. Every circumstance of their position and of ours seems to say, 'See that you do not merely establish an English kingdom in those soils; if you do, that kingdom will not be a blessing to the colonists, to the natives, or to the mother country. See that you do not merely send forth preachers in your ships to tell the people that all they have believed hitherto -- if they have believed anything -- is false, and that we hold a doctrine which sets it all aside. See that you raise up in the midst of them what they shall feel to be as real a kingdom as the one which is presented to them in the persons of governors and judges; a kingdom which does not only deal equal justice to natives and to settlers, but which claims both alike for its citizens, endues both alike with its highest privileges; a kingdom which comes to subvert nothing, but to restore that which is decayed and fallen; to adopt into itself every fragment of existing faith and feeling; to purify it and exalt it; to cut off from it only that which the conscience of the native confesses to be inconsistent with it; to testify that wherever there is a creature having human limbs and features, there is one of that race for which Christ died, one whom He is not ashamed to call a brother.'

In such countries as New Zealand and Australia, such a testimony as is borne by the establishment of a Christian kingdom of peace and righteousness is everything; for there, of course, only the rudest and most incoherent spiritual theories and speculations will be found to exist. In India the case is altogether different; yet there, more than anywhere,

231

is it needful that the signs of a spiritual kingdom should be introduced, that Christianity should be regarded as something more than a fine theory. For how did the simple tenets of Mahomedanism prevail over the complicated creeds and philosophies of the Hindoos but because the former came forth in the shape of an organic society, and the latter were only forms of thought connected principally with the physical universe? The Christian Church ought to understand the positions both of the Hindoo and the Mussulman, in respect to the strange masses of feelings and opinions which are exhibited in the traditions of the one, and to the struggle after consistency and unity which are visible in the actual history of the other. Would that the supporters of Indian missions had taken this ground when they were assailed by the cowardice and indifference of the merchant-emperors thirty years ago! Would that they had been able to reply to those who had accused them of disturbing the faith of the natives, and so endangering English dominion -- No; it is your godlessness and rapacity which endanger their faith; you are making them infidels while you pretend to indulge their superstitions: we go to save their faith by delivering them from their superstitions and your example; we go, that England may not perish in that day when she shall be called to give account of the crimes which you have committed. But it was not fully understood at that time that Christianity was anything else but a sect, or a collection of sects, sent into the world to displace Pagan and Mahomedan sects; therefore, the years which have followed have produced their natural effect, and we have now to deal for the most part with a generation of open or disguised infidels. Still the good men of that day, guided by a higher wisdom than their own, were led to ask strenuously of the English legislature, that a Bishop might be sent out to them. They felt that they wanted a Church. A heart was put into a country which had hitherto only been directed by wise heads or skilful hands; a heart which is still beating, and which we trust may yet send a life-blood into every part of that vast empire. The issue is with God; but He has taught us by sufficiently manifest indications in what way He wills that we should fulfil our part in the work.

7. I have not yet spoken of the spirit in which we should act towards the members of foreign Churches, be they Romish or Protestant. But enough has been said in former parts of this work to indicate the course which an Englishman, who is not tied down by systems, must strive to pursue in reference to them. What I have been chiefly wishing to shew is, that here we have the means of acting upon the principles which all men everywhere ought to act upon if they could; herein it seems to me lies the blessing for which we have to give thanks. Our Church has no right to call herself better than other Churches in any respect, in many she must acknowledge herself to be worse. But our position, we may fairly affirm, for it is not a boast but a confession, is one of singular advantage. If what I have said be true, our faith is not formed by a union of the Protestant systems with the Romish system, nor of certain elements taken from the one and of certain elements taken from the other. So far as it is represented in our liturgy and our

232

articles, it is the faith of a Church, and has nothing to do with any/ system at all. That peculiar character which God has given us, enables us, if we do not slight the mercy, to understand the difference between a Church and a System, better perhaps than any of our neighbours can, and, therefore, our position, rightly used, gives us a power of assisting them in realising the blessings of their own. By refusing to unite with them on the ground of any one of their systems, by seeking to unite with them on the grounds of the universal Church, we teach them wherein lies their strength and their weakness; by determining that we will be a nation distinct from all others, we encourage each of them to be a nation distinct from us and from all others. By shewing them how our Church life and our national life are interwoven, we teach them that the bonds which make them one with us are necessary to the support of that peculiar character and position which make them independent of us.

But for such tasks as these -- for reconciling the different sects in our own land, for dealing with the wild feelings respecting government and society which are abroad, for bringing the different classes into co-operation, for entering into the strong passions of Scotch Calvinists and Irish Romanists, for taming the savages of the antipodes, for restoring the strange reliques of ancient civilisation among the natives of British India, for suggesting any practical hints, or giving any practical help to our brethren on the Continent; what need have we of another discipline and another spirit than that which we seem at present to possess! Shall we obtain either the one or the other by sitting still, by affirming that these tasks are too great for creatures so infirm and fallen, by waiting for some sudden inspiration? This cannot be. These works are set before us; in one way or other, we are trying to carry them on, and must carry them on. The necessity is laid upon us; the only point to be considered is how we can support it. Do we tremble at the great efforts of thought which are presupposed in these outward undertakings, the careful studies in history, ecclesiastical and civil, the acquaintance with the powers and the distinctions of words as the signs of thought, the intimacy with the symbols which nature and art have furnished to the mythologist, the patient toil with which these must be weighed in our minds before we can cast ourselves into the feelings of other men, while yet we do not lose our own? Assuredly this is required of us, not the whole of each student -- for the Church is one body, and hath many members -- but something of every one, and the habit and disposition of all. But there is nothing in all this to stagger the countrymen of Bacon and of Newton. Study is painful and intolerable to Englishmen if they cannot connect it with action. They cannot pursue it for its pleasure or its comeliness; make them feel that there is an end in it, that it is necessary for their business, and they will be as diligent slaves in the reading of books as in the making of roads. Our systems and our parties have confused us in every direction; they lead us to fancy that all things are moving round in a weary circle, or are imprisoned in lifeless notions. At the same time they tempt every man to suppose that he is to be everything, and to know everything, and to do everything; for he feels that if he has not the whole of his system before him, each part of it becomes mischievous and false. And he cannot trust other men to do their work while he does his own; for he feels that he belongs to a party rather than to a Church, and therefore he has no security that each person has his orders and duties assigned to him. Thus we are at the same time indolent and overdiligent, ignorant and encyclopaedic. Once break this spell, and we shall again begin to connect our specific studies with a general humanity, and so at once preseve their limitations and make them universal.

But there is another and the more serious subject. I have spoken of a different discipline, but we need a different spirit in order to that discipline. Not a different spirit from that which we received in our baptism, but an altogether different one from the spirit of party and of selfishness, which we have allowed to enter into us and possess us in our manhood. To exorcise this, that the other may really inform us and rule us, should surely be our first object. And we cannot drive it out of others until we have striven that it may be banished from outselves. If we, who form the clergy of the land, believe that we are its heart, we must suppose that the purification of the body generally depends upon our purification; we must feel that every evil which we call upon others to repent of has its origin and root in us, and that we must repent of it first. I fear that the habit of apologising for our institution, when it has been ignorantly attacked by those who know nothing of its meaning or its blessing, may have operated injuriously upon our lives. We have defended the arrangements of Providence and the order of the Church, till, unawares, we have begun to defend ourselves, who have so grievously sinned against those arrangements and that order, and have hindered men from perceiving what they are. For this fault, if we have committed it, we must wish to make amends; since we must know that there can be no national confession or national reformation, if we, who ought to be the foremost in both, as having the most to answer for, are trying to make excuses for ourselves, hiding the evil which we are inwardly conscious of, or imputing it to circumstances, most of which are very favourable to us, none of which ought to be our masters.

But if shame and humilation are needful for English clergymen generally, they must be especially needful in those who have presumed to speak of our sins, and to offer any suggestion for our amendment. It is too probable that they would have known nothing of the evil of systems and parties in others if they had not felt it in themselves; nay, that the irritation of the beam in their own eye has made them more eager to detect the mote in their brother's eye. I have in this book attacked no wrong tendency to which I do not know myself to be liable. I hope I am conscious to a certain degree, though very insufficiently, of the danger I am in of substituting the denunciation of it for the practical correction of it in the only sphere over which I have any control. I am not ignorant, also, that the hints which I have offered in opposition to systems may, themselves, be turned by myself or by others into a system; and that neither its weakness and inconsistency, nor the insignificance of its originator, may prevent it from connecting itself with some new party. I believe that some of whom I have spoken in this chapter began to fulfil their mission with as sincere a desire that their words might never become the symbols of a faction as I can feel now. I do not, therefore, confide in myself. But since a school, which should be formed to oppose all schools, must be of necessity more mischievous than any of them; and since a school, which pretended to amalgamate the doctrines of all other schools, would be, as I think, more mischievous than that, I do pray earnestly, that if any such schools should arise, they may come to naught; and that, if what I have written in this book should tend even in the least degree to favour the establishment of them, it may come to naught. On the other hand, if there by anything here which may help to raise men above their own narrow conceptions and mine, may lead them to believe that there is a way to that truth which is living and universal, and above us all, and that He who is Truth will guide them in that way -- this which is from Him and not from me, I pray that He will bless. 'Let all thine enemies perish, O Lord;' all systems, schools, parties which have hindered men from seeing the largeness, and freedom, and glory of Thy kingdom; 'but let them that love thee,' in whatever earthly mists they may at present be involved, 'be as the sun when he goeth forth in his strength.'

By the Author:

Man's Knowledge of God
No Cross, No Crown: A Study of the Atonement
The Almost Chosen People: The Religion of Abraham Lincoln
A Plan of Church Union: Catholic, Evangelical, Reformed
Thoreau: Mystic, Prophet, Ecologist
Freedom's Holy Light: American Identity and the Future of
Theology

Editor:

Protestant Churches and Reform Today
The Recovery of Unity; the Thought of F.D. Maurice (with John F.
Porter)
Thomas Traherne's Centuries of Meditations
The Spirit of Anglicanism
Anglican Spirituality